UN⊕HABITAT

State of the
World's Cities 2010/2011

Bridging The Urban Divide

publishing for a sustainable future

London • Washington, DC

First published by Earthscan in the UK and USA in 2008 for and on behalf of the United Nations Human Settlements Programme (UN-HABITAT).

United Nations Human Settlements Programme (UN-HABITAT)
P.O. Box 30030, Nairobi, Kenya
Tel: +254 20 7621 234
Fax: +254 20 7624 266/7
Website: www.unhabitat.org

DISCLAIMER

The designations employed and the presentation of the material in this report do not imply the expression of any opinion whatsoever on the part of the Secretariat of the United Nations concerning the legal status of any country, territory, city or area, or of its authorities, or concerning delimitation of its frontiers or boundaries, or regarding its economic system or degree of development. The analysis, conclusions and recommendations of this reports do not necessarily reflect the views of the United Nations Human Settlements Programme or its Governing Council.

The Report is produced with official data provided by governments and additional information gathered by the Global Urban Observatory. Cities and countries are invited to update data relevant to them. It is important to acknowledge that data varies according to definition and sources. While UN-HABITAT checks data provided to the fullest extent possible, the responsibility for the accuracy of the information lies with the original providers of the data. Information contained in this Report is provided without warranty of any kind, either express or implied, including, without limitation, warranties of merchantability, fitness for a particular purpose and non-infringement. UN-HABITAT specifically does not make any warranties or representations as to the accuracy or completeness of any such data. Under no circumstances shall UN-HABITAT be liable for any loss, damage, liability or expense incurred or suffered that is claimed to have resulted from the use of this Report, including, without limitation, any fault, error, omission with respect thereto. The use of this Report is at the User's sole risk. Under no circumstances, including, but not limited to negligence, shall UN-HABITAT or its affiliates be liable for any direct, indirect, incidental, special or consequential damages, even if UN-HABITAT has been advised of the possibility of such damages.

HS/1249/09E (paperback)
HS/104/10E (hardback)

ISBN: 978-1-84971-176-0 (Earthscan paperback)   ISBN: 978-92-113-2211-8 (UN-HABITAT paperback)
ISBN: 978-1-84971-175-3 (Earthscan hardback)   ISBN: 978-92-113-2217-0 (UN-HABITAT hardback)

Design and layout by
Michael Jones Software,
Nairobi, Kenya.

For a full list of Earthscan publications contact:

Earthscan
Dunstan House
14a St Cross Street
London EC1N 8XA, UK
Tel: +44 (0)20 7841 1930
Direct: +44 (0)20 7841 1930
Fax: +44 (0)20 7242 1474
E-mail: earthinfo@earthscan.co.uk
Website: www.earthscan.co.uk

22883 Quicksilver Drive, Sterling, VA20166-2012, USA

Earthscan publishes in association with the International Institute for Environment and Development.

A catalogue record of this book is available from the British Library.

Library of Congress Cataloging-in-Publications Data has been applied for.

Printed and bound in Malta by Gutenberg Press Ltd.
The paper used for this book is FSC-certified. FSC (the Forest Stewardship Council) is an international network to promote responsible management of the world's forests.

Mixed Sources
Product group from well-managed
forests, and other controlled sources
www.fsc.org Cert no. TT-CoC-002424
© 1996 Forest Stewardship Council

Foreword

The emerging picture of the 21st century city fits many descriptions. Some are centres of rapid industrial growth and wealth creation, often accompanied by harmful waste and pollution. Others are characterized by stagnation, urban decay and rising social exclusion and intolerance. Both scenarios point to the urgent need for new, more sustainable approaches to urban development. Both argue for greener, more resilient and inclusive towns and cities that can help combat climate change and resolve age-old urban inequalities.

The 2010/2011 State of the World's Cities Report, *Bridging the Urban Divide*, examines the social, economic, cultural and political drivers of urban poverty and deprivation. It argues that much inequality and injustice stems from inadequate policy-making and planning by local authorities and central governments alike. Typical remedies include removing barriers that prevent access to land, housing, infrastructure and basic services, and facilitating rather than inhibiting participation and citizenship. The report also emphasizes that lasting gains are best achieved through a combination of local action and national enabling policies.

As we grapple with old and new challenges in a rapidly urbanizing world, this timely report can help inform research, policy dialogue and development planning for years to come. I commend its findings to all who are working to create the just, green and dynamic environments that the inhabitants of the world's towns and cities need to thrive.

Ban Ki-moon
Secretary-General
United Nations

Introduction

This *State of the World's Cities Report (2010/11)* is published in a very important year – a key milestone that marks the halfway point towards the deadline for the "slum target" of the Millennium Development Goals. Government efforts to reduce the number of slum dwellers show some positive results.

According to new estimates presented in this Report, between the year 2000 and 2010 over 200 million people in the developing world will have been lifted out of slum conditions. In other words, governments have collectively exceeded the Millennium Target by at least a multiple of two.

However, this achievement is not uniformly distributed across regions. Success is highly skewed towards the more advanced emerging economies, while poorer countries have not done as well. For this reason, there is no room for complacency, because in the course of the same years the number of slum dwellers increased by six million every year. Based on these trends it is expected that the world's slum population will continue to grow if no corrective action is taken in the coming years.

This Report highlights the unprecedented challenges which urbanization throws at the world's cities today – particularly in the South – and the attendant *urban divide* which we all have to address collectively to stem the multiple deprivations that follow from unequal growth. These challenges include grinding poverty, environmental degradation, income inequalities, historical socio-economic inequalities, marginalization and various forms of exclusion.

Achieving sustainable urban development is likely to prove impossible if the *urban divide* is allowed not only to persist, but to continue growing, opening up an enormous gap, even in some cities a gulf, an open wound, which can produce social instability or at least generate high social and economic costs not only for the urban poor, but for society at large.

This edition of the Report underlines the choices available to policymakers across the range of economic, social, cultural and political challenges that are needed to bridge the *urban divide*. It charts a new course of action, with the steps and levers needed to achieve a more inclusive city, emphasizing the need for comprehensive and integrated responses that go beyond a compartmentalized, short-term perspective.

The Report benefits enormously from context-specific knowledge drawing in large part on regional perspectives and information, in a bid to inspire evidence-based local policy responses. In that sense, this Report contributes to bridge the gap between scientific information and societal action, which is a simple, but fundamental requisite, to promote equity and sustainability for more harmonious cities.

Anna K. Tibaijuka
Under-Secretary-General and Executive Director
United Nations Human Settlements Programme
(UN-HABITAT)

Acknowledgements

Core Team
Director: Oyebanji Oyeyinka
Coordinator: Eduardo López Moreno
Statistical Adviser: Gora Mboup

Principal Authors: Eduardo López Moreno, Oyebanji Oyeyinka, Gora Mboup
Editorial Management: Thierry Naudin, Rasna Warah
Editorial Support: Darcy Varney

Support Team
Contributors: Padmashree Sampath, Cecilia Zanetta, Miloon Kothari, Shivani Chaudhry, Christopher Williams
Research: Gianluca Crispi, Raymond Otieno Otieno, Anne Amin
Graphs: Gianluca Crispi, Azad Amir-Ghassemi, Raymond Otieno Otieno
Maps: Jane Arimah
Statistics: Julius Majale, Philip Mukungu, Souleymane Ndoye, Wandia Riunga, Barbara Agonga-Williams, Wladimir Ray
Administrative Assistance: Anne Idukitta, Elizabeth Kahwae, Mary Dibo

UN-HABITAT Advisory and Technical Support
Claudio Acioly, Ben Arimah, Alioune Badiane, Daniel Biau, Mohamed Halfani, Lucia Kiwala, Guenter Karl, Joseph Maseland, Naison Mutizwa-Mangiza, Oyebanji Oyeyinka, Andrew Rudd, Wandia Seaforth, Sharad Shankardass, Paul Taylor, Anna K. Tibaijuka, Emily Wong, Mariam Yunusa.

International Advisory Board
Robert Buckley, William Cobbett, Ali Farzin, Daniel Hoornweg, Maria da Piedade Morais, Marc Redwood, Dina K. Shehayeb, Germán Solinis, Yu Zhu.

Financial Support
Government of Norway, Kingdom of Bahrain, International Development Research Center (Canada).

Additional Contributions:
Background documents for policy analysis on the inclusive city:

Latin America and the Caribbean: Alain Santandreu (El Callao – Peru); César Valencia (Portoviejo – Ecuador); Cristina Reynals (Buenos Aires – Argentina); Daniel Ruben Cenci (Curitiba – Brazil); Dominique Mathon (Port-au-Prince – Haiti); Jaime Vásconez (Quito – Ecuador); José Luis Paniagu (Oruro – Bolivia); Ricardo Montezuma (Bogotá – Colombia); Tomás Martínez Baldares (Cartago – Costa Rica); Vanessa Marx (São Paulo – Brazil).
Africa: Babatunde Agbola (Abuja – Nigeria); F. K. E. Nunoo (Accra – Ghana); Rosemary Awuor-Hayangah (Durban and Johannesburg – South Africa); C. O. Olatubara, O J Omirin and F. F. Kasim (Ibadan – Nigeria), Catherine Adeya (Mombasa – Kenya); Agevi Elijah (Nairobi – Kenya).
Asia: Society for Development Studies (Jaipur, New Delhi and Mumbai – India); Muhammed Taher and Kazi Maruful Islam (Rajshahi – Bangladesh); Muhammed Taher, Rezaul Karim and Ghulam Murtaza (Khulna – Bangladesh); Muhammed Taher and Iftekhar U. Chowdhury (Chittagong – Bangladesh); Muhammed Taher and Nurul Islam Nazem (Dhaka); Jayasundera Warnakula (Colombo).

Input to boxes:
Shivani Chaudhry, Miloon Kothari, Eduardo López Moreno, Thierry Naudin, Francisco Perez Arellano, Raquel Rolnik, Padmashree Sampath, Pablo Vaggione, Darcy Varney, Rasna Warah, Emily Wong.

Additional research:
Azad Amir-Ghassemi, Charlotte Clayton, Martha Mathenge, Elizabeth Mwaniki, Onyema Onwuka, Claudia Umanzor Zelaya.
Additional contributions in map production: Victoria Abankwa, Kangwa Chama, Bharat Dahiya, Ali Farzin, Maria Dolores Franco Delgado, Eden Garde, Alberto Paranhos, Chris Radford, Dania Rifai, Ali Shabou, Kulwant Singh, Jonathan Stewart, Mansour Tall, Jaime Vásconez, Yu Zhu.

Country/region information:
Claudio Acioly; Marlene Fernandes and Maria da Piedade Morais (Brazil); Nefise Bazoglu (Turkey); Ali Farzin, (Iran and China); Simone Cecchini, Cecilia Martinez and Jorge Rodriguez (Latin American countries); Omondi Odhiambo (Lake Victoria); Keith Smith and Pinky Vilakazi (South Africa); Kulwant Singh (India), Vinod Tewari (India), Yu Zhu (China).

Cover montage: Boston Street ©Jorge Salcedo/Shutterstock and Kathmandu, Nepal ©Dhoxax/Shutterstock.

Contents

Part 03: Bridging the Urban Divide

©Mark Henley/Panos Pictures

Overview and Key Findings

The world is inexorably becoming urban. By 2030 all developing regions, including Asia and Africa, will have more people living in urban than rural areas. In the next 20 years, *Homo sapiens,* "the wise human", will become *Homo sapiens urbanus* in virtually all regions of the planet.

Cities – whether large or small, whole neighbourhoods, city centres, suburban or peri-urban areas – offer human beings the potential to share urban spaces, participate in public and private events and exercise both duties and rights. These opportunities in turn make it possible to cultivate societal values and define modes of governance and other rules that enable human beings to produce goods, trade with others and get access to resources, culture, and various forms of riches or well-being.

Cities can be open or closed with regard to residents' ability to access, occupy and use urban space, and even produce new spaces to meet their needs. Cities can also be open or closed in terms of residents' ability to access decisions and participate in various types of interaction and exchange. Some residents find the city as the place where social and political life takes place, knowledge is created and shared, and various forms of creativity and art are developed; other residents find that the city denies them these opportunities. Cities can therefore be places of inclusion and participation, but they can be also places of exclusion and marginalization.

The Urban Divide

Cities are constantly changing. They are built, rebuilt, transformed, occupied by different groups, and used for different functions. In the search for better spatial organization for higher returns, more efficient economies of scale and other agglomeration benefits, cities generate various degrees of residential differentiation. In most urban areas of the developed world, the segmentation of spaces for different uses is relatively visible, although social heterogeneity and mixed uses remain widespread. In contrast, in many cities of the developing world, the separation of uses and degrees of prosperity are so obvious that the rich live in well-serviced neighbourhoods, gated communities and well-built formal settlements, whereas the poor are confined to inner-city or peri-urban informal settlements and slums.

Cities, particularly in the South, are far from offering equal conditions and opportunities to their resident communities. The majority of the urban population is prevented from, or restricted in, the fulfillment of their basic needs because of their economic, social or cultural status, ethnic origins, gender or age. Others, a minority, benefit from the economic and social progress that is typically associated with urbanization. In some of these cities, the *urban divide* between "haves" and "have nots" opens up a gap – if not, on occasion, a chasm, an open wound – which can produce social instability or at least generate high social and economic costs not only for the urban poor, but for society at large.

Cities are, more often than not, divided by invisible borders. These split the "centre" from the "off-centre", or the "high" from the "low", as the urban divide is colloquially referred to in many parts of the South. These man-made demarcations are often completely different along a spatial and social continuum, reflecting the only difference experienced by their respective populations: socio-economic status. Closer assessment of the urban space in many cities of the developing world sheds forensic light on the fragmentation of society, marking out differences in the way space and opportunities are produced, appropriated, transformed and used. Some areas feature significant infrastructure, well-kept parks, gardens and up-market residential areas. In contrast, other areas are characterized by severe deprivation, inadequate housing, deficient services, poor recreation and cultural facilities, urban decay, and scarce capital investment in public infrastructure. These tangible differences in access come as symptoms of the intangible yet enduring divisions in society that apportion unequal opportunities and liberties across residents.

The physical divide takes the form of social, cultural and economic exclusion. Large sections of society are frequently excluded on grounds of predetermined attributes over which they have no control at all, such as gender, age, race, or ethnicity, or over which they have very little control, such as where they live (slums *vs.* rich neighbourhoods) or what they own (income and social status). However, this narrow perspective overlooks the actual and potential contributions of marginalized groups to the building of cities and nations, and therefore can only delay progress toward sustainable and *inclusive* development.

The urban divide is the face of injustice and a symptom of systemic dysfunction. A society cannot claim to be harmonious or united if large numbers of people cannot meet their basic needs while others live in opulence. A city cannot be harmonious if some groups concentrate resources and opportunities while others remain impoverished and deprived.

Yet cities are not – and should not be – "the world which man created, and therefore the world in which he is henceforth condemned to live". Cities are, on the contrary, vehicles for social change: places where new values, beliefs and ideas can forge a different growth paradigm that promotes rights and opportunities for all members of society. Based not only on moral and ethical arguments but also practical access to opportunity, the concept of an "inclusive city", or "a city for all", encompasses the social and economic benefits of greater equality, promoting positive outcomes for each and every individual in society.

Urban Trends

Urbanization: A Positive Force for Transformation

By the mid-20th century, three out of 10 people on the planet lived in urban areas. At that time, and over the following three decades, demographic expansion was at its fastest in cities around the world. Subsequently, a slow but steady process of deceleration took over. Today, half the world's population lives in urban areas and by the middle of this century all regions will be predominantly urban, with the tipping point in Eastern Africa anticipated slightly after 2050. According to current projections, virtually the whole of the world's population growth over the next 30 years will be concentrated in urban areas.

Although many countries have adopted an ambivalent or hostile attitude to urbanization, often with negative consequences, it appears today that this worldwide process is inevitable. It is also generally positive, as it brings a number of fundamental changes, namely: (a) in the employment sector, from agriculture-based activities to mass production and service industries; (b) in societal values and modes of governance; (c) in the configuration and functionality of human settlements; (d) in the spatial scale, density and activities of cities; (e) in the composition of social, cultural and ethnic groups; and (f) in the extension of democratic rights, particularly women's empowerment.

Using a wealth of significant and comparative new data, this Report identifies the trends, both similar and dissimilar, that characterize urbanization in various regions and countries; it does so against a background of significant recent changes, such as accelerated expansion or shrinking of cities, ageing populations, urban and regional dynamics and regional location factors, among others. In this respect, it is worth mentioning two significant trends that can either help bridge or exacerbate the urban divide:

- Cities are merging together to create urban settlements on a massive scale. These configurations take the form of mega-regions, urban corridors and city-regions. They are emerging in various parts of the world, turning into spatial units that are territorially and functionally bound by economic, political, socio-cultural, and ecological systems. Cities in clusters, corridors and regions are becoming the new engines of both global and regional economies, and they reflect the emerging links between urban expansion and new patterns of economic activity. However, as they improve inter-connectivity and create new forms of interdependence among cities, these configurations can also result in unbalanced regional and urban development as they strengthen ties to existing economic centres, rather than allow for more diffused spatial development.

The challenge here is for local authorities and regional governments to adopt policies that maximize the benefits of urbanization and respond to these forms of inter-connectivity and city interdependence. The rationale is to promote regional economic development growth, as well as to anticipate and manage the negative consequences of urban/regional growth, such as asymmetrical regional and urban development that has the potential to compound the urban divide.

- More and more people both in the North and South are moving outside the city to "satellite" or dormitory cities and suburban neighbourhoods, taking advantage of accommodation that can be more affordable than in central areas, with lower densities and sometimes a better quality of life in certain ways. Spatial expansion of cities is triggered not only by residents' preference for a suburban lifestyle, but also by land regulation crises, lack of control over peri-urban areas, weak planning control over land subdivisions, improved or expanded commuting technologies and services, as well as greater population mobility. Whether it takes the form of "peripherization" (informal settlements) or "suburban sprawl" (residential zones for high- and middle-income groups), sub-urbanization generates negative environmental, economic and social externalities. In developing countries, the phenomenon comes mainly as an escape from inadequate governance, lack of planning and poor access to amenities. Rich and poor seek refuge outside the city, which generates further partitioning of the physical and social space.

Cities must aim policies at current urban challenges (slums, affordable land, basic services, public transport) and more particularly anticipate expansion with sound planning policies and related actions that control the speculation associated with urban sprawl. Cities must also grant rights to the urban poor, along with affordable serviced land and security of tenure if further peripherization is to be avoided.

The Wealth of Cities

The prosperity of nations is intimately linked to the prosperity of their cities. No country has ever achieved sustained economic growth or rapid social development without urbanizing (countries with the highest per capita income tend to be more urbanized, while low-income countries are the least urbanized). Thanks to superior productivity, urban-based enterprises contribute large shares of gross domestic product (GDP). In other countries, it is a group of cities that accounts for a significant share of national GDP. The clustering of cities into mega-regions, urban corridors and city-regions operating as single economic entities sets in motion self-reinforcing, cumulative growth patterns that are making a significant contribution to the world's economic activity. High urban densities reduce transaction costs, make public spending on infrastructure and services more economically viable, and facilitate generation and diffusion of knowledge, all of which are important for growth. Hand in hand with economic growth, urbanization has helped reduce overall poverty by providing new opportunities, raising incomes and increasing the numbers of livelihood options for both rural and urban populations. Urbanization, therefore, does indeed play a positive role in overall poverty reduction, particularly where supported by well-adapted policies. However, when accompanied by weak economic growth, or when distributive policies are nonexistent or ineffective, urbanization results in local concentration of poor people rather than significant poverty reduction.

Cities have the potential to make countries rich because they provide the economies of scale and proximity that generate enhanced productivity. Economic growth can turn urban centres into effective "poverty fighters" if benefits and opportunities are redistributed through adequate policies. Cities can also significantly reduce rural poverty.

Slums: Good News are Shadowed by Bad News

In many developing countries, urban expansion has often been characterized by informality, illegality and unplanned settlements. Above all, urban growth has been strongly associated with poverty and *slum* growth. Fortunately, a number of countries have, to some extent, managed to curb the further expansion of slums and to improve the living conditions prevailing there. Uneven as they may have been

around the world, efforts to narrow the most unacceptable form of urban divide as represented by slums have yielded some positive results. According to UN-HABITAT estimates, between the year 2000 and 2010, a total 227 million people in the developing world will have moved out of slum conditions. In other words, governments have collectively exceeded the slum target of Millennium Development Goal 7 by at least 2.2 times, and 10 years ahead of the agreed 2020 deadline.

Asia stood at the forefront of successful efforts to reach the slum target, with governments in the region together improving the lives of an estimated 172 million slum dwellers between the year 2000 and 2010; this represents 74 per cent of the total number of urban residents in the world who no longer suffer from inadequate housing. China and India have improved the lives of more slum dwellers than any other countries, having together lifted no less than 125 million people out of slum conditions in the same period. After China and India, the most significant improvements in slum conditions in Asia were recorded in Indonesia, Turkey and Viet Nam. At sub-regional level, the greatest advances were recorded in Southern and Eastern Asia (73 and 72 million people, respectively), followed by South-East Asia (33 million). In contrast, Western Asia failed to make a contribution, as the number of slum dwellers in the sub-region increased by 12 million.

Across *Africa*, the lives of an estimated 24 million slum dwellers have improved in the last decade, representing 12 per cent of the global effort to narrow this form of urban divide. North Africa is the only sub-region in the developing world where both the number (8.7 million) and proportion of slum dwellers have steadily declined (from 20 to 13 per cent). Egypt, Morocco and Tunisia were the most successful countries. In sub-Saharan Africa, though, the total proportion of the urban population living in slums has decreased by only 5 per cent (or 17 million people). Ghana, Senegal, Uganda, Rwanda and Guinea were the most successful countries in the sub-region, reducing the proportions of slum dwellers by over one-fifth in the last decade.

Some 13 per cent of the progress made towards the global slum target occurred in *Latin America and the Caribbean*, where an estimated 30 million people have moved out of slum conditions since the year 2000. Over the past decade, Argentina, Colombia and Dominican Republic have been able to reduce their proportions of slum dwellers by over a third, making them the most successful countries in the region.

The successful municipalities took the responsibility for slum reduction squarely on their shoulders, backing commitments with bold policy reforms, and preventing future slum growth with equitable planning and economic policies. Recognition of the existence of slums must combine with long-term political commitment backed by adequate budget resources, policy reforms and institutional strengthening, strong monitoring and scaling up of successful local projects, if slums are to be tackled effectively.

In all developing regions, improving the lives of slum dwellers calls for macro-level programmes that include housing infrastructure and finance, improved water and sanitation, and adequate living spaces. However, these macro-level programmes must be associated with micro-level schemes, including micro-credit, self-help, education and employment.

The fact that an additional 227 million urban dwellers have gained access to improved water and sanitation as well as to durable and less crowded housing shows that a number of countries and cities are taking the slum target seriously. This enhances the prospects for millions of people to escape poverty, disease and illiteracy, and to lead better lives thanks to a narrower urban divide.

Kibera, Nairobi, Kenya. Urbanization can result in high levels of inequality. ©**Nairobi River Basin Project/UNEP**

Improving the lives of slum dwellers is the best way to achieve all the Millennium Development Goals. Improved housing conditions and provision of water and sanitation will not only save lives among the very poor, but also support progress in education and health.

Over the past 10 years, the *proportion* of the urban population living in slums in the developing world has declined from 39 per cent in the year 2000 to an estimated 32 per cent in 2010. And yet the urban divide endures, because in *absolute* terms the numbers of slum dwellers have actually grown considerably, and will continue to rise in the near future. Between the year 2000 and 2010, the urban population in the developing world increased by an estimated average of 58 million per annum; this includes 6 million who were not able to improve their conditions and joined the ranks of slum dwellers. At the same time, UN-HABITAT estimates that through upgrading or prevention of informal settlements, developing countries lifted an annual 22 million people out of slum conditions between the year 2000 and 2010. Based on these trends, the world's slum population is expected to reach 889 million by 2020.

Good news is coming with bad news. UN-HABITAT estimates confirm that the progress made on the slum target has not been enough to counter the demographic expansion in informal settlements in the developing world. In this sense, efforts to reduce the numbers of slum dwellers are neither satisfactory nor adequate.

Against this background, it is up to national governments to revise and increase the slum target to a number that takes into account both existing and potential new slums. Those nations that have been performing well so far must maintain or increase efforts to improve the living conditions of slum dwellers, while providing adequate alternatives to prevent new slum formation. Those governments that are falling behind in slum reduction must bring radical changes to their attitudes and policies vis-à-vis slums and urban poverty at large.

Efforts must focus on those regions facing the greatest development challenges in slum reduction: sub-Saharan Africa and Western Asia. Others in need of special attention are those countries which, for all their overall progress toward the slum target at national level, are still faced with huge spatial inequalities in some regions and cities. Finally, efforts are also required in those cities which, although they are doing relatively well, still feature large pockets of poverty where people remain marginalized.

Divided Cities

The urban divide does not just refer to a fragmented space or a community riven by socio-economic disparities. More often than not, economic lines of divide tend to coincide with social, cultural and political barriers. Various forms of exclusion continue to marginalize vast amounts of human capital ready to be mobilized for the sake of a sustainable city.

A divided city is one that fails to accommodate its poorer residents, regardless of the social and cultural riches they might contribute. Social divisions can permeate interactions amongst individuals even in the absence of significant ethnic, racial or other factors of segregation. Fresh divisions constantly emerge and become entrenched; patterns of social inclusion and exclusion preserve benefits for specific social segments based on physical location, shared interests, historic inequalities or other criteria.

If the four dimensions of the inclusive city – social, political, economic and cultural – are to be turned from a mere conceptual paradigm into reality, they must be implemented within a rights-based framework, and one that is easy to enforce. Short of this, prevailing patterns of exclusionary development, selective benefit-sharing, marginalization and discrimination will continue unabated in cities. City efforts to design and implement strategies for inclusiveness must be based on a clear and cogent representation of the way these four dimensions can be integrated concurrently into the day-to-day lives of the population.

Only through explicit and deliberately inclusive processes will it be possible to identify the locally appropriate, innovative and high-leverage actions and policies which government, public officials and major institutions can deploy to set in motion self-reinforcing processes that will bridge the urban divide.

Income Inequality in Cities: Contrasting Numbers

In general terms, income inequalities in *developed countries* are low. However, altogether, income inequalities in developed countries increased between the mid-1980s and 2005. Little is known about inequalities in European urban areas specifically, as available data is generally not disaggregated to individual cities. Still, nationwide aggregates do not always accurately reflect disparities in general urban or city-specific incomes. The most surprising variations between national and city-specific Gini coefficients of income or consumption disparities are found in the United States of America, where around 2005 the national coefficient stood at 0.38, but exceeded 0.5 in many major metropolitan areas including Washington, D.C.; New York City; Miami; and others. These values are comparable to the average Gini coefficients of cities in selected Latin American countries, where income inequality is particularly steep.

Income inequalities are higher in the *developing world* than in developed nations. New data presented by UN-HABITAT on Gini coefficients shows mixed results in the various regions of the South.

In general, urban inequality in *Latin America and the Caribbean* is declining, although it remains quite high. An analysis of income distribution trends in 17 selected countries in the region shows that in nine of them, urban Gini coefficients have fallen slightly between the late 1990s and 2006. However, in the urban areas of five other Latin

American countries, income inequalities have slightly risen or remained stable. The recent improvement in economic conditions in various countries across the region has resulted in a narrower income gap between rich and poor. However, the current financial and food crises are likely to dampen the chances for sustained economic growth in coming years, and short of appropriate pro-poor policies, inequalities may rise again, instead of declining further.

Trends in the economic divide in *Africa's* urban areas are mixed. Among the 13 countries under review, eight showed lower values (if only marginally for some) and five featured moderate to significant increases. The region's urban areas, in sub-Saharan Africa in particular, retain the highest degrees of poverty in the world, together with the highest prevalence of slum populations in urban areas. In African urban areas, progress in poverty reduction has been rather slow overall, but these mixed results in the distribution of income and consumption point to the hope of future improvements.

In *Asia*, the economic urban divide is widening. Although income and consumption inequality is low to moderate overall, average incomes have increased in almost all Asian countries, and poverty has fallen nearly everywhere in the region, with the exception of Bangladesh.

African cities appear to be the most unequal in the world (sample of 37 cities with an average Gini coefficient of 0.58). Next come Latin American cities (24 cities, with a Gini average of 0.52). Asian cities (30) feature a comparatively low degree of income inequality, as measured by a Gini coefficient of 0.384. Eastern Europe (8) and CIS cities (10) feature the lowest average Gini values and, presumably, the greatest degrees of equality, at 0.298 and 0.322, respectively.

Highly unequal income or consumption patterns in cities in the developing world point to institutional and structural failures, as well as to broader economic problems such as imbalanced labour markets or a lack of pro-poor policies. The more unequal the distribution of income or consumption in urban areas, the higher the risk that economic disparities will result in social and political tension.

Space Inequality: The Poverty Trap

The spatial divide in developing country cities does not just reflect income inequalities among households; it is also a by-product of inefficient land and housing markets, ineffective financial mechanisms and poor urban planning. While income inequalities are a major divisive social factor, the spatial inequalities visible in so many cities are an outgrowth of both socioeconomic disparities and larger processes of urban development, governance and institutionalized exclusion of specific groups.

When slum areas are physically isolated and disconnected from the main urban fabric, residents become cut off from the city, often enduring longer commuting times and higher transportation costs than they would if their neighbourhoods

were more integrated into urban networks. On top of low incomes and shelter deprivations, these residents find themselves underprivileged in terms of access to the urban advantage. Combined, the physical and social distance between poor and rich neighbourhoods represents a *spatial poverty trap* marked by six distinct challenges: (a) severe job restrictions; (b) high rates of gender disparities; (c) deteriorated living conditions; (d) social exclusion and marginalization; (e) lack of social interaction, and (f) high incidence of crime.

Absence of policy coordination between or within national and local government constrains cities' ability to meet the requirements of urban development and to deploy strategies that mitigate spatial inequality.

More gender-specific schemes, like maternity and childcare benefits, vocational training, protecting women's rights at the workplace, and micro-credit are required if women are to be lifted out of the spatial poverty trap.

Inequality of Opportunities

In every country in the world, access to the "urban advantage" and distribution of the related benefits is largely determined by various organizations and institutions – including, crucially, the formal land and labour markets as well as public utilities. The problem in developing countries is that most of these institutions are weak or dysfunctional, exposing them to undue influence from, or capture by, vested domestic or foreign interests. In some cities, necessary public institutions are lacking altogether, in which case essentially private vested interests fill the void and act as substitutes for institutions that would otherwise prioritize the interests of society at large. In both situations, the markets for land, basic services and labour are skewed in favour of private interests, enabling them to claim more than their fair shares of the benefits of the "urban advantage". In this process, uneducated people and young slum dwellers, particularly women, are deprived of the formal, secure livelihoods that could lift them up and out of the dire socioeconomic outcomes associated with the informal, insecure conditions in which they are forced to live.

As reflected in the limited resources available for good schooling, health and other facilities in many cities, unequal opportunities create "minorities in the marketplace" whose individual members are automatically excluded from a wide range of outcomes associated with economic growth and globalization – including demand for a skilled and healthy labour force.

The particular ways cities are planned, designed and built says much about what is valued there, and planning processes can either help or hinder development of opportunities for all. Basic services make a significant contribution to the "urban advantage", and together with employment feature high among the aspirations of those who move to cities in search of a brighter future.

Today, about 85 per cent of all new employment opportunities around the world occur in the informal economy and young people in slums are more likely to work in the informal sector than their non-slum peers. Despite some advantages, informal employment ends up trapping slum-dwelling and other low-income young people in perpetual poverty. Unfortunately, slum areas remain a "blind spot" when it comes to policy interventions, job creation and youth support.

So far, the benefits of the "urban advantage" keep eluding some specific groups, and women in particular. Poverty consistently exposes young urban females to steeper challenges than male peers when it comes to acquiring the knowledge and skills they need to live healthy, fulfilling lives.

Local authorities should adjust laws and regulations to lower the costs and increase the benefits for those willing to formalize their businesses. Local authorities should also provide assistance to small enterprises, enabling them to upgrade skills and improve access to both productive resources and market opportunities.

Large-scale, labour-intensive infrastructure and urban improvement works could provide gainful employment to the poor as well as their fair share in the "urban advantage". These labour-intensive programmes are to be combined with vocational training and skill development activities.

The Social Divide

The economic divide does more than deprive the poor of the proper shelter, basic utilities and dignified employment that are typically associated with the "urban advantage" and to which they are entitled. Beyond the functional goods and services that provide for decent living conditions, the repercussions of poverty can reach into life in its most physical and social dimensions.

Based on a systematic comparison of slum with non-slum populations within the same city, and groups of slum dwellers suffering various types of shelter deprivations, this Report demonstrates with compelling evidence that hunger, health and poor education outcomes have strong social class gradients, as measured by the intensity of shelter deprivations.

Hunger in cities. More and more urban populations are experiencing hunger and often with more intensity than those in rural areas. New data presented by UN-HABITAT on malnutrition in urban areas – as measured by the incidence of underweight children – shows significant differences in food security across socioeconomic groups in cities. As the relentless rise in food prices in urban areas combines with persistently low incomes, the urban poor cannot afford to purchase adequate amounts and types of food. Paradoxically, even in those countries with enough food for the whole population, only the richest can access it, while the poorest struggle every day to ensure one meal for their offspring.

Based on strong empirical evidence, this Report shows that the current food crisis is not the first of its kind. In many places, food insecurity has affected the daily lives of urban poor and rural families for at least the past two decades. Data reveals that in the developing world, serious malnutrition has been widespread in urban slums and rural areas since 1990, regardless of local food crises. Over the past 15 years, more than four out of 10 children suffered from stunted development in Asia and Africa; in the poorest nations of Latin America and the Caribbean, the proportion was three to five out of 10. Just like poverty, hunger in cities is only the outcome of an inequitable distribution of available resources. Children from poor families are often born into hunger, grow up in hunger, and might die in hunger if no remedial action is taken.

The structural food crises the urban poor keep experiencing on an ongoing basis call for fundamental policy remedies, including with regard to production, marketing, distribution, handling, and control of food for the urban market.

Slum upgrading is strongly linked to health and nutrition programmes, and altogether should be part of a comprehensive approach to improved lives for the urban poor.

Eradicating hunger will require multiple interventions, and not only those related to food availability. Use of safe water, improved sanitation and durable housing materials, combined with provision of sufficient living areas to ease overcrowding, will improve the chances of better health outcomes and life conditions for slum dwellers.

The health divide. The poor are typically driven to the least developed areas of a city, often places that are poorly integrated to the urban fabric, where dilapidated environments lead to worse health outcomes and greater risks of premature deaths than in improved and well-maintained urban areas. This Report argues that cities where a higher degree of equality prevails – including lower income disparities, lower incidence of slums and only small numbers of slum dwellers with various shelter deprivations – the occurrence of ill health tends to be noticeably less frequent. Conversely, public health is generally poorer in more unequal cities that feature stark material differences in housing and basic service provision. Better housing conditions are therefore essential to ensuring a healthy population. For instance, in cities featuring large numbers of households with all four basic shelter deprivations, the prevalence of diseases such as diarrhea rises twofold compared with the whole city, and about threefold or more when compared with the non-slum areas of the same city.

Moreover, child mortality rates remain highly associated with diarrhoeal diseases, malaria and acute respiratory infections related to overcrowding and air pollution; these in turn result from various environmental health hazards such as lack of sanitation and hygiene, lack of access to safe water, poor housing conditions, poor management of solid wastes, and many other hazardous conditions. Children in substandard environments are exposed to contaminated air, food, water and soil, and to conditions where parasite-carrying insects breed.

The fight against childhood diseases must look beyond the traditional realm of the household to encompass the modern environment of disease: the neighbourhood, and the city as a whole, with all their attendant risks and harms.

Education: Opportunities and inequalities. Access to education is greater in cities than in rural areas. In most countries of the South, the "urban advantage" is quite clear for both rich and poor in urban settings. However, not all cities are alike in their accommodation of young people's education and employment needs. Social and cultural barriers continue to deny slum dwellers the opportunity to complete their basic education. Children from slum communities are less likely to enroll in school and complete primary education; and youth living in the same communities have noticeably fewer opportunities to attend secondary school if compared with their peers in non-slum areas. These initial inequalities intensify at higher levels of education, perpetuating and reproducing an unfair system that restricts the physical and intellectual potential of millions of young urban dwellers, whose future is denied or jeopardized for lack of equitable distribution policies. The dilemma for many children of poor families is not what to study in the future, but a simple and shocking one: food, or school. Education remains a luxury for the urban poor in the face of current crises.

This Report sheds light on the particular challenges faced by slum populations with regard to this fundamental right, highlighting the fact that if the urban/rural gap in education has been reduced over time, the divide between rich and poor populations has been widening, and is cause for great concern. The Report also shows with fresh data that social inequalities are not only a matter of class hierarchy, but also of gender disparities. Still, efforts to improve the education of girls in some countries have resulted in significant increases in their enrolment numbers, but today a slight regression in boys' enrolment and participation is becoming a worrying trend that calls for gender-sensitive responses.

The education of girls and young women generates powerful poverty-reducing synergies and yields enormous intergenerational gains. It is positively correlated with enhanced economic productivity, more robust labour markets, higher earnings, and improved societal health and well-being.

Taking Forward the Right to the City

The "right to the city" has evolved over the past 50 years as a challenge to the exclusionary development, selective benefit-sharing, marginalization and discrimination that are rampant in cities today. More than a new legalistic device, the right to the city is the expression of the deep yearnings of urban dwellers for effective recognition of their various human rights. The concept has been deployed in various ways across regions, countries and cities of the world. In some places it has been used as a theoretical and political framework focusing on enforcement, empowerment, participation, self-fulfillment, self-determination and various forms of human rights protection at the city level. In other places, the concept has served as a platform for action and a practical framework for enforcement, whereas in some cities, the concept is absent from the political discourse, either not used at all or banned outright.

Where the right to the city has been implemented, higher degrees of inclusion have not necessarily ensued, though. Large numbers of people, particularly in the developing world, do not fully benefit from the "urban advantage", do not participate in decision-making and do not enjoy effective fundamental rights and liberties, while others do, living in decent, healthy and environmentally friendly places with full exercise of their citizenship. Some other countries have made significant efforts to close the urban divide as part of a less specific "rights-based" approach, or only recognizing some particular aspects of the right to the city. Despite these ambiguities, the right to the city remains a powerful vehicle for social change.

Brazil in 1988 was the first country to include the right to the city in its constitution. As an expert from São Paulo commented in the UN-HABITAT policy analysis on the inclusive city, "nowadays, talking about rights is talking about the right to the city". Ecuador recognized several housing-related rights in its 2008 constitution, including the right to the city. In that country, a respondent to the survey component of the policy analysis in Portoviejo associated this right with unrestricted access to services, freedom of opinion and participation, and equal access to opportunities: "This right is, in its broader sense, endorsed by decision-makers, as well as recognized and implemented by the community in its everyday life through widespread practice."

Many other cities in the developing world devise and deploy policies in compliance with national legal commitments to more inclusive communities; although they fall short of explicit references to the right to the city *per se*, they endorse some particular aspects of the notion. For example, Rosario, Argentina's third largest city, has declared itself a *"Human Rights City"* with a formal commitment to openness, transparency and accountability. In Australia, the

Victoria Charter of Human Rights and Responsibilities (2006) refers explicitly to equal rights, including freedom, respect, equality and dignity for all. Some other countries and cities endorse aspects of democratic governance that are explicitly or implicitly consistent with the "right to the city" concept: Dakar's *Civic and Citizens' Pact* (2003); India's *Citizen's Charter* (1997); and Porto Alegre's *Participatory Budgeting* and *Local Solidarity and Governance Programme (2004)*.

A number of cities in India, Ghana, South Africa, Colombia, Brazil, Ecuador, Peru and other Latin American countries are also taking forward the right to the city concept in a variety of spheres (social, economic, political, and cultural), even if progress is often rather slow and sometimes suffers from repeated setbacks. In some other cities and countries, particularly in South-Eastern and Eastern Asia and North Africa, economic growth policies have gone hand in hand with positive social developments and the populations enjoy a decent quality of life, but political rights and freedom are lagging behind. Other cities and countries, mainly in sub-Saharan Africa and Western Asia, are about to deploy legal and political frameworks based on equality and rights.

This Report identifies the factors hindering implementation of the right to the city and other forms of inclusion needed to bridge the urban divide. In addition to a variety of factors – historical socioeconomic inequalities, grinding poverty, environmental degradation and more frequent climate change-related natural disasters, among other threats – the Report highlights poorly defined inclusive mechanisms and institutions. It also points to deficiencies in the instruments that make it possible to understand and anticipate some of the factors generating further inequalities (i.e., scarcity of land and concentration of ownership in very few hands; lack of redistributive policies; ineffective housing markets, etc.). Moreover, only very few municipal leaders have demonstrated a proper sense of vision or political commitment to overcome the urban divide.

UN-HABITAT policy analysis shows that more often than not, policy aims and processes do not match because they fail to acknowledge the inter-linkages among the four spheres or dimensions of the inclusive city – economic, social, political, and cultural. Admittedly, cities will, time and again, adopt new rules and regulations in a bid to address some exclusion-related issues; but these fail to spell out specific goalposts, sustained processes or tangible results that can be monitored. Moreover, institutional frameworks tend over time to embed negative instead of positive attitudes, and to entrench informal social arrangements that are impervious to change. The Report details the most important factors that prevent cities from bridging the urban divide and taking forward the right to the city. These include (1) poor coordination among various tiers of government; (2) absence of data for informed policy choices; (3) influence of vested interests; (4) inadequate adjustment to changing economic conditions; and (5) exclusion of marginalized groups and discrimination of minorities.

Against this background, it is not surprising that more than two-thirds of respondents to the UN-HABITAT policy analysis survey perceived urban reforms as serving primarily the interests of the rich, with politicians and civil servants coming next (except in Africa, where they are viewed as the major beneficiaries). The urban poor stand to share only to a minimal extent, if at all, in any benefits accruing from urbanization and related reforms. As one of the experts from Latin America commented, "When one is [economically] poor, one is also poor and excluded in a cultural, social and political sense". The majority of excluded groups in slum areas typically fall victim to a sort of *triple jeopardy*: (1) they are poor and uneducated; (2) many are migrants or from ethnic minorities; and (3) many are female.

This Report identifies the key principles underlying the right to the city, providing the basic underpinnings needed by those municipalities interested in a rights-based approach to inclusion that does not overtly endorse the "right to the city" concept. The Report also discusses some critical aspects that are needed to guarantee an effective right to the city for all. In particular, this right must be seen as a vision for an alternative, well-devised, ideal city; instead of a right to any city, especially today's dominant, defective model, this is an entitlement to an urban environment where mutual respect, tolerance, democracy and social justice prevail.

Adoption and implementation of a strong human rights-based approach upholds the dignity of all urban residents in the face of multiple rights violations, including the right to decent living conditions. The right to the city can provide municipal authorities with the platform they need for a wide range of policies and initiatives that promote an "inclusive" urban environment.

The right to the city calls for a holistic, balanced and multicultural type of urban development. Therefore, it must pervade all policy areas, including land use, planning, management and reform, and it must do so in close cooperation with government agencies and civil society.

The Regional Dynamics of Inclusion

The urban divide results from social, economic, political, and cultural exclusion. Taken individually, each of these dimensions has far-reaching consequences for urban dynamics and the way policy initiatives can influence inequality. However, this Report shows with compelling evidence that these four dimensions overlap and interact to a substantial degree. Therefore, understanding the dynamic linkages among them is essential to any prompt and sustainable transition from a partially to a completely inclusive city. Any government committed to promoting inclusiveness should act in a proactive way across the four dimensions. UN-HABITAT policy analysis highlights significant associations among them, and these findings can be readily used by municipal and other public authorities to guide their own efforts and policies on the way to more inclusive cities.

Economic inclusion is tied closely to the social and political dimensions of inclusion. Some cities grow and prosper, others are less successful. In any of these cases, genuine economic inclusion leading to equitable allocation of opportunities and income is, to a very large extent, determined by the political, cultural and social equality parameters that are specific to any given city.

UN-HABITAT analysis shows that in African surveyed cities, economic inclusion appears to be strongly associated with the planning functions of municipal, state/provincial and national government, as well as with the active involvement of non-governmental organizations that advocate stronger political will, freedom of expression and human rights. The connection between economic inclusion and social and political freedoms comes as a response to extensive rent-seeking by the political and economic elites that dominate the urban economy. For all purposes and effects, this correlation echoes a call to democratize the business sector in order to open it up and provide opportunities for all, instead of systematically denying these to most citizens due to weak institutions, inadequate regulatory frameworks, and poor government management of the economic sphere.

In *Asia,* economic inclusiveness in surveyed cities is associated with government-induced employment (through infrastructure development, for example), together with fiscal incentives and sound contractual and legal frameworks. Freedom of expression is also strongly associated with economic inclusiveness in this region. This can be explained by the expansion of the middle class as a result of economic prosperity in various countries, which in turn is accompanied by greater demands not just for the sake of improved social and economic conditions, but also for transparency and accountability.

In *Latin American and Caribbean* cities under review, multiparty democracy and freedom of the press are both strongly associated with economic inclusiveness. Despite significant progress in democratic governance, expert opinion suggests that political institutions, rule of law and accountability in this region do not always work properly and still fall short of the expectations of urban populations. This political call to amend dysfunctional social and economic institutions is echoed in survey respondents' perceptions that urban policies, reforms and decisions benefit the rich by up to three times as much as they do slum dwellers and the poor.

Reform of government institutions, combined with modernized public policies and novel forms of participation, are of crucial importance if economic inclusion of the poor is to be improved.

Africa's national, local and municipal authorities must improve coordination of their planning and implementation functions if the urban divide is to be narrowed across the continent.

Social inclusiveness calls for a multidimensional approach. Once again, findings show that coordination at all levels of government is critical to bridging the social divide. Interestingly, among all policy interventions, government health care programmes appear to be the most effective bridge over the social divide; in *Africa,* public transport features as the second most effective way of reducing social inequalities.

In the Asian cities under review, UN-HABITAT analysis shows that improvements in social inclusiveness are closely associated with the political role of non-governmental organizations advocating stronger political commitment by government, along with freedom of expression and other human rights. This strong link suggests that these organizations should play an even more proactive role in the political sphere; they could, for instance, encourage the citizenry to regroup and put public authorities under more pressure, as is already the case in Latin American cities. Civil society must also explore new frontiers if it is effectively to support the institutional strengthening required to promote equality, political rights and civil liberties.

In *Latin American and Caribbean* cities under review, social inclusion is associated with several policy variables, particularly in three areas: change in existing rules to promote employment, improvements in political governance, and freedom of cultural expression. The experts participating in the UN-HABITAT policy analysis were of the view that an enabling, efficient legal framework would stimulate formal job creation and therefore it is an essential pre-requisite for social and economic inclusion. Experts also considered that institutions and enforcement mechanisms would enable communities to raise their voices in order to ensure that their demands are heard and mainstreamed both in legal frameworks and policy decisions. Finally, in some cities culture is promoted as a means of social inclusion. In Bogotá, for instance, culture builds collective identity and conviviality as an antidote to violence, illustrating its potential role in social transformation.

A healthy, well-educated population is a major asset for any city, and knowledge is a prerequisite for enhanced civic participation in the social, political and cultural spheres.

Where cities fail to deploy institutions and procedures that are more responsive to the needs of ordinary people (including the poor), exclusion and social inequality will continue to interfere with effective basic rights and liberties for everyone, a phenomenon that can pose threats to social and political stability.

Political inclusiveness and democratic governance.
It comes as no surprise that freedom of expression and the press, multiparty elections and a constitutional guarantee of cultural expression were all found to be positively linked to political inclusiveness in the *African* cities under review – even though these components of democratic politics are at different stages of advancement across countries, and making relatively slow progress overall. The statement of an expert respondent to the policy analysis in Abuja that "the city is dominated by the politics of the rich and *godfatherism*", seems to echo a general sentiment in various other African cities. However, some aspects of democracy (e.g., proper election standards, viability of basic democratic institutions, courts and legislatures) and social participation are becoming more dominant in the political discourse in the region. In Ghana, Liberia, Rwanda and South Africa, public administrations have been more responsive.

In *Latin America and the Caribbean*, too, freedom of expression and the press is, naturally enough, associated with political inclusion, as are multiparty elections. In this region, the factors behind inequalities remain as challenging as ever, and an expert in Bogotá noted that "poverty and exclusion act as restricting factors for some groups, so that civil and political freedoms for them often end up being more symbolic than effective". Although social participation is recognized as a civic right, and good practice in this respect is not absent across the continent, experts rated it very low. Still, in general terms, the political process is looking very encouraging in a number of cities and countries in this region, as it is beginning to usher in a more positive political and institutional environment. Various instances of best practice demonstrate the close links between political inclusiveness, democratic governance and full exercise of civic and political rights. Other instances show a clear connection between cultural expression and political inclusion (e.g., Bogotá's Declaration of Cultural Rights).

The empirical link between democratic governance and social inclusion highlights the need for institutions and enforcement mechanisms that favour participatory decision-making, while guaranteeing effective freedom of speech and the press.

Using culture for social, economic and political inclusion. In cities as diverse as Buenos Aires, Port-au-Prince, Chittagong, Abuja or Mombasa, cultural diversity and city inclusion find themselves challenged by a similar set of factors, namely, extremely inequitable provision of cultural facilities and access to culture, technology and information among poorer areas and more affluent neighbourhoods. This cultural divide undermines the capacity of the poor to take advantage of modern-day cultural and other opportunities for self-development and enjoyment.

Numerous cities are, nevertheless, struggling to promote culture in underprivileged areas and enabling some forms of cultural rights and expressions; they do so through three main channels: (1) *ad hoc* provision of shared spaces for cultural events; (2) promotion of intercultural programmes; and (3) the protection and celebration of specific monuments and buildings that are part of the architectural heritage. In most such cases, though, the rationale behind the promotion of cultural expression and heritage preservation is to impose fixed values and single, one-way meanings on places and narratives, which are made to reflect only the history of the country's or city's ethnic majority and oligarchies. Consequently, various other cultural and ethnic groups fail to recognize themselves in that particular history or local identity, adding to their sense of systematic exclusion. In all developing regions, the poor and slum dwellers appear to be systematically excluded from cultural life, along with the elderly, young people and foreign migrants. Poverty in Asia, Africa and Latin America conspires against cultural inclusion. An expert in Quito characterized this relationship in no uncertain terms: "An individual who is poor economically will very often be poor socially and culturally, too". In *Asian* and *African* cities, where culture is historically entrenched in various forms of inequalities that persist across generations, freedom of expression appears to be strongly linked with cultural inclusion. In the *Latin American and Caribbean* cities under review, cultural inclusiveness is positively correlated with laws that promote equitable employment, as well as with fiscal incentives, micro-credit and formal municipal promotion of culture. Cities and countries that are bridging the cultural divide combine effective access to education, the judiciary and other public and private services, as well as sports and leisure activities and amenities, recognizing that cultural diversity is essential to the construction of citizenship. This recognition is fundamental if traditional behaviour, attitudes and practice are to be transformed for the purposes of an enhanced democratic culture.

Cities should encourage anything that can foster multiple and complementary identities in order to reduce any polarization between various groups, particularly in a multi-cultural, multi-linguistic, multi-ethnic type of society. Recognition of cultural diversity entails the deployment of spaces and conditions that favour various forms of active participation, in accordance with the different societal, cultural and organizational forms that characterize any given population.

Five Strategic Steps to an Inclusive City

An inclusive city can be defined and individually experienced in many different ways by its residents. Still, inclusive cities share a few basic features that can take different forms in various conditions: they provide the opportunities and supportive mechanisms that enable all residents to develop their full potential and gain their fair shares of the "urban advantage". In an inclusive city, residents perceive themselves as important contributors to decision-making, ranging from political issues to the more mundane routines of daily life. Active participation guarantees all residents a stake in the benefits of urban development. The concepts of human relations, citizenship and civic rights are all inseparable from urban inclusiveness.

UN-HABITAT policy analysis has identified a series of practical strategic steps and catalysts for change that make it easier for municipal authorities to bridge the urban divide. The practical strategic steps that contribute to the promotion of an inclusive city are the following: (1) assessing the past and measuring progress; (2) establishing new, more effective institutions, or strengthening existing ones as needed; (3) building new linkages and alliances among various tiers of government; (4) developing a sustained, comprehensive vision to promote inclusiveness; and (5) ensuring an equitable redistribution of opportunities.

1) Assessing the past and measuring progress. The beauty and the challenge of urban space is that no two cities are alike. Each has its own history, economy, politics, social dynamics, cultural beat and, above all, human potential. Cities do not become divisive overnight; rather, as this report shows, exclusion and marginalization build and reproduce over time due to fierce and unequal competition for land, labour, capital, resources, and the like. Understanding the specific factors behind the urban divide and the way it makes itself felt in any given city is a crucial step for those municipal authorities committed to promoting inclusion. Such understanding can help determine the direction of change and anticipate the institutional and financial requirements for reform. It also establishes a starting point from which future policies and practices can be assessed, enabling city managers to monitor progress and evaluate performance.

2) More effective, stronger institutions. In the cities of the developing world, existing rules and institutions are generally perceived as creations of the rich and powerful that frequently cater to their sole interests, with little regard for those of other social groups, particularly the poor. However, a new development paradigm is placing institutions at the centre of efforts to promote sustainable development and reduce poverty and inequality, recognizing their moral leverage and power of social transformation. Evidence from successful cities shows that the *way* municipalities perform their duties is just as important as the *nature* of what they achieve. Inclusive cities conduct in-depth reviews of their systems, structures and institutional mechanisms to pave the way for genuine change, including the more effective and stronger institutions that are part of a structural and societal transformation process.

3) Building new linkages and alliances among the various tiers of government. Evidence from the UN-HABITAT expert survey shows that it takes no less than the three tiers of government (city, state/provincial and national) to make a city inclusive, and even a fourth one – metropolitan-area coordinating bodies – depending on local circumstances. Unfortunately, in the developing world, reality is all-too-often at odds with this finding, as government coordination remains patchy, poor and informal. Cities that manage both to develop innovative programmes and actions and deploy greater "entrepreneurship" achieve more if they establish strategic alliances that combine policies and resources with other tiers of government as well as the private sector. Efficient linkages among various public authorities and civil society also ensure greater sustainability of local programmes. Experience shows that at the root of successful collaboration lies an institutional and managerial capacity to share resources such as staff, skills, funding, information and knowledge for mutual benefit or gain.

4) Demonstrating a sustained vision to promote inclusiveness. Cities need a clear "vision" of their future – a long-term plan that combines creativity, realism and inspiration on top of providing a framework for strategic planning. A city's "vision" builds upon its specific identity, comparative advantage, geographic endowments and defining historical and cultural dimensions. It is not just a city's function, structure and form that its vision projects into the future, but also a community's dreams and aspirations. For this reason, any city "vision" should always be context-driven and developed with the participation of all segments of the population. Unfortunately, at present, in a majority of cities, urban planning practice seems to be divorced from any long-term city vision, and many major decisions are influenced by pressures from various stakeholders. Thus, an open, transparent process that integrates various kinds of urban stakeholders has more chances to address entrenched problems of exclusion, proposing solutions that are appropriate both culturally and politically. Such inclusive development of a vision and planning in turn enhances the potential for collective ownership, as the proposed action plan is endorsed by the broadest possible constituency. A city's vision must be optimistic and ambitious, and at the same time realistic. It should be innovative if it is to break with the inertia of the past and bring about a qualitative leap towards the future. A vision should turn into a workable plan with clearly defined funding sources and accounting mechanisms. In this sense, far from being a fiction, a "vision" is a plan, a roadmap, and a commitment that is made by city authorities (who are the leaders, custodians and promoters of the vision) and the other tiers of government and civil society (who are major stakeholders in the process).

5) Ensuring the redistribution of opportunities. Cities are places of opportunity. They act as the engines of national economies, driving wealth creation, social development and employment. The urban environment acts as the primary locus for innovation, industrial and technological progress, entrepreneurship and creativity. Strong empirical evidence confirms that the concentration of people and productive activities in cities generates economies of scale and proximity that stimulate growth and reduce the costs of production, including the delivery of collective basic services such as piped water, sewers and drains, electricity, solid waste collection, public transport, health care, schools and many other public amenities and services. However, as it concentrates people and productive activities, a city can become a problem if it is inadequately planned or poorly governed, or when distributional policies are lacking or dysfunctional. The distribution of opportunities across the population can, therefore, become skewed or inequitable. Still, all these challenges are outnumbered by opportunities: cities will continue to stand at the crossroads of an interdependent world, producing goods, services and ideas within an institutional framework that can either overcome or exacerbate the urban divide.

Equal Opportunities: Catalysts for Distributive Change

The five strategic steps described above provide municipal authorities with the overall strategic framework they need to bridge the urban divide and move towards a more inclusive city. This dynamic framework is designed to support local rights-based policies that tackle exclusion in its various dimensions and redistribute opportunities across urban populations. In this respect, UN-HABITAT policy analysis has identified five catalysts for distributive change that municipal authorities can activate in cooperation with provincial and national government. These catalysts overlap with the four dimensions of exclusion/inclusion as well as with the recognized international rights implicitly subsumed in the "right to the city". More specifically, improvements in the living conditions of the urban poor, investment in human capital and fostering employment opportunities are designed to affirm social and economic inclusion and rights, and the other two catalysts explicitly focus on political and cultural inclusion and rights. Socioeconomic inclusion calls for land tenure reform and capital investment in infrastructure, which create the conditions for people to fulfill their individual potential. The catalysts for distributive change involve local government practices that foster political inclusion, as well as budgeting and planning procedures that achieve cultural inclusion through direct involvement of ethnic minorities in decision-making. The five policy catalysts are as follows:

a) *Improve quality of life, especially for the urban poor.* Creating the conditions for improved access to safe and healthy shelter, secure tenure, basic services and social amenities such as health and education, is essential to any individual's physical, psychological, social and economic development and well-being.

b) *Invest in human capital formation.* Cities and regions are well-placed to ensure strategic coordination between the institutions and various stakeholders involved in human capital formation, and to design policies that are well-adjusted to local needs. Such capital formation is a condition for socioeconomic development and a more equitable distribution of the urban advantage,

c) *Foster sustained economic opportunities.* Cities can stimulate sustained economic growth for poor and underprivileged populations through promotion of labour-intensive projects. These include primarily public works and the construction industry, which can give opportunities for support to small-scale enterprises and the informal sector. Moreover, and in close cooperation with national government, a number of cities in the developing world have launched various forms of social security or protection schemes in a bid to expand access to economic opportunities for those traditionally excluded from mainstream wealth creation and economic development. In this respect, conditional cash transfers (CCTs) stand out as the most efficient poverty reduction mechanism. These schemes enhance incomes in the short run and capabilities in the long run.

d) *Enhance political inclusion.* Today, more and more municipal and national authorities share the same basic philosophy: bringing government within the reach of ordinary people through enhanced mutual engagement. Some of these municipalities are constantly trying out new modes of political participation, creating permanent fora for dialogue and negotiation. The physical space is becoming a political space in terms of systems of representation and participation, and in this sense is a fundamental aspect of local democracy.

e) *Promote cultural inclusion.* Culture has historically been left out of the conventional international development agenda, or relegated to its fringes. However, more and more scholars and experts have come to realize that some cities in the South have opted for a more comprehensive perspective on development, one where culture features as one of the levers of success. More and more local development policies and strategies are by now mainstreaming some of the cultural dimensions of urban life, such as social capital, tradition, symbols, meaning, sense of belonging and pride of place, on top of optimal use of local cultural resources by local communities. A number of cities today are using culture as a transformational tool to integrate ethnic minorities, preserve regional values, safeguard linguistic and religious diversity, resolve conflicts, protect the heritage in the built environment, and in the process promote economic development. Beyond the sole cultural sphere, these policies together can go a long way towards bridging the urban divide in its other – social, political and economic – dimensions.

It takes five catalysts to integrate the poor and marginalized into mainstream urban life: improved quality of life, investment in human capital formation, sustained economic opportunities, enhanced political inclusion, and cultural inclusion.

STATE OF THE WORLD'S CITIES 2010/2011

BRIDGING THE URBAN DIVIDE

PART 01

Urban Trends

1.1
Cross-currents in global urbanization

Quick Facts

1. In the developing world, the region with the greatest proportion of people living in urban centres is Latin America and the Caribbean, whereas sub-Saharan Africa – and Eastern Africa in particular – has the lowest percentage of urban dwellers.

2. Urbanization remains a driving force of demographic change, though it is slowing down at different paces in different parts of the world.

3. Suburbanization and urban sprawl are happening in different places throughout the world, spreading low-density urban patterns and negative environmental, economic and social externalities.

4. Urban sprawl in an environment of poverty exacerbates the urban divide.

Policy Points

1. Suburbanization in developing countries comes mainly as an escape from poor governance, lack of planning and poor access to amenities. Rich and poor escape to find refuge outside the city, which generates further partitioning of the physical and social space.

2. Conurbations are turning into mega-regions, city-regions and urban corridors, and outside these engines of global and regional economies isolated cities have fewer chances to prosper.

3. Worldwide urbanization is inevitable, and generally positive, but equality or inequality in cities is influenced by policy choices.

4. Too many countries have adopted an ambivalent or hostile attitude to the urbanization process, with negative consequences.

Our Shared Urban Future

The United Nations predicts that by the year 2030, more people in every region of the world will live in urban than in rural areas, even in Asia and Africa, which are now the least urbanized parts of the globe.[1] Our shared future will largely come about through the social, political, economic, and cultural dynamic that is urbanization – the convergence of human activity and aspiration in all cities, regardless of size.

The urbanization process is characterized not only by demographic shifts from rural to urban areas, or by the growth of urban populations, but also by changes in various aspects of society:

- in the employment sector, from agriculture-based activities to mass production and service industries;
- in societal values and modes of governance;
- in the configuration and functionality of human settlements;
- in the spatial scale, density and activities of places; and
- in the composition of social, cultural and ethnic groups and the extension of democratic rights, particularly women's empowerment.

Although urbanization takes different forms and its incidence is not uniform, the experiences of diverse countries around the world exhibit some remarkable similarities, as well as distinct differences.

This chapter identifies the trends, both convergent and divergent, that characterize urbanization in various regions and countries against a background of significant recent changes, such as accelerated expansion or shrinking of cities, ageing populations, urban and regional dynamics and location factors, among others. Analysis of global trends helps raise awareness of where there is a need to maximize gains and locate or relocate investments and opportunities, and provides information about how to plan for more sustainable development. Such analysis also points to the need to design economic recovery policies, rethink urban and regional strategies and create new opportunities; it also offers insights into to the best ways of anticipating urbanization and managing the negative consequences of urban growth, such as asymmetrical regional and urban development and various types of disparities.

Convergent Urban Growth Patterns

A slower though more pervasive urbanization

If current projections are anything to go by, virtually the whole of the world's demographic growth over the next 30 years will be concentrated in urban areas – a stark contrast with the pattern that prevailed between 1950 and 1975, a period characterized by a much more balanced split between urban and rural areas.[2] At the same time, the pace of urbanization in the world is not accelerating, not even in the developing world. On a global scale, the urban population is expected to grow at an average annual rate of roughly 1.5 per cent from 2025 to 2030. The decade when urban demographic expansion was at its fastest across the world was the 1950s, with an annual growth rate of over 3 per cent. By the late 1980s, this pace had slowed to an annual 2.7 per cent. Between 2010 and 2015, the annual growth of the global urban population is expected to slow even further, to 1.9 per cent.[3] Developing countries are also experiencing a slowdown in overall population growth, from an annual 4.1 per cent in the early 1960s to 2.5 per cent in 2010; similarly, urban population growth in the developing world is expected to fall to an annual 1.8 per cent between 2025 and 2030.

For all this notable slowdown in urban population growth rates around the world, current trends and projections suggest that urbanization is to continue in both developed and developing regions of the world. More specifically, by 2050 urban dwellers will likely account for 86 per cent of the population in the more developed and 67 per cent in the less developed regions. Overall, it is expected that 7 out of 10 people will be living in urban areas by 2050. In the less urbanized regions of the world, namely, Africa and Asia, the proportion of the urban population is expected to increase to 61.8 per cent and 66.2 per cent, respectively, by the middle of the century.

Urbanization is strongly linked to the development process

Already, half of the world's population is urban, and it can only become more so in the future. Even though various countries are on different paths of economic development and are making the urban transition at different times and with different urban growth patterns, it remains quite clear that urbanization is an inevitable outcome of the development process. The real challenge is for governments to adopt policies that maximize the benefits of urbanization.

A country's degree of urbanization, as measured by the share of its urban population in relation to total population, is also an apt indicator of its wealth. Most nations with high per capita incomes are among the most urbanized, just as most of those with low per capita incomes are among the least urbanized. Empirical evidence clearly demonstrates that as a country

▲
Souzhou, China. Urbanization and economic growth are inextricably linked even at the regional level. ©**Tan Wei Ming/Shutterstock**

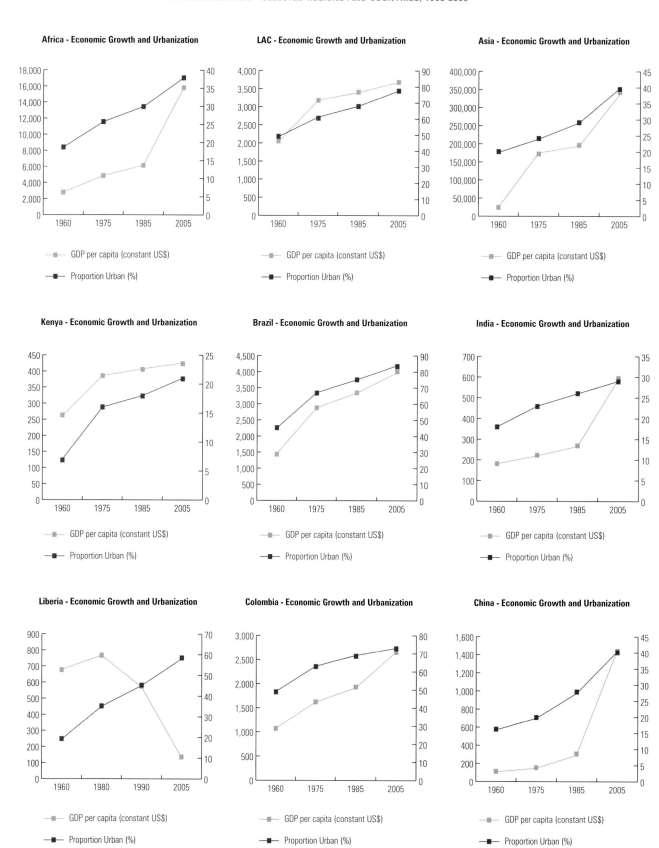

Source: UNDESA, World Urbanization Prospects, 2007 revision - World Bank, World Development Indicators.

▲
Kibera, Nairobi, Kenya. Urbanization can result in severe inequality. ©**Manoocher Deghati/IRIN**

becomes more urban, its per capita income also tends to rise, as shown in Figure 1.1.1. In this sample, only Liberia, a country recently ravaged by civil war, has experienced a decline in per capita income while its population was becoming more urban, indicating that internal conflicts (which in this particular case drove thousands of rural people to seek the security of towns and cities) have serious consequences for economic growth.

The link between urbanization and economic development is clear in Asia, where rapid urbanization has been the major factor behind the growth dynamic, in the process also contributing to overall reductions in poverty rates.[4] In Latin America, economic development and urbanization have historically been linked in a process of industrialization and modernization, even though this has resulted in high degrees of inequality between and within countries. In Africa, the link between urbanization and economic development is more tenuous, particularly in sub-Saharan countries; however, recent research suggests a positive link between the two variables in most African countries, as is generally the case in other regions.[5] For instance, Rwanda in the late 1990s experienced a very high annual urban growth rate of more than 17 per cent as the country rebuilt after a severe conflict; the pace slowed down to a relatively high 7 per cent between 2000 and 2005, and to just over 4 per cent between 2005 and 2010 (estimates). At the same time, rapid urbanization in Rwanda over the last decade has gone hand in hand with healthy economic indicators as annual growth rates have ranged between 3 and 9 per cent since 2002.[6] Although today less than 20 per cent of Rwanda's population is urban, the proportion is expected to rise to nearly 30 per cent by 2030, compared with just 20 per cent in neighbouring Uganda and Burundi.[7]

Urbanization and economic growth are inextricably linked not only at the national level, but in regions within individual countries, too. Those regions experiencing economic growth also tend to urbanize quickly, and those urbanizing faster typically experience higher rates of economic growth. Cities along China's eastern seaboard are a good example, but there are many others, such as the National Capital Region in the Philippines, the Mekong River Delta in Viet Nam, Maputo and the Southern Region of Mozambique, and Tangier-Tetouan in northern Morocco, to name just a few. Those regions that are economically successful are not only more urbanized than others in the same country: they are also experiencing urban population growth rates that are roughly two to three times the national average.

Whether urbanization influences economic growth, or the reverse, remains a moot point. What is quite clear, though, is that the level of urbanization (or the proportion of people living in urban areas) is associated in some places with numerous, positive societal outcomes, such as technological innovation, various forms of creativity, economic progress, higher standards of living, enhanced democratic accountability, and women's empowerment.[8] In this sense, urbanization can be a positive force for economic development, and also one that has desirable social and political outcomes; indeed, some of the world's fastest-growing cities are also among the best governed, and some provide the best quality of life in their respective nations.[9] In those cases where urbanization has not been concomitant with significant improvements in quality of life or governance, other, divisive factors may be at play, such as extreme inequalities, conflict, inadequate or ineffective policies, which can block development or substantially set back progress.

Novel urban configurations: Mega-regions, urban corridors and city-regions

As the world becomes more urban, new residents will continue to be distributed across cities of all sizes and much along the current prevalent pattern.[10] In some instances, though, cities are merging together to create urban settlements on a massive scale. These new configurations take the form of mega-regions, urban corridors and city-regions (see Map 1.1.1). Mega-regions are natural economic units that result from the growth, convergence and spatial spread of geographically linked metropolitan areas and other agglomerations.[11] They are polycentric urban clusters surrounded by low-density hinterlands, and they grow considerably faster than the overall population of the nations in which they are located.[12] Urban corridors, on the other hand, are characterized by linear systems of urban spaces linked through transportation networks.[13] Other dynamic and strategic cities are extending beyond their administrative boundaries and integrating their hinterlands to become full-blown city-regions.[14] These are emerging in various parts of the world, turning into spatial units that are territorially and functionally bound by economic, political, socio-cultural, and ecological systems.[15] All of these urban configurations – cities in clusters, corridors and regions – are becoming the new engines of both global and regional economies.

Mega-regions today are accumulating even larger populations than any mega- or meta-city (defined by UN-HABITAT as a city with a population that exceeds 20 million), and their economic output is enormous. The population of China's Hong Kong-Shenzen-Guangzhou mega-region, for example, is about 120 million, and it is estimated that Japan's Tokyo-Nagoya-Osaka-Kyoto-Kobe mega-region is likely to host 60 million by 2015.[16] In Brazil, the mega-region that stretches from São Paulo to Rio de Janeiro is home to 43 million people. Although more widespread in North America and Europe, mega-regions are taking shape in Asia and other parts of the world as cities converge apace, with the typical huge demographic concentrations, large markets, significant economic capacities, substantial innovative activities and high numbers of skilled workers that come with them. Recent research shows that the world's 40 largest mega-regions cover only a tiny fraction of the habitable surface of our planet and are home to fewer than 18 per cent of the world's population, even as they account for 66 per cent of global economic activity and about 85 per cent of technological and scientific innovation.[17]

Urban corridors, in contrast, present a type of spatial organization with specific economic and transportation objectives. In urban corridors, a number of city centres of various sizes are connected along transportation routes in linear development axes that are often linked to a number of mega-cities, encompassing their hinterlands. New developments in some fringe areas experience the fastest growth rates and the most rapid urban transformation. An example is the industrial corridor developing in India between Mumbai and Delhi, which will stretch over 1,500 kilometres from Jawaharlal Nehru Port (in Navi Mumbai) to Dadri and Tughlakabad (in Delhi).[18] Another good example is the manufacturing and service industry corridor in Malaysia's Kuala Lumpur, clustered within the Klang Valley conurbation that stretches all the way to the port city of Klang.[19] In Africa, the greater Ibadan-Lagos-Accra urban corridor, spanning roughly 600 kilometres across four countries, is the engine of West Africa's regional economy.[20] Another urban corridor is the 1,500 kilometre-

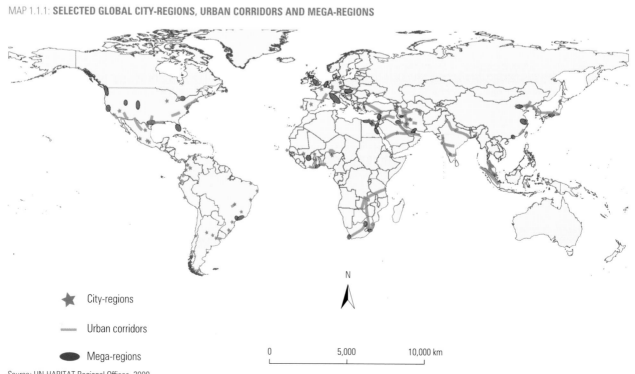

MAP 1.1.1: **SELECTED GLOBAL CITY-REGIONS, URBAN CORRIDORS AND MEGA-REGIONS**

★ City-regions

--- Urban corridors

⬬ Mega-regions

0   5,000   10,000 km

N

Source: UN-HABITAT Regional Offices, 2009

Tokyo, Japan. The Tokyo-Nagoya-Osaka-Kyoto-Kobe mega-region is likely to host 60 million by 2015.
©**Ssguy/Shutterstock**

long belt stretching from Beijing to Tokyo via Pyongyang and Seoul, which connects no less than 77 cities with populations of 200,000 or more. More than 97 million people live in this urban corridor, which, in fact, links four separate megalopolises in four countries, merging them into one, as it were.[21]

Urban corridors are changing the functionality of cities and even towns both large and small, in the process stimulating business, real estate development and land values along their ribbon-like development areas. They are also improving inter-connectivity and creating new forms of interdependence among cities, leading to regional economic development growth. In some cases, however, urban corridors can result in severe urban primacy and unbalanced regional development, as they strengthen ties to existing economic centres rather than allowing for more diffused spatial development.

City-regions come on yet another, even larger scale as major cities extend beyond formal administrative boundaries to engulf smaller ones, including towns. In the process, they also absorb semi-urban and rural hinterlands, and in some cases merge with other intermediate cities, creating large conurbations that eventually form city-regions. Many such city-regions have grown enormously over the last 20 to 30 years, owing to the effects of agglomeration economies and comparative advantages. The extended Bangkok Region in Thailand, for example, is expected to expand another 200 kilometres from its current centre by 2020, growing far beyond its current population of over 17 million. In Brazil, Metropolitan São Paulo already spreads over 8,000 square kilometres, with a population of 16.4 million.[22] The full extent of South Africa's Cape Town city-region, when including the distances from which commuters travel to and from every day, reaches up to 100 kilometres. Some of these city-regions are actually larger in both surface area and population than some entire countries like Belgium, the Czech Republic or the Netherlands.

Mega-regions, urban corridors and city-regions reflect the emerging links between city growth and new patterns of economic activity. These regional systems are creating a new urban hierarchy and the scope, range and complexity of issues involved require innovative coordination mechanisms for urban management and governance. The World Bank has identified the three main issues that these configurations face, namely:

- *Coordination,* "conceiving the development of cities in parallel with the development of regions and sub-regions, rather than isolated nodes in economic space", a process that calls on metropolitan, regional and even national planners to work together;
- *Broader plans for regional planning/development,* "requiring dispersion of specific urban functions (i.e., solid waste treatment, airports, skills and training centres) within a continuous region, rather than crowding them in a large city"; and
- *Coping with horizontal fiscal disparities,* and more specifically "designing mechanisms to transfer fiscal resources among urban governments in a region".[23]

Suburbanization is becoming more prevalent

More and more people, particularly young families and the affluent middle-aged, are living in satellite or dormitory cities and suburban neighbourhoods, taking advantage of accommodation that can be more affordable than in central areas, with lower densities and a better quality of life in certain ways. In some cases, spatial expansion of cities is triggered by factors other than residents' preference for a suburban lifestyle. These include land regulation crises, lack of control over peri-urban areas, weak planning control over land subdivisions that leads to various forms of speculation, improved or expanded commuting technologies and services, as well as greater population mobility. Some of the other factors behind suburbanization are characteristic of poorly managed cities, such as pollution, traffic congestion, lack of car parks and poor public amenities. Spatial expansion is also triggered by changes in lifestyles that are disseminated through large urban centres, propelled by the globalization of consumption patterns, in turn bringing more homogeneity across diverse areas of the world.[24]

The suburban growth pattern of urbanization has long been strongly associated with North American cities; over the past decade, though, there have been signs that suburbanization, or what is known as a form of "horizontal spreading", "dispersed urbanization" or urban sprawl, is happening in many metropolitan areas of the world. Urban sprawl has always been a pejorative term for the uncontrolled expansion of urban areas, characterized by voracious consumption of land for the purposes of low-density development. Under the many forms it takes in various cities of the world, sprawl happens when population growth and the physical expansion of a city are misaligned. The Los Angeles metropolitan area in the United States is a classic case in point: between 1970 and 1990, its population grew by 45 per cent, while its built surface area expanded by 300 per cent.[25]

Urban sprawl is increasingly happening in developing countries as well, as real estate developers are promoting the image of a "worldclass lifestyle" outside the city. Research in Guadalajara, Mexico, between 1970 and the year 2000 showed that the surface area of the city grew 1.5 times faster than the population.[26] Similar research shows that urban sprawl is consuming considerable amounts of land in cities as diverse as Antananarivo in Madagascar, Beijing in China, Johannesburg in South Africa, Cairo in Egypt and Mexico City in Mexico, to name just a few.

In both developing and developed countries, sprawl involves four dimensions: a population that is widely scattered in low-density developments; residential and commercial areas that are spatially separate; a network of roads characterized by overstretched blocks and poor access; and a lack of well-defined, thriving activity hubs, such as "downtown" areas and city centres. Other features typically associated with sprawl include overdependence on motorized transport coupled with a lack of alternatives, a relative uniformity of housing options, and pedestrian-unfriendly spaces.[27]

Cairo and Los Angeles: the two faces of urban sprawl. ©**Dumitru/Shutterstock and iofoto/Shutterstock**

For instance, most South African cities are expanding primarily through development of new housing areas which, being located beyond the existing urban periphery, are relatively unplanned. As a result, the urban periphery consists of pockets of housing developments that are isolated and separated from each other by trunk roads or open spaces.

In many developing countries, urban sprawl generates a configuration involving two main, contrasting types of development in one and the same city: (1) a form of "peripherization" that is characterized by large peri-urban areas with informal and illegal patterns of land use, combined with a lack of infrastructure, public facilities and basic services, and often accompanied by a lack of both public transport and adequate access roads; and (2) in contrast, a form of "suburban sprawl" characterized by residential zones for high- and middle-income groups and highly valued commercial and retail complexes that are well-connected by individual rather than public transport. In most cases, residential areas coexist with huge commercial centres located along main highways.[28] In some developing countries, urban sprawl is the consequence of poverty, not affluence, as informal unplanned settlements on the periphery spring up in response to a lack of affordable housing options within the city itself. In this sense, urban sprawl results from a lack of policy attention to current urban challenges (slums, land, services, transport), and more particularly an inability to anticipate urban growth, including through provision of land for the urbanizing poor. Denial of permanent land rights to the urban poor is one of the main factors behind the "peripherization" associated with urban sprawl in developing countries.[29]

From a social and spatial perspective, urban sprawl contributes to the urban divide. It has a negative impact not only on the infrastructure and sustainability of cities, but also on social cohesion, often exacerbating social segregation and segmentation. The spatial separation of social groups, particularly along socio-economic lines, results in spatial disparities in wealth and quality of life across various parts of cities and metropolitan areas, dilapidated city centres, and suburbs. To put it in a nutshell: sprawl is a symptom of a divided city. Suburbanization in developing countries happens mainly as an escape away from poor governance, lack of planning and poor access to amenities. "Rich and poor find refuge in escaping the city"[30], which generates further partitioning of the physical and social space.

Urban sprawl has a wide range of implications. In most cases, it will lead to an increase in the cost of public infrastructure and of residential and commercial development. Sprawl adds to the costs and inefficiencies of transportation, resulting in high energy consumption. Sprawling metropolitan areas consume much more energy than compact cities and require larger outputs of materials such as metal, concrete and asphalt because homes, offices and utilities are farther apart.[31] Sprawl also creates fiscal problems for cities, as it takes place outside of urban administrative boundaries. While suburban municipalities benefit from tax revenues with increased development, it is central cities or downtown municipalities that foot the bill for many daytime services used by suburban residents.

Moreover, in many places, urban sprawl causes significant losses of prime farmland as new developments absorb arable land. In the absence of proper planning, urban sprawl also contributes to the degradation of a number of environmental resources; for instance, it has caused substantial damage to environmentally sensitive areas around several cities in Latin America, including Panama City and its surrounding Canal Zone, Caracas and its adjacent coastline, San José de Costa Rica and its mountainous area, and São Paulo and its water basins. Informal provision of services to the poor in peri-urban areas is also very wasteful and expensive (to the poor in the short term, and to the city in the long term) and is a further significant cause of urban dysfunctionality.

Divergent Urban Growth Patterns

While similar modes of urbanization and urban growth are evident in many cities around the world, there are also significant differences in the patterns of urbanization among regions and even greater variations in the degree, pace and nature of individual country and city growth. This section discusses the most distinct and unique patterns of urbanization and urban growth in various regions of the world.

No uniform "tipping point" across regions

Sometime during the year 2008, and for the first time in human history, the world's population became more urban than rural. Although more people overall are now living in urban centres than in rural areas, not all regions have yet experienced their own urban transitions; in fact, some regions are not expected to reach the urban population "tipping point" for another 20 to 30 years. (See Table 1.1.1)

TABLE 1.1.1: **URBANIZATION LEVEL PER REGION AND TIPPING POINT (URBAN VS. RURAL POPULATION)**

Region	Tipping point before 2010 (year)	2010 urban (%)	Tipping point after 2010 (year)	2050 urban (%)
World		50.6		70
MORE DEVELOPED REGIONS	Before 1950	75		86
Europe	Before 1950	72.6		83.8
Eastern Europe	1963	68.8		80
Northern Europe	Before 1950	84.4		90.7
Southern Europe	1960	67.5		81.2
Western Europe	Before 1950	77		86.5
LESS DEVELOPED REGIONS		45.3	2020	67
Africa		40	2030	61.8
Sub-Saharan Africa		37.3	2032	60.5
Eastern Africa		23.7		47.6
North Africa	2005	52		72
Southern Africa	1993	58.8		77.6
Western Africa		44.6	2020	68
Asia		42.5	2023	66.2
Eastern Asia		48.5	2013	74.1
South-central Asia		32.2	2040	57.2
South-eastern Asia		48.2	2013	73.3
Western Asia	1980	66.3		79.3
Latin America and the Caribbean	1962	79.4		88.7
Central America	1965	71.7		83.3
South America	1960	83.7		91.4
Rest of the World				
North America	Before 1950	82.1		90.2
Oceania	Before 1950	70.6		76.4

Source: UN DESA, 2008b and UN-HABITAT 2009.

In the more developed regions (Europe, North America and Oceania), the tipping point from a predominantly rural to a majority urban population occurred in the mid-1950s, while in some countries, such as the United States, it took place as early as the beginning of the 20th century.[32] In the developing world, the first and only region to become predominantly urban before 2008 was Latin America and the Caribbean, where at least half of the population has been living in places formally designated as "cities" and "towns" since the early 1960s. Three distinct factors combined to bring about this evolution: (1) a very unequal agrarian structure, with little capacity to retain the rural population; (2) political centralism, which concentrated power in the capitals of individual federated states, and (3) government policies favouring import substitution (in some countries since the 1930s, in others since the 1950s).[33] A relatively early urbanization trend is also notable in two sub-regions of the developing world, Southern and North Africa, which passed the "urban tipping point" in 1993 and 2005, respectively, despite significant efforts to prevent urbanization.[34]

In today's world, different regions find themselves at different levels on the urbanization scale. At one extreme, North America boasts the highest proportion of people living in urban areas, at 82.1 per cent. The second and third most urbanized regions are Latin America and the Caribbean and Europe, with 79.4 per cent and 72.6 per cent of their populations living in urban areas, respectively. At the other end of the spectrum, Africa and Asia have the lowest proportions of urban residents in the world, with 40 per cent and 42.5 per cent of their populations in urban areas, respectively, or significantly below the global average of 50.6 per cent.

Northern Europe is the world's most urbanized sub-region with, on average, 84.4 per cent of its population projected to live in urban areas by 2010. The sub-region of South America comes next, with 83.7 per cent of its population projected to live in cities and towns, slightly more than North America, which ranks third. The next most urbanized sub-region is Western Europe (77 per cent). At the other end of the urbanization spectrum, Eastern Africa ranks last by far, with just 23.7 per cent of its population projected to live in urban areas by 2010. The proportion is higher in South-Central Asia (32.2 per cent), while in Eastern- and South-Eastern Asia rates of urbanization remain relatively low, with the urban population accounting for just under 50 per cent in both sub-regions (Table 1.1.1).

Caution is in order here as urbanization rates and trends in different regions are, of course, largely affected by the formal definition of what constitutes a "city" or "urban area" in every country, which in turn seriously affects comparability across regions and countries. What constitutes an urban area differs from one country to another. For example, in Uganda, a settlement with a population of more than 2,000 is classified as urban, whereas in Nigeria and Mauritius the benchmark is 10 times higher; in China, those settlements with more than 3,000 residents are considered "urban", while only those with 60,000 or more are "cities". Urban areas are also typically defined by the administrative and legislative functions they serve, further complicating the designation of urban settlements.

Considering the challenges of definition and the fact that many successive degrees of urbanization separate truly rural places and major cities, it is expected that the tipping point for "urban Asia" and "urban Africa" will happen in 2023 and 2030, respectively. South-Central Asia, the least urbanized sub-region in Asia, will not achieve the urban transition until 2040, primarily because in the two large countries in the region, India and Bangladesh, seven out of every 10 in the population still live in rural areas today. The least urbanized part of Africa, the Eastern sub-region where urbanization was not strongly linked to industrialization or modernization until recently,[35] will remain predominantly rural until after 2050, when projections suggest that only 47.6 per cent of the population will be living in urban areas. However, huge demographic and social transformations are occurring in this sub-region, which is currently experiencing the highest urban growth rate in the world (3.87 per cent in 2000-2005); this points to the need for local and national policies that respond positively to current urbanization challenges.

By 2050, 70 per cent of the world population is likely to be living in urban environments. In this respect, some of the patterns emerging in specific projections are worthy of note. South America will be the most urban region in the world (91.4 per cent), followed by Northern Europe (90.7 per cent) and North America (90.2 per cent). The least urbanized regions by the middle of the 21st century will remain Africa (61.8 per cent) and Asia (66.2 per cent): they will be slightly below the global average of 70 per cent. It must be stressed that in those two continents, the already more urbanized sub-regions – North and Southern Africa, and Eastern and Western Asia – will see further increases in the urban segment of the population to the point where, by 2050, their respective shares of urban dwellers will be larger than those currently prevailing in Europe.

The fact that by 2050 Latin America and the Caribbean, and particularly South America, is projected to feature the highest proportion of urban population in the world somewhat challenges the notion that urbanization can be taken as a proxy for the level of development in general.[36] Notwithstanding definition problems, and considering that urban data has not been harmonized and urban projections are devoid of adjustment factors, it is possible that over the next 40 years, some countries in the South American sub-region will have significantly reduced poverty and inequalities to the standards of today's developed nations, while others will not. It is unlikely that by 2050 the sub-region will rank among the first in the Human Development Index and boast one of the highest GDPs per capita; still, the region shows some promise in terms of human development indicators: average life expectancy is comparable to North America's, and infant mortality is the lowest among developing regions.[37] Moreover, the changing structure of urban patterns in Latin America and the Caribbean, characterized by a rapid increase in the number of secondary cities and the reduction of urban primacy, is another distinctive feature of the region that is certain to bring more prosperity to secondary cities.

Lima, Peru. By 2050, South America will be the most urban region in the world with 91.4 per cent of its population residing in urban areas. ©**Yory Frenklakh/Shutterstock**

Not all cities in developing nations are experiencing rapid population growth

By the middle of the 21ˢᵗ century, the total urban population of the developing world will more than double, from 2.5 billion in 2010 to 5.3 billion in 2050.[38] Between 1995 and 2005 alone, the urban population of the developing world grew by an average of 1.2 million per week, or around 165,000 every day.[39] Not all cities contribute equally to this rapid growth, and neither is it unprecedented or out of control.

Many cities, including Kolkata, Chennai, Recife, Santiago, Monterrey, Algiers, Alexandria, Maputo and Lusaka are experiencing relatively low annual growth rates (1 to 2 per cent), and further slowdowns are likely over the coming years. Somewhat surprisingly, a number of other cities in the developing world find themselves experiencing population declines (particularly in central areas), such as Rabat, La Paz, Belo Horizonte, San Luis Potosi, Dengzhou, Madurai, Bandung and Manila, to name just a few.

On the other hand, recent high annual growth rates of over 4 per cent have rapidly transformed many cities in the developing world, including Bamako, Abuja, Kinshasa, Ouagadougou and Sana'a, suggesting that on current trends their populations will double in about 17 years. Some of the fastest-expanding cities have seen their populations double in fewer than eight years, owing to phenomenal annual growth rates of over 8 per cent (see Figures 1.1.2-4). Some cities in China, such as Shenzhen and Shangqiu, experienced exceptionally high annual growth rates of over 17 per cent in the 1990s.

Across Africa, rapid urban expansion is widespread, with 13 agglomerations experiencing annual growth rates of over 4 per cent. Between 2005 and 2010, Africa experienced the highest urban growth rates in the world—an annual 3.3 per cent average—and the pace is expected to remain relatively high over the next 15 years. On the other hand, demographic growth is slowing down in Asian and Latin American cities, and this is expected to continue over the next decade.

Generally speaking, high rates of urban growth still characterize urban change in the developing world, where the annual average was 2.5 per cent between 1990 and 2006.[40] However, that is not uniformly the case; for every 100 cities in the developing world, 15 grew at high annual rates of over 4 per cent, compared with 2 to 4 per cent for another 32 cities. On the other hand, more than half (53 out of 100) grew rather slowly: 1 to 2 per cent for 22 of these, and under 1 per cent for another 19. Moreover, 11.4 per cent of cities saw both their economies and their populations regress between 1990 and 2006. Declining urban populations is a relatively new phenomenon in the developing world, though not yet as prevalent as in the developed world where a significant 40 per cent of cities have seen a fall in their populations.[41] Demographic contraction may, however, pave the way for a new urban trend that is starting to unfold in the developing world.

▲
Manila, Philippines. Population growth is slowing down in Asian cities, and in Manila numbers are actually declining. ©**Shadow216/Shutterstock**

FIGURE 1.1.2: **AVERAGE ANNUAL GROWTH RATE OF SELECTED FAST GROWING CITIES IN AFRICA BETWEEN 1990 AND 2006**

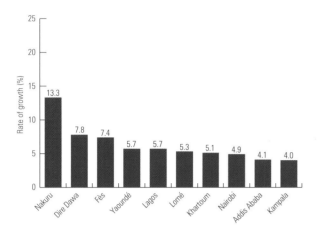

FIGURE 1.1.3: **AVERAGE ANNUAL GROWTH RATE OF SELECTED FAST GROWING CITIES IN ASIA BETWEEN 1990 AND 2006**

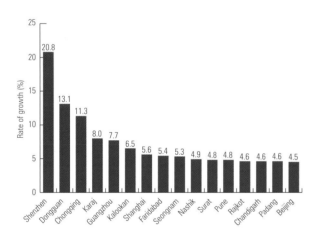

FIGURE 1.1.4: **AVERAGE ANNUAL GROWTH RATE OF SELECTED FAST GROWING CITIES IN LATIN AMERICA AND CARIBBEAN REGION BETWEEN 1990 AND 2006**

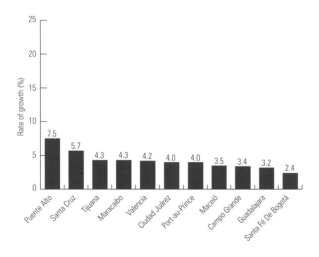

Source: Demographic Yearbook, Various Years 1990 - 2006.

BOX 1.1.1: HIGH URBAN GROWTH RATES, BUT EASTERN AFRICA REMAINS PREDOMINANTLY RURAL

Although they can boast some of the highest urban growth rates, East African countries remain the least urbanized in the world and will only begin to experience an urban transition by the middle of this century. Only 22.7 per cent of the region's population was classified as "urban" in 2007, with some countries featuring significantly lower proportions. The least urbanized countries include Burundi (10.1 per cent), Ethiopia (16.6 per cent), Rwanda (18.2 per cent) and Uganda (12.8 per cent). It is worth noting here that countries with similar income levels and human development indicators, such as Benin in Western Africa and Angola in Central Africa, feature higher rates of urbanization – 40.8 per cent and 55.8 per cent, respectively.

In East Africa between 2005 and 2010 (estimate), annual urban growth rates range from a high of 6.8 per cent in Burundi to a low of 1.4 per cent in the Seychelles. Countries with relatively high annual urban growth rates over 4 per cent include Eritrea, Ethiopia, Malawi, Mozambique, Rwanda, Somalia, Tanzania and Uganda. It must be noted that while most East African countries are expected to see a deceleration in the growth of their urban population rates in the next decade, a few may instead experience a surge. For instance, having featured an annual rate of 3.9 per cent between 2005 and 2010 (estimate), Kenya's urban population growth is expected to accelerate to 4.2 per cent between 2015 and 2020. Similarly, projections suggest that Uganda's urban growth rates are bound for a significant rise, from the current 4.4 per cent to over 5 per cent in the next decade.

However, high urban growth rates in East Africa are not anywhere near the "tipping point" where a national population becomes predominantly urban. United Nations projections indicate that by 2030, only 33.7 per cent of the region's total population will be urban. For most countries – except those already highly urbanized, such as Djibouti, Mauritius, Reunion and Seychelles – the transition will only occur after 2040, with the exception of Mozambique, Somalia and Zimbabwe, where it is expected by 2030.

The low rates of urbanization in East Africa result from a variety of factors, including low industrialization, over-dependence on subsistence agriculture, inadequate or outdated land policies, lack of pro-urban development strategies, insufficient investment in secondary and small cities, past colonial policies that discouraged rural-to-urban migration, and apparent lack of political will to address the "urban question" and turn cities and towns into engines of national growth.

Another particular aspect of the urbanization process in the least urbanized East African countries is that of "divided loyalties" – conflicts between communal loyalty and obligations to ancestral rural land, or to clan and family ties, on the one hand, and the need to adapt to and participate in a modern, urbanizing world, on the other hand. This phenomenon prevents many rural migrants from fully embracing the city as their home or engaging with local authorities to demand better services and rights. Consequently, many cities in the region can be described as hosting "transplanted villagers" who are yet to be turned into truly urban citizens whose loyalties, investments, livelihoods and future prospects are intimately linked with the cities where they live.

Sources: UN DESA, 2008b; Warah, 1999.

▲
Nairobi. Kenya's urban population growth is expected to accelerate to 4.2% between 2015 and 2020. ©**Attila JÁNDI/Shutterstock**

END NOTES

1. All urban data are from UN Department of Economic and Social Affairs (DESA), 2008b, unless otherwise indicated.
2. Cohen, 2004.
3. UN DESA, 2008b.
4. Asian Development Bank, 2008.
5. Njoh, 2003.
6. Central Intelligence Agency, n.d.
7. "Urban population" refers to the "*de facto* population living in areas classified as urban according to the criteria used by each area or country". UN DESA, 2008.
8. Kasarda & Krenshaw, 2006.
9. Satterthwaite, 2007.
10. Cohen, 2004.
11. Florida, 2008.
12. Florida, et al., 2007.
13. Whebell, 1969.
14. Jacobs, 1961.
15. Knight, 2008.
16. Asian Development Bank, 2008.
17. Florida, et al., 2007.
18. Noronha, 2007.
19. Brunn, et al., 2003.

20. UN-HABITAT & United Nations Economic Commission for Africa, 2008.
21. Yeung & Lo, 1996.
22. Cohen, 2004.
23. Indermit & Homi, 2007.
24. Ojima & Hogan, 2009.
25. Ojima & Hogan, 2009.
26. Fausto Brito, 2008.
27. European Environmental Agency, 2006.
28. In some cases exclusive, gated communities are virtually "cities within cities", often housing their own schools, malls, churches or mosques and, of course, the essential 18-hole golf course. Refer for instance to Douglass & Liling, 2007. "Globalizing the City in Southeast Asia: Utopia on the Urban Edge – The Case of Phu My Hung, Saigon", IJAPS, Vol. 3, No. 2, November 2007, downloaded the 11/11/2009 from http://www.usm.my/ijaps/articles/1%20douglas(1-42)1.pdf.
29. W. Corbett, personal communication, 21 November, 2009.
30. D. Shehajeb, personal communication 2009.
31. McElfish, 2007.
32. Science Daily, 2007.

33. J. Rodriguez, personal communication, 23 October, 2009.
34. UN DESA, 2008b.
35. UN-HABITAT & United Nations Economic Commission for Africa, 2008.
36. Sharma, 2003.
37. UN-HABITAT, 2008. [SWCR]
38. UN DESA, 2008b.
39. Figures based on calculations using *World Urbanization Prospects: The 2007 Revision* Population Database, urban population of the less developed regions between 1995 and 2005. See http://esa.un.org/unup/.
40. UN-HABITAT elaborations, using Demographic Yearbook, UN Statistical Division, 1990-2006. The Demographic Yearbook details the population of capital cities and cities of 100,000 and more for the latest available year and mainly on "city proper". On the other hand, the World Urbanization Prospects data (City Population and City Population Growth Rate) in the Statistical Annex details data on urban agglomerations (i.e. City proper plus suburban fringes) with 750,000 inhabitants or more.
41. UN-HABITAT, 2008.

©agophoto/Shutterstock

1.2
The wealth of cities

Quick Facts

1. Urbanization and economic growth typically happen in tandem; however, equitable distribution of benefits and opportunities remains a challenge.

2. Demographic expansion in cities nowadays stems more from natural growth than rural-urban migration, including in sub-Saharan Africa.

3. Urbanization, when accompanied by weak economic growth, results in a concentration of poor people in cities rather than in significant poverty reduction.

4. Countries with the highest per capita income tend to be more urbanized, while low-income countries are the least urbanized.

Policy Points

1. Cities have the potential to make countries rich because they provide the economies of scale and proximity that generate enhanced productivity.

2. Urban centres that are economically growing can be real poverty fighters if adequate policies are implemented; they can also significantly reduce rural poverty.

The City-Nation Nexus

The prosperity of nations is intimately linked to the prosperity of their cities. No country has ever achieved sustained economic growth and rapid social development without urbanizing. Evidence shows that the transition from low-income to middle-income country status is almost always accompanied by a transition from a rural to an urban economy.[1]

Thanks to their superior productivity, urban-based enterprises contribute large shares of the gross domestic product (GDP) of nations. In some countries, such as Korea, Hungary and Belgium, it takes only a single city to contribute the more substantial share of national wealth – almost half in the case of Seoul, and roughly 45 per cent in the case of Budapest and Brussels.[2] In other countries, it is a group of cities that accounts for a significant share of national GDP. In South Africa, for example, six major cities concentrating 31 per cent of the total population together contribute as much as 55 per cent of national GDP.[3] In both India and China, the five largest cities contribute approximately 15 per cent of national GDP in 2004 – roughly three times what could have been expected based solely on their relative shares of the population.[4]

Cities have the potential to make countries rich because they provide the economies of scale and proximity to make growth more efficient. High densities in cities reduce transaction costs, make public spending on infrastructure and services more economically viable, and facilitate the generation and diffusion of knowledge, all of which are important for growth. Regardless of whether cities fuel economic growth or are, instead, its by-product, it is indisputable that cities have become major hubs of economic activity, both within individual countries and as contributors to the global economy.

Table 1.2.1 and Figure 1.2.1 show the relative shares of a group of selected cities from both developed and developing countries in terms of land size, population and gross domestic product (GDP) relative to the country as a whole. In all cases, the *economic* output of the cities is much higher than the corresponding *land* inputs. In addition, all but one of the selected cities contribute a larger share of the country's GDP than their share of the total population. Guangzhou and Brussels offer the most telling examples, with a GDP share that is 5 and 4.4 times higher, respectively, than their share in their respective national populations.[5] The only exception is Sydney, which produces a lower share of GDP than the proportion of the Australian population that calls the city home.

Exclusive focus on the GDP contribution of urban areas can be misleading, though. Rather than individual areas, it is often clusters of cities that function as a single economic entity and set in motion self-reinforcing, cumulative growth patterns.[6] For instance, Johannesburg, Pretoria and the East Rand function as more of a single city-region – a cluster of economically linked and interdependent cities – than as three geographically separated cities. The three have substantial geographical advantages: they are relatively close to the largest international airport in Africa, and they are well connected through a highway network to the ports of Durban, Richards Bay and Cape Town as well as to those in neighbouring Maputo in Mozambique and Walvis Bay in Namibia. Taking this "cluster" city as a whole, its

FIGURE 1.2.1: **SHARE OF NATIONAL GDP AND POPULATION OF SELECTED CITIES**

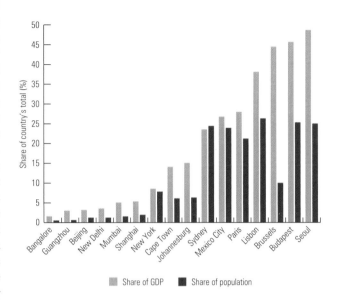

Share of GDP   Share of population

Sources: New York, Sydney, Mexico City, Paris, Lisbon, Brussels, Budapest, Seoul: OECD, 2008. Bangalore, New Delhi, Mumbai, Guangzhou, Beijing, Shanghai: van Dijk, 2007. Johannesburg, Cape Town: Naudé & Krugell, 2004.

TABLE 1.2.1: **LAND, POPULATION AND GDP OF SELECTED CITIES AS A SHARE OF THE COUNTRY TOTAL**

City	Per cent of GDP	Per cent of Population	Per cent of Land	Relative Share of GDP versus Population
Bangalore	1.5	0.5		2.9
Guangzhou	2.9	0.6	0.1	5.1
Beijing	3.1	1.2	0.2	2.6
New Delhi	3.5	1.2	0.0	3.0
Mumbai	5.0	1.5	0.0	3.3
New York	8.5	7.8	0.1	1.1
Shanghai	13.6	1.9	0.1	7.1
Cape Town	14.0	6.1	0.2	2.3
Johannesburg	15.0	6.3	0.14	2.4
Sydney	23.5	24.4	0.02	1.0
Mexico City	26.7	23.9	0.1	1.1
Paris	27.9	21.2	0.5	1.3
Lisbon	38.0	26.3	3.2	1.4
Brussels	44.4	10.0	2.3	4.4
Budapest	45.6	25.3	0.8	1.8
Seoul	48.6	25.0	0.6	1.9

Sources: New York, Sydney, Mexico City, Paris, Lisbon, Brussels, Budapest, Seoul: OECD, 2008. Bangalore, New Delhi, Mumbai, Guangzhou, Beijing, Shanghai: van Dijk, 2007. Johannesburg, Cape Town: Naudé & Krugell, 2004.

▲
Brussels, Belgium. The capital accounts for nearly half of Belgium's GDP and only 2.3% of its land area. ©**Jeroen Beerten/Shutterstock**

contribution to South Africa's GDP is greater than 31 per cent.[7] The fact that Johannesburg is host to two-thirds of all South Africa's corporate headquarters and 60 per cent of the top 100 companies underscores its economic importance.[8]

Cities also concentrate a large share of economic activity worldwide. When adjusting the actual GDP per capita by the costs of living in individual cities (i.e., purchasing power parity – PPP) and ranking them by GDP, the top 25 cities accounted for roughly 15 per cent of the world's GDP in 2005.[9] This share increases to around one-fourth of the world's GDP when the top 100 cities are included (see Figure 1.2.2). The largest cities in the major developed economies are at the top of the global GDP rankings, with Tokyo, New York, Los Angeles, Chicago, Paris and London being the top six in 2005. Tokyo alone accounts for almost 2 per cent of the world's GDP.

The economic power of these cities is comparable to that of many national economies. Tokyo and New York have an estimated GDP similar to those of Canada or Spain, while London's GDP is higher than that of Sweden or Switzerland. Four megacities in developing countries are currently in the top 30 GDP ranking – Mexico City, Buenos Aires, São Paulo, and Rio de Janeiro – accounting for 1.5 per cent of the global GDP. Fast-growing cities such as Shanghai, Mumbai, Istanbul and Beijing are expected to move into the global top 30 by 2010.[10]

The larger contribution of some cities to the country's GDP relative to their share of the population points to the advantages of urban areas. Specifically, cities benefit from the efficiency gains and consumption benefits arising from location advantages, economies of scale and agglomeration economies, including lower prices for inputs, greater access to specialized services, lower transaction costs, and more fluid knowledge sharing. In turn, these advantages attract fast growing sectors of the economy, including services and manufacturing, into cities – in fact, urban agglomeration seems to be a prerequisite for industrialization. The competitive advantages of cities are even more important in developing countries, where poor transportation and communication infrastructure in the hinterland exacerbates the cities' location advantages that enable firms to access not only the larger domestic markets within the cities themselves, but also export markets.[11]

Data indicates that predominantly urban regions have a consistently higher GDP per capita than those that are predominantly rural. On average, in 2005, those in OECD countries generated a GDP per capita that was 57 per cent higher than predominantly rural regions: US $30,882, compared with US $19,623.[12] The same relationship holds for all OECD countries at the national level, with the exception of South Korea, where GDP per capita is significantly higher in predominantly rural regions than in urban ones: US $23,886 and US $16,274 in 2005, respectively. This unusual pattern reflects a two-pronged government policy: significant subsidies stabilize agricultural production in order to maintain food security; and expanding non-agricultural industries have been turned into a main source of income in rural areas, in a bid to promote economic equality with urban areas.[13] In all other OECD countries, GDP per capita is consistently

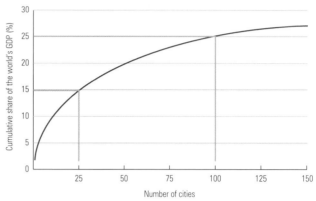

FIGURE 1.2.2: **CUMULATIVE SHARE OF THE RICHEST CITIES AND URBAN AREAS IN GLOBAL GDP, 2005**

Source: Based on data from City Mayors, n.d.

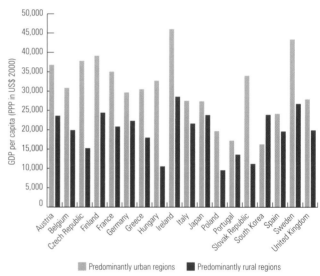

FIGURE 1.2.3: **REGIONAL GDP PER CAPITA BY DEGREE OF URBANIZATION FOR SELECTED OECD COUNTRIES, 2005 (PPP 2000)**

■ Predominantly urban regions ■ Predominantly rural regions

Source: Data from OECD Regional Statistics.

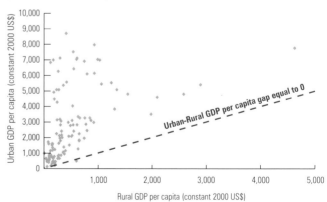

FIGURE 1.2.4: **RURAL AND URBAN GDP PER CAPITA, 2005 (CONSTANT US$, 2000)**

Source: World Bank, 2007.
Note: Rural share of GDP is estimated based on the share of the agricultural sector, while the urban share is estimated based on the combined share of GDP produced in the manufacturing and service sectors. These are divided by the rural and urban population to obtain the rural and urban GDP per capita, respectively.

higher in predominantly urban areas. The urban-rural gap in terms of GDP per capita ranges between 15 per cent for Japan and 210 per cent in Hungary (see Figure 1.2.3).

Whether urbanization causes economic growth or economic growth causes urbanization, it is indisputable that urbanization and growth go together. As shown in Figure 1.2.5, over the past four decades countries around the world have experienced, on average, increases in both their urban population and per capita income. While the urban population worldwide increased from 33 to 42 per cent between 1960 and 2000, per capita income more than doubled over the same period.[14]

▲
Tokyo, Japan. The city alone accounts for almost two per cent of the world's GDP.
©Galina Barskaya/Shutterstock

FIGURE 1.2.5: **TRENDS IN URBANIZATION AND GDP PER CAPITA FOR ALL COUNTRIES, 1960-2000**

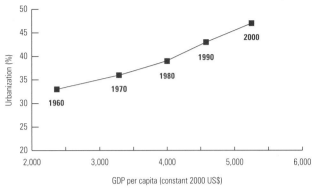

Source: World Bank, 2007.

FIGURE 1.2.6: **URBANIZATION AND GDP PER CAPITA ACROSS COUNTRIES, 2007**

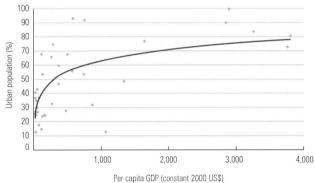

Source: World Bank, 2007.

TABLE 1.2.2: **AVERAGE URBAN POPULATION AND GDP PER CAPITA BY INCOME LEVEL AND BY REGION, 2007**

	GDP Per Capita (Constant 2000 US$)	Urban Population (% of Total)
By Level of Income		
High income	28,755	78
Middle income	2,011	48
Low income	415	32
By Region		
Latin America & Caribbean	4,580	78
Europe & Central Asia	3,004	64
Euro Area	21,879	73
Middle East & North Africa	1,869	57
East Asia & Pacific	1,644	43
South Asia	647	29
Sub-Saharan Africa	601	36

Source: World Bank, 2007.

The data also suggests a strong empirical relationship between urbanization and per capita income across countries.[15] As shown in Figure 1.2.6, countries with the highest per capita income tend to be more urbanized, with at least 70 per cent of their population living in urban areas. Likewise, the populations of middle-income countries tend to be at least 50 per cent urban, while low-income countries are the least urbanized.

The positive relationship between economic growth and urbanization is also evident when countries are aggregated by income level. As shown in Table 1.2.2, high-income countries exhibit both the highest GDP per capita and urbanization levels, while low-income countries are at the other end of the spectrum, with the lowest GDP per capita and urbanization levels.[16] Likewise, those regions that exhibit the highest levels of urbanization are also the ones with the highest GDP per capita, as illustrated by the fact that Latin America and the Caribbean, with the highest proportion of urban population in the developing world, also has a higher GDP per capita than Asia and Africa.

Looking at the sub-regions of the developing world, the only exception to the rule is sub-Saharan Africa: although countries there tend to be more urbanized than those in Southern Asia, their GDP per capita is lower (36 per cent and US $601 in sub-Saharan Africa, compared with 29 per cent and US $647 in Southern Asia). This phenomenon, which some authors refer to as "pathological urbanization" (see Box 1.2.1) or "urbanization without growth" does not really "describe what has been happening in most African countries"[17], which like all other regions of the world feature a normal, linear relationship between urbanization and economic growth. As explained by Kessides, in Africa this relationship "has simply not been sufficient to propel most of the countries into the realm of per capita income increases needed to overcome poverty sustainably".[18] It is expected, however, that the relatively high economic growth rates which several African countries have experienced these past few years will cause proportional increases in the urban population, as cities stand to attract more migrants not just from villages, but from other cities as well. This trend is in line with those in urban Europe in the latter part of the 19th century, when the Industrial Revolution led to a surge in urban populations and rising incomes. It was only in the early part of the 20th century that the problems associated with rapid urban growth – including slum proliferation and inequality – were addressed in a significant manner to reduce overall poverty.

It is important to note that rural-urban migration is just one of the three drivers of urbanization in today's world, accounting for only about 25 per cent. The other two factors are natural population increases and reclassification of rural into urban areas (see Box 1.3.2).[19] Rural-urban migration plays a relatively more significant role in regions with initial low rates of urbanization, such as Eastern and Southern Asia, sub-Saharan Africa, and North Africa and the Middle East. Conversely, it comes as no surprise that natural demographic growth within cities is relatively more important in regions where large parts of the population are already urban, such as Latin America and the Caribbean, Europe and Central Asia.

Urbanization and poverty

Overall, the relationship between urbanization and poverty is a positive one, as the incidence of poverty tends to be less pronounced in urban than in rural areas. This urban/rural divide tends to prevail across the world. Figure 1.2.7 shows the poverty rates in cities and the countryside with respect to the national rural and urban poverty lines, for 50 developing countries and between 1998 and 2007.[20] The figure suggests that on the whole, the incidence of poverty is more than 60 per cent higher in rural than in urban areas. Specifically, almost half (48.9 per cent) of the rural population in these countries is below the rural poverty line, while less than a third (30.3 per cent) of the urban population is below the urban poverty line. The relatively low prevalence of urban poverty is largely a result of the fact that the high costs of non-food items in cities are not considered in the poverty equation. If the cost of living were factored in, the prevalence of urban poverty would certainly rise.

At the country level, this positive relationship between urbanization and poverty holds for all but five countries, or 90 per cent of the cases.[21] In other words, the urban-rural poverty gap is positive in 45 of the 50 countries. In countries such as Viet Nam and Rwanda, the incidence of poverty in rural areas is roughly 5 times higher than in urban areas. Other countries, such as Burundi, show a small gap, as poverty is widespread in both rural and urban areas. The exceptions are Sri Lanka and the West Asian countries of Georgia, Armenia and Azerbaijan, where urban areas feature a higher incidence of poverty than rural areas. The gap is substantial in the case of Sri Lanka, where urban poverty is more than three times higher than rural poverty. However, the relationship is less pronounced or negligible in the West Asian countries.

▲
Yerevan, Armenia. In some West Asian countries, urban areas feature a higher incidence of poverty than rural ones. ©**Chubykin Arkady/Shutterstock**

FIGURE 1.2.7: **RURAL AND URBAN POVERTY HEADCOUNT RATIO AT RURAL AND URBAN NATIONAL POVERTY LINES, 1998-2007** **(% OF RURAL AND URBAN POPULATION)**

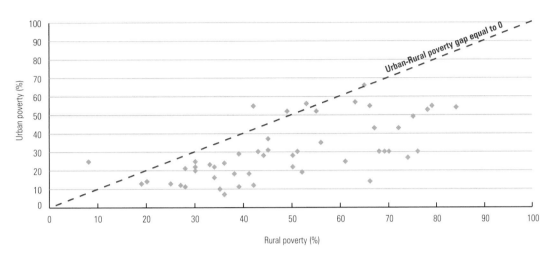

Source: World Bank, 2007.

▲
Rural Viet Nam. In countries such as Viet Nam and Rwanda, the incidence of poverty in rural areas is roughly five times higher than in urban areas.
©Szefei/Shutterstock

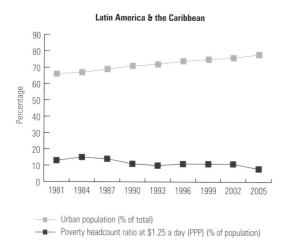

Latin America & the Caribbean

Urban population (% of total)
Poverty headcount ratio at $1.25 a day (PPP) (% of population)

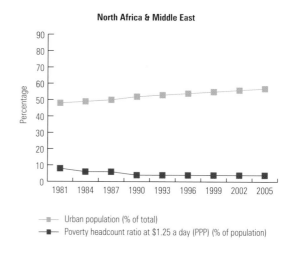

North Africa & Middle East

Urban population (% of total)
Poverty headcount ratio at $1.25 a day (PPP) (% of population)

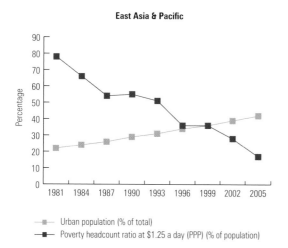

East Asia & Pacific

Urban population (% of total)
Poverty headcount ratio at $1.25 a day (PPP) (% of population)

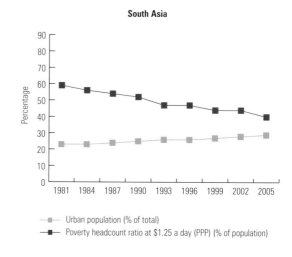

South Asia

Urban population (% of total)
Poverty headcount ratio at $1.25 a day (PPP) (% of population)

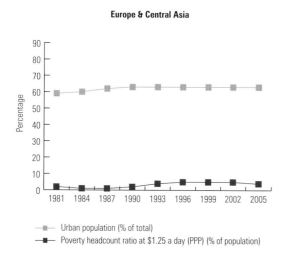

Europe & Central Asia

Urban population (% of total)
Poverty headcount ratio at $1.25 a day (PPP) (% of population)

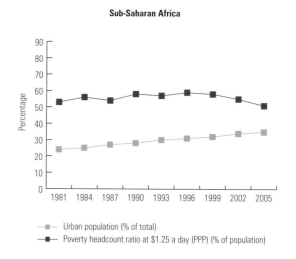

Sub-Saharan Africa

Urban population (% of total)
Poverty headcount ratio at $1.25 a day (PPP) (% of population)

Source: World Bank, 2007.

Seoul, South Korea. The city contributes close to 50 per cent of the country's wealth.
©Leonidovich/Shutterstock

While the traditional rural-urban comparison does indeed reveal that, as a whole, urban populations are better off than those living in rural areas, this situation conceals some profound differences in living conditions *within* urban areas – a major dimension of the urban divide. When disaggregating the data at the rural, urban, slum and non-slum levels, it becomes apparent that there are remarkable similarities between living conditions in rural areas and slums with regard to social indicators such as health and education.[22]

Given the lower incidence of relative poverty in urban areas, the overall poverty rate (urban and rural) can be expected to decline as the share of the urban population rises – assuming that the distribution of income within urban or rural areas remains unchanged. Urban growth is, therefore, both positive and necessary for rural poverty reduction. The inverse relationship between urbanization and poverty is indeed apparent in trendlines for both, over time and in various regions of the world (Figure 1.2.8); this is particularly the case in Eastern Asia, where urbanization has steadily increased and poverty drastically declined. Cities can be real poverty fighters. Although less dramatic, the same pattern of rising urbanization and declining poverty is also evident in Southern Asia. On the other hand, three regions – Latin America and the Caribbean, North Africa and the Middle East, and East/Central Europe and Central Asia – illustrate the dismal legacy of poverty reduction strategies since the late 20th century. Although the population became more urban in Latin America and the Caribbean and North Africa and the Middle East during the past two decades, the reduction in poverty experienced during the 1980s came to a halt in the 1990s. A similar phenomenon occurred in East/Central Europe and Central Asia, where poverty increased during the 1990s as the degree of urbanization remained largely unchanged. In sub-Saharan Africa, a majority of the population will become urban over the next 30 years and this "urban transition" represents both an opportunity and a challenge. Local and central authorities must develop sound policies and strategies to ensure that urban areas become real engines of national economic growth, with the potential to reduce poverty and enhance quality of life for all; otherwise, urban growth will result in a concentration of poor people in cities instead of rural areas, and there will be no significant overall poverty reduction.[23]

Empirical evidence also indicates an inverse relationship between the degree of urbanization and the overall incidence of poverty in individual countries: as shown in Figure 1.2.9, countries that are more urbanized tend to feature lower poverty rates relative to the national poverty line. The opposite seems to be the case for countries that are little urbanized, where the incidence of poverty tends to be higher.[24]

The empirical relationship between urbanization and poverty does not imply causality – that is, urbanization *per se* does not result in overall poverty reduction. More likely, the relationship between urbanization and poverty reflects a strong relationship between these two situations and other factors like pro-poor policies and economic growth. Hand in hand with economic growth, urbanization has helped reduce overall poverty by providing new opportunities, raising incomes and increasing the numbers of livelihood options for both rural and urban populations. Urbanization, therefore, does indeed play a positive role in overall poverty reduction, particularly where supported by well-adapted policies.[25]

In summary, cities tend to be centres of economic power, both within local regions and as contributors to the national economy. Their influence results not only from their share of the world's population but also from their location and economic advantages, including economies of agglomeration and scale. The prosperity of cities usually mirrors the prosperity of countries, as an increase in urbanization generally goes hand in hand with higher GDP per capita, and in some countries contributes to a decline in overall poverty at the national level. However, cities can also be places of high inequality, as increased prosperity often does not result in more egalitarian distribution of wealth or income. But, does this urban divide really matter as long as the prosperity of cities results in poverty reduction? This important question, as well as what causes inequality, is further explored in Part 2 of this Report.

FIGURE 1.2.9: **POVERTY HEADCOUNT RATIO RELATIVE TO NATIONAL POVERTY LINE BY DEGREE OF URBANIZATION, 1998-2007**

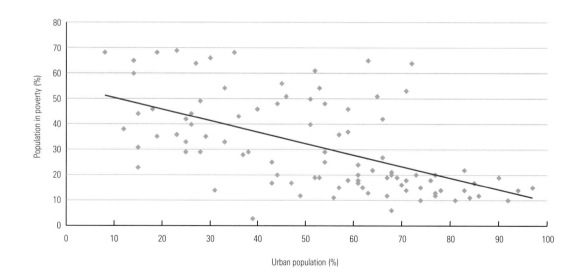

Sources: World Bank, 2007; European Community, 2007.

Phnom Penh, Cambodia. Increased prosperity does not result in more egalitarian distribution of wealth. ©**Swissmacky/Shutterstock**

BOX 1.2.1: IS URBANIZATION IN AFRICA "PATHOLOGICAL"?

In the past two decades, researchers, economists and analysts have tended to view urbanization in Africa through a prism of "abnormality" or "exceptionalism". They have described the continent's rapid urban growth – averaging approximately 4 per cent per year in the 1980s and 1990s – as "pathological" or "dysfunctional"; this suggests that, unlike the rest of the world, urbanization in Africa has often not been accompanied by sustained economic growth or reduced poverty. Furthermore, African countries experiencing what has been termed "urbanization without growth" have been diagnosed as either "failed states" or under-industrialized, agrarian economies that have been unable to diversify or improve productivity.

While it is true that economic growth did not keep pace with rising urban populations in several countries, particularly in the 1980s and 1990s, more recent evidence paints a different picture. A UN-HABITAT review of data from 36 African countries shows that half of the countries, including Angola, Ethiopia, Liberia, Malawi, Mozambique and Sudan, experienced relatively high (over 5 per cent) economic growth rates in 2006 and 2007, with Angola, Ethiopia and Sudan growing at double-digit rates of 21.1 per cent, 11.1 per cent, and 10.2 per cent, respectively. In many of these countries, average annual urban growth rates between 2005 and 2010 were not significantly higher than the continental average of 3.3 per cent. In fact, in South Africa and Botswana, where more than 60 per cent of the population is urban and which featured GDP growth rates of more than 5 per cent in 2006 and 2007, annual urban growth rates between 2005 and 2010 (estimate) were significantly lower than the continental average, at 1.35 per cent and 2.51 per cent, respectively. Growth in the formal economy of many African countries has been fuelled mainly by the industrial (including construction and mining) and services sectors, which tend to be urban-based. Of all the economic sectors, including agriculture, the services sector has grown the fastest in Africa since the 1990s.

Despite robust economic growth in several countries, though, approximately one-third of the 36 African countries under review have experienced substantial shifts in population without commensurate poverty reduction. Even though just one country experienced negative GDP growth in 2006 and 2007, GDP growth per capita provides a different perspective. One-third of the countries, including Burundi, Eritrea, Guinea, Mali, Niger and Togo, featured negative GDP per capita growth rates during 2006 and 2007, with Zimbabwe experiencing the worst at -6.0 per cent. In some countries, such as Kenya, relatively high economic growth rates from 2003 to 2007 have been undercut by recent civil

TABLE 1.2.3: ANNUAL URBAN AND GDP (%) GROWTH RATES IN SELECTED AFRICAN COUNTRIES

Country	Average annual urban growth rate 2005-2010 (%)	Percentage urban 2010 (%)	Gross domestic product (GDP) growth 2006-2007 (%)
Angola	4.4	58.5	21.1
Botswana	2.51	61.1	5.3
Burundi	6.78	11.0	3.6
Chad	4.67	27.6	0.6
Congo, Dem. Rep.	5.07	35.2	6.5
Ethiopia	4.29	17.6	11.1
Ghana	3.48	51.5	6.3
Kenya	3.99	22.2	7.0
Liberia	5.65	61.5	9.4
Nigeria	3.78	49.8	5.9
Rwanda	4.21	18.9	6.0
South Africa	1.35	61.7	5.1
Sudan	4.29	45.2	10.2
Tanzania	4.2	26.4	7.1
Uganda	4.4	13.3	7.9
Zimbabwe	2.24	38.3	-5.3

Sources: World Bank, 2009; UN DESA, 2008.

strife and political factors, which hindered economic growth and productivity in 2008 and 2009.

Furthermore, the concerns of outside observers have been justified by the experiences of many African countries where high economic growth rates have not led directly to reductions in slum populations or urban poverty. This would point to a pattern of "pathological" urban growth which, fundamentally, reflects a lack of political will to tackle urban poverty in a systematic way, but can also derive from the poor performance of policies and programmes in many countries. As discussed in Part 2 of this Report, development strategies and related interventions have, to a large extent, been dictated by powerful interest groups. In some cases social policies, including those involving donor assistance, have proved to be extremely ineffective. High slum prevalence in many African cities can also be attributed to structural and political failures in the distribution of public goods, as well as to lack of human and financial resources to address urban poverty. Against this background, economic growth in many cases has had little impact on either poverty or inequality, or both. In other words, sustained economic growth has not been in a position to drive the urbanization process with desirable results. In the fastest growing African economies, such as oil-rich Angola and Sudan, slum dwellers constitute the majority – more than 80 per cent – of the urban population. Poor agricultural yields and civil war have been blamed for the high urban and slum growth rates in these countries, as rural migrants have flocked to cities to escape hunger or conflict. While natural population growth in African cities is increasingly the norm (more people are born in cities than migrate to them), continued civil

strife and environmental crises in some countries are still pushing rural populations to urban areas, where the majority of the migrants end up in slums or poorly-serviced neighbourhoods.

Although rural poverty rates tend to be higher than those in urban areas, the gap is rapidly closing. In Kenya, for instance, the urban and rural poverty rates in 1997 were 49 per cent and 53 per cent, respectively. Projections for 2020 indicate that urban poverty will account for more than 40 per cent of total poverty in several African countries, including Benin, Cameroon, Kenya, Mauritania, Mozambique, Nigeria, Senegal and Tanzania. These projections suggest that rapid urbanization may lead to a shift in the locus of poverty in Africa from rural to urban areas, leaving cities with a larger share of total poverty in the coming decades.

However, statistics often fail to reflect Africa's underground economies, where the bulk of the urban population works in the informal sector. In fact, many African cities that may appear as "a patchwork of shantytowns, refugee camps, industrial zones and gated residential communities" are actually clusters of economic activities that are linked through both formal and informal networks. One study showed that in the years 1999 and 2000, the informal economy accounted for 42 per cent of 23 African countries' gross national product (GNP). Evidence from several African countries has also shown that the informal economy keeps growing even as the formal sector is stagnant. It is estimated, for instance, that informal activities account for 93 per cent of all new jobs and 61 per cent of urban employment in Africa. Although this largely invisible economy is not in a position to propel the continent out of poverty, it plays an important role in Africa's urban transformation and development.

Sources: Spence et al., 2009; Kessides, 2006; World Bank, 2009; UN DESA, 2008b; Fay & Opal, 2000.

▲
Sanaa, Yemen. The country features the highest proportion of people living below the national poverty line in Western Asia. ©**Vladimir Melnik/Shutterstock**

END NOTES

1   Commission on Growth and Development, 2009.
2   OECD, 2008.
3   Naudé & Krugell, 2004.
4   Van Dijk, 2007.
5   Sources: for New York, Sydney, Mexico City, Paris, Lisbon, Brussels, Budapest, Seoul: OECD, 2008; for Bangalore, New Delhi, Mumbai, Guangzhou, Beijing, Shanghai: van Dijk, 2007, and Naudé & Krugell, 2004. This data should be interpreted carefully, as in some cases different data sources were used for each factor, for which there could be some discrepancy regarding the boundaries of cities.
6   For an in-depth description and examples of growth and innovation dynamics in urban clusters in Africa, see, for example, Oyelaran-Oyeyinka & McCormick, 2007.
7   Naudé & Krugell, 2004.
8   Centre for Development and Enterprise (CDE), 2002.
9   Gross Domestic Product (GDP) is calculated on a Purchasing Power Parity (PPP), which adjusts the actual GDP per capita based on the costs of living in that country or city. The GDP figures in the table reflect the PPP-adjusted per capita value multiplied by the population of the city and the surrounding urban area in order to arrive at a total PPP-adjusted number for the GDP of the city (City Mayors, n.d.).
10 City Mayors, n.d.
11 For a comprehensive review of the literature on urbanization and economic growth, see Spence *et al.*, 2008.
12 The OECD regional typology classifies regions into predominantly urban, intermediate and predominantly rural. It is based on (1) population density, (2) the percentage of population living in rural communities and (3) the size of the urban centers located within a region. GDP per capita (PPP in U.S. dollars at year 2000 value) corresponds to the 18 OECD countries for which per capita data is collected at the regional level. (OECD, n.d.)
13 Liu *et al.*, 2009.
14 Per capita income measured in constant year-2000 U.S. dollars.
15 Annez & Buckley, 2008.
16 World Bank (2007), *World Development Indicators*.
17 Washington, D.C.: Author
18 Kessides, 2006.
19 Kessides, 2006.
20 Commission on Growth and Development, 2009.
21 Out of the 211 countries included in the World Bank's *World Development Indicators* dataset (2007), 50 countries had data on urban and rural poverty between 1998 and 1997.
22 The higher incidence of poverty in rural relative to urban areas is also found when using International poverty lines (see Ravallion *et al.*, 2006).
23 UN-HABITAT, 2006.
24 World Bank, 2007.
25 $R^2 = 0.3059$. A total of 94 countries are included, for which data on poverty rate relative to the national poverty line was available between 1997 and 2007 in either the World Bank *World Development Indicators* or European Commission. (n.d.) Eurostat statistics database. Accessed through: http://epp.eurostat.ec.europa.eu/portal/page/portal/eurostat/home/
26 Ravallion *et al.*, 1996.

Quick Facts

1. The Millennium "slum target" has been achieved, improving the lives of 227 million people, but only because it was set too low at the outset; 100 million was only 10 per cent of the global slum population.

2. China and India alone achieved the global slum target by improving the lives of 125 million slum dwellers.

3. North Africa is the only sub-region in the developing world where both the number and proportion of slum dwellers have steadily declined.

4. No single country has managed to halve their slum populations. The more successful (Indonesia, Morocco, Argentina, Colombia, Egypt, Dominican Republic) reduced slum incidence by 30 to nearly 50 per cent.

Policy Points

1. The population of slum dwellers around the world continues to grow at around 10 per cent every year, intensifying the problem worldwide.

2. Unless governments adopt ambitious, well-devised targets for their own countries and allocate adequate budget resources, the lives of slum dwellers will effectively remain unchanged.

3. Individual countries must revise and increase the slum target to take into account both existing and potential new slums. This is an essential building block if the urban divide is to be bridged.

4. Countries and cities that take the slum target seriously are increasing the prospects for millions to escape poverty, disease and illiteracy, and simply to lead better lives.

5. Countries that have managed substantially to reduce their own slum populations give hope to others and show that adequate policies can bring positive change.

6. Improving the lives of slum dwellers is the best way to achieve all the Millennium Development Goals. Improving housing conditions and providing for water and sanitation will not only save lives among the very poor, but will also support progress in education and health.

1.3
Slum Dwellers:
Proportions are Declining, but Numbers are Growing

Good news on the slum target, Millennium Development Goal 7

The living conditions of slum dwellers have made bleak news for years, shedding the crudest - and cruelest - light on the urban divide. In 2006, UN-HABITAT reported that thousands of people were joining the ranks of the slum population every month in the towns and cities of developing countries, where one in every three residents already lived in a slum.[1] Along with new data on the global slum population, UN-HABITAT presented a "worst-case" slum scenario, in which growth rates were projected to continue unabated with the number of residents rising from nearly one billion in 2005 to 1.4 billion by 2020.[2]

At the time, the data put the urban divide under sharp focus and sparked fresh interest in slums. The outcome was a series of reports and publications predicting increasingly desperate situations for the world's slum dwellers. Since the growth in urban populations in developing countries is often characterized by informality, illegality and unplanned settlements, and is, above all, strongly associated with urban poverty, many authors assumed that *urban* growth in the poorest countries would be synonymous with *slum* growth. Fortunately, though, a number of countries have, to a significant extent, managed to curb the further expansion of slums and to improve the living conditions prevailing there. This suggests that the world can reduce the urban divide and steer away from the worst-case scenario for urban growth.

Since the year 2000, when the international community committed to the Millennium Development Goals (MDGs) and associated targets, the global effort to narrow the starkest, slum-related form of urban divide has yielded some positive results. United Nations data suggests that the overarching goal of reducing absolute poverty by half can be achieved, although higher food prices in the last year may push 100 million people deeper into poverty.[3] When, under Goal 7, target 11 (as the slum target was originally known), member states pledged significantly to improve the lives of at least 100 million slum dwellers by 2020, they could not have known that the target would be achieved 10 years ahead of schedule.[4]

Delhi, India. Asia was at the forefront of successful efforts to reach the Millennium slum target between the year 2000 and 2010. ©**Paul Prescott/Shutterstock**

▲
Cape Town, South Africa. Many slum households suffer from only one shelter deprivation and could be improved easily. ©Ivonne Wierink/Shutterstock

TABLE 1.3.1: **URBAN POPULATION LIVING IN SLUMS, 1990-2010**

Major region or area	URBAN SLUM POPULATION (THOUSANDS)					
	1990	1995	2000	2005	2007	2010
Developing Regions	656,739	718,114	766,762	795,739	806,910	827,690
North Africa	19,731	18,417	14,729	10,708	11,142	11,836
Sub-Saharan Africa	102,588	123,210	144,683	169,515	181,030	199,540
Latin America and the Caribbean	105,740	111,246	115,192	110,105	110,554	110,763
Eastern Asia	159,754	177,063	192,265	195,463	194,020	189,621
Southern Asia	180,449	190,276	194,009	192,041	191,735	190,748
South-Eastern Asia	69,029	76,079	81,942	84,013	83,726	88,912
Western Asia	19,068	21,402	23,481	33,388	34,179	35,713
Oceania	379	421	462	505	524	556

Major region or area	PROPORTION OF URBAN POPULATION LIVING IN SLUMS (%)					
	1990	1995	2000	2005	2007	2010
Developing Regions	46.1	42.8	39.3	35.7	34.3	32.7
North Africa	34.4	28.3	20.3	13.4	13.4	13.3
Sub-Saharan Africa	70	67.6	65	63	62.4	61.7
Latin America and the Caribbean	33.7	31.5	29.2	25.5	24.7	23.5
Eastern Asia	43.7	40.6	37.4	33	31.1	28.2
Southern Asia	57.2	51.6	45.8	40	38	35
South-Eastern Asia	49.5	44.8	39.6	34.2	31.9	31
Western Asia	22.5	21.6	20.6	25.8	25.2	24.6
Oceania	24.1	24.1	24.1	24.1	24.1	24.1

Source: UN-HABITAT estimates (based on United Nations Population Division, World Urbanization Prospects: The 2007 Revision).

According to UN-HABITAT estimates, between the year 2000 and 2010 a total 227 million people in the developing world will have moved out of slum conditions. In other words, governments have collectively exceeded the Millennium target by at least 2.2 times.

Not only have slum dwellers experienced significant improvements in their day-to-day lives, but millions have also ceased being slum dwellers under the UN-HABITAT definition (see Box below). Another reason to rejoice is that all regions in the developing world have contributed to this success, even though some countries have been more successful than others.

While the world has reason to celebrate this welcome overall dent in the urban divide, there is no room for complacency. More than 200 million slum dwellers do enjoy better living conditions today than they did 10 years ago, but their absolute number in the developing world is not on the decline, quite the contrary: the number of slum dwellers in the developing world has risen from 767 million in the year 2000 to an estimated 828 million in 2010 (see Table and Map 1.3.1). This means that 61 million new slum dwellers have been added to the global urban population since the year 2000. Current UN-HABITAT estimates confirm that the progress made on the slum target has not been enough to counter the growth of informal settlements in the developing world. In this sense, efforts to reduce the number of slum dwellers - and the urban divide at its most unacceptable - are neither satisfactory nor adequate, especially when considering that 50.6 per cent of the world's population - or 3.49 billion - now live in urban areas.[5]

Regional Trends

Many countries and regions have narrowed the urban divide through significant reductions in both the numbers and proportions of slum dwellers, but some are lagging behind or, worse, are actually regressing. As shown in Map 1.3.2, **Asia** was at the forefront of successful efforts to reach the Millennium slum target between the year 2000 and 2010, with governments in the region improving the lives of an estimated 172 million slum dwellers; these represent 75 per cent of the total number of urban residents in the world who no longer suffer from inadequate housing. The greatest advances in this region were recorded in Southern and Eastern Asia, where 145 million people moved out of the "slum dweller" category (73 million and 72 million, respectively); this represented a

24 per cent decrease in the total urban population living in slums in the two sub-regions. Countries in South-Eastern Asia have also made significant progress with improved conditions for 33 million slum residents, or a 22 per cent decrease. Only Western Asia has failed to make a contribution as the number of slum dwellers in the sub-region *increased* by 12 million. This setback can largely be attributed to the conflict-related deterioration of living conditions in Iraq, where the proportion of urban residents living in slum conditions has tripled from 17 per cent in the year 2000 (2.9 million) to an estimated 53 per cent in 2010 (10.7 million).

Across *Africa*, the lives of 24 million slum dwellers have improved in the last decade, representing 11 per cent of the global effort to narrow this form of urban divide. North Africa has made significant gains (see Map 1.3.3), with improved conditions for 8.7 million. In sub-Saharan Africa, though, the proportion of the urban population living in slums has decreased by only 5 per cent (or 17 million); as for the future, data suggest persistent challenges as growth rates remain high for both urban and slum populations (estimated at slightly less than 4 per cent on an annual basis). Every year, 10 million more people are added to the urban population of sub-Saharan Africa; approximately one-third of these, or 3 million, move to "formal" urban areas and act both as agents and beneficiaries of formal urban and economic growth. The remaining two-thirds, or 7 million, live in informal settlements or slum conditions. Of these, only 2 million can expect to lift themselves out of the slum conditions where the other 5 million will remain confined on the wrong side of the urban divide.

Some 13 per cent of the progress made towards the global Millennium slum target has occurred in *Latin America and the Caribbean*, where 30 million people have moved out of slum conditions since the year 2000. In proportional terms, the reduction is 19.5 per cent. This leaves Latin America lagging behind North Africa for improved slum conditions, while remaining far ahead of sub-Saharan Africa, where the slum-induced urban divide remains stark (Map 1.3.4).

On a global scale, the overall outlook is cause for optimism. The fact that an additional 227 million urban dwellers have gained access to improved water and sanitation as well as to durable and less crowded housing shows that a number of countries and cities are taking the slum target seriously. This enhances the prospects for millions of people to escape poverty, disease and illiteracy, and to lead better lives thanks to a narrower urban divide.

UN-HABITAT SLUM INDICATORS

A slum household consists of one or a group of individuals living under the same roof in an urban area, lacking one or more of the following five amenities: (1) durable housing (a permanent structure providing protection from extreme climatic conditions); (2) sufficient living area (no more than three people sharing a room); (3) access to improved water (water that is sufficient, affordable and can be obtained without extreme effort); (4) access to improved sanitation facilities (a private

toilet, or a public one shared with a reasonable number of people); and (5) secure tenure (*de facto* or *de jure* secure tenure status and protection against forced eviction). Since information on secure tenure is not available for most countries included in the UN-HABITAT database, however, only the first four indicators are used to define slum households, and then to estimate the proportion of the urban population living in slums.

Slum proportions of selected countries in Africa (1990)

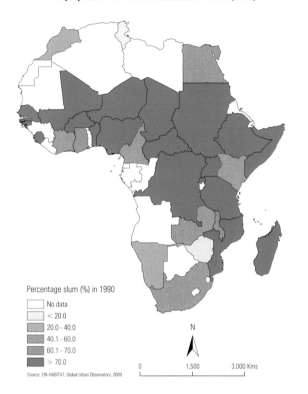

Percentage slum (%) in 1990

- No data
- < 20.0
- 20.0 - 40.0
- 40.1 - 60.0
- 60.1 - 70.0
- > 70.0

N

0   1,500   3,000 Kms

Source: UN-HABITAT, Global Urban Observatory, 2009.

Slum proportions of selected countries in Africa (2000)

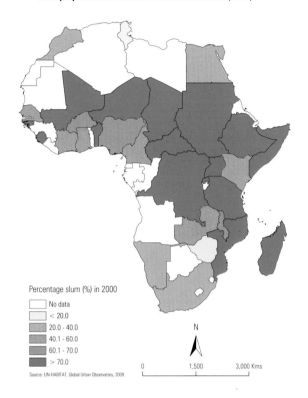

Percentage slum (%) in 2000

- No data
- < 20.0
- 20.0 - 40.0
- 40.1 - 60.0
- 60.1 - 70.0
- > 70.0

N

0   1,500   3,000 Kms

Source: UN-HABITAT, Global Urban Observatory, 2009.

Slum proportions of selected countries in Africa (2005)

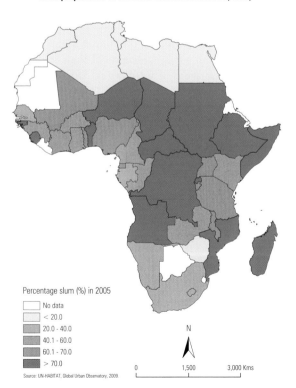

Percentage slum (%) in 2005

- No data
- < 20.0
- 20.0 - 40.0
- 40.1 - 60.0
- 60.1 - 70.0
- > 70.0

N

0   1,500   3,000 Kms

Source: UN-HABITAT, Global Urban Observatory, 2009.

Slum proportions of selected countries in Africa (2010)

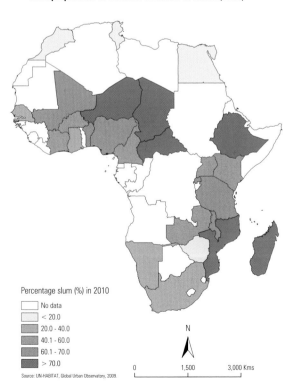

Percentage slum (%) in 2010

- No data
- < 20.0
- 20.0 - 40.0
- 40.1 - 60.0
- 60.1 - 70.0
- > 70.0

N

0   1,500   3,000 Kms

Source: UN-HABITAT, Global Urban Observatory, 2009.

MAP 1.3.2: **PERCENTAGE CHANGE IN SLUM PROPORTIONS IN SELECTED COUNTRIES IN LATIN AMERICA AND THE CARIBBEAN BETWEEN 1990 AND 2010 (ESTIMATE)**

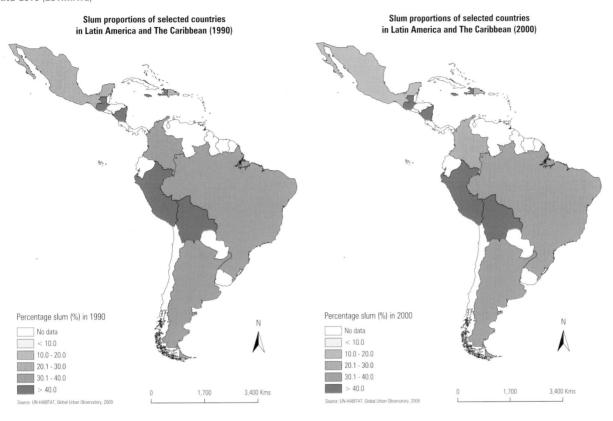

Slum proportions of selected countries in Latin America and The Caribbean (1990)

Percentage slum (%) in 1990

- No data
- < 10.0
- 10.0 - 20.0
- 20.1 - 30.0
- 30.1 - 40.0
- > 40.0

N

0   1,700   3,400 Kms

Source: UN-HABITAT, Global Urban Observatory, 2009.

Slum proportions of selected countries in Latin America and The Caribbean (2000)

Percentage slum (%) in 2000

- No data
- < 10.0
- 10.0 - 20.0
- 20.1 - 30.0
- 30.1 - 40.0
- > 40.0

N

0   1,700   3,400 Kms

Source: UN-HABITAT, Global Urban Observatory, 2009.

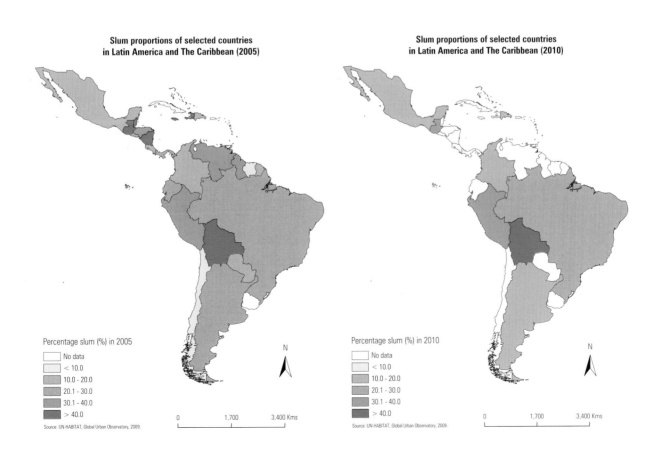

Slum proportions of selected countries in Latin America and The Caribbean (2005)

Percentage slum (%) in 2005

- No data
- < 10.0
- 10.0 - 20.0
- 20.1 - 30.0
- 30.1 - 40.0
- > 40.0

N

0   1,700   3,400 Kms

Source: UN-HABITAT, Global Urban Observatory, 2009.

Slum proportions of selected countries in Latin America and The Caribbean (2010)

Percentage slum (%) in 2010

- No data
- < 10.0
- 10.0 - 20.0
- 20.1 - 30.0
- 30.1 - 40.0
- > 40.0

N

0   1,700   3,400 Kms

Source: UN-HABITAT, Global Urban Observatory, 2009.

MAP 1.3.3: **PERCENTAGE CHANGE IN SLUM PROPORTIONS IN SELECTED COUNTRIES IN ASIA BETWEEN 1990 AND 2010 (ESTIMATE)**

Slum proportions of selected countries in Asia (1990)

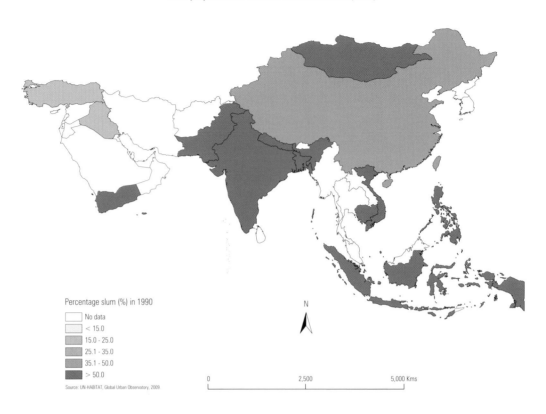

Percentage slum (%) in 1990

- No data
- < 15.0
- 15.0 - 25.0
- 25.1 - 35.0
- 35.1 - 50.0
- > 50.0

N

0   2,500   5,000 Kms

Source: UN-HABITAT, Global Urban Observatory, 2009

Slum proportions of selected countries in Asia (2000)

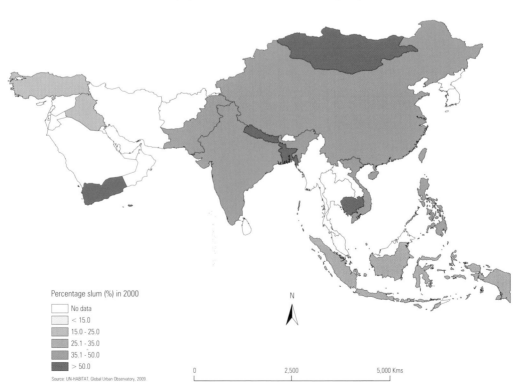

Percentage slum (%) in 2000

- No data
- < 15.0
- 15.0 - 25.0
- 25.1 - 35.0
- 35.1 - 50.0
- > 50.0

N

0   2,500   5,000 Kms

Source: UN-HABITAT, Global Urban Observatory, 2009

Slum proportions of selected countries in Asia (2005)

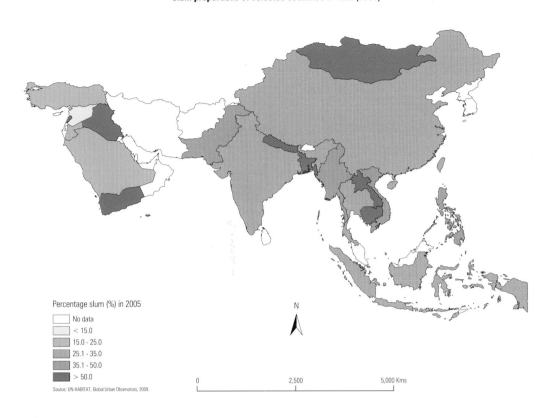

Percentage slum (%) in 2005

- No data
- < 15.0
- 15.0 - 25.0
- 25.1 - 35.0
- 35.1 - 50.0
- > 50.0

N

0   2,500   5,000 Kms

Source: UN-HABITAT, Global Urban Observatory, 2009.

Slum proportions of selected countries in Asia (2010)

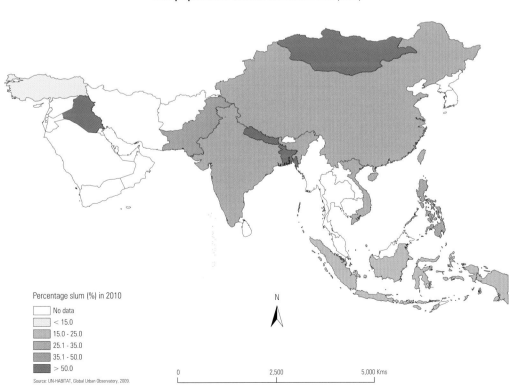

Percentage slum (%) in 2010

- No data
- < 15.0
- 15.0 - 25.0
- 25.1 - 35.0
- 35.1 - 50.0
- > 50.0

N

0   2,500   5,000 Kms

Source: UN-HABITAT, Global Urban Observatory, 2009.

BOX 1.3.1: **THE VARIOUS PROFILES OF SLUM CITIES**

▲
Addis Ababa, Ethiopia. The country is experiencing a growth rate of over 10 per cent, but slum prevalence remains very high. ©**Manoocher Deghati/IRIN**

No universal pattern of shelter deprivations or types of slums emerges clearly, and there is no universal prescription for slum improvement. Still, when rapid urban growth does not come with basic urban infrastructure, slums expand and the urban divide widens.

Contrary to "cities with slums" where the divide between rich and poor is quite clear, in "slum cities" the two categories live side by side. They lack at least one element of adequate shelter, on top of environmental hazards like excessive pollution and lack of solid waste management, among others. They are typically located in countries where poverty is endemic, urban infrastructure is absent, and housing is inadequate overall.

Slum cities are prevalent throughout sub-Saharan Africa. In Central African Republic, Chad and Ethiopia, slum cities are entrenched, with as many as 91 per cent of even non-slum households living in extremely deprived settlements. The same situation prevails in Niger, Nigeria, Tanzania and Togo. The lack of basic services is to be attributed largely to inadequate planning, construction and social services, leaving cities at risk of becoming more deeply mired in pollution, disease and social ills. Rapid urban growth without a proportional increase in basic urban infrastructure can only widen the urban divide, as it leads to further slum expansion.

A high concentration of slum households also characterizes the urban areas of Southern Asia, owing to lack of housing as well as widespread poverty and instability. In Bangladesh, endemic poverty is such that 71 per cent of urban households lack durable housing, sufficient living area or improved sanitation. In India, 44 per cent of all urban households are classified as slums, and 16 per cent of households lack improved sanitation. In Afghanistan, Pakistan and Sri Lanka, political instability and conflict have deteriorated basic service provision and shelter conditions in cities, resulting in a high prevalence of slums.

The same holds in Iraq and Lebanon, with refugees and displaced persons compounding the situation. Elsewhere in Western Asia, Yemen features the highest proportion of people living below the national poverty line, at 41 per cent; 65 per cent of households are classified as slum dwellers, and 26.4 per cent suffer from multiple shelter deprivations.

In Latin America and the Caribbean, Guatemala, Haiti, Nicaragua and Bolivia feature the highest proportions of slum households. In Haiti and Bolivia, more than half of these suffer from multiple shelter deprivations, with slum prevalence rates of 76 per cent and 61 per cent, respectively. In both countries, lack of sanitation and sufficient living area are the most widespread shelter deprivations.

Source: UN-HABITAT Global Urban Observatory, 2009.

MDG Progress in Individual Countries

Some countries have made substantial progress and are clearly moving ahead not only in slum reduction but also in slum prevention. In absolute numbers, China and India have improved the lives of more slum dwellers than any other country, having together lifted no less than 125 million people out of slum conditions between the year 2000 and 2010 (estimate) (see Figure 1.3.1).

In this resolute effort to bridge the urban divide over the past decade, China has recorded the most spectacular progress in the world, with improvements to the day-to-day conditions of 65.3 million urban residents who were living with one or more factors of shelter deprivation. In proportional terms, China's urban slum population fell from 37.3 per cent in the year 2000 to an estimated 28.2 per cent in 2010, a 25 per cent relative decrease (see Figure 1.3.2). Although disparities have grown with the country's rapid economic growth, China has managed to improve living conditions through economic reforms and modernization policies that have used urbanization as a propelling force of national growth. Pro-growth policies, with targeted pro-poor dimensions, have generally resulted in a reduction in the number of slum dwellings. More significantly, targeted programmes directed at old villages within the boundaries of expanding cities and newly developed slums (which provide cheap housing for the more than 8 million migrant workers who flock to the cities every year) have mixed both regulation and development mechanisms to prompt modernization - and have met success. A particularly successful strategy has been facilitating access of slum dwellers to more than 20 million new and affordable housing units through government equity grants (as a mortgage instrument). These procure leases on cheap housing built by property developers, who are given preferential tax rates as an incentive for the development of affordable homes. On top of this, a new tier of self-governance seems to also have emerged in the new housing estates, with residents electing committees to oversee and manage urban safety and security, environmental conservation and the needs of young and elderly people.[6]

Like China, India has been successful in improving the lives of slum dwellers, having helped 59.7 million of these out of dire conditions since the year 2000. Slum prevalence fell from 41.5 per cent in 2000 to an estimated 28.1 per cent in 2010, a relative decrease of 32 per cent. India has taken up urban poverty alleviation and slum improvement as important components of its urban development policies through four specific strategies: (1) enhancing the productivity of the urban poor by building skills and providing access to micro-credit; (2) improving the living conditions of the poor through provision of basic services and *in-situ* development of slum settlements; (3) providing security of tenure to poor families living in unauthorized settlements and improving their access to serviced low-cost housing and subsidized housing finance; and (4) empowering the urban poor through community development and encouraging their participation in decision-making.[7]

FIGURE 1.3.1: BRIDGING THE URBAN DIVIDE THROUGH SLUM IMPROVEMENT: THE MOST SUCCESSFUL COUNTRIES

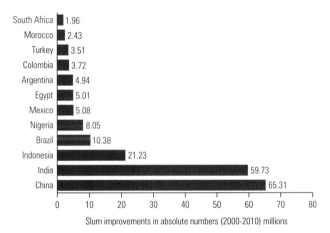

Slum improvements in absolute numbers (2000-2010) millions

Source: UN-HABITAT - GUO, 2009. Note: 2010 data are predictions.

FIGURE 1.3.2: BRIDGING THE URBAN DIVIDE THROUGH SLUM IMPROVEMENT

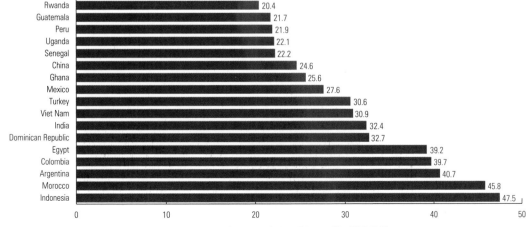

% of population lifted out of slum condition (2000-2010)

Source: UN-HABITAT - GUO, 2009. Note: 2010 data are predictions.

After China and India, the most significant improvements in slum conditions in **Asia** were recorded in Indonesia, Viet Nam and Turkey. In South-East Asia, Indonesia improved the lives of 21.2 million slum dwellers, a 33 per cent proportional decrease (from 34.4 per cent of the urban population in the year 2000 to an estimated 23 per cent in 2010). Turkey scored as the best-performing country in Western Asia, reducing its proportion of slum households by slightly less than one-third, from 17.9 per cent in the year 2000 to an estimated 12.4 per cent in 2010. Another country that managed to narrow the urban divide was Viet Nam, where slum incidence dropped from 48.8 per cent in the year 2000 to an estimated 33.7 per cent in 2010 - a 30.9 per cent decrease. This is commensurate with poverty reduction over the same period,[8] and it is worth noting here that Viet Nam has also made significant progress on most of the other Millennium Development Goals.

The more successful developing countries are found in **North Africa**. Egypt, Morocco and Tunisia have achieved the most substantial reductions in the proportions of people living with shelter deprivations. In Morocco, an estimated 2.4 million people moved out of slum conditions over the past 10 years, reflecting a 45.8 per cent reduction in slum prevalence between the year 2000 (24.2 per cent) and 2010 (an estimated 13 per cent), thanks to strong political leadership, clear targets and adequate budget resources. Egypt reduced its proportion of slum dwellers by 39 per cent, as slum prevalence fell from 28.1 per cent of the urban population in the year 2000 to an estimated 17.1 per cent in 2010, in the process improving living conditions for five million people. Such significant narrowing of the urban divide in Morocco and Egypt alone accounted for two-thirds of North Africa's progress.

Among other major regions of the world, **Latin America and the Caribbean** has made relatively good progress on the slum target. However, aggregate figures conceal the region's heterogeneity. Argentina, Colombia and Dominican Republic, the most successful countries in the region, were able to reduce their proportions of slum dwellers in the last decade by over a third. Haiti, Mexico, Nicaragua, Guatemala and Peru achieved reductions ranging from 21 to 27 per cent. Brazil managed to reduce its slum population by 16 per cent. Other countries in the region have been less successful, achieving only negligible progress toward the Millennium target and a narrower urban divide.

Latin America's four most populated countries - Argentina, Colombia, Mexico and Brazil - account for 79 per cent of the region's estimated improvements in the lives of slum dwellers. Among these, Argentina and Colombia have proved the more successful, reducing by two-fifths their slum population thanks to improved housing and better access to water and sanitation. As it emerged from the economic crisis of the late 1990s and early 2000s, Argentina managed to improve the lives of nearly five million people residing in slum neighbourhoods, significantly reducing the prevalence of *invasiones* (as slums are known locally). In Colombia, an estimated 3.7 million slum dwellers have benefited from well-targeted slum upgrading and prevention strategies, lowering slum prevalence from 22.3 per cent in the year 2000 to an estimated 13.5 per cent in 2010. Mexico made fair progress with improved conditions for five million slum dwellers in the last decades, as slum prevalence dropped from 19.9 per cent in the year 2000 to an estimated 14.4 per cent in 2010. Brazil, the world's 10th largest economy, was able to improve the living conditions of an estimated 10.4 million people between the year 2000 and 2010, as slum incidence regressed from 31.5 to 26.4 per cent. The main factors behind Brazil's success include economic and social policies that have improved incomes for poor urban households; a decreasing population growth rate and slowing rural-urban migration; the development of low-income housing policies that subsidize construction material costs, sites and services, and provide for slum upgrading and land tenure regularization; new social housing and urban infrastructure projects; the creation of a Ministry of Cities; and the adoption of a constitutional amendment safeguarding citizens' right to housing.[9]

▲
Fès, Morocco. North Africa is the only sub-region in the developing world where both the number and proportion of slum dwellers have steadily declined. ©**kirych/Shutterstock**

BOX 1.3.2: SOME CITIES ARE JUST ONE OR TWO STEPS FROM BRIDGING THE DIVIDE... BUT OTHERS ARE ONLY "RECLASSIFIED" VILLAGES

▲
Addis Ababa, Ethiopia. Slums in sub-Saharan Africa are noted for the extent of their deprivations.
©Manoocher Deghati/IRIN

The prevalence of slum households varies dramatically across cities of the developing world. In some, a relatively small percentage of households experience shelter deprivations, or many experience only one barrier to adequate housing. In other cities, a majority of households live in dwellings that lack two or more basic shelter amenities, threatening the health, safety and well-being of residents.

Slums in the cities of many sub-Saharan African countries have become notorious for the extent and intensity of their deprivations, and yet living conditions for people in housing classified as "slums" are not uniformly alarming. Indeed, the divide between slums and more conventional urban environments seems so narrow as to be relatively easy to bridge - if only policymakers recognized the opportunity and acted accordingly. Indeed, in a number of sub-Saharan African cities, some of the living conditions that prompted concern in the past are undergoing noteworthy improvement; in some places, slum households now are only one or two basic amenities short of "adequate" housing. In Southern Africa, countries like Namibia and Zimbabwe feature the relatively low slum concentrations that can also be observed in middle-income countries of Asia and Latin America and the Caribbean. In the Southern Africa sub-region, it could take a simple programme targeting housing

or sanitation to help many families out of slums, enabling them fully to enjoy urban life with all their basic shelter needs met. In South Africa, for example, 3 out of 10 urban homes are "slum households", and as many as 22 per cent of households suffer from only one shelter deprivation - primarily lack of improved sanitation (10 per cent) or of sufficient living area (9 per cent).

Because no universal pattern of shelter deprivations or types of slums is evident across the cities of the developing world, there is no universal prescription for slum improvement. In all of the cities where the urban landscape is dominated by slums, improving the lives of slum dwellers first requires the implementation of macro-economic programmes that can lift households from deprivation to adequate living standards, providing for the missing elements in their environments: housing infrastructure and finance, improved water, improved sanitation, or durable housing units with adequate living space. However, these macro-level programmes must be associated with micro-level schemes, including micro-credit, self-help, education and employment. Housing services may be available, but families will use them only if they are affordable. Moreover, urban infrastructure projects, when focused on slum upgrading, should include economic development and employment programmes if families are to af-.

ford public services. Efforts must also ensure that durable, properly sized land and housing is affordable and accessible to poor families so that they can also afford health care, education and other essential services.

Slums are often viewed as the result of poor management of demographic growth on the part of major cities, but cities of all sizes struggle with the inability to provide adequate affordable land and housing and the extended water supplies and sanitation facilities needed to serve expanding populations. Slums can be easier to improve in smaller than in larger cities, as small cities often feature fewer social, cultural and economic barriers to urban development. In small cities, developing master plans and engaging in urban planning with the participation of families and communities is often more straightforward than in large cities, and institutions can be more easily coordinated to implement services. In cities of all sizes, improving the lives of slum dwellers and bridging the urban divide depends on increased development of non-agricultural sectors, services and industries for sustainable urbanization, providing access to well-paid jobs, formal land and housing policies as well as structured credit.

Planning for growth can be particularly difficult where "cities" are actually just agglomerations of contiguous settlements that feature the same densities as those of more typical urban areas, but are administered independently. Such fragmented urban areas may not provide the infrastructure and economic activities that make cities liveable and viable. In some places, even areas where rural activities are predominant can be classified as "cities" the moment they meet certain population thresholds. In Mali and Madagascar, for example, any place with a population of 5,000 inhabitants or more qualifies as "urban". The reclassification of a location from rural area to "city" or "town" can imply the presence of administrative institutions, such as a city council in charge of planning, land allocation and provision of basic services; however, development of such much-needed amenities as sewerage systems and housing schemes to ensure access to adequate dwellings often does not follow, leaving small cities and towns as deprived as villages or rural communities. Clearly, creating "urban" places without adequate infrastructure for the resident population densities is a recipe for slum cities.

Source: UN-HABITAT Global Urban Observatory, 2009.

Slum target reached, but the numbers keep growing

The year 2010 marks the halfway point towards the deadline for the "slum target". In their efforts to improve the lives of at least 100 million slum dwellers by 2020, the governments of the world have already collectively exceeded the target by more than two times. Part 2 of this Report shows how improvements in housing can also have an impact on access to health, education and job opportunities for those living in slum neighbourhoods.

Over the past 10 years, the proportion of the urban population living in slums in the developing world has declined from 39 per cent in the year 2000 to an estimated 32 per cent in 2010. And yet the urban divide still exists, because in absolute terms the numbers of slum dwellers have actually grown considerably, and will continue to rise in the near future. Therefore, the fact that the world as a whole has reached the Millennium slum target 10 years in advance does not mean that efforts to improve the lives of slum dwellers should slow down or altogether stop. Rather, the fact that the target was reached this early makes it quite clear that it was simply set too low.

In the developing world between the year 2000 and 2010, the urban population is estimated to have increased by an average of 58 million per year. During the same period, the absolute number of slum dwellers is reckoned to have increased by nearly half this number (28 million) every year. UN-HABITAT estimates that in developing countries, 22 million people have been lifted out of slum conditions every year over that decade, through slum upgrading or prevention.

▲
Mathare, Nairobi, Kenya. The projections for slum reduction in sub-Saharan Africa are as not as optimistic as for other regions of the world. ©**Manoocher Deghati/IRIN**

This means that an average of 6 million people became slum dwellers every year. These estimations show that nearly half of the urban growth in the developing world can be attributed to slum expansion (48 per cent) and a significant proportion of it is improved over time (38 per cent), but still about 10 per cent of this informal growth remains in deprived conditions every year.

Simple projections extrapolating data from the previous decade show that by 2020, and short of drastic action to curb current trends, the slum population worldwide is likely to grow annually by 6 million every year, or another 61 million people, to reach a total of 889 million by 2020.

New slum estimates presented in Table 1.3.1 show that today, nearly a third (32.7 per cent) of the urban population in developing regions live in the inadequate housing conditions that are a major aspect of the urban divide. In particular, the projections for slum reduction in **sub-Saharan Africa**, where approximately 61.7 per cent of urban residents are slum dwellers, are as not as optimistic as for other regions of the world. The precarious nature of the development pathway of sub-Saharan Africa appears clearly in a number of trends that have to do not just with slums but also with other development and urban divide indicators such as infant and maternal mortality, employment and hunger. Despite the efforts of some countries and cities to expand basic services and improve housing conditions in slum areas, inaction by others has prevented overall progress from keeping pace with a rapidly increasing urban population. In the past decade, the number of urban residents in the sub-region increased by some 100 million, slightly more than half (55 million) of whom were new slum dwellers, while another 16 million moved from the "slum dweller" to the "urban non-slum resident" category. This means that while the proportion of the urban population living in slums underwent a moderate reduction (from 65 per cent in the year 2000 to an estimated 61.7 per cent in 2010), the actual slum population increased in absolute numbers by five million every year. The data provides no evidence that this pattern, and the urban divide that comes with it, will change, and it is likely that nearly half of the growth in sub-Saharan Africa's urban population will take place against a background of poverty and deprivation between now and 2020.

In Benin, Ethiopia, Malawi and other countries that rank among the lowest on the Human Development Index compiled by the United Nations Development Programme (UNDP), slum prevalence is expected to remain at a very high 70 per cent. The future is not looking bright for conflict-affected countries in sub-Saharan Africa, either: in Central African Republic and Côte d'Ivoire, the proportion of slum dwellers has increased by around one-tenth. The most conspicuous case of slum population increase was observed in Zimbabwe, with a surge (from 3.3 to 17.9 per cent) resulting from massive forced evictions in 2005. These have added to the numbers of people living in overcrowded conditions, and a deteriorating economy has also had severe effects on the country's urban poor.

BOX 1.3.3: WOMEN BEAR THE BRUNT OF PROBLEMS ASSOCIATED WITH SLUM LIFE

The vast Kibera settlement in Nairobi receives much media attention as one of the largest, most densely populated slums in Africa, but there are surprisingly few comprehensive studies with reliable statistics relating specifically to the women who live there. Much of the documentation about women in Kibera is based on case studies, interviews and qualitative analysis.

Kibera is a vast slum located approximately seven kilometres southwest of Nairobi's city centre. A large concentration of women live there in what can easily be described as the worst conditions slums have to offer. The slum is characterized by severe poverty, poor access to clean water, overflowing open sewers, huge heaps of rubbish, overly crowded mud houses, constant threat of eviction, and widespread criminality, delinquency and unemployment.

Although men in Kibera also suffer from problems associated with slum life, numerous studies on informal settlements in the region suggest that women bear the brunt of problems brought on by inadequate housing and insecure tenure. Unequal power relations between women and men generally leave Kibera women at a disadvantage in areas such as accessing land, property and other productive resources, and securing remunerated work.

Indeed, research by the Centre on Housing Rights and Evictions (COHRE) found that: *"Informal settlements in Nairobi are ... often home to thousands of women who were driven by in-laws out of their rural and urban homes and land upon the death of their husbands. In two separate missions to Kenya, as well as through research on women's inheritance rights in sub-Saharan Africa, COHRE found that family pressure, social stigma, physical threats and often extreme violence directed at the widow force her to seek shelter elsewhere."*

The study reinforces findings from numerous others showing that widows are particularly vulnerable to eviction because of customary and traditional practices in sub-Saharan Africa that override international commitments, such as the Convention on the Elimination of All Forms of Discrimination Against Women. Such practices often compromise the rights of Kenyan widows to keep their land and housing when disputes with in-laws arise. Property grabbing from widows whose husbands have died of AIDS is also reportedly widespread and is one of the factors that push women to migrate to Kibera.

Kibera slum, Nairobi, Kenya. ©**Sven Torfinn/Panos Pictures**

Because of their low incomes, these women have few housing alternatives when or if they are evicted. There is also some evidence to suggest that single, unmarried mothers in informal settlements such as Kibera have the poorest choice in housing since many landlords are unwilling to rent to them, believing them to be unreliable tenants.

The burden of women's domestic roles in Kibera also puts them at more of a disadvantage when basic services like water, sanitation and electricity are lacking. Like women in many parts of the developing world, those in Kibera are usually responsible for water collection and management of waste in the home. Long queues of women waiting with rows of yellow jerrycans are a common sight in the slum. Up to 85 per cent of women in Kibera draw water from private and community-owned water kiosks.

As in other slums where sanitation facilities are poor or non-existent, going to the toilet at night or in the early morning is a considerable security concern for women. Because they have to venture down narrow, unlit alleyways, many would rather use a plastic bag (the so-called "flying toilets") rather than braving the dark and the inherent risk of rape and sexual harassment.

Compared with men, who are more likely to secure work outside the slum, women spend more time around the home and are more likely

than males to take care of household waste. In doing so, they are exposed to environmental hazards such as breathing in harmful fumes from the burning of rubbish, which add to the health risks they already experience by cooking indoors with charcoal, kerosene or firewood in the absence of electricity or cheaper fuel.

Even if women do not get sick themselves, their unpaid labour when caring for people with diarrhoea (leading killer of children under 5 - and malaria, both of which are exacerbated by lack of improved sewerage) takes time away from education or income-generating activities.

The Kenya Water for Health Organization estimates that the average household in Kibera comprises seven people, and that many households are female-headed. A 10-by-10 square foot dwelling for seven people is indicative of severe overcrowding and its attendant problems, such as lack of privacy, ease of disease transmission - especially respiratory infections - and increased risk of "negative social behaviour patterns", such as domestic violence and child abuse. The cycle of violence continues outside the home as well: poverty often pushes girls in slums to engage in risky sexual behaviour or prostitution in exchange for food, shelter, gifts, or cash. As a result, HIV infection in the slum remains extraordinarily high, with estimates as high as 20 per cent - more than twice the national average.

Sources: COHRE & Hakijami Trust, 2007; COHRE, 2008; Ilako & Kimura, 2004; Marras, n.d.; UN-HABITAT, 2002; UN-HABITAT, 2006.

North Africa is the only sub-region in the developing world where both the number and the proportion of slum dwellers have been steadily declining since the year 2000. Despite an urban growth rate of 2.4 per cent[10] (or an additional 2.2 million urban dwellers every year) over the past decade, the share of slum dwellers in the sub-region fell from 20 per cent to an estimated 13.3 per cent over the same period, or about 2.9 million in absolute numbers. This substantial reduction in the urban divide can be attributed to effective government policies for slum upgrading and prevention.

Asian cities are host to an estimated 61 per cent of all the slum dwellers in the developing world. In **Southern Asia,** the poorest sub-region, more than one-third (35 per cent) of the urban population experiences at least one shelter deprivation as defined by UN-HABITAT. The sub-region also features the highest incidences of infant mortality and other social problems in Asia.[11] Fifty-three per cent of the slum dwellers in Southern Asia, or 103 million people, are concentrated in India, the most populated country in the sub-region. Despite India's substantial reduction in slum prevalence, projections are that the slum population in Southern Asia will still grow by some half million per year, totaling 200 million by 2020. This is even more likely as economic growth rates are slightly declining in India.[12] In Bangladesh, slum prevalence remains very high at 70 per cent. Regional spillovers from the global financial crisis are also likely to cut into government revenues and concomitant abilities to invest in the delivery of housing and basic services that are essential to narrowing the urban divide.

South-Eastern Asia features the second-highest rate of slum prevalence in the region (an estimated 31 per cent in 2010). For all the achievements of countries like Indonesia, Viet Nam and, to some extent, the Philippines, where slum growth has decelerated significantly, other social indicators such as maternal mortality remain unacceptably high[13] in the sub-region as a whole. This is primarily a result of conditions prevailing in Cambodia, Lao People's Democratic Republic and Myanmar, where slum prevalence is high and development indicators point to low quality of life. Improvements in the lives of slum dwellers take longer in South-Eastern Asia; by current trends and short of drastic action, the number of residents in slum areas is to grow by slightly more than 2 million every year, reaching 109 million by 2020. It is also likely that urban poverty, and the urban divide, will increase in some of the South-Eastern Asian emerging economies that have been severely affected by the collapse in demand for consumer durable goods and the deterioration of global financial conditions; both of these could result in more victims of shelter deprivations in the coming years.

In Eastern Asia, 28.2 per cent of the urban population dwell in slums. More than 90 per cent of Eastern Asia's slum dwellers, or 171 million, live in China. In fact, China is home to a full one-fifth of the world's slum population - the same as the country's share in the global population. Thanks to China's own significant achievements, Eastern Asia as a whole has reduced slum incidence by an estimated 25 per

cent. However, in view of ongoing rapid urban growth, it is anticipated that the number of slum dwellers in the sub-region will continue to increase by a total 30 million over the next 10 years, reaching 219 million by 2020. In countries with liberalized open economies and a high dependence on external demand, such as Korea, unemployment and poverty may increase as a result of the global financial crisis, making the conditions of those already living with shelter deprivations even worse.

The proportion of slum dwellers in **Western Asia** should be relatively low by 2010, at an estimated 24.6 per cent of the urban population. In terms of slum prevention, however, the sub-region has made little progress, owing to deteriorating living conditions in Iraq, Lebanon and Jordan. The slum population in the sub-region has grown by more than half since the year 2000 (from 23 million to 36 million), as a consequence of ongoing political turmoil, a related increase in the refugee population, and disruptions in the delivery of basic services and housing. The implications of the region's instability are also evident in other Millennium Development Goal indicators, such as the high proportion of underweight children under 5 and the high maternal mortality rate - two indicators on which Western Asia has made little progress compared with other developing regions.[14] Against this background, Turkey stands out for having reduced by slightly less than one-third its slum population and improved the lives of nearly 3.5 million people over the last 10 years; no other country has contributed more to MDG compliance in Western Asia. Turkey has achieved this by systematically legitimizing self-built housing, allowing for *in-situ* upgrading, and providing public transport and basic service infrastructure to informal settlements in the largest cities. In recent years, however, forced evictions and "urban renewal" strategies in some Turkish cities have replaced informal housing with large-scale estates that have resulted in the displacement of the poorest residents.[15] If the Western Asia sub-region remains engulfed in conflicts and various forms of instability, it is likely that the existing urban divide, as reflected in high numbers of slum dwellers, will be there to stay, growing by around 24 million to reach 48 million in the next 20 years.

Latin America and the Caribbean experienced a significant (20 per cent) reduction in the proportion of slum dwellers in its urban population over the last decade. However, slum incidence remains relatively high: 23 out of 100 urban residents in the region live in *tugurios, favelas* or *campamentos,* as the precarious settlements are locally known. The region is quite heterogeneous in terms of human development indicators and slum incidence. Haiti, the poorest country in the region and one of the poorest in the world, has a slum prevalence of 70 per cent. Bolivia and Nicaragua similarly feature very high slum prevalence, with nearly every other urban resident living in informal neighbourhoods that lack one or more basic services. Approximately one-third of the total urban population in Peru and Guatemala live in slums, compared with roughly one-quarter in Argentina and Brazil. Elsewhere in the region, slum incidence is low in Colombia, Dominican

Republic and Mexico, with less than 15 per cent of the urban population living in slums; the lowest proportions are found in Chile and several Caribbean countries, where the urban divide is less pronounced.

Latin America exhibits the greatest inequalities in the distribution of welfare and wealth in the developing world. However, between 2002 and 2006, the region achieved significant social and economic progress. Generally speaking, poverty and unemployment have been reduced; in some countries, income gaps have narrowed and job numbers increased, underlying the current positive trend in the region. According to the Economic Commission for Latin America and the Caribbean, poverty decreased by more than 4 per cent between 2002 and 2006.[16] The current global financial crisis and the 2008 food crisis may reverse some of these trends, and could particularly affect health and education services for the very poor. The potential effect on slum indicators

and the urban divide is difficult to estimate, but the trends of the past two decades suggest that the slum population in Latin America and the Caribbean will, like Southern Asia's, continue to grow by half a million people every year, reaching 120 million by 2020.

Slums: The need for a higher goal and a more realistic target

Because of the many cross-currents behind urban, demographic and policy realities, another 172 million people have become slum dwellers even as, 10 years ahead of the 2020 deadline, the world collectively exceeded by a wide margin the 100 million reduction target set under Millennium Development Goal 7, target 11. The number of urban residents living in slum conditions is now estimated at some 828 million.

▲
Jakarta. Indonesia has achieved a substantial reduction in the number of slum dwellers. ©**Kzenon/Shutterstock**

BOX 1.3.4: FROM BLIND SPOT TO SPOTLIGHT: FIVE POLICY STEPS TO SLUM REDUCTION

▲
Bogotá. In Colombia, an estimated 3.7 million slum dwellers have benefited from well-targeted slum upgrading and prevention strategies.
©Tifonimages/Shutterstock

Slums have only on occasion proved to be what most public authorities wished they would: a transient phenomenon, which growth and higher incomes would eliminate over time. In too many cities today, all-too visible slums remain blind spots for policymakers - caught as they are between token gestures, clearance or mass eviction, or administrative "pass the buck". The odd attempt at institutional response and reform typically founders on lack of support, funding or coordination. Still, municipalities in a number of countries (representing about one-third of those known as "developing") have managed to reduce the absolute and relative numbers of slum-dwellers among their populations.

How did they do it? The successful governments took the responsibility for slum reduction squarely on their shoulders, backing commitments with bold policy reforms, and preventing future slum growth with equitable planning and economic policies. Recent policy evidence collected by UN-HABITAT in 44 successful countries suggests that slum reduction takes a combination of five specific, complementary approaches: (1) awareness and advocacy; (2) long-term political commitment; (3) policy reforms and institutional strengthening; (4) implementation and monitoring; (5) and scaling-up of successful local projects.

Awareness and advocacy. For local authorities and other stakeholders, awareness requires slum monitoring systems and indicators to collect information and analyse trends, like those that have been successful throughout Viet Nam, Brazil and Indonesia. Advocacy involves disseminating messages on improved living conditions for slum dwellers, as governments

in Brazil, India and Mexico have done. Civil society organizations can also encourage political commitment and champion the views and rights of slum dwellers and the poor in general - either as watchdogs like *Réseau Social Watch Bénin* that monitor Millennium Development Goals and poverty reduction strategies, or as partners in government-funded programmes, like Mexico's *Hábitat y Rescate de Espacios Públicos (Reappropriation of public space)*. Organizations like Shack/Slum Dwellers International on occasion perform both an advocacy and an executing role.

Long-term political commitment. Over the past 15 years, consistent political commitment to large-scale slum upgrading and service provision to the urban poor has enabled China, India, Turkey, Dominican Republic, Colombia, Egypt, Morocco and Tunisia to reduce and stabilize slums. Other countries, including Ghana, Senegal and Argentina have fairly recently stepped up action, and yet others have begun to gather the necessary political support for land and tenure policy reforms, including Burkina Faso, Senegal and Tanzania.

Policy reform and institutional strengthening. The policy reforms required for slum upgrading and prevention involve housing, land and infrastructure provision and finance. Indonesia, Nicaragua and Peru have integrated large numbers of urban poor into the legal and social fabric; other countries, like India, have deployed major pro-poor reforms and programmes for land and housing provision or are adopting more inclusive approaches. Costa Rica, Ecuador and Colombia look to avoid relocations and instead work on settlements *in situ*, improving existing living conditions. Most of the more successful countries - including Indonesia, Iran, Mexico, Philippines, South Africa and Turkey - look beyond the housing sector and fight slums as part of broader-ranging urban poverty reduction strategies. Policies have tended to shift from entitlement to co-participation, where financial viability and down-payments condition access to public subsidies for both new housing and improvements. Creation of a Human Settlements Ministry gives higher visibility and continuity to the cause as demonstrated in Burkina Faso. Municipal decentralization through community-based consultation mechanisms is another avenue that has succeeded in Cambodia, Malawi and Zambia.

Implementation and monitoring. Countries that performed well on the Millennium slum target (including Indonesia and South Korea) deployed transparent and pro-poor policies backed up by adequate human and technical resources. Others, such as Colombia, Chile, the Philippines and South Africa, also trained urban planning and management professionals and involved them in housing and basic service delivery programmes. The most successful countries (China, Viet Nam, Chile, Sri Lanka and Peru) coordinated slum policy implementation between central regional and municipal authorities and the private sector. Other countries set themselves national targets: Cambodia (100 slum communities upgraded every year); Chile, Brazil, Morocco and Thailand (all of which enacted clear slum targets and benchmarks as part of urban poverty reduction). Indonesia uses results-based monitoring and satisfaction surveys.

Scaling-up. Replication and scaling-up of successful, local one-off or pilot slum-upgrading projects have served Brazil, Mexico, Colombia, South Africa, Sri Lanka and Indonesia well with measurable impacts on national indicators of slum growth. As originally modest-scale programmes were upgraded in Brazil, Egypt, Nicaragua and Turkey, the private sector and civil society became involved, or the schemes benefited from additional funding for replication and mainstreaming into government policies. In Burkina Faso and Senegal, reforms started in the 1980s in the capital city and expanded into large-scale physical and tenure upgrading schemes for irregular settlements across the country. Other countries, including China, Chile and South Africa, engaged in large-scale public subsidies to the housing sector, in a bid to reach the poorest groups and meet the rising costs of social housing. In most cases, success mobilized huge domestic (and, on occasion, external) resources to promote innovative strategies, including for slum prevention.

Policy analysis shows that on top of a combination of these five elements, success on the Millennium slum target involves proper coordination between cohesive, well-designed and adequately resourced centralized interventions on the one hand, and local authorities on the other hand.

Sources: Bazoglu, 2007; Chowdhury, 2006; López Moreno, 2003; UN-HABITAT, 2008.

When the international community adopted the Millennium Declaration and implicitly endorsed the "Cities without Slums" target in the year 2000,[17] experts in development agencies thought that 100 million was both a significant number and a realistic target within 20 years. By 2003, though, when UN-HABITAT - the agency in charge of monitoring the "Cities without Slums" target - made a first estimate of the global slum population, it appeared that 100 million represented only about 10 per cent of that total, which in 2001 stood at over 900 million.

Even if the Millennium target was low and somehow poorly defined, as it failed to specify what a "significant improvement" in the lives of slum dwellers would entail, it was welcome at the time insofar as it provided the set figure and deadline that had been missing in the Habitat Agenda (1996). The Millennium Declaration also came as the first clear commitment by the international community to address an explicitly urban issue, in the process raising the profile of cities and slums on the global agenda.

In 2003, UN-HABITAT, together with expert groups, developed a set of five indicators of deprivation (see Box p.33) in order to monitor and measure improvement in slum conditions. Unfortunately, unlike other Millennium Development Goals, the slum target was not set as a proportion, such as halving the proportion of people living on less than one US dollar a day, or reducing by two-thirds the under-5 mortality rates[18] with reference to a specific baseline (in this case, the year 1990). Instead, the slum target was set as an absolute number, and for the world as a whole. This makes it difficult, if not outright impossible, to set country-specific targets. A more effective alternative could have been, for instance, for every country to halve the proportion of slum dwellers in the urban population between the year 2000 and 2020. As the target stands, instead, governments do not know the numbers of slum dwellers whose conditions they must improve as part of the global target of 100 million. Clearly, this target has diluted responsibilities and hindered a number of governments from making serious commitments. Further adding to the unambitious nature of the target is its extended 2020 deadline, instead of 2015 for all other Millennium Development Goals.

Looking ahead to 2020, there is no question that the world has proved that it can collectively achieve a slum target that will narrow the urban divide by making a real difference to urban populations. Without any doubt, urban poverty and slums can be reduced, and the urban divide with them. Governments and local authorities know what to do. However, success requires a collective, medium-term effort on the part of all member States. Even though the target was low and easily achievable, progress has been made in various countries. From a practical as well as a symbolic point of view, this first achievement is eminently meaningful for all those

In Haiti, more than half of slum dwellers suffer from multiple shelter deprivations.
©Dermot Tatlow/Panos Pictures

▲
Viet Nam is one of the countries leading the developing world in reducing poverty, nearly halving its poverty rate between 1990 and 2000. ©**Chris Stowers/Panos Pictures**

involved. From a practical perspective, the success of the better-performing countries gives hope for others; it conveys a clear message that positive results are within reach. It shows that for those countries lagging far behind, this is the time for action. It is time to define a reasonable target, formulate appropriate policies, set up strategies and procedures that are clear, concise and easy to follow, and to dedicate significant financial and human resources to effective results.

From a symbolic point of view, the success of some countries is showing the world that it is possible to reduce urban poverty. It is also showing which countries are honouring their pledge to meet the slum target and which are failing to "keep the promise" - a promise that is not only about numbers, but, more importantly, about people: the 828 million people living in deprived housing conditions, without improved water or adequate sanitation, often in dilapidated dwellings without sufficient living space or secure tenure.

The current global financial climate poses a risk that some advances in slum upgrading and prevention may be reversed. Another risk is that some gains can be undone by government inaction or poor responses that do not take population growth into account. Progress in improving the lives of slum dwellers will depend largely on the way governments address slums as part of the broader agenda of reducing urban poverty and inequality.

The world has another 10 years to make further progress on the slum reduction target by the 2020 deadline. Governments must recognize that 100 million slum dwellers was a minimum threshold, not a ceiling. Together they must revise and raise the target to a number that takes into account both existing and potential new slums. This is an essential building block if the urban divide is to be bridged, if only over time.

Countries that have been performing well so far must maintain or increase efforts to improve the living conditions of slum dwellers, while providing adequate alternatives to prevent new slum formation. Those governments that are falling behind in slum reduction must bring radical changes to their attitudes and policies vis-à-vis slums and urban poverty at large.[19]

In this respect, a multi-pronged policy response to the persistent challenge of slums is a key target in its own right, and one that has the potential to influence the achievement of other Millennium Development Goals. Improving housing conditions and providing for water and sanitation will not only save lives among the very poor, but it will also support progress in education and health. This first step out of poverty will be another, major one across the urban divide.

Policymakers around the world must bridge the urban divide at the regional, national, local and city levels, Policies must focus on those countries and regions facing the greatest development challenges in slum reduction: sub-Saharan Africa and Western Asia. Other areas and countries in need of special attention are those which, for all their overall progress toward the slum target at the national level, are still faced with huge spatial inequalities in some regions and cities. Finally, policies must also focus on those cities which, although they are doing relatively well, still feature large pockets of poverty where people remain marginalized. It is increasingly apparent that failure to set and meet a more ambitious slum target will jeopardize the achievement of other MDGs.[20] Only political will, adequate policies and the right technical choices can effectively tackle slums, which represent the most unacceptable face of the urban divide.

END NOTES

1. UN-HABITAT, 2006.
2. Ibid.
3. United Nations DESA (2008a). The Millennium Development Goals Report 2008. New York: Author.
4. When signing the Millennium Declaration in the year 2000, the international community - 147 Heads of State and 191 nations - adopted the Millennium Development Goals (MDGs). Goal 7, target 11, commits governments significantly to improve the lives of at least 100 million slum dwellers by 2020. It is important to note that no estimate of the global number of slum dwellers existed in the year 2000. The first estimate, by UN-HABITAT, came in 2003 and was close to the one-billion mark; this meant that target 11 was not just short on ambition, but also based on an arbitrary figure.
5. United Nations DESA (2008b), World Urbanization Prospects: the 2007 revision. New York: Author.
6. A. Farzin, personal communication, 27 October, 2009.
7. V. Tewari, personal communication, 27 October, 2009.
8. Viet Nam is one of the countries leading the developing world in poverty reduction, having nearly halved its poverty rate from 58 per cent in 1990 to some 32 per cent in the year 2000, well ahead of

the 2015 deadline. Source: Embassy of the Socialist Republic of Viet Nam in the United States, 2002.
9. M. Fernandez, personal communication, 27 October, 2009.
10. United Nations DESA (2008b), World Urbanization Prospects: the 2007 revision. New York: Author.
11. The death rate for children under 5 is 81 per 1,000 live births in Southern Asia, compared with 47 in Western Asia, 35 in South-Eastern Asia, and 24 in Eastern Asia. United Nations DESA, MDG Report, 2008.
12. Despite the fact that India's economy is less exposed to the decline in global demand than other countries owing to the small share of trade in its economy, the World Economic Outlook 2009 estimated that economic growth in India declined from 9 per cent in 2007 to 4.5 per cent in 2009. International Monetary Fund (2009, April). World Economic Outlook: Crisis and Recovery. Washington, D.C.: Author.
13. The maternal mortality rate in South-Eastern Asia was 300 deaths per 100,000 live births in 2005, the second highest in Asia after Southern Asia. United Nations DESA, 2008.
14. The percentage of underweight children in Western Asia was 14 in 1990 and 13 in 2006. The sub-region

remained stagnant while this indicator improved in other developing regions. The same holds with regard to maternal deaths in Western Asia, which declined from 190 in 1990 to 160 per 100,000 live births in 2006. United Nations DESA, 2008.
15. N. Bazoglu, personal communication, 23 October 2009.
16. In 2006, 39.8 per cent of the population of Latin America and the Caribbean (or some 209 million people) lived in poverty. This represented a decrease of more than 4 per cent on 2002 (44 per cent). Coward, 2006.
17. The Millennium Declaration addresses development concerns related to peace, security, human rights and governance. By 2002, the Declaration included eight interconnected and mutually reinforcing development goals that were merged under the designation of "Millennium Development Goals", along with 18 agreed development targets and 40 indicators.
18. Targets of Millennium Development Goals 1 and 4.
19. López Moreno, 2007.
20. Ibid.

PART
02

The Urban
Divide

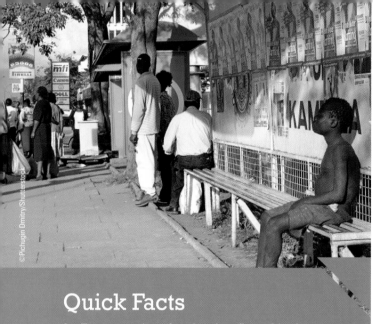

2.1
The Urban Divide
Overview and Perspectives

Quick Facts

1. Fragmentation of society is reflected in clear differences in the way space and opportunities are produced, appropriated, transformed and used.

2. Economic and social exclusion typically results in cultural and political exclusion.

3. A divided city exacerbates inequalities and contributes to the stratification of the population into a social hierarchy marked by exclusion; ethnic minorities are often finding themselves in the same category as the poor and unempowered.

4. Further partitioning the city are divisive factors like fear, anxiety and insecurity that contribute to partitioning further the city.

Policy Points

1. Inclusive policies for cities should acknowledge the dynamics of the urban divide and support informal business institutional arrangements as well as affordable delivery of land and housing.

2. Residents can gradually realize their individual city rights through access to better services, including health and education, jobs and opportunities. Freedom of expression, equal opportunities for business development, recognition of cultural rights and adequate housing are all equally important.

3. Strategies for inclusiveness must be based on a clear and cogent representation of the way the four dimensions of equality – economic, social, political and cultural – can be integrated concurrently into the day-to-day lives of the population.

4. The "right to the city" encapsulates the four dimensions of equality, which, combined, will guarantee inclusiveness.

Divided spaces and opportunities

Cities are more often than not divided by invisible borders. These split the "back" from the "front"; or the "higher" and "lower" areas, as the urban divide is known colloquially in many parts of the South. These man-made fractions often run along a spatial and social continuum, reflecting the only difference between their respective populations – socio-economic status.[1] Closer assessment of the urban space in many cities of the developing world unambiguously exposes the fragmentation of society, with clear differences in the way space and opportunities are produced, appropriated, transformed and used. Some areas feature significant infrastructure, well-kept parks, gardens and up-market residential areas. In contrast, other areas are characterized by severe deprivation, inadequate housing, deficient services, poor recreation and cultural facilities, urban decay and scarce capital expenditures. These tangible differences in access come as symptoms of the intangible, yet enduring divisions in society that apportion unequal opportunities and liberties across all urban residents.

In diverse urban landscapes, sharp contrasts abound across neighbouring streets, buildings, public spaces, gardens, markets or offices. In places, these urban components merge and blend into one another; in others, they are separated by walls, doors, symbolic features or geographic factors such as topography, rivers or lakes. Whether differentiated spaces are contiguous or separated, they add to any social gaps and deepen divisions across the city.

Cities as diverse as Nairobi, Buenos Aires, Johannesburg, Mexico and Rio de Janeiro are similar in that pockets of wealth and poverty co-exist in close proximity, sometimes just one or two blocks from one another. In Mumbai, a city of stark contrasts, skyscrapers face makeshift roadside settlements and the largest slums in Asia. In other cities, wealth and poverty are more clearly demarcated. For instance, in the northern neighbourhoods of Quito, poverty affects fewer than 2 per cent of the population, while in the *barrios* to the south, the proportion is close to 95 per cent.[2] Examples such as these highlight the large disparities between better-off minorities and the many poor, which are also reflected in different degrees of access to cultural facilities, public goods, transportation and open spaces in most cities in the developing world.

Social segregation also transpires in economic statistics, with sharp differences in incomes across neighbourhoods and districts within one and the same city. For instance, in one of the wealthiest neighbourhoods in Buenos Aires, average per capita income is 1,400 pesos (or US $370), or three times the average 371 pesos earned by the poorer residents. Such disparities are also reflected in land values in the Argentinean capital: the cost of one square metre in the rich neighbourhood is 116 per cent higher than in the poorer one.[3]

Amartya Sen has amply demonstrated that it is incumbent on development strategies to pool and mobilize skills and abilities across the whole spectrum of society. This is the reason that the urban divide as a concept cannot be defined exclusively in terms of fragmented space and socio-economic disparities. Since a sustainable city requires engagement with all segments of the resident population, the social divide must also be taken to involve the unequal opportunities across social categories, age groups and gender regarding such resources as access to knowledge, technology and gainful employment that may hinder such effective engagement. Large sections of society are frequently excluded on grounds of predetermined attributes over which they have no control at all (such as gender, race, ethnicity, age) or little control such as where they live (slums *vs.* rich neighbourhoods) or what they own (income and social status); however, this narrow perspective overlooks the actual and potential contributions of marginalized groups to building cities and nations, and therefore can only delay progress toward sustainable and *inclusive* development.

Various forms of exclusion continue to marginalize vast amounts of human capital that is only waiting to be mobilized for the sake of sustainable cities. In New Delhi, for example, 52 per cent of men were employed in 2006, as opposed to only 9.4 per cent of women.[4] Likewise in the same year, 82 per cent of the total labour force in Chittagong was male and only 18 per cent female.[5] In many cities of the developing world, women are less educated than men; but even where women have achieved higher education levels, their income-generating capabilities remain the same as, or even inferior to, those of men. For instance, in the metropolitan area of San José, Costa Rica, women earn, on average, 20 per cent less than men, despite the fact that they have a higher proportion of college degrees.[6]

These divisions are reinforced by spatial and socio-economic differences within a city, illustrating the various degrees of access made available by private-sector suppliers of goods and services. From Port-au-Prince to Ibadan to Nairobi to Dhaka, erratic power supply affects poor neighbourhoods more than affluent areas. Blackouts, lack of adequate transportation and inferior educational and health facilities for the urban poor are all clear symptoms of a divided city, where middle-class and rich households are better served simply because they can pay or they have the capacity to negotiate the provision of services and facilities for their specific neighbourhoods. In many cities, public facilities predominantly used by the poor are described as overcrowded and badly managed by poorly paid and unmotivated staff, combining waste of resources with little focus on results. In contrast, privately owned and managed schools, universities and health centres generally feature better equipment, more qualified staff and more advanced facilities that can only be afforded by the middle and upper classes. In Mumbai, for instance, half of slum neighbourhoods have no primary schools.[7] In Port-au-Prince, the disparity in enrollment rates at primary level is significant: 59 per cent of children from poor households are enrolled, as opposed to 79 per cent of those from better-off households.[8] Such tangible divisions in one and the same city create new social lines of divide and reinforce those already separating the privileged from the disadvantaged; this is the case in Port-au-Prince, with its separate schools for the *gran nèg,* or the rich, and for the *malheureux,* or the underprivileged.

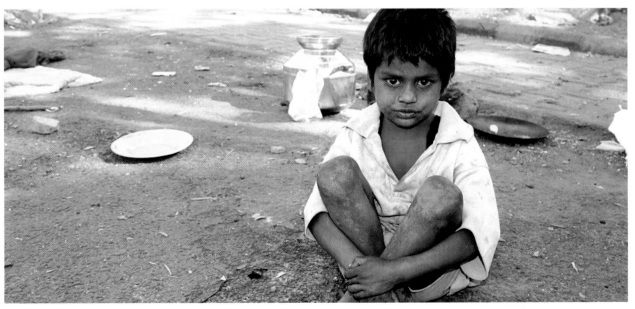

▲
Mumbai. In India's economic capital, half of slum neighbourhoods have no primary schools. ©**The final miracle/Shutterstock**

Social divisions can permeate interactions amongst individuals even in the absence of significant ethnic, racial or other factors of segregation. Fresh divisions constantly emerge and become entrenched; patterns of social inclusion or exclusion preserve benefits for specific social segments based on their physical location, shared interests or other criteria.

More often than not, economic and social exclusion result in cultural and political exclusion as well. On top of the features mentioned above, a divided city is also one that fails to accommodate poorer residents, regardless of the cultural richness they might lend to the city as a whole. Hip-hop groups in cities throughout Africa and the Americas, samba schools in São Paulo and *tribus urbanas* in Quito, for example, represent vital aspects of youth culture, but they remain on the margins of society, typically creating messages about, and communicating only with, members of their own self-selected groups. Though their voices may communicate important truths about the cultural realities of large populations in cities, such groups often remain excluded from, and marginalized by, the urban mainstream.

Urban segmentation can also result from institutionalized divisions of space and social belonging, such as the specific form of citizenship formalized in China's "*Houku*", or certificate of urban residence. At the other end of the range of divisive factors are the intangible feelings of fear, anxiety and insecurity that contribute to partitioning Rio de Janeiro into safe and "no-go areas", or that designate *zones de droit* and *non-droit* in Port-au-Prince, or those that signal "no-law neighbourhoods" in Mexico City. The urban divide not only generates stigma, but to some extent also feeds on it. In cities in Asia, Africa or Latin America, some spaces are known for what they lack, as in the "*barrios sin domicilios*", or neighbourhoods without addresses. Symbolic dividing lines can also refer to the history of a city: the "flooded district", or the "burnt area", often conspicuously devoid of the amenities and resources common to less damaged areas.

▲ Art or Vandalism? In Bristol, UK the City Council is voting on whether to keep or remove graffiti. ©**1000 Words/Shutterstock**

The divide has inter-generational consequences for society

Slums are the face of a divided city. The divisive nature of any city finds its graphical reflection in numbers such as the proportion of slum dwellers to the overall population, or the degrees of deprivation in slums. In some places ("cities with slums"), informal settlements are located in one part of the city, with the better-off neighbourhoods in another. In that sense, a certain degree of homogeneity can be found in the residential areas of an otherwise heterogeneous city. A good example of this is Greater Mumbai, where the slum population in the western suburbs is as high as 43 per cent, whereas in the city proper it is only 17 per cent. A similar pattern features in New Delhi District, where 3.4 per cent of the population lives below the poverty line, whereas in the North West District, this proportion is more than 30 per cent.[9] A slum area is typically associated with reduced numbers of schools, clinics and other public and private amenities. In La Paz for instance, mothers from slum areas are three times more likely not to receive prenatal professional care than those from non-slum areas. This shows quite clearly that in a vital area like reproductive health, unequal access to services can have fatal consequences for mothers and children in a divided city: in Bolivia's capital in 2005, the probability of dying before the age of 5 for slum-born children was 1.38 times higher than for those born in non-slum areas.[10]

It is apparent, therefore, that low incomes and multidimensional deprivations increase risks and exacerbate the overall vulnerability of the poor. The partitioning of urban and social space not only derives from the historical partition of wealth and poverty, but is also a result of pronounced, enduring intergenerational inequities. Indeed, children of impoverished parents face a broad range of risks: malnutrition, lack of educational opportunities and resources, and greater incidence of diseases than their better-off counterparts, coupled with lower access to proper health care and lower life expectancy. Underprivileged children are also faced with unequal opportunities when it comes to the social and cultural expression of their specific identities, aspirations and feelings within society. They are frequently relegated to the second or third ranks in the urban hierarchy of tangible and intangible amenities or benefits. For instance in Bogotá, up to one-third of the housing stock in the underprivileged municipality of Usme is located in environmentally hazardous areas.[11] In Nairobi, more than 200 informal settlements housing more than half the population are crammed into a tight space that represents only 5 per cent of the city's residential land. Similarly in Dhaka, 34 per cent of available space is planned for allocation to 4.4 million upper- and middle-income people outside the city centre, compared with only 4 per cent for 4.5 million low-income residents. This uneven distribution of space, and the associated poverty, interfere with the exercise of equal rights within the city – the primary reason being that a substantial portion of the population is faced with restricted access to employment and income, on top of other obstacles to the development of their abilities and their opportunities to live a better life.

A divided city not only exacerbates inequalities, it also contributes to the stratification of the population into a social hierarchy marked by exclusion. In the Peruvian city of Oruro, the Andean population – Quechua-speaking, predominantly female and illiterate, and with a high probability of becoming parents in adolescence – is systematically excluded and marginalized. In Jaipur, India, the "Schedule Casts" and "Schedule Tribes" that represented only 12.5 and 3.4 per cent, respectively, of the city's residents in 2008, accounted for as much as 53 per cent of the overall slum population.[12] Undoubtedly, the high concentration of socially marginalized groups among slum residents is an indicator of the urban divide in any city. Ethnic minorities are finding themselves, more often than not, in the same category as the poor and unempowered. In the metropolitan region of São Paulo, 4.4 per cent of the population over 15 years was illiterate in 2004. From this universe, illiteracy among the white population was only 3.4 per cent, compared with 6.6 per cent among the black or brown population. In a gender perspective, male illiteracy among the white population was 2.5 per cent, compared with 4.1 per cent for females; in contrast, among the black or brown, 5.7 per cent of males were illiterate compared with 7.4 percent for females. It is worth noting that because of unequal access to higher education, in the same year 20 per cent of whites had college degrees, as opposed to only 5.9 per cent of blacks or browns.[13]

Inclusive cities: A positive approach to the urban divide

The urban divide involves a range of negative factors that are an integral part of the transformative process cities are undergoing, especially in the developing world. Still, divided cities should not necessarily be thought of as a negative phenomenon. This evolving, multi-dimensional process calls for a more nuanced understanding of city development. For example, slums play a fundamental role in capital formation in cities in the developing world, and also demonstrate substantial economic potential. In New Delhi, up to one-third of investment in housing is accounted for by slum dwellers.[14] Similarly, informal sector activities today contribute as much as 80 to 90 per cent of all new job opportunities in Latin America.[15] A positive development strategy calls for the transformation of informal activities in order to create more productive enterprise clusters.

The urban divide also incidentally creates human capital in the form of social and cultural practices and arrangements that allow people to save money, share resources, build businesses and create opportunities in mutually beneficial ways. These include initiatives such as community social funds, music and art groups that provide education and cultural expression, as well as informal institutional mechanisms that promote service delivery to the marginalized. Recognition and promotion of the economic potential of slums, or of social and cultural

▲
Dhaka. In the capital of Bangladesh, 34 per cent of available space is planned for allocation to 4.4 million upper-income people outside the city centre, compared with only 4 per cent for 4.5 million low-income residents. ©**Manoocher Deghati/IRIN**

THE URBAN DIVIDE – OVERVIEW AND PERSPECTIVES

55

initiatives that reflect the creativity of society, require a holistic approach – one that enables all segments of the population to participate in the economic growth and prosperity of cities in a collective effort to promote long-term, sustainable urban development.

An *inclusive city*, as defined for the purposes of this report, is one that provides *all* residents – regardless of race, ethnicity, gender or socio-economic status – with adequate housing and decent basic services, and facilitates equal access to social amenities, opportunities and other public goods that are essential to the general and environmental well-being of everyone *(social inclusion)*.

An inclusive city upholds citizens' rights and liberties, and promotes social and political participation for the sake of better-informed and more democratic decision-making *(political inclusion)*.

An inclusive city is one that fosters economic development by way of equal opportunities for business and access to employment, and promotes pro-poor economic policies *(economic inclusion)*.

An inclusive city promotes social integration and celebrates diversity. It values people's cultural rights, recognizing the human capital of all segments of society, which it strives to enhance through promotion of creative artistic expression and heritage activities *(cultural inclusion)*.

▲
Morocco. Cities must develop a vision that integrates everyone.
©**Bensliman Hassan/Shutterstock**

In this definition, residents' environmental rights come under the dimensions of social and cultural equality, since they address the intergenerational aspects of individuals' rights to live in safe and sound environments.

Against this background, municipal efforts to design and implement strategies for inclusiveness must be based on a clear and cogent representation of the way the four dimensions of equality – economic, social, political and cultural – can be integrated *concurrently* into the day-to-day lives of the population. Residents can gradually realize their individual city rights through access to better services, including health and education, jobs and opportunities. Freedom of expression, equal opportunities for business development, recognition of cultural rights and adequate housing are all equally important. Cities are the places where partnerships can be forged, constructive debates can be held, and negotiation and consensus can take place in a collective effort to promote development.[16]

Therefore, it is for committed and proactive local governments to build new relationships and alliances with central and state/provincial authorities. Inclusive policies for cities should acknowledge the dynamics of the urban divide; in this respect, they should focus more particularly on any positive components that could be integrated to formal municipal norms and practices, such as the informal economy, social capital and informal institutional arrangements, including affordable land delivery and housing systems, etc. Only through explicit and deliberately inclusive schemes and procedures will it be possible to identify the locally appropriate, innovative and high-leverage actions and policies which government, civil service and major institutions can deploy to set in motion self-reinforcing processes that will overcome the urban divide.[17]

Inclusive cities: A rights-based dynamic

If the four dimensions of equality – social, political, economic and cultural – are to be turned from a mere conceptual paradigm into reality, they must be implemented within a rights-based framework, and one that is easy to enforce. Short of this, the prevailing patterns of exclusionary development, selected benefit-sharing, marginalization and discrimination will continue unabated in cities. Moreover, entrenched types of socio-economic behaviour such as rent-seeking and patronage will also persist unchecked (as would, more generally, any challenge to what is known to economists as "Pareto optimality", through promotion of opportunities for a few at the expense of others).

Such a rights-based framework is predicated upon three requirements, though:
- Cities must develop a vision that integrates everyone.
- Cities must put forward plans and implementation mechanisms that are adequately monitored and can be revised depending on outcomes.
- Cities must set up new institutions, or improve and strengthen existing ones, in order to ensure that they are inclusive, accountable and efficient.

If met, these three requirements would, along with others, guarantee that a city provides the framework that integrates the dreams, aspirations, freedoms and rights of its entire population.

The "right to the city" encapsulates the four dimensions of equality, which, combined, will guarantee inclusiveness. The fundamental principle of the right to the city is that human rights are interdependent and indivisible. This calls for the simultaneous achievement of all human rights for all residents in any city. This, in turn, means that all human rights – political, economic, social, and cultural – must receive equal priority in city governance, planning, management and implementation. The right to the city should also encompass the rights to self-determination and freedom of assembly and organization, and the right to development (social, political, cultural, spiritual and economic), both individual and collective. Endorsement and implementation of a strong human rights-based approach, therefore, is the only way to preserve and uphold the dignity of all urban dwellers while addressing the multiple violations and problems which millions in cities around the world are facing today.

The right to the city is not to be viewed as yet another legal concept; rather, it represents a dynamic and pragmatic combination of the multiple human rights to which urban dwellers are entitled, and that they want fulfilled. The concept and implementation of the right to the city must be grounded in the basic, universally recognized human rights principles of non-discrimination, indivisibility, gender equality, gradual realization, non-retrogression, subsidiarity, solidarity and cooperation (see Chapter 3.1). With its implicit universal ambit and egalitarian underpinning, the right to the city suggests that special attention must be given to any individuals or groups – including gender – in a situation of vulnerability; the notion also strongly if tacitly subsumes responsibility and sustainability as core principles.

Cities for all in the developing world

An inclusive city, as defined in this report, addresses economic as well as social, political and cultural equality across all segments of society. The notion of inclusiveness as comprising these four dimensions derives from Sen's "capabilities" perspective.[18] This perspective stresses how important it is to view economic opportunities in conjunction with all other forms of political, social and cultural rights in societies that work together to build up "capable" social capital in developing countries. Only when the four forms of opportunities converge can they usher in optimal conditions for production of the human capital required to enable sustainable development.

FIGURE 2.1.1: **THE RIGHT TO THE CITY**

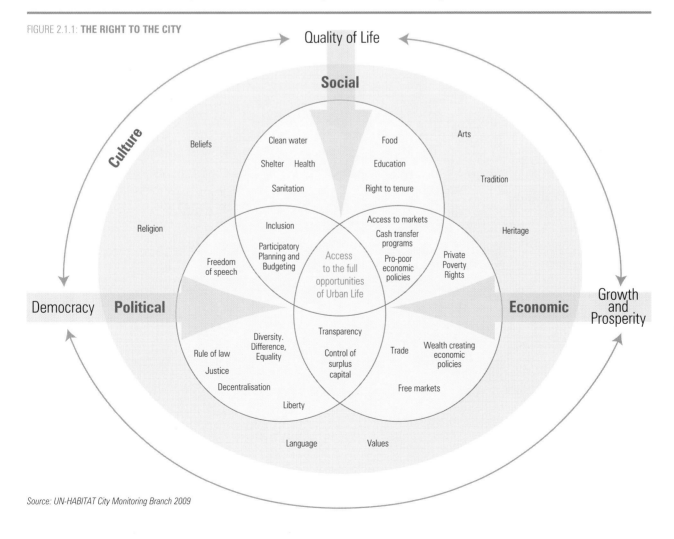

Source: UN-HABITAT City Monitoring Branch 2009

Hongkong, China. Pro-democracy rally. ©**Ndrpggr/Shutterstock**

BOX 2.1.1: **POLICY ANALYSIS ON THE INCLUSIVE CITY: SURVEY METHODOLOGY**

In 2009 UN-HABITAT conducted a policy assessment on inclusive urban policies in 27 cities in the developing world: Africa (7 cities), Asia and Latin America and the Caribbean (10 cities each). The analysis was carried out by expert focus groups in every city. Each group was comprised of some 15 experts from community associations, non-governmental and other civil society groups, the media, lawyers, urban planners, municipal officials and the business sector.

The questionnaire sent out to the 27 city-specific focus groups took in the four dimensions of the "inclusive city", including the local institutional and organizational capacities associated with them. The assumption behind the survey was that the "right to the city" encapsulates the four dimensions of equality which, combined, bring about inclusiveness.

To a significant extent, cities were selected based on availability of "hard" indicators (such as Gini coefficients, gross domestic product per capita, labour structure, etc.); in a next step, this quantitative data was combined with qualitative information provided by individual expert groups (for their perceptions on the various variables). Prior to the focus group meeting, every group prepared a background document for their respective city. These reports analyzed the laws, regulations, policies and actions that have contributed to make cities more inclusive, specifying which stakeholders had brought about the positive changes. This Report quotes from a number of these expert background papers in order better to reflect both perceptions of local realities, and understanding of the "inclusive city" concept.

UN-HABITAT tested the basic assumption behind the survey against the expert group answers to the questionnaire. Descriptive statistical analysis was combined with econometric techniques in order to understand the correlations and associations between various aspects of inclusion/exclusion and policy interventions. The econometric models informed the substantive sections of Part 3 ("Bridging the Urban Divide") of this Report and guided policy analysis. The results of the survey questionnaire were analyzed against UN-HABITAT quantitative data, the background reports from every city and other relevant information, in order to make sure that progress towards inclusive cities could be attributed to policy decisions and related actions. Additional policy research was conducted through literature and Web searches, in order to shed more light on the causality of policy changes.

END NOTES

[1] López Moreno, 2009.

[2] Vásconez Jaime, City Report on Inclusiveness on Quito, UN-HABITAT background study for the State of the World's Cities Report 2010, prepared by the "Centro Internacional de Gestión Urbana" (CIGU), August 2009.

[3] Cristina Reynals, City Report on Inclusiveness in Buenos Aires, UN-HABITAT background study for the State of the World's Cities Report 2010, August 2009.

[4] Society for Development Studies, City Report on New Delhi, UN-HABITAT background study for the State of the World's Cities Report 2010, August 2009.

[5] Taher & Chowdhury, City Report on Chittagong, UN-HABITAT background study for the State of the World's Cities Report 2010, August 2009.

[6] Tomás Martínez Baldares, City Report on Cartago,

UN-HABITAT background study for the State of the World's Cities Report 2010, August 2009.

[7] Society for Development Studies, City Report on Mumbai, UN-HABITAT background study for the State of the World's Cities Report 2010, August 2009.

[8] Dominique Mathon, City Report on Port-au-Prince, UN-HABITAT background study for the State of the World's Cities Report 2010, August 2009.

[9] Society for Development Studies, City Report on Mumbai, op cit.

[10] FAFO, "Cities and Citizen Report for La Paz", UN-HABITAT Monitoring Urban Inequities Programme, document produced for this report, 2009.

[11] Montezuma Ricardo, City Report on Bogotá, UN-HABITAT background study for the State of the World's Cities Report 2010, August 2009.

[12] Society for Development Studies, City Report on Jaipur, UN-HABITAT background study for the State of the World's Cities Report 2010, August 2009.

[13] Vanessa Marx and Rodrigo Nobile, City Report on São Paulo, UN-HABITAT background study for the State of the World's Cities Report 2010, August 2009.

[14] Society for Development Studies (2009c).

[15] Ocampo (2008).

[16] Awuor-Hayangah (2009a).

[17] E-mail communication with Peter Boothroyd, moderator of the e-debate on the urban divide for the World Urban Forum, University of British Columbia, 09/09/09.

[18] Sen, 1999.

©Madanmohan Rao

2.2
The Economic Divide
Urban Income Inequalities

Quick Facts

1. Economic development tends to go hand in hand with more equitable income distribution, except in Latin America (where income inequality is stark), Eastern Europe and CIS (where income inequality is low).

2. In the developing world, the concentration of inequalities is higher in urban than in rural areas, except in Latin America.

3. The magnitude of urban economic inequality, or the severity of the economic divide, is not a function of city size.

4. Overall the economic urban divide remains sharp; it is slightly decreasing in Latin America and is increasing moderately in Asia. Trends are mixed in Africa, and transition countries are becoming less egalitarian.

5. The stark rich-poor divide is most noticeable in African and Latin American cities. In both regions, the gap is often extreme compared with cities in Asia, Eastern Europe and the CIS.

Policy Points

1. Whether economic growth results in broader distributions of incomes or consumption in urban areas is a matter for socioeconomic policy and structural reforms.

2. In developing countries, the more unequal the distribution of income or consumption in urban areas, the higher the risk that economic disparities will result in social and political tension.

3. Highly unequal income or consumption patterns in cities in the developing world point to institutional and structural failures, as well as to broader economic problems such as imbalanced labour markets or a lack of pro-poor policies.

4. Even when measured in strictly economic terms, inequality can point to several types of urban deprivation, such as lack of basic public services like water and sanitation, some of which are directly linked to the Millennium Development Goals.

Global and city trends in income inequality

Any full understanding of an inclusive city requires a multidimensional assessment framework. Such a framework must, indeed, account for practical social, economic, political and cultural opportunities, as well as the interdependencies among them. A wide variety of measures is used to gauge the economic and social condition of the world's cities, and the most frequently used measurements of the economic dimension of the urban divide are income and consumption inequalities.

Inequality is usually measured on a national scale, but attention is increasingly paid to general urban and city-specific inequalities. As a further step in the research into urban inequalities presented by UN-HABITAT in the previous (2008/9) edition of the *State of the World's Cities* report, this chapter identifies and measures income and consumption inequalities in a larger sample of cities from both developed and developing countries, based on updated data. It reviews ongoing trends and recent changes in the urban divide as measured by economic inequality, including some of the causal factors. For the purposes of this report, UN-HABITAT has analyzed Gini coefficients for both income and consumption at the general urban level, and, where possible, for specific cities.

Two related cautionary points about UN-HABITAT data must be stressed here. First, *income inequality* cannot be mistaken with *poverty*: notionally at least, countries can be so broadly well-off, or poor, as to feature minimal inequality *(see below under "The more equal cities")*. Second, Table 1 presents *groupings* of countries that correspond to specific Gini coefficient brackets and that in no way whatsoever can be understood as *rankings*. The import of these groupings is to suggest that the more *income* inequality, the higher the potential for social and, ultimately, political tension. This potential is mitigated by the institutional and other arrangements that prevail in any particular location. Such institutional arrangements (such as welfare) typically tend to be stronger in developed than in developing countries. Across all countries, though, a broader definition of these arrangements also includes provision of services such as health care, education, housing and basic facilities, etc.;

access to these can be unequal within individual cities, with the potential of enhancing or mitigating equality as measured in pure economic terms.

When measured in terms of *consumption (household expenditures)* instead of income, high Gini coefficients also denote unequal access to basic goods, which may act as a hindrance to poverty reduction strategies and achievement of Millennium Development Goals. Consumption-based Gini coefficients are not immune from perverse effects and can reflect some type of deprivation instead of "more equal" access to urban services. For instance, poor households in slum settlements typically spend relatively high proportions of their low incomes on water when, for lack of alternatives, they buy it from street vendors at a multiple of the prices charged by water distribution utilities. More generally, both income and consumption inequalities are linked to broader economic factors like labour markets, capital investment in public services, lack of pro-poor policies, etc. Further potential distorting factors originate with economic and other patterns. The services sector features a very wide range of income levels, from the highest in any given city or economy to the lowest available in the formal sector (cleaning, catering, waste disposal). The informal economy similarly features a broad range of incomes, which at the top of the range can both be very substantial and go unreported for tax and statistical purposes. Corruption and fraud are two further, unreported distorting factors that are more likely to affect mid- to top-range incomes. Finally, urban dwellers in the middle to top income brackets typically tend to consume more imported products, including food, than those on low incomes.

The economic urban divide across the world: An overview

Developed country cities: Inequality is relatively low

In general terms, income inequalities in developed countries are low. Little is known, however, about inequalities at the urban level, as available data is generally not disaggregated to metropolitan areas or individual cities. The exceptions are Australia, Canada, Japan and the United States of America. Information on Gini coefficients in developed, highly urbanized nations is generally provided on a nationwide scale. Based on this data, national degrees of income inequality in developed countries range from a low Gini coefficient of 0.23 in Denmark and Sweden to a high of 0.385 in Portugal.

Very low degrees of inequality are found in countries with Gini values under 0.3, which is the average for 27 selected developed nations that report nationwide Gini values. All countries in this category are European and include (in order of ascending Gini values): Denmark, Sweden, Luxemburg, Austria, Czech Republic, Slovakia, Finland, France, Belgium, The Netherlands, Switzerland, Norway, Iceland and Germany. The low degrees of inequality reflect the regulatory, distributive and redistributive capacity of European welfare states.[1] Relatively low degrees of inequality that still exceed the sample average for developed countries (between 0.301 and 0.385) are found in some other European countries such as Spain, Greece, Ireland, United Kingdom, Italy, Poland and Portugal (in ascending order), and also in Australia, Canada, Japan, New Zealand and the United States of America.

▲
Linz, Austria. Income inequalities in developed countries are generally low. ©**Marek Slusarczyk/Shutterstock**

BOX 2.2.1: **MEASURING INEQUALITY: THE GINI INDEX**

The term "inequality" has many different meanings. In this report, it is used primarily to describe how an indicator of economic well-being is distributed over a particular population.

The Gini index is the most widely used summary measure of inequality. It measures the distribution of either income or household consumption expenditures as a ratio between 0 and 1, where 0 indicates perfect equality (a proportional distribution of resources), and 1 indicates perfect inequality (where one individual has all of the income or other resources and no one else has any).

Since income is split between consumption and savings, income-based are always higher than consumption-based Gini coefficients, and savings accumulation, or lack thereof, is a major

determinant of wealth or poverty. For instance, in 2003 the Gini coefficient in Addis Ababa was 0.560 for expenditure and, 0.612 for income. The Gini coefficient can also be used to estimate other non-income inequalities, such as in health, education, assets and access to infrastructure.

The meaning of the Gini index can be understood in terms of the "income gap" created by unequal resource distribution. For example, when the Gini coefficient is 0.47 – which is the case in the states of Alabama, Florida, Louisiana, Mississippi, and Texas in the United States of America – it means roughly that the poorest 20 per cent of the population (the fifth quintile) earns 3 per cent of the total income, whereas the wealthiest 20 per cent (first quintile) earns 50 per cent of the total income.

The measurement of household income and consumption inequalities is subject to different approaches in different countries. Some countries – such as India, Mozambique and Togo – base their inequality estimations on household expenditure rather than income because the statisticians responsible for reporting inequality data presume that survey questions about consumption patterns will produce more accurate results and less suspicion than those about earnings. Other countries – such as South Africa, China and Brazil – base their inequality estimates on income because they assume that household reluctance to disclose earnings will also extend to expenditure. Still others, like Sri Lanka, assess income inequality using both income and expenditure.

Sources: UN-HABITAT, Global Urban Observatory Database, 2009; Asian Development Bank, 2007.

Altogether, income inequalities at national level in developed countries increased between the mid-1980s and 2005.[2] Growth in nationwide income inequality has been particularly stark in Poland and Germany, both of which experienced increases of up to 17 and 10 per cent, respectively, between the year 2000 and 2005 – the most significant rises in income inequality of all of the developed countries under review. Computations based on OECD data[3] for 25 developed nations, however, show that the average Gini value changed by less than 1 per cent between the year 2000 and 2005. Some countries have even experienced a 4 to 7 per cent decline in Gini values in recent years, particularly the United Kingdom, Greece and Spain.

From a policy perspective, analyzing urban-level Gini coefficients is fundamental to understanding and addressing urban poverty. Yet, for all their wealth of information on urban indicators and data, developed countries typically do not report city-specific Gini coefficients, particularly in Europe. Those that are available for specific metropolitan areas or cities suggest that *nationwide* aggregates do not always accurately reflect disparities in general urban or city-specific incomes. For example, the national Gini coefficient for Canada in the mid-1990s was 0.283, whereas the value for the country's urban areas was 0.36, indicating a higher degree of inequality in cities than in rural areas. Likewise, Australia reported a national Gini coefficient of 0.317 in the year 2000, but the value for the major cities was slightly higher, at 0.332 in 2001. The most surprising variations between national and city-specific Gini data are found in the United States of America, where around 2005 the national coefficient stood at 0.381, but exceeded 0.5 in many major metropolitan areas including Washington, D.C., New York City, Miami

and others. These values are comparable to the average Gini coefficients of cities in selected Latin American countries, where income inequality is particularly steep (see Map 2.2.1). When comparing national aggregates with city-specific values, it is clear that huge variations can be found within one and the same country. Even in highly urbanized societies, national Gini coefficients conceal income inequalities at the sub-national level.

Developing countries: Wide differences in income inequality in urban areas across regions and countries

Income inequalities are generally greater in developing than in developed countries. In the developing world, disparities between urban and rural areas are often also quite stark; consequently, national and local Gini values must be disaggregated to provide an accurate picture of the disparities in each environment. The following review of developing countries delves into general urban as opposed to city-specific inequalities. Whereas in developed nations, Gini coefficients are based only on income, in developing countries the calculations are based either on income or consumption (see Box 2.2.1).

The overall pattern that emerges from a review of the expanded UN-HABITAT database on urban income inequalities in developing countries features values that differ significantly across regions, countries and cities, as well as a persistence of such differences over time. Table 2.2.1 illustrates the breadth of urban Gini coefficients based on income across selected developing countries. Five distinct groups emerge from the analysis, ranging from "low" to "extremely high" income inequality.

TABLE 2.2.1: **THE ECONOMIC URBAN DIVIDE: COUNTRY GROUPINGS BY GINI COEFFICIENTS (BASED ON INCOME, VARIOUS YEARS)**

GROUP 1 Low inequality (less than 0.299)	GROUP 2 Relatively Low inequality (0.300 to 0.399)	GROUP 3 Relatively High inequality (0.400 to 0.449)	GROUP 4 High inequality (0.450 to 0.499)	GROUP 5 Very High inequality (0.500 to 0.599)	GROUP 6 Extremely High inequality (0.600 or more)
Belarus	China	Cameroon	Philippines	Argentina	Namibia
Romania	Poland	Uganda	El Salvador	Brazil	Zambia
Bulgaria	Lithuania	Côte d'Ivoire	Uruguay	Chile	South Africa
Armenia	Algeria	Viet Nam	Venezuela	Colombia	
Kyrgyz Republic	Georgia	Nepal	Panama	Dominican Republic	
Hungary	Tajikistan	Malaysia	Peru	Ecuador	
Albania		Moldova	Mexico	Guatemala	
Kosovo		Turkmenistan	Costa Rica	Nicaragua	
Serbia		Azerbaijan	Paraguay	Ethiopia	
Uzbekistan		Russia	Nicaragua	Kenya	
Kazakhstan			Bolivia	Nigeria	
			Honduras	Zimbabwe	
			Thailand*	Botswana	
				Sri Lanka	

*Based on the average of urban Gini coefficients at provincial level.
Source: Statistical Annex in this Report.

MAP 2.2.1: **URBAN INEQUALITIES (INCOME) IN SELECTED CITIES AND COUNTRIES IN LATIN AMERICA AND THE CARIBBEAN (1998-2007)**

The developing world encompasses Africa, most of Asia, and Latin America and the Caribbean; the review in this chapter also includes those transition countries in Eastern Europe and the Commonwealth of Independent States (CIS) for which urban-level Gini coefficient data based on income is available. Since most of the countries in Asia and Africa base their Gini coefficient estimates on consumption instead of income, they are not included here.

Low inequality: Countries in this bracket feature urban Gini coefficients under 0.299. Their urban areas generally feature broad provision of basic services and the social and redistributive policies that allow for an equitable income distribution. Only Eastern European and CIS countries exhibit low degrees of urban income inequality, likely owing in part to the influence of their former Socialist regimes with their strong social institutions, safety nets and strict controls on wages. Belarus is where urban income inequality is at its lowest, followed by Romania, Kyrgyz Republic, Bulgaria, Armenia, Hungary, Albania, Kosovo and Serbia. In several countries in this "low inequality" bracket, income inequality and poverty are increasing, though, probably because of the post-Socialist erosion of public institutions, the abrupt opening-up of weak economies and declining gross domestic product, among other factors.

Relatively low inequality: In this bracket, urban Gini coefficients range between 0.300 and 0.399, just below the international alert line of 0.4 above which inequalities may have serious negative political, social and economic consequences for societies if not properly addressed. These countries are divided evenly between those with Gini coefficients under 0.34 (China, Poland and Lithuania) and those with values higher than 0.34 (Algeria, Georgia and Tajikistan). Countries in this bracket typically feature healthy economic expansion, a degree of political stability and relatively homogenous societies with only narrow income and consumption disparities across social segments.

Relatively high inequality: This corresponds to Gini coefficients between 0.400 and 0.449. This bracket comprises a mix of countries from four regions: Africa, Asia, Eastern Europe and the CIS. In Africa, the urban areas of Cameroon, Uganda and Côte d'Ivoire feature the lowest income-based Gini values, owing to recent policies that have strengthened institutions and redistributive mechanisms against a background of economic growth. In Asia, on the other hand, cities in Viet Nam and Nepal, and to a lesser extent Malaysia, exhibit relatively high income inequality with increasing urban Gini coefficients. In Eastern Europe, the highest urban Gini coefficient is to be found in Moldova (0.400). In the CIS, cities in Azerbaijan, Turkmenistan and Russia stand out for their high degrees of income inequality compared with the sub-region's average (0.334). Some recent evidence points to increasingly pronounced income inequalities in Russia in the recent past, resulting from growing unemployment, higher cost of living and an erosion of the redistributive institutions.[4]

High inequality: In this bracket, urban Gini coefficients range between 0.450 and 0.499 – above the threshold where city and other public authorities should address inequality as

a matter of urgency. Most of the cities in this bracket are in Latin America and the Caribbean.[5] General urban Gini values in El Salvador, Uruguay, Venezuela, Panama, Peru, Costa Rica, Paraguay, Mexico, Honduras and Bolivia are all high, although just under the region's average (0.505). In Asia, inequality is high in the urban areas of the Philippines and Thailand. In this bracket, inequalities are approaching dangerously high levels; if the current trend continues, challenging conditions in many cities could discourage capital expenditure and lead to sporadic protests and riots. High income inequality is often linked to weak labour markets, inadequate capital investment in public services and lack of pro-poor social programmes.[6]

Very high inequality: This is the bracket where Gini values ranging from 0.500 to 0.599 point to institutional and structural failures in income distribution. Again, the majority of countries in this bracket are in Latin America and the Caribbean, a region where urban areas have been characterized by high income inequality for many years. In some African countries, urban income inequalities are also becoming dangerously high, particularly in Nigeria, Kenya, Ethiopia and Zimbabwe. In Asia, Sri Lanka is the only country where urban areas feature very high income inequalities, with a Gini coefficient of 0.55 – far higher than the region's average of 0.416.

Extremely high inequality: Whereas the urban areas in several countries in this review have experienced very serious income inequalities in recent years, only a few fall into the "extremely high" bracket where Gini coefficients reach as high as 0.600 or more. Such extreme values often result from dysfunctional labour markets, sluggish economic growth, structural problems of wealth distribution and institutional failure that reflect long-standing patterns of inequality. All the countries in this group are in Southern Africa, with urban areas in the Republic of South Africa featuring the highest degree of income inequality in the world (as measured by Gini coefficients).

The magnitude of consumption inequalities in urban areas

Recent estimates show that in Africa's urban areas (see Map 2.2.2), Togo's stand out as the least unequal, with a consumption Gini coefficient of 0.31, or one-third below the continent's average urban Gini value for consumption (0.45). If anything, though, this relatively equitable income distribution reflects the almost uniform degree of poverty that characterizes Togo's urban areas. This stands in sharp contrast with the low degree of inequality prevailing in Scandinavian cities, which instead reflects strong distributional institutions. Other countries where consumption-based Gini coefficients for urban areas are below Africa's average include Morocco, Egypt, Mauritania, Democratic Republic of Congo, Central African Republic and Ethiopia, in ascending order (see Figure 2.2.1). Serious distributional problems are found further south in Malawi and Namibia, with "very high" Gini values (0.52 and 0.58, respectively) denoting that consumption largely remains concentrated in a small segment of the population.

▲
Granada, Nicaragua recorded the most significant decrease in its Gini coefficient between the year 2000 and 2005. ©**Felix Mizioznikov/Shutterstock**

FIGURE 2.2.1: **CONSUMPTION INEQUALITY AT NATIONAL-URBAN LEVEL IN AFRICA**

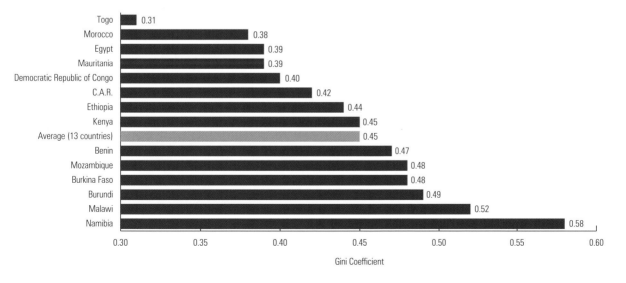

	Gini Coefficient
Togo	0.31
Morocco	0.38
Egypt	0.39
Mauritania	0.39
Democratic Republic of Congo	0.40
C.A.R.	0.42
Ethiopia	0.44
Kenya	0.45
Average (13 countries)	0.45
Benin	0.47
Mozambique	0.48
Burkina Faso	0.48
Burundi	0.49
Malawi	0.52
Namibia	0.58

Source: UN-HABITAT, Global Urban Observatory, 2009. Data from UN-ECLAC, UN-ESCAP, UNU and other sources (see Statistical Annex).

MAP 2.2.2: **URBAN INEQUALITIES (CONSUMPTION/INCOME) IN SELECTED CITIES AND COUNTRIES IN AFRICA (1993-2007)**

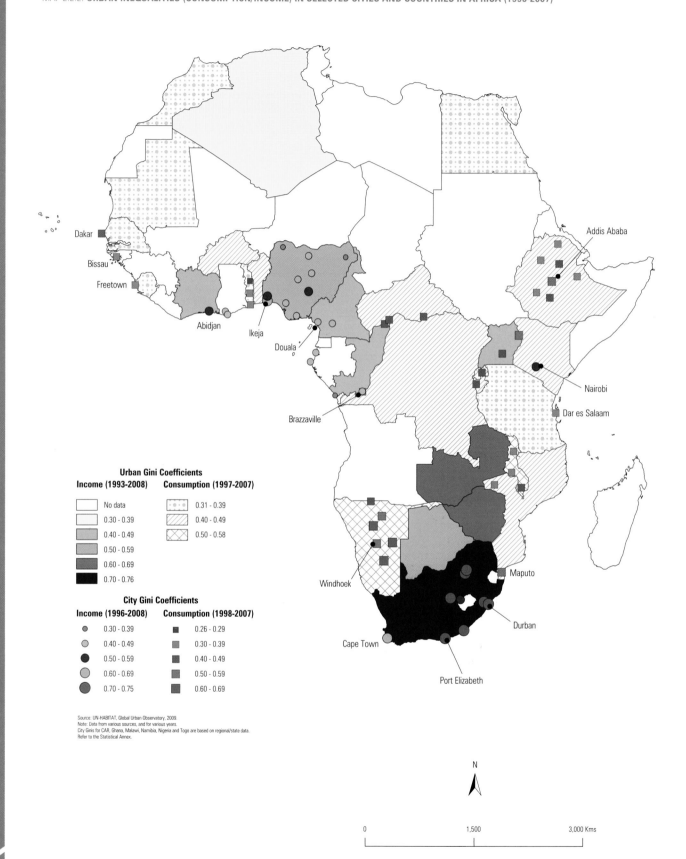

Dakar
Bissau
Freetown
Abidjan
Ikeja
Douala
Brazzaville
Addis Ababa
Nairobi
Dar es Salaam
Windhoek
Maputo
Durban
Cape Town
Port Elizabeth

Urban Gini Coefficients

Income (1993-2008)	Consumption (1997-2007)
No data	0.31 - 0.39
0.30 - 0.39	0.40 - 0.49
0.40 - 0.49	0.50 - 0.58
0.50 - 0.59	
0.60 - 0.69	
0.70 - 0.76	

City Gini Coefficients

Income (1996-2008)	Consumption (1998-2007)
0.30 - 0.39	0.26 - 0.29
0.40 - 0.49	0.30 - 0.39
0.50 - 0.59	0.40 - 0.49
0.60 - 0.69	0.50 - 0.59
0.70 - 0.75	0.60 - 0.69

Source: UN-HABITAT, Global Urban Observatory, 2009.
Note: Data from various sources, and for various years.
City Ginis for CAR, Ghana, Malawi, Namibia, Nigeria and Togo are based on regional/state data.
Refer to the Statistical Annex.

N

| 0 | 1,500 | 3,000 Kms |

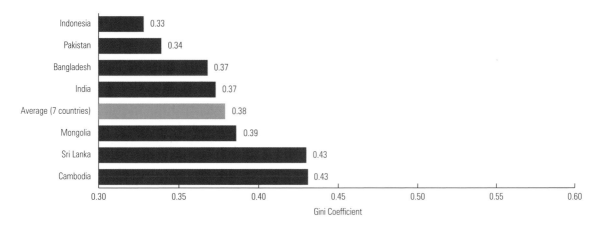

Source: UN-HABITAT, Global Urban Observatory, 2009. Data from UN-ECLAC, UN-ESCAP, UNU and other sources (see Statistical Annex).

The consumption-based Gini values for the urban areas of all these countries are above the region's average as measured by the sample, with Namibia's coefficient exceeding that average by as much as 30 per cent.

By comparison, household expenditure in Asia's urban areas is relatively less unequal. On this count, Indonesia features the lowest Gini value in the whole region (0.328) and is closely followed by Pakistan, Bangladesh and India, whose urban areas all exhibit Gini values under the Asian average of 0.379. The distribution of household expenditures in urban Sri Lanka and Cambodia is more unequal, with Gini values of 0.43. This suggests unequal access to basic goods that may hinder poverty reduction strategies, even against a background of economic growth.

Income inequality and level of development

When comparing income inequality in the urban areas of countries in brackets 1 and 2 in Table 1 – those with "low" and "relatively low" Gini values – with the extent of the urban divide in countries appearing in brackets 3 to 6 – from "relatively high" to "extremely high" urban income inequality – it is clear that economic development somehow goes hand in hand with broader income distribution. In general terms, countries with low Gini coefficients belong to high-income groups, except for some in Eastern Europe and the CIS (bracket 2) that are classified as moderate-income countries. On the other hand, high Gini coefficients are widespread in countries ranging from medium- to low-income levels, and particularly in poorer countries in Asia and Africa.

This relationship between higher development and broader income distribution holds in all of the countries in the UN-HABITAT sample; the only exception is Latin America and the Caribbean, where GDP per capita is significantly higher than in the other countries with very unequal incomes. As shown in Figure 2.2.3, countries in Latin America are clustered high on the Y axis, denoting high Gini coefficients, and around the middle of the X axis, denoting moderate per capita GDP. This relationship is even more obvious when compared with Eastern European countries featuring relatively similar GDPs per capita to those in Latin America, which is much more unequal.

Figure 2.2.3 also shows that most of the countries are noticeably clustered according to the Gini-based bracket that reflects their degree of inequality. For instance, countries in brackets 1 and 2 ("low" and "relatively low" income inequality in urban areas) are located at the lower right quadrant of the graph (low Gini values and relatively high GDP), and those

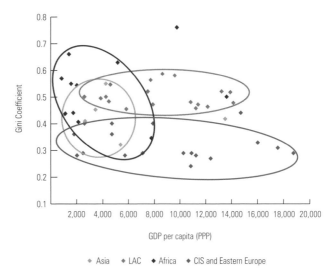

Source: UN-HABITAT, Global Urban Observatory, 2009.
Data from UN-ECLAC, UN-ESCAP, UNU, World Bank and other sources.

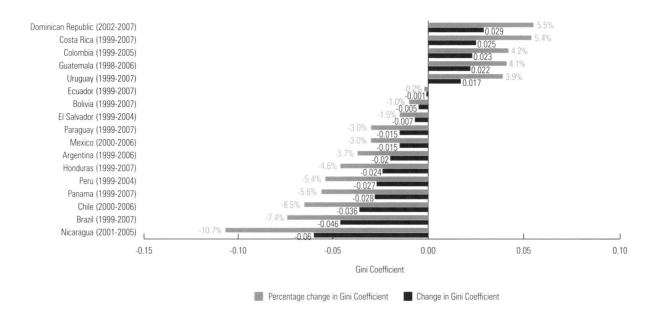

Source: UN-HABITAT, Global Urban Observatory, 2009. Data from UN-ECLAC, UN-ESCAP, UNU and other sources (see Statistical Annex).

in brackets 5 and 6 ("very high" and "extremely high" income inequality) appear in the top left quadrant (high Gini values and low GDP). Malaysia, Botswana and South Africa are interesting exceptions, with a GDP per capita significantly higher than other Asian and African countries in bracket 5, which are characterized by moderately unequal distributions of income.

The concentration of inequalities is higher in urban than in rural areas.

Nationwide averages of inequality conceal differences across rural and urban Gini values, as well as among degrees of inequality across cities. In most countries, the average income gap between urban areas is greater than the average difference between national income and rural income. Exceptions are Morocco, Lesotho, Central African Republic, Cameroon and Botswana, where the total national Gini coefficient is higher than the Gini coefficient for the urban areas overall.

The degree of inequality in both income and consumption is substantially greater in urban than in rural areas in general. Exceptions include Algeria, Sierra Leone, Central African Republic, Botswana and China, where inequality is slightly higher in rural areas. In Asia and Africa, inequalities are growing faster in urban than in rural areas. Latin America and the Caribbean is the only region in the developing world where indices of income inequality in both urban and rural areas are almost identical.[7] In Latin America, the historically

unequal allocation of land in rural areas has combined with ineffective redistributive policies in urban areas to reinforce ingrained patterns of inequality. The land distribution patterns established under Spanish colonial rule have institutionalized *latifundia* and *hacienda* estates where indigenous people were forced to work in indentured servitude; subsequent agricultural modernization favoured large companies over individual smallholder farmers, further marginalizing indigenous agriculturalists. This historical, path-dependent process was further consolidated under military dictatorships and structural adjustment policies, and tackling this combined legacy today is quite a challenge for land reform policies. In urban areas, redistributive policies such as basic service delivery and cash transfers have failed to make a deep and lasting impact on either urban or rural poverty.[8]

Regional trends in the economic urban divide

In the previous edition of this report, UN-HABITAT showed that inequality has increased since the 1980s, particularly in transition and some emerging economies. New information shows more mixed results on developing countries: Latin America and the Caribbean has made some progress in recent years; Africa shows no clear pattern of increase or decrease of inequalities and Asia exhibits a moderate overall increase. However, a closer examination of changes in urban Gini coefficients per region shows specific differences, which are reviewed in the next section.

Latin America and the Caribbean: A slight narrowing in the divide

In general, urban inequality in Latin America and the Caribbean is declining, although it remains quite high. An analysis of income distribution trends in 17 selected countries in the region shows that in nine countries urban Gini coefficients have fallen slightly from around 1999 to around 2006. Nicaragua recorded the most significant decrease in its Gini coefficient, which dropped by approximately 10 per cent as the country experienced a moderate economic recovery between the year 2000 and 2005, with annual GDP growth improving to about 4 per cent.

The next best performing countries in the region were Brazil, Chile, Panama and Peru where income-based Gini coefficients narrowed during this period by 7.4, 6.5, 5.6, and 5.4 per cent, respectively. In Honduras, Mexico and Paraguay, Gini coefficients dropped by a range of 4.6 per cent to 3 per cent. Argentina stands out as a basket case: from 0.54 in 1999, its Gini coefficient had risen to 0.58 by 2002 in the aftermath of a severe economic crisis; a robust recovery ensued with five consecutive years (2003-2008) of over 8 per cent annual real growth in GDP, which by 2006 had reduced the Gini value to 0.52.

However, in the urban areas of five other Latin American countries (Uruguay, Guatemala, Colombia, Costa Rica and Dominican Republic), income inequalities have slightly risen or remained stable, regardless of economic growth rates above the region's average.

The recent improvement in economic conditions in various countries across the region has resulted in a narrower income gap between rich and poor. However, the current financial and food crises are likely to hamper the chances for sustained economic growth in the coming years, and short of appropriate pro-poor policies, inequalities may rise again, instead of declining further.

Africa: Mixed shifts in the economic urban divide

Trends in the economic divide in Africa's urban areas are mixed, or so suggests the sample in the UN-HABITAT survey of Gini coefficients for various periods. Among the 13 countries under review, eight showed lower values (if only marginally for some) and five featured moderate to significant increases. The region's urban areas, and in sub-Saharan Africa in particular, retain the highest degrees of poverty in the world, together with the highest prevalence of slum populations in urban areas. In African urban areas, progress in poverty reduction has been rather slow overall, and these mixed results in the distribution of income and consumption can only point to the hope of future improvements.

According to recent national surveys on income and expenditures conducted in selected African countries, the most significant reductions in Gini values in urban Africa took place in Côte d'Ivoire between 2002 and 2008, and in Uganda between 2003 and 2006, when the respective coefficients decreasing from 0.51 to 0.44, and from 0.48 to 0.43, respectively. Côte d'Ivoire experienced this significant narrowing in the economic urban divide even as annual GDP growth rate was rather poor (under 1 per cent), reflecting the civil strife in the country at the turn of the century. In contrast, the significant decline in income inequalities in Uganda coincided with annual growth rates of around 6 per cent – which goes to show that economic growth does not necessarily go hand in hand with increasing inequalities. This is the case in a few other African countries: Benin, Rwanda and Tanzania all managed to reduce urban consumption inequalities in a dynamic economic environment where GDP growth ranged between 4 and 6.5 per cent.

In the urban areas of several other African countries, the economic divide as measured by Gini coefficients has increased, signaling a widening gap between rich and poor in terms of access to basic resources. Burkina Faso, Egypt and Ethiopia have seen their urban consumption Gini coefficients increase by 7.8, 13.2 and 11.8 per cent, respectively. In Zambia, too, urban income inequality has increased by 8.2 per cent, pushing the country into the "extremely high" inequality bracket – even as Zambia's GDP grew at an annual rate of about 5.5 per cent between 2003 and 2006. In Mozambique, consumption inequalities have widened only marginally.

Asia: The economic urban divide is widening

Asian countries are characterized by low to moderate degrees of income and consumption inequality overall (see Map 2.2.3). With the exception of the 1997/8 financial crisis, economic growth in Asia has been robust over the past two decades, more than doubling in real terms from 2.7 per cent to 5.8 per cent between 1990 and 2007.[9] As a result, average incomes have increased in almost all Asian countries, and poverty has fallen nearly everywhere in the region, with the exception of Bangladesh.

In the urban areas of seven Asian countries, Gini coefficients have been rising, compared with decreases in five other countries. Nepal, one of the few Asian countries that has undergone an economic recession in recent years, features the most significant increase, with its urban Gini coefficient soaring from 0.26 in 1985 – at the time, one of the lowest in the world – to 0.43 in 1996. In updated (2007) data, the Gini coefficient at country level was still high as economic conditions remained unfavourable.[10] Mongolia provides a variation on the same theme: the country's urban consumption-based Gini coefficient rose some 16 per cent from 2003 to 2006 – an annual increment of about 5 per cent – which was twice the rate of its economic growth during that period, pointing to a need for more effective redistribution policies. In the early years of the 21st century, China has also experienced remarkable and sustained economic growth that has contributed to lifting millions of people out of poverty; yet at the same time, income inequalities have been increasing in both urban and rural areas. According to UN-HABITAT

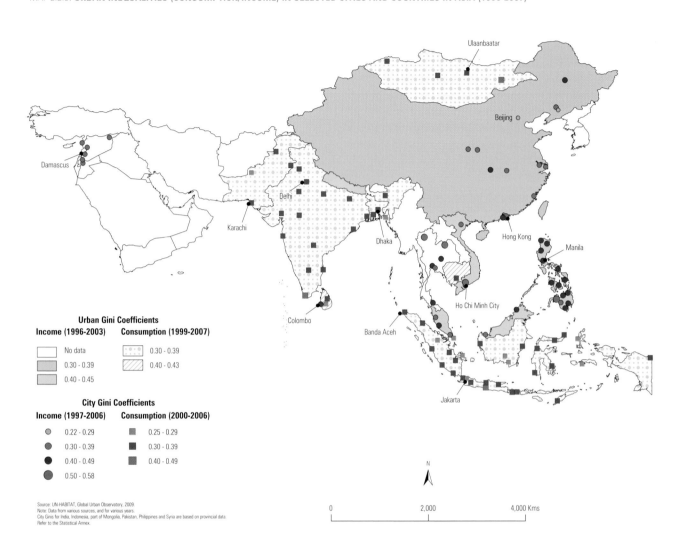

Urban Gini Coefficients

Income (1996-2003)	Consumption (1999-2007)
No data	0.30 - 0.39
0.30 - 0.39	0.40 - 0.43
0.40 - 0.45	

City Gini Coefficients

Income (1997-2006)	Consumption (2000-2006)
0.22 - 0.29	0.25 - 0.29
0.30 - 0.39	0.30 - 0.39
0.40 - 0.49	0.40 - 0.49
0.50 - 0.58	

Source: UN-HABITAT, Global Urban Observatory, 2009.
Note: Data from various sources, and for various years.
City Ginis for India, Indonesia, part of Mongolia, Pakistan, Philippines and Syria are based on provincial data.
Refer to the Statistical Annex.

N

0   2,000   4,000 Kms

data, income inequality in China's urban areas (as measured by Gini values) grew from 0.23 in 1988 to 0.32 in 2002, and has continued to rise. Though still relatively low, these Gini values represent a 39 per cent increase over the period.

In urban Viet Nam, income inequalities increased by 17 per cent between 1993 and 2002 against a background of rapid economic growth. In urban Bangladesh in the 1990s, inequalities in consumption increased by an even steeper 20 per cent, compared with 9 per cent in India and 6.3 per cent in Pakistan in the early 2000s. In India, the widening economic urban divide came in sharp contrast to annualized GDP growth of over 5 per cent in the early 2000s. India provides an apt demonstration of the practical implications of the difference between income-based and consumption-based Gini coefficients. The country compiles urban Gini coefficients based on consumption only (i.e., excluding savings, namely, assets), which in this case minimizes the extent of urban economic inequalities.[11]

The increasing share of the top 1 per cent of income-earners in India's total national income points to an even steeper surge in income inequality, especially since the early 1990s.[12]

In the urban areas of five other Asian countries, the economic divide has narrowed in recent years, as reflected in income- or consumption-based Gini coefficients. Sri Lanka recorded the sharpest decline between 1990 and 2006: a drop of 11.3 per cent, or an annualized decline of -0.7 per cent. In the meantime in the country at large, Gini values also fell (from 0.62 in 1990 to 0.55 in 2006). These improvements in both general urban and nationwide values coincided with a period of sustained (4.9 per cent) economic growth, but the degree of consumption inequality remains high (at 0.43), suggesting that the benefits of overall prosperity are not as broadly distributed in Sri Lanka as they could be. Malaysia, Cambodia and the Philippines are the three other Asian countries where the urban economic divide narrowed in recent years.[13]

Kathmandu, Nepal. The country has seen its urban Gini coefficient soaring from 0.26 in 1985 to 0.43 in 1996. ©**Dhoxax** /**Shutterstock**

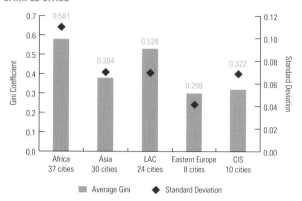

Source: UN-HABITAT, Global Urban Observatory, 2009.
Data from UN-ECLAC, UN-ESCAP, UNU and other sources (see Statistical Annex).

FIGURE 2.2.6: **REGIONAL GINI AVERAGES FOR URBAN INCOME DISTRIBUTION IN SAMPLE COUNTRIES**

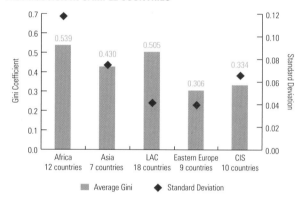

Source: UN-HABITAT, Global Urban Observatory, 2009.
Data from UN-ECLAC, UN-ESCAP, UNU and other sources (see Statistical Annex).

The magnitude of the divide in specific cities

National averages tend to conceal any substantive differences between inequalities in a country's urban areas overall and those in specific cities. The disparities between the urban rich and the urban poor as measured in terms of income and consumption distribution in specific cities vary considerably across developing regions, with the stark rich-poor divide most noticeable in African and Latin American cities, as suggested earlier. In both regions, the gap is often extreme compared with cities in Asia, Eastern Europe and the CIS, where the degree of inequality remains relatively low.

Using an expanded dataset of city-specific Gini coefficients, UN-HABITAT has calculated simple averages for regions based on 109 cities selected for their noteworthy variations. The 37 African cities in the sample display the highest average Gini coefficient (based on income) of all regions, at 0.581. Next come the 24 selected Latin American cities, with an average Gini coefficient of 0.528. Taken together, the 30 selected Asian cities feature a comparatively low degree of income inequality, as measured by a Gini coefficient of 0.384. This average is just below the 0.40 threshold, above which inequality is considered unacceptably high. Among the cities in the sample, those in Eastern Europe (8) and the CIS (10) feature the lowest average Gini values and, presumably, the greatest degrees of equality, at 0.298 and 0.322, respectively. (Figure 2.2.5).[14]

Indices of income inequality aggregated at the national urban level differ from the averages of the selected cities. Although a clear pattern fails to emerge, the averages of city-specific Gini coefficients in Africa and Latin America are higher than those for the two regions' aggregated urban Gini value, whereas in Asia, Eastern Europe and the CIS, the

Johannesburg, South Africa. Of all the cities in the UN-HABITAT sample, Johannesburg is one of the most unequal in the world. ©**Madanmohan Rao**

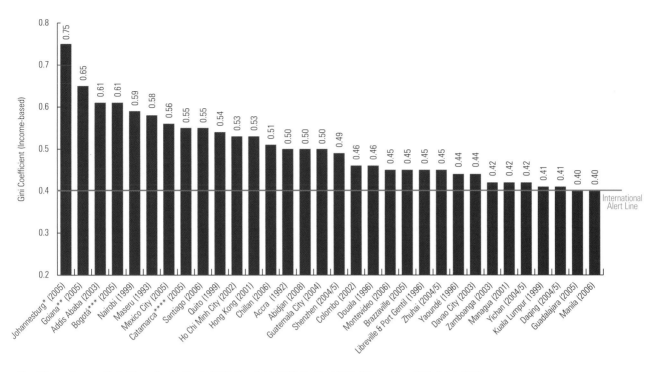

* In addition to other seven South African cities: East London (0.75), Bloemfontein (0.74), East Rand (0.74), Pietermaritzburg (0.73), Pretoria (0.72),
Port Elizabeth (0.72), Durban (0.72) and Cape Town (0.67)
** In addition to other six Brazilian cities: Fortaleza (0.61), Belo Horizonte (0.61), Brasilia (0.60), Curitiba (0.59), Rio de Janeiro (0.53) and São Paulo (0.50)
*** In addition to other three cities in Colombia: Barranquilla (0.57), Calí (0.54) and Medellín ((0.51)
**** In addition to other two cities in Argentina: Buenos Aires (0.52) and Formosa (0.44)

Source: UN-HABITAT, Global Urban Observatory, 2009. Data from UN-ECLAC, UN-ESCAP, UNU and other sources (see Statistical Annex).

converse is true. Variations between inequalities at the city and urban levels are notable in Africa, Latin America and Asia: while the average Gini coefficient for individual sampled *cities* in Africa stands at 0.581, its collective equivalent for the region's *urban areas* overall is 0.539, a difference of 4 per cent (see Figure 2.2.5 and 2.2.6). In Eastern Europe and the CIS, variations between these two types of average are negligible: in Eastern Europe, for instance, the city-specific income-based Gini coefficient is 0.298, compared with 0.306 for its general urban equivalent. These variations confirm the assumption that national trends cannot account for what is happening in every city or sub-region in the same country, because the factors of inequality are determined by history and culture, and are largely influenced by local policies and actions.

As for measures of the economic divide based on consumption rather than income, general urban or city-specific data are available only for countries in two regions: Africa and Asia. Urban Africa consistently shows much higher degrees of inequality than Asia, based on both consumption and income. Even though, as might have been expected, values for consumption are lower than for income, here again Africa remains characterized by high degrees of inequality, with Gini coefficients of 0.394 for the average of 49 selected cities and towns, and 0.45 for urban areas

in 15 countries. Asia similarly exhibits lower inequalities in consumption, with an average Gini value of 0.326 for six selected cities and 0.379 for urban areas in seven countries.

The most unequal cities

Of all the cities in the UN-HABITAT sample, Buffalo City (East London), Johannesburg and Ekurhuleni (East Rand), among other South African cities, are the most unequal in the world, with extremely high Gini coefficients of 0.71 or more. They are followed by the Brazilian cities of Goiana, Fortaleza, Belo Horizonte and Brasilia: all of these feature income Gini coefficients above 0.60, making them the most unequal cities in Latin America and the most unequal in the world after South Africa (Figure 2.2.7).

Colombian cities such as Bogotá, Barranquilla and Calí, and Lagos in Nigeria, top the list of those where the urban economic divide is at its sharpest, alongside Chiangmai and Udonthani in Thailand,[15] all of which feature income Gini coefficients above 0.55 (which is considered "very high" inequality). They are closely followed by some cities in Argentina (Catamarca and Buenos Aires), Chile (Santiago and Chillan) and Ecuador (Quito), all of which record income Gini values between 0.55 and 0.51.

BOX 2.2.2: **MEASURING INEQUALITY: SOURCES AND TYPES OF DATA**

In the 2008/9 edition of this report, UN-HABITAT drew from a relatively large dataset of Gini coefficients for 94 cities in 47 countries, and an additional 68 countries with data aggregated at the national urban level. For the current report, UN-HABITAT has expanded its dataset to city-level data for 119 cities in 61 countries; national-level urban data for 72 countries; and sub-regional data for 216 predominantly urban states, provinces and districts in 15 countries. In total, the enlarged UN-HABITAT database includes data on income and consumption distribution in a total 90 countries. The database has also been updated. Urban inequalities at the national or city level are calculated in the current report from data collected between 1988 and 2008. The previous report cited data from 1983 to 2005.

Roughly 57 per cent of the Gini coefficients presented in this report are based on income,

and the remaining 43 per cent on consumption. For the purposes of analyzing inequalities, estimates for income and consumption have been systematically separated. Data on Gini coefficients is derived from of a mix of sources. The Economic Commission for Latin America and the Caribbean has compiled Gini coefficients for UN-HABITAT at the urban, rural and selected city levels, based on data from household surveys and census information from 1989 to 2007, and calculating two or three points in time, where possible. The United Nations Economic and Social Commission for Asia and the Pacific has produced Gini coefficients through a similar arrangement, calculating the values at the national, provincial or state, urban and city levels based on various sources, including national surveys, census data and special surveys that were conducted by the national statistical offices in selected countries in different years.

UN-HABITAT complemented the set of Gini coefficients for the region with information from the Asian Development Bank, the World Bank and the national statistical offices and planning units of various governments, as necessary.

Gini coefficients for cities and urban areas in Africa have been collected from various sources, as there is no central depository of such data in the region. UN-HABITAT approached national statistics offices, ministries of finance and planning and other government departments involved in poverty reduction and country strategy papers, including the International Monetary Fund and the South African Cities Network. UN-HABITAT calculated Gini coefficients for the small cities and towns in the Lake Victoria Region in Tanzania, Uganda and Kenya based on its own urban inequality surveys. Such surveys were also conducted by UN-HABITAT in Addis Ababa, Casablanca and Dakar.

Other highly unequal cities stand out as more isolated cases, with values well above the national average. They include (in decreasing order): Addis Ababa, Nairobi, Maseru, Mexico City, Ho Chi Minh City, Hong Kong and Port-au-Prince, all featuring Gini coefficients above 0.52, which ranks as "very high".

For all these cities, the Gini coefficients are based on income. When values are based on consumption expenditures, they are invariably lower. Addis Ababa, with a Gini coefficient of 0.56,[16] and Maputo and Casablanca, both with Gini coefficients of 0.52, feature the highest values in the world for consumption-based inequality. There can be little doubt that if data on *income* distribution in Maputo, Casablanca or other similar cities were available, it would show even greater degrees of inequality.

The most equal cities

The cities in the broader, updated UN-HABITAT sample returning lower Gini coefficients than those reviewed above are more likely to offer more equitable environments, with adequate housing and affordable basic services. Still, this does not mean that measuring *economic* equality in a city will reveal whether it affords residents all of the opportunities of an ideal equitable city. The Gini coefficient may be the most widely used measure of how equitable a city is, but as an indicator it suffers from two major drawbacks: (1) the Gini coefficient fails to capture the proportion of a country's population that is poor, and (2) it does not measure the non-economic dimensions of an equitable or egalitarian city, as described above. The Gini method is a useful measure of a fairly narrow kind of inequality, which is the difference in income (or consumption) of a typical individual from the incomes of those right above and below them; but clearly,

income inequality tells only part of the story of inequality in any given place.

Among UN-HABITAT's sample of cities, Jakarta, Chittagong, Dhaka, Khulna, Lomé, Freetown, Dar es Salaam, Phnom Penh, Bissau and Dakar stand out as the most egalitarian in the developing world, as measured by consumption-based Gini coefficients (with a range of 0.27 to 0.37).

The problem is that the "most equal" developing-world cities in the UN-HABITAT sample are in fact "equally poor cities", as they feature similar distribution of consumption expenditures across rich and poor. However, all these cities fail to provide water, sanitation or housing to all residents, and they feature some of the highest incidences of slums in their respective regions. The "most equal cities" in the sample also perform poorly on various social indicators. In Bangladesh, for example, Chittagong and Dhaka – with consumption-based Gini coefficients of 0.29 and 0.31, respectively – suffer from high rates of under-5 mortality, reaching 97 deaths per 1,000 children at urban level nationwide and up to 130 in the most deprived slum settlements. In Dakar, a city with relatively low consumption inequality (0.37), the literacy rate among women was 63 per cent in the year 2000, compared with 90 per cent for men; this combined into a female-to-male literacy ratio of 0.7, reflecting a marked gender disparity in the Senegalese capital. Likewise, in Jakarta and Dar-es-Salaam, overall literacy rates for women stand around 94 per cent, but in slums and the most deprived areas they drop to 63 and 50 per cent, respectively.

Another feature of the "equally poor" cities in the UN-HABITAT sample is that economic growth proceeds at different paces. Some are dynamic and growing fast; others are experiencing slower paces of development. As they continue growing, though, cities must fulfil two related duties for the sake of their populations: (1) they must ensure that any

FIGURE 2.2.8: **MOST EQUAL CITIES (INCOME-BASED GINI). SELECTED CITIES IN THE DEVELOPING WORLD (1997-2006)**

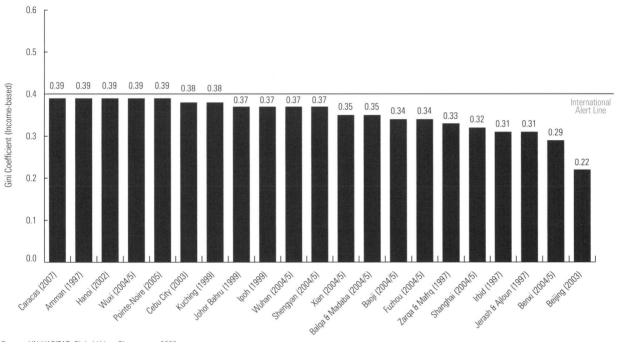

Source: UN-HABITAT, Global Urban Observatory, 2009.
Data from UN-ECLAC, UN-ESCAP, UNU and other sources (see Statistical Annex).

In Jakarta, Indonesia overall literacy rates for women stand around 94 per cent, but in slums and the most deprived areas they drop to 63 and 50 per cent.
©**Esther de Jong/IRIN**

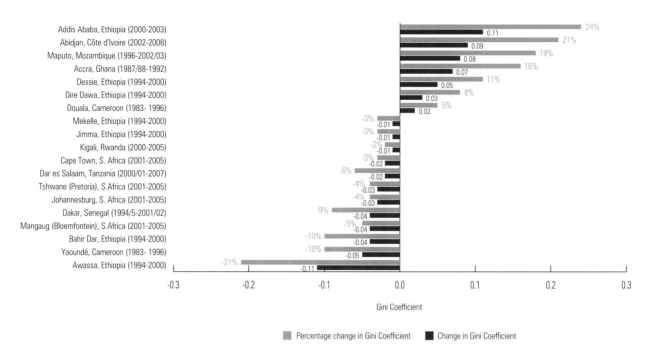

Source: UN-HABITAT, Global Urban Observatory, 2009.
Data from UN-ECLAC, UN-ESCAP, UNU and other sources (see Statistical Annex).

progress toward more egalitarian distribution of consumption is going to remain over time, and (2) they must enhance economic and social opportunities for the poor, women and other vulnerable groups, in the process reducing the systemic social deprivations that prevent certain segments of society from achieving the benefits of an egalitarian city.

A review of income-based coefficients in the UN-HABITAT sample shows that Beijing is the "most equal" city in the world, with a Gini value as low as 0.22 in 2003. It is followed by Benxi, (0.29) and several other Chinese cities including Shanghai, Baoji and Xian, which all boast Gini coefficients below 0.37. Several cities in Jordan are also characterized by very low income Gini coefficients (between 0.31 and 0.35), including Amman, Jerash, Ajloun, Irbid, Zarqa, Mafrq, Balga, and Madaba.[17] Hanoi in Viet Nam and Caracas in Venezuela also feature relatively low income inequality, with Gini coefficients below 0.39.

Where and how is the economic urban divide decreasing?

A review of recent trends in inequality conducted by UN-HABITAT bears only on a limited sample of 48 cities for which data is available: 19 in Africa, 22 in Latin America and only seven in Asia. It must be stressed here that the results depict only general patterns, but can nevertheless point to potential drivers of change.[18]

In 27 out of these 48 cities, Gini coefficients are seen to decrease, though to a very small extent in some cases. In 11 of those cities – eight in Africa, two in Latin America and

one in Asia – the decrease in Gini coefficients is significant (by more than 1 per cent per year), ultimately changing by more than 10 per cent. Over the period recorded in the UN-HABITAT sample, inequality actually increased in 21 cities. Of these, significant increases of more than 1 percent per year were notable in five cities in Africa, two in Latin America and two in Asia.

In the Ethiopian cities of Awasa, Bahir Dar and Jimma, Gini coefficients based on consumption declined substantially (by 21 per cent, 10 per cent and 3 per cent, respectively) between 1994 and the year 2000. Several factors may have been at play behind these reductions in consumption inequality: access to education, health services, nutrition, and water and sanitation have improved throughout the country, on top of significant development in infrastructure, roads, power lines and telecommunications.[19] A recovery in food production in the mid-1990s, coupled with relatively strong economic growth, may have significantly reduced poverty for many households, especially in places most affected by recurrent droughts.[20] It also appears that expenditures on housing have not significantly affected consumption distribution, as rents paid to *kebeles* – the smallest administrative units or associations of residents – in Awasa, Bahir Dar and Jimma may have experienced a lower increase than the Ethiopian capital of Addis Ababa in recent years (Figure 2.2.9).

Elsewhere in Africa, urban economic inequality has also declined in Accra, Ghana, by a significant 16 per cent between 1987/8 and 1992, and in Dakar the household level Gini coefficient declined by 9 per cent (0.458 to 0.419) between

FIGURE 2.2.10: **LATIN AMERICAN AND CARIBBEAN CITIES – CHANGES IN GINI COEFFICIENTS**

Bogotá, Colombia (1991-2005)	0.116 — 24%
Catamarca, Argentina (1994-2005)	0.057 — 12%
Calí, Colombia (1991-1998)	0.050 — 10%
Quito, Ecuador (1990-1999)	0.042 — 8%
Mexico City, Mexico (1992-2005)	0.037 — 7%
Curitiba, Brazil (1990-2005)	0.033 — 6%
Buenos Aires, Argentina (1990-2005)	0.024 — 5%
Medellín, Colombia (1991-1998)	0.022 — 4%
Goiana, Brazil (1999-2005)	0.009 — 1%
Santiago, Chile (1990-2006)	0.003 — 0%
Brasilia, Brazil (1990-2007)	-0.008 — -1%
Fortaleza, Brazil (1990-2005)	-0.032 — -5%
Guatemala City, Guatemala (1989-2004)	-0.045 — -8%
Belo Horizonte, Brazil (1990-2005)	-0.049 — -7%
Montevideo, Uruguay (1990-2006)	-0.055 — -11%
Guadalajara, Mexico (1992-2005)	-0.055 — -12%
Chillan, Chile (1990-2006)	-0.056 — -10%
Caracas, Venezuela (1990-2007)	-0.059 — -13%
Managua, Nicaragua (1993-2001)	-0.060 — -13%
São Paulo, Brazil (1990-2007)	-0.061 — -11%
Rio de Janeiro, Brazil (1990-2007)	-0.080 — -13%
Formosa, Argentina (1999-2005)	-0.088 — -17%

Percentage change in Gini Coefficient   ▮ Change in Gini Coefficient   Gini Coefficient

Source: UN-HABITAT, Global Urban Observatory, 2009.
Data from UN-ECLAC, UN-ESCAP, UNU and other sources (see Statistical Annex).

1994/5 and 2001/2. In Dakar, the changes can be associated with rapid economic growth and Senegal's intensive emphasis on infrastructure development, which generated jobs and promoted self-employment. Remittances from abroad have also been a significant source of income for Dakar's poor households. According to a 2008 study by Senegal's Ministry of Economy, remittances amounted to 500 billion CFA Francs (about US $1.1 billion) in 2007, a figure that has remained relatively stable in recent years. Cash transfers go primarily into household expenditures and investment in property. It is estimated that without these international transfers, poverty in Senegal would affect 53 per cent of the population, or 16 per cent more than with remittances.[21]

In South Africa, the cities of Mangaug, Tshwane (Pretoria), Johannesburg, and Cape Town experienced moderate (3 to 5 per cent) reductions in Gini coefficients between 2001 and 2005. This largely reflects significant economic and social improvements, particularly the introduction of a social (minimum) wage and subsidized rates in basic service delivery, education and housing.[22] Since 1994, the government of South Africa has effectively been redistributing wealth and welfare resources, spending public funds and deploying social programmes to bring about a more equitable distribution of public goods among the population. Back in 1975, the government's share of social spending on the country's black population was only 28 per cent, compared with 55 per cent on the white population. The share of social spending on the black population increased to 51 per cent in 1990, 67 per cent in 1993, and 80 per cent by 1997. In contrast, the share of social spending on the country's white population decreased from 55 per cent in 1975 to 33 per cent in 1990, 17 per cent in 1993, and 9 per cent in 1997. By 1997, race-based spending allocations were roughly proportionate to each group's share of South Africa's population.[23]

In Latin America and the Caribbean, several Brazilian cities have recently (between 2005 and 2007) experienced significant declines in their income Gini coefficients, including São Paulo (18 per cent), Rio de Janeiro (12 percent) and Brasilia (6 per cent). Decreases in income inequality in these cities are concomitant with those in overall urban Gini values in Brazil, which fell from 0.63 in 1999 to 0.60 in 2004 and 0.58 in 2007. The gradual drop in the Gini coefficient can be attributed in part to three well-documented factors: demographic trends, education policy and social protection. Declines in the size of Brazilian families and improvements in family dependency rates and access to education have helped reduce inequality. In the early and mid-1990s, universal admission to primary schooling and reductions in the rates of grade repetition led to a drop in the Gini coefficient by about 0.2 points per year from 1995 onward. Direct government cash transfers to households through the *Bolsa Familia* programme have also reduced income inequality, and increases in other forms of social protection, such as an increased minimum wage, have led to a further decrease of 0.2 Gini points per year.[24] These well-designed and targeted social policies have stimulated aggregate demand and consumption, enlarging the domestic market, which in turn spurred further increases in income and purchasing power (see Figure 2.2.10).[25]

In which cities are income inequalities growing and why?

The most significant increases in Gini coefficients in the UN-HABITAT sample cities have occurred in Colombia, where measures of income inequality climbed by 24 per cent in Bogotá between 1991 and 2005, 10 per cent in Calí and 4 per cent in Medellín between 1991 and 1998. Three well-documented factors can account for the increases in income distribution in Colombian cities. First, the informal sector has led in new job creation, in the process demonstrating that the formal economy is not in a position to accommodate Colombia's growing workforce. According to estimates by the International Labour Organization, eight out of every 10 jobs created in the 1990s were low-quality jobs in the informal economy.[26] Second, wage discrepancies in Colombia are becoming much more significant between skilled and less-skilled workers, with better-skilled workers earning increasingly more. Similarly, wages of college graduates relative to high school graduates in Colombia increased by 21 per cent between 1991 and 1995, and similar gaps have been recorded between workers who had graduated from secondary school and those who had not.[27] In Colombia's manufacturing sector, the wages of non-production or white-collar workers increased in relation to production or blue-collar workers; overall, differences in occupation accounted on average for 15 per cent of labour income inequality in the 1990s.[28] Third,

increases in private investment, exports, capital inflows and currency overvaluation have resulted in greater inequality in Colombia. However, in recent years, the economy has grown by more than 6 per cent annually, and increased government social spending (in the form of subsidies to the poor) has helped to offset increases in income inequalities that might result from economic prosperity.

Income inequalities also increased in Mexico City by 7 per cent (from 0.52 to 0.56) between 1992 and 2005. Among other factors, the rise in the city's Gini coefficient reflects declining trade union affiliation and falling real minimum wages coupled with a shift in trade that has resulted in higher wages for more qualified workers. In Argentina, Buenos Aires experienced rising inequality (around 5 per cent) from 1990 to 2005, a period marked by macro-economic stabilization policies, more open international economic flows, deregulation and structural reforms, including privatization. This 15-year trend was characterized by the closure of manufacturing firms, layoffs in privatized companies and widespread unemployment, which culminated in the 2000/1 economic crisis. Recovery materialized only around 2003, but had no clear influence on overall socioeconomic conditions until 2005.[29]

In Africa, the most significant increases in inequality in recent years have occurred in Addis Ababa, where the Gini coefficient for consumption rose by 24 per cent between

BOX 2.2.3: INCOME INEQUALITY AND CITY SIZE

Economists have long supported the idea that inequality is a natural consequence of urban growth and development. As a country's population becomes more and more urban and both the labour force and the productive sector shift from more equitable traditional and agricultural activities to less equitable modern, industrial activities, inequalities are expected to increase until aggregate incomes rise to a point where all members of society reach a common standard of living. Recently, economists have applied this concept to cities of various sizes, arguing that income inequality increases as city size grows, or that large cities tend to feature higher income disparities (as measured by Gini coefficients) than smaller ones. However, what may be evident in the developed world has not been observed in the South.

Based on an expanded database of city-specific Gini coefficients and a larger sample that includes small and intermediate cities in developing countries, UN-HABITAT has identified wide variations in Gini values across the city size spectrum. For example in a large city like Hong Kong, the Gini coefficient stands at

0.53, compared with only 0.22 in China's capital Beijing. In Jordan, the small cities of Jerash and Irbid feature low Gini coefficients (0.31), or nearly half those of similar-sized Monoregala and Rathnapura in Sri Lanka.

One of the most significant findings in this analysis is that average Gini coefficients for small, intermediate and large cities in the sample are quite similar, and no clear trend emerges whereby large cities are "more unequal" than smaller ones, or vice-versa. The poor relationship found between city-specific Gini values and population size challenges the previously accepted view that narrow wage distributions (i.e., low Gini values) are a defining feature of small and intermediate cities while larger ones, as the typical hosts to both highly paid workers (with advanced technical and professional training) and poor immigrants, naturally feature much broader income disparities. On the contrary, UN-HABITAT surveys of urban inequalities in 17 towns around Lake Victoria in East Africa found Gini coefficients similar to, or higher than, those in the capital cities of their respective countries. For instance, the consumption-based

Gini coefficient for Bukoba, with a population of about 100,000, stands at 0.34, the same as for Dar es Salam. Likewise, the Kenyan towns of Migori and Kisii feature income Gini coefficients of 0.558 and 0.631, respectively, compared with Nairobi's 0.58. Clearly, city size is not necessarily – nor even evidently, according to UN-HABITAT's analysis of urban settlements in the developing world – a determinant of inequality. Cites and countries can feature such drastically different cultural and political histories, policies and paths to development that it is not possible to establish a direct relationship between city size and the distribution of income.

This is why city authorities and policymakers must be well aware of the particular ways in which their cities are growing and changing over time. Improved living conditions for low-income and middle-class residents, and bridging not just the economic but also social, racial and cultural divides through redistributive policies, conscious urban planning and subsidies for housing and other needed amenities, would all go a long way toward building economically integrated communities in cities of all sizes.

Sources: Asian Development Bank, 2007; Haworth, Long & Rasmussen, 1978; Nord, 1980; Demographic Yearbook, from 1990 to 2006; Dreier Peter

the year 2000 and 2003; and in Abidjan, where the Gini coefficient increased by 21 per cent between 2002 and 2008. Significant increases in consumption inequality were also recorded in the Ethiopian cities of Dessie and Dire Dawa (11 and 8 per cent, respectively), and in Maputo, capital of Mozambique, where consumption-based Gini values rose by 18 per cent between 1996 and 2003. While the proportion of people in Mozambique living below the poverty line fell by 15 per cent nationwide between 1996 and 2003, growth in consumption has been much faster for better-off than poorer residents, clearly suggesting that economic growth in Maputo may not be as equitable as in other parts of the country.[30]

The high degree of consumption inequality in Addis Ababa can be attributed to a combination of factors, particularly the enduring effects of the policy choices made under the country's structural adjustment programme, with its lifting of subsidies on basic services, public expenditure cuts, tax reform and credit restrictions, all of which contributed to the persistence of poverty and inequality, particularly in the capital city.[31] The economic and political transition in the country has brought increased capital expenditure that is more beneficial for people with relatively better skills and high initial asset accumulation, most of whom are located in the capital city.[32] Gradual deregulation of social housing in the hands of *kebeles* has resulted in a disproportionate increase in housing rents for the urban poor in Addis Ababa.

▲
Addis Ababa. In Africa, the most significant increases in inequality in recent years have occurred in the Ethiopian capital. ©**Manoocher Deghati/IRIN**

All unequal cities are not so in the same way

UN-HABITAT data and analysis confirm that urban income inequalities take different forms across different cities and carry a variety of dimensions with them. It frequently happens that the income-based Gini coefficient for a city does not reflect the "bundle of commodities and services" available to residents; this has led an increasing number of countries to adopt consumption or household expenditure as a more accurate benchmark of inequality. Cities, and countries such as India, that make various subsidies available to low-income groups tend to feature lower consumption inequality, as they enable people to access basic goods for free or at reduced rates. Similarly, Canadian cities tend to be less unequal than those in the United States, as Canada maintains a range of social policies that target the poor and the vulnerable.

At times, inequalities in urban incomes conceal other types of divides, or fail to capture achievements in public service delivery or literacy. UN-HABITAT data shows that while Brazilian cities generally tend to experience extremely high degrees of income inequality, they fare better than highly unequal cities in poor African countries when it comes to access to piped water and sanitation. For instance, in 2007, even though Brazil's capital city Brasilia featured a very high (0.60) income Gini coefficient, 90 per cent of the population had access to piped water and 85 per cent to sanitation.

BOX 2.2.4: INCOME INEQUALITY DOES NOT TELL THE WHOLE STORY

For all its relevance as an indicator of wealth distribution, income inequality is not sufficient to describe what is actually happening in a community, or how that community might change for better or worse. Focusing on income inequality and overlooking other social, cultural and political indicators of well-being is to see only one side of the picture.

A consensus is emerging among academics and policymakers that inequality is multidimensional and cannot be viewed solely through the prism of income. It is now generally accepted that human beings can have access to a variety of assets, freedoms and opportunities, besides income, on which they can rely not just to survive but also to express their social and other identities. More often than not, these forms of social capital are not reflected in economic surveys, which are more concerned with earned income figures for various groups. Surveys also fail to capture "the hidden economy" of households, such as unpaid labour or in-kind and cash assistance from relatives and friends. The various dimensions of "wealth" are fundamental to Amartya Sen's concept of "entitlements" and the "capabilities" approach to development, which holds that the quality of an individual's life should be measured not by their income, but by the rights and freedoms s/he enjoys.

Sources: Grusky & Kanbur, 2006; Sen, 1999; UNDP, 1990, p. 9.

BOX 2.2.5: A LEGACY OF DEEP DIVIDES: URBAN INEQUALITY IN THE UNITED STATES

New York City has one of the highest degrees of black segregation. ©**Andrew F. Kazmierski/Shutterstock**

For many people in the United States, moving up from the lowest economic ranks to the middle class, and from the middle class to the top income echelons, is becoming increasingly difficult. The richest 1 per cent of households now earns more than 72 times the average income of the poorest fifth of the population, and 23 times that of the middle fifth. In just one year, between 2005 and 2006, the richest 1 per cent of the U.S. population increased

their earnings by US $95,700, while the bottom fifth took home only US $600 more than the previous year, and the middle fifth stagnated, earning only US $300, or 0.6 per cent, more than they had in 2005.

The United States has more cities with a Gini coefficient of 0.50, or higher than any other wealthy country. Gini coefficients based on 2006 data for 247 American cities with populations over 100,000 range from 0.35 to 0.57. Forty cities feature Gini coefficients above 0.50, indicating high income inequality due to poverty and racial segregation, post-industrial economic restructuring and combinations of inner-city decline and suburban sprawl.

In "the other America", poor black families and the chronically unemployed are clustered in ghettos, lacking access to quality education, secure tenure, lucrative employment and political power. Higher inequality often corresponds with greater segregation, especially for black residents. The most unequal city, Atlanta, Georgia, has the third-highest degree of black segregation, followed by New York City, Wash-

ington, D.C, Fort Lauderdale, and Miami (all with Gini coefficients above 0.52).

In Chicago, discriminatory mortgage lending and public housing development from the 1960s onward conspired to isolate many low-income black families in the central city. Lack of affordable housing outside the city centre, coupled with high unemployment and poor education, has further undermined social mobility and economic advancement. In Washington, D.C., the vast majority of black residents live on the eastern side of the metropolitan area, far from the economic prosperity, wealth, job growth, and quality schools now concentrated in the west.

Earning power and income prospects depend on a geography of opportunity, i.e., access to good-quality institutions, decent housing and amenities that foster good health and prosperity. Even where standards of living are high, the marginalization and spatial segregation of specific groups creates cities within a city: distinctly deprived areas that further reinforce unequal opportunities and the distance between abject poverty and affluence.

Sources: Gini data from the U.S. Census Bureau, 2006 American Community Survey; index of dissimilarity data from CensusScope, based on 2000 U.S. Census data
Sources: Beauregard, 2008; CensusScope, n.d.; Katz, 2002; Kneebone & Berube, 2008; Massey & Fischer, 2000; Massey & Fischer, 2003; McCarthy, 1999; OECD, 2008; Schill & Wachter, 1995; Sherman, 2009; Steffel Johnson, 2006; Von Hoffman, 2009

On the other hand, Ethiopia's capital city Addis Ababa also featured a very high Gini coefficient (0.612) in 2003, but only two-thirds of the population had access to piped water and only 44 per cent to adequate sanitation. While these numbers show that near-universal access to services does not necessarily result in lower income inequality, they also demonstrate that measures of income inequality do not necessarily capture those determinants of quality of life that are associated with social indicators like health and well-being.

In some cities, significant income inequality is often closely related to other types of inequalities. With its relatively high consumption Gini coefficient of 0.64 in 2006, Lagos is among the most unequal cities in sub-Saharan Africa. This is reflected in shelter indicators such as living area and sanitation, as well as in high unemployment rates among males. Nearly two-fifths of Lagos residents live in overcrowded housing, and a quarter have no access to adequate sanitation. The city is also unable to provide jobs for its growing population, with 40 per cent of males and 12 per cent of females unemployed in 2006. On the other hand in Mexico, income inequality in Guadalajara is relatively low compared with other Latin American cities, and this situation happens to be matched by healthy shelter and social indicators; residents enjoy near-

universal access to safe water and sanitation, and almost all are literate.

Surprisingly, slum prevalence or "ghettoization" may or may not influence income inequality in any particular city. In some of the most unequal cities in Latin America and the United States, for instance, it is only a relatively small proportion of the population that lives in slums or urban ghettos, and yet inequality remains high. In those cities where poverty and wealth are concentrated in specific areas, income inequality measures may also fail to capture important dimensions of the urban divide. For instance, Simi Valley, California, on the outskirts of Los Angeles, enjoys a relatively low degree of income inequality (with a Gini coefficient of 0.37) because it is a relatively homogenous and wealthy "bedroom community", whose members are isolated from impoverished or less wealthy communities within the city of Los Angeles. Washington, D.C., on the other hand, is significantly more unequal (0.537), which is reflected in the spatial division of the U.S. capital by both wealth and race factors, with its significant, and largely poor, black and Hispanic communities concentrated in certain areas. The same pattern can also be seen in New Orleans, with large pockets of wealth amid populations that suffer from endemic poverty.

BOX 2.2.6: **CORRUPTION FEEDS INCOME INEQUALITY**

Corruption and income inequality deprive communities and the poor not only of material wealth, but also of opportunities and livelihoods. Generally defined as the misuse of public office for private gain, corruption can take the form of "grand corruption", when legislative and executive bodies implement economic policies for the benefit of a small segment of the population; "legislative corruption", when under lobbyists' influence lawmakers favour specific interest groups; and "bureaucratic corruption", when officials seek bribes.

All types of corruption take advantage of structural deficiencies in the political, judicial and economic institutions of developing countries that are already stacked against the poor.

Empirical research into the causal relationship between corruption and income inequality suggests that it would take only a 10 per cent decrease in corruption to increase GDP growth by 2.8 per cent in Africa, 2.6 per cent in Latin America and the Caribbean, and 1.7 per cent in OECD and Asian countries. Africa is where corruption is most detrimental to economic growth, and Latin America where the phenomenon most deeply affects income equality. Researchers infer that a one-standard-deviation decrease in corruption would lower the Gini coefficient of income distribution (on a 0 to 1 scale) by 0.05 point in the OECD area, 0.14 point in Asia, 0.25 point in Africa, and 0.33 point in Latin America.

Corruption has pervasive social and economic consequences, and policymakers' failure to tackle these as part of broader efforts to promote equity and equality only encourages a vicious cycle of interrelated increases in both corruption and income inequality. Corruption stymies economic growth and therefore can affect income distribution, economists have shown; sociologists have found that the reverse is also true: income inequality can increase corruption if the phenomenon is considered as acceptable behaviour in an unequal society.

Corruption makes public spending less efficient, especially in vital welfare and education areas. In Uganda, only 13 per cent of central government spending on some educational programmes reached its destination between 1991 and 1994.

Specific policies, or attempts to strengthen financial and legal monitoring schemes, are not enough to tackle corruption; also required are quick and efficient prosecution of offenders and anti-poverty, redistributive policies. Targeting corruption without addressing its systemic counterpart, inequality, may doom anti-corruption efforts to failure.

Sources: Delavallade, 2006; Gyimah-Brempong, 2002; Gyimah-Brempong, 2006; Lambsdorff, 2006; Subramanian & Chakrabarti, 2003; Svensson, 2005; Uslaner, 2005; You & Khagram, 2005; Weisman, 2006.

END NOTES

1 Mingione & Vicari Haddock, 2008.
2 OECD, 2008. Values for OECD countries refer to national Gini values (urban + rural).
3 OECD, 2008.
4 Some recent studies computed the Gini coefficients in some cities within the country individually, on the basis of which they estimate that the urban rich in the national computations are under-estimated and the urban poor are over-estimated (in other words, the Gini value does not reflect the reality of recent changes of economic distribution in the country). Gustafsson & Nivorzhkina, 2005.
5 African countries with similar Gini coefficients are not included here, since their values are based on consumption.
6 UN-HABITAT, 2008.
7 Variations are minimal. Only in Paraguay and Bolivia is inequality substantially higher in rural areas; it is slightly higher in Honduras, Panama and Ecuador.
8 E-mail communication with Jorge Rodríguez Vignoli, ECLAC, Celade, 28 July, 2009.
9 ESCAP, 2008.
10 Nepal's GDP growth was 2.5 per cent in 2007, whereas it grew at 5.2 per cent between 1990 and 1995. ESCAP, 2008.
11 Asian Development Bank, 2007.
12 Asian Development Bank, 2007.
13 UN-HABITAT data for Malaysia is limited to 1999, and changes in urban Gini coefficients for Cambodia and the Philippines are marginal.
14 The African average has a standard deviation of 0.1140. The average for Latin America is 0.0691, and the average for Asia is 0.0669. The corresponding standard deviations for the Gini averages are 0.0369 for Eastern Europe and 0.0722 for the Commonwealth of Independent States.
15 Data for Chiangmai and Udonthani in Thailand is at the provincial level. It is worth noting, however, that the population of both provinces is approximately 95 per cent urban.
16 The Gini coefficient for Addis Ababa in 2003 was calculated by UN-HABITAT based on its Urban Inequities Survey and estimates. However, other sources indicate a Gini consumption coefficient of 0.48 and 0.45 for 1994 and 2000, respectively.
17 Data for Jordan is relatively old and may not reflect recent increases in income inequalities.
18 Analysis can be distorted by short, cyclical economic fluctuations, or by discrepancies among definitions, methods of data collection, change of components in the computation method, and other problems of comparability of data across two different points in time.
19 Ethiopian Ministry of Finance and Economic Development, 2006; International Monetary Fund, 2004.
20 Awasa, for instance, has become a seat of regional government, which resulted in more professionals moving into the city. In addition, the booming of the coffee trade in the late 1990s may have boosted the economy of the city, contributing to increases in consumption. See Alemayehu Gebremedhin, 2005.
21 Diop, 2008.
22 UN-HABITAT, 2008.
23 Department for International Development (DFID) (UK). (n.d.). Inequality in Middle Income Countries: South Africa Case "Section 2. An overview of inequality, poverty and growth in SA", http://www.sarpn.org.za/documents/d0000671/P686-Gelb_Inequality_in_SA_section2.pdf, downloaded on 17/09/09. n.d.
24 International Policy Center for Inclusive Growth, UNDP, 2009.
25 International Policy Center for Inclusive Growth, UNDP, 2009.
26 Ocampo, 2008.
27 Cárdenas & Bernal, 1999.
28 Cárdenas & Bernal, 1999.
29 E-mail communication with Artemio Abba, Director, Buenos Aires Observatory of Metropolitan Studies, 3 August, 2009.
30 James, Arndt & Simler, 2005.
31 Alemayehu Gebremedhin, 2005.
32 Okojie & Shimeles, 2006.

2.3
The Spatial Divide
Marginalization and its Outcomes

The spatial dimension of inequality: The poverty trap

Quick Facts

1. The urban spatial divide is more than the physical expression of income inequalities among households; it is also a by-product of inefficient land and housing markets.

2. A spatial poverty trap occurs when physical distance to the city centre (and the associated benefits and opportunities) turns into social distance.

3. The poverty trap involves a combination of six factors: poor job opportunities, living conditions and social interactions; and high rates of gender disparities, social exclusion and criminality.

4. Schemes and policies to reduce social disparities have been reported in only one-third of the African, Asian and Latin American countries under review.

5. Inequality in all its forms is detrimental to any society, and when it becomes excessive inequality poses a danger to social stability and sustained economic growth.

Policy Points

1. Absence of policy coordination between or within national and local government constrains cities' ability to meet the requirements of urban development and to deploy strategies that mitigate spatial inequality.

2. Social policies should not be devised exclusively as nationwide programmes if they are effectively to address the determinants of spatial inequality in cities and, more generally, the urban divide.

3. More gender-specific schemes, like maternity and childcare benefits, vocational training, protecting women's rights at the workplace, and micro-credit are required if women are to be lifted out of the spatial poverty trap.

Inequalities in cities are not only about income and consumption expenditures; they also reflect entrenched patterns of urban development and ownership of physical space. Whereas cities in the developed world tend to facilitate social and economic mixing by encouraging diverse land uses, providing various types of housing (social, low-income, middle class), and developing transportation systems that facilitate urban mobility, numerous cities of the South are characterized by stark segregation between rich and poor. Socioeconomic clustering in cities of the developing world is a consequence of limited service and transportation infrastructure, coupled with lack of housing choice. The poor, unable to afford land or shelter in the limited areas of the city that are fully serviced, have access only to the least desirable and most densely developed spaces. The rich, on the other hand, can invest in private housing on secluded properties, often paying for their own water systems, electricity generators and road maintenance.

Income inequality effectively restricts available options when it comes to choosing the best residential location based on factors such as proximity to jobs, schools and institutions; neighborhood preferences and housing types; access to credit opportunities and economic incentives; and other factors. While income inequalities are a main dividing factor between different social areas, the spatial inequalities visible in so many cities are also an outgrowth of broader-ranging processes of urban development, governance and institutionalized exclusion of specific groups.

As discussed in Chapter 1.3, the separation between rich and poor takes many forms in the cities of the developing world. In some, particularly in sub-Saharan Africa, large numbers of slum households are clustered in specific areas that dominate the cityscape, and can represent as much as 80 per cent of all urban neighbourhoods. This is the case, for instance, in Bangui, Central Africa Republic; N'Djamena, Chad; Niamey, Niger; and the cities of Addis Ababa, Maputo and Luanda. In other cities, such as Kathmandu, Almaty, Managua, Guatemala City and Cotonou, to name just a few, poor neighborhoods hosting a mix of slum and non-slum households are clearly visible at the periphery of the city, in the decaying urban centres, or in scattered "slum islands" in the interstices of formal, fully serviced settlements. The spatial divide in such cities constitutes more than the physical expression of income inequalities among households; it is also a by-product of the inefficient land and housing markets that force non-poor and middle-income households to reside in slum areas for lack of better alternatives.

When slum areas are physically isolated and disconnected from the main urban fabric, residents become cut off from the city, often enduring longer commuting times and higher transportation costs than they would if their neighbourhoods were more integrated into city systems. Residents of such settlements find themselves facing problems related not only to low incomes or shelter deprivations, but also to the social distance between themselves and those who have greater access to the opportunities and amenities of the city. Combined, the physical and social distance between poor and rich neighbourhoods represents a *spatial poverty trap* marked by six distinct challenges:

Severe job restrictions. Opportunities for work around slum settlements in remote areas may be restricted, leaving residents vulnerable to unemployment. For example, in Mexico, 20 per cent of workers spend more than three hours commuting to and from work every day. Long-distance commuting is exacerbated by inefficient and costly public transport systems, which add to the fragmentation of the urban economy and further divide the urban space, to the detriment of slum dwellers.

Gender disparities. Evidence shows that women from isolated slum areas are effectively forced to work closer to home than men because of the variety of risks they may face, such as exposure to crime and difficulty in accessing transport. Women often also need to be closer to home than men to care for family members and carry out household responsibilities. In the Sanjay slum in Delhi, for instance, 75 per cent of men have been found to work within 12 kilometres of their homes, whereas 75 per cent of women worked within a radius of only 5 kilometres of home, showing how their employment opportunities are restricted.

Worsening living conditions. Spatial mismatches between job location and place of residence can leave more remote slum-dwellers little alternative but to spend the night in public spaces, squat in temporary units devoid of adequate services, or share houses in overcrowded conditions. In Rio de Janeiro, some workers sleep on beaches during the week, saving commuting time as well as transportation costs that

▲
In Delhi, India, 75 per cent of men have been found to work within 12 kilometres of their homes, whereas 75 per cent of women worked within a radius of only 5 kilometres.
©**Paul Prescott/Shutterstock**

consume at least 20 per cent of their wages. Similarly in Dhaka and Mumbai, slum-dwelling workers are often found sleeping on the pavement, travelling home only for weekends and holidays.

Social exclusion and marginalization. In neighbourhoods with poor connections to the city, permanent access to health and education facilities is difficult, not only on account of physical accessibility, but also because of the costs and time involved in transportation. In Mumbai, for instance, 50 per cent of slums have no access to primary schools, a percentage that is even higher in the informal areas on the outskirts of the city. In Chittagong, the number of kindergarten schools for relatively well-to-do households is on the increase, while many children in distant slums have almost no access to education.

Lack of social interaction. Physical segregation in terms of distance, time and costs reduces the opportunities for members of different income groups to interact. As a result, social capital in its various forms is built only among the poor, or based on other affinities such as ethnicity. In such conditions, the positive effects of social capital are neutralized, because interaction among unemployed people for instance, does not increase employment opportunities. In those distant and isolated neighbourhoods that effectively function as *spatial poverty traps,* it is more likely that social interaction can eventually encourage crime, as a strong sense of rejection can lead to anti-social behaviour.

High incidence of crime. When confined to remote locations, slum dwellers are also penalized by reduced access to the various opportunities the city has to offer. Long-distance commuting in dark, underserved areas increases the risk of crime. The poor are more defenceless than other social groups and often rank among the prime victims of urban crime. However, they also rank among the perpetrators. In São Paulo, for instance, the number of homicides in some isolated neighbourhoods has been reported to be more than five times as high as in the safest districts.

The survey conducted in 2009 by UN-HABITAT in 27 selected cities in Africa, Asia and Latin America points to some of the fundamental policy roots of spatial inequality. *(See Chapter 2.1 for the survey methodology.)* In the absence of policy coordination between national, local or other tiers of government, cities are clearly constrained in their ability to meet the requirements of regional development and to deploy strategies that would mitigate spatial inequality. The survey shows that in cities in Latin America, both national and local authorities were involved in urban policy initiatives, while in Asia and Africa, national policies were predominant without commensurate regional or local implementation at the city level.

Another important factor behind policy dysfunction is that social policies are often formulated as national programmes, with little if any consideration for local conditions or geographical scope, in the process overlooking regional asymmetries and specific needs. When determined solely at national level, social policies ignore the specific spatial inequalities that must be addressed in the congested and highly competitive urban and regional environments. Regarding social disparities, only fewer than 35 per cent of all respondents to the UN-HABITAT questionnaire reported that schemes were in place to reduce them in African, Asian and Latin American cities. Respondents also reported that such urban public services or goods as waste collection, recreation facilities, public parks and free spaces were largely unavailable in all three regions. Inter-regional comparisons show that Latin America fares significantly better than the other two regions, although the level remains quite low.

On gender equality, UN-HABITAT survey returns suggest that apart from setting minimum percentages for female employees in the public and private sectors, all other gender-specific schemes (maternity and childcare benefits, provision of specific skills and vocational training, protecting women's rights at the workplace, micro-credit facilities) are largely lacking in all three regions, with fewer than 25 per cent of respondents reporting that any of these were in place, particularly in remote and isolated slum settlements. Moreover, the incidence of policy initiatives in support of informal sector employment – either through job enhancement or legalization of certain informal sector activities – was, again, found to be very low in all three regions.

The central role played by economic inclusiveness may be best understood from a contrarian perspective: economic exclusion automatically tends to drive individuals out of the social, political and cultural spheres, resulting in a "capabilities" constraint.[1] In this process, the poor are made poorer by the other forms of marginalization they are subjected to, and are excluded from those opportunities that help create capabilities of any kind in the first place. As the survey findings for Bogotá demonstrate, poverty acts as a major hindrance to any effective "right to the city".

The interrelationships between the economic and other three dimensions of inclusiveness (or otherwise) are such that, over time, social, political and cultural exclusion tend to undermine the very possibility of equal economic opportunities. Countries and cities are subject to changing historical factors that make their development path-dependent, and they are challenged by internal factors that only add to divisiveness. These include divisions based on racial, ethnic, religious and other political allegiance factors. Despite efforts to provide an equal basis for all individuals in society in the three regions (through the national constitution, affirmative action laws and other such regulatory measures), enforcement of these rights seems to be weak and tends to reinforce various forms of exclusion over time. UN-HABITAT survey findings clearly show this to be the case. Over the past two to three decades, public authorities in the three regions under review have largely failed to deploy the sustainable policies required to reduce the urban divide on a scale commensurate with their respective urban growth rates. Even more importantly, survey returns on average point to a clear lack of coordination between (in most cases) national policies and (in some instances) the local level as well as to poor concerted action to address the spatial divide which, in many cases, turns into a poverty trap.

BOX 2.3.1: WOMEN'S "INEQUALITY SPACES"

▲ Luanda, Angola. Residents of Boa Vista slum in Luanda often walk several kilometers to collect water. ©**Jaspreet Kindra/IRIN**

Most household surveys fail to capture any differences in access to services, or control over resources, among members of the same household. This comes in stark disregard of the fact that intra-household inequalities are increasingly recognized as detrimental to the social and economic advancement of women.

UNIFEM's *Progress of the World's Women 2008/9* report notes that owing to women's limited decision-making power within the household, their relationship to the public sphere or to markets is often mediated by men. This means that women may not be in a position to make important decisions about what services the household should prioritize, as they are often under pressure to favour the needs of males over those of others in the family. Women's lack of agency in the household has severe consequences with regard to their access to services such as health care and education.

Demographic and Health Surveys conducted between 1999 and 2005 showed that more than half of married women in sub-Saharan Africa and South Asia had no say over decisions regarding their own health care. In both regions, women also wielded little decision-making power over daily household purchases. Moreover, more than 40 per cent of married women in both sub-Saharan Africa and South Asia reported that they were not allowed to visit relatives when they

chose. The notion that women "rule the roost" was evidently not borne out by DHS statistics, which further showed that one in five women in sub-Saharan Africa did not even have the final say over what food to cook.

Stark differences have been noted, however, between married women in South Asia and others in the eastern part of the continent. Married women in East Asia are among the most emancipated in the developing world. Surveys show that large numbers in this region not only make final decisions regarding their own health care, but are almost completely in charge of what to purchase for the household and what to cook for dinner. While this may reflect gender-based roles in which women are expected to carry out domestic chores, women in this region also exercise control over other aspects of their lives. Unlike their sisters in South Asian countries such as India, Afghanistan and Pakistan, more than 90 per cent of women in this region do not need their spouses' permission to visit relatives.

At a much more fundamental level, lack of a voice when deciding which services to prioritize has serious consequences. For instance, in most societies, women are in charge of domestic chores, such as washing, cleaning and cooking. When access to water is limited or non-existent, it is for women to ensure that their families have enough water for drinking and bathing. Retriev-

ing water can involve walking long distances for long stretches of time. Recent research on sub-Saharan Africa suggests that women spend some 40 billion hours a year collecting water – the equivalent of a year's worth of labour by the entire workforce in France. Capital expenditure on access to water provision for households would release substantial amounts of women's time on a day-to-day basis, opening up fresh opportunities, including self-improvement. Similarly, when women have little say if any in their own health care, they are in no position to make important decisions about the number of children they should have or whether or not to use contraception. In extreme cases, it may also mean that they are likely not to get treatment when they need it, and are therefore vulnerable to debilitating injuries and early death. Similarly, women's lack of decision-making powers in other areas concerning the household, including children's opportunities, hardly puts them in a good position to make sure their children go to school or receive adequate nutrition.

Since any country's development is intimately linked to how well or badly its female population is faring, it is clear that women's low status within the household is severely hampering progress in South Asia and sub-Saharan Africa – the two regions that have consistently been rated by the United Nations as the world's poorest with the worst health, education and shelter indicators.

Source: UNIFEM, 2008.

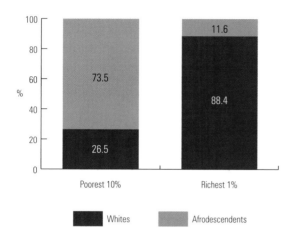

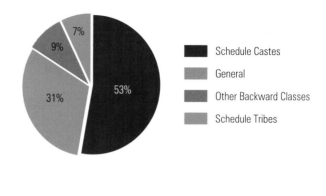

Excluding the rural population of the states of RO, AC, AM, RR, PA and AP.
Source: IBGE, National Sample Household Survey.

Source: National Institute of Urban Affairs, 2008, Urban Poverty Reduction Strategy in Selected Cities of India.

The intangible dimensions of spatial inequality

Spatial inequality reaches beyond physical space constraints to include "inequality space". This specific component has a different effect across social categories such as women and children, ethnic groups and races, the elderly and the disabled. On the whole, these groups have been largely overlooked in policy discourses on inequality, and not just in urban contexts. For example, until recently, most household surveys failed to capture the inequalities women have to face up to within the household. Although the surveys collected data on gender-disaggregated indicators, such as literacy among boys compared with girls, they did not adequately reflect girls' or women's lack of access to other resources and opportunities. Updated data in Demographic and Health Surveys shows that intra-household inequalities often take the form of a lack of decision-making power among women in the household.[2] A large proportion of women in South Asia and sub-Saharan Africa, for instance, have no final say in decisions regarding their own health. (See Box 2.3.1.)

Household surveys often fail to capture other aspects of "voicelessness" in women's conditions, such as whom to marry and when, especially where arranged marriages are the norm. While *gender* inequality is generally understood as a central dimension of general inequality, social scientists have been struggling to integrate these dimensions into mainstream data collection methodologies, partly because of the difficulties inherent in collecting and measuring such data. Similarly, income inequality measures often fail to reflect racial and ethnic differences in access to resources. Research in India, Indonesia, Mexico and Tanzania shows that although in general the poor systematically receive lower quality health care than the rich, the situation is often worse for ethnic minorities. In Mexico, for instance, indigenous groups were shown to receive worse health care from both public and private providers, regardless

of income.[3] The proportion of people living in extreme poverty in Brazil – one of the world's most unequal countries with a Gini coefficient of 0.566 – is relatively low (4.2 per cent) compared with other middle-income emerging economies; still, poverty incidence remains linked to skin colour and area of residence. In 2005, poverty levels were three times higher in rural areas than in cities, and were particularly severe among Afro-descendents. Brazil's 2007 National Monitoring Report indicates that blacks represented 73.5 per cent of the poorest 10 per cent of the population, although they contributed less than 8 per cent of the population.

Still in Brazil, many black and indigenous children remain out of primary school, and 7.5 million people still live in extreme poverty.[4] In some cities, socially marginalized groups are heavily concentrated in slums, and therefore suffer most from lack of access to decent shelter and opportunities; this is especially the case when their neighbourhoods are located far away from the city, and the long commutes penalize them in terms of cost and time. In the Indian city of Jaipur, for instance, underprivileged ("scheduled") castes and tribes[5] contribute 61 per cent of the slum population, although they represent only a combined 16.1 per cent of the total city population.[6]

Results of the 2009 UN-HABITAT survey show that in all the 27 selected cities in the three regions under review, those places where the urban poor and slum dwellers earn a living are systematically excluded from mainstream economic, social, cultural and political programmes and initiatives. When asked to rank the most vulnerable groups in their respective cities for the purposes of the UN-HABITAT survey, experts reckoned that along with the disabled and the elderly, slum dwellers and the urban poor were the most vulnerable in terms of exclusion. The economic marginalization of the urban poor was further evidenced by the reported length of their daily commutes: an average one to two hours one way, amounting to nearly four hours a day.

FIGURE 2.3.3: **PROPORTION (%) OF MARRIED WOMEN WITH NO SAY OVER HOUSEHOLD DECISIONS**

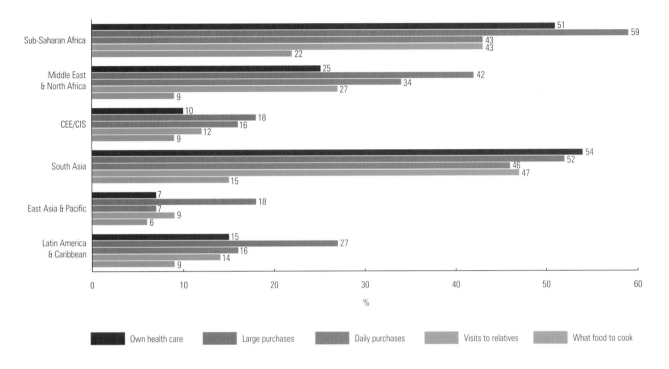

Own health care   Large purchases   Daily purchases   Visits to relatives   What food to cook

Source: DHS Database.

▲
A large proportion of women in sub-Saharan Africa have no final say in decisions regarding their own health or what to cook for dinner. ©**Manoocher Deghati/IRIN**

FIGURE 2.3.4: **INEQUALITY AND INCIDENCE OF POVERTY RELATIVE TO NATIONAL POVERTY LINE**

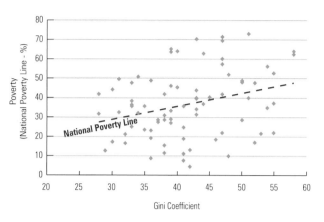

Sources: Poverty line between 1988-2002 available in World Development Indicators (World Bank, 2005); Gini coefficient: latest available between 1998-2007 in World Development Indicators (World Bank, 2007).

FIGURE 2.3.5: **AVERAGE ANNUAL GROWTH RATE IN PER CAPITA INCOME AND POVERTY REDUCTIONS BY REGION 1980s, 1990s, 2000s**

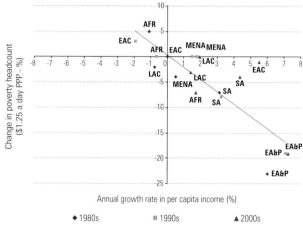

AFR: *Sub-Saharan Africa*
EAP: *East Asia & Pacific*
MENA: *Middle East & North Africa*

EAC: *Europe & Central Asia*
LAC: *Latin America & Caribbean*
SA: *South Asia*

Source: Periods: 1981-1990; 1990-1999; 1999-2005; World Development Indicators (World Bank, 2007).

FIGURE 2.3.6: **SOCIAL, ECONOMIC, POLITICAL AND CULTURAL INCLUSIVENESS OF SELECTED AFRICAN CITIES**

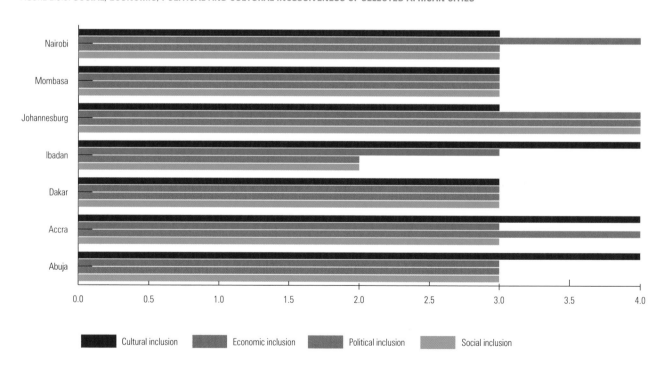

Source: UN-HABITAT survey on city inclusiveness, 2009.

How other deprivations reinforce the spatial divide

A significant body of literature on income distribution provides evidence that inequalities are detrimental to any society in terms of social stability and economic inefficiency. High-income groups in feudal or monopolistic economies may, for instance, protect themselves from free competition by buying political influence, in the process distorting markets and making democratic governance institutions less accountable. Highly unequal societies are also associated with reduced social mobility.

Whatever the various combinations of the six factors behind the poverty traps outlined above, they militate in favour of a shift in emphasis – one from inequalities in *outcomes* to inequalities in *opportunities*. This shift is critical to any proper understanding not just of *equality outcomes* in any given city, but also, and more importantly, of the *root causes of the urban divide*. In turn, shifting the emphasis from outcomes to opportunities enhances the importance of inequality on both normative and instrumental grounds. On normative grounds, inequalities of opportunity are deemed unethical from the point of view of social justice, as they are determined by morally irrelevant circumstances. On instrumental grounds, inequalities of opportunity are deemed important from an efficiency perspective, as they can have negative repercussions on economic performance.[7]

The potential negative impact of unequal opportunities is also important with regard to poverty reduction, particularly in developing countries. Whatever the trend in economic growth, the more unequal the distribution of income and the less the poor stand to benefit, in accounting terms.[8] Inequality might also be linked to persistent poverty even in growth scenarios: evidence shows that greater land-related and educational inequality reduces income growth for the poorest quintile about twice as much as that of all quintiles.[9] These dynamics might highlight the positive relationship between poverty and inequality across countries, as shown in Figure 2.3.4. Specifically, countries with greater income inequality (as measured by the Gini coefficient) tend to feature higher incidences of poverty relative to respective national poverty lines.[10]

To the extent that inequality can slow down growth as it introduces inefficiencies in the allocation of resources, it can also have an indirect effect on poverty reduction. As shown in Figure 2.3.5, poverty reduction in all regions is closely associated with average annual growth in per capita income.[11] The most remarkable example is that of East Asia, where high growth over the past three decades (thanks to pro-poor policies) has brought about substantial reductions in poverty, reducing the percentage of the population living on US $1.25 or less from 78 per cent in 1981 to 17 per cent in 2005. Conversely, those regions with stagnant or weak economic growth and without clear pro-poor policies have failed to achieve significant reductions in poverty: in sub-Saharan African countries, the percentage of the population living on US $1.25 a day has remained almost constant at around 50 per cent over the past three decades.[12]

Far from being yet another significant, specific phenomenon, inequality should clearly become a central focus of development policies. Inequality is as much about social justice, political freedom and cultural expression as it is about economic opportunities, which, in turn, determine income, wealth and social standing. Failure to account for the social, political, cultural and economic dimensions of exclusion and inequality results in a distribution of opportunities that is predetermined by unfair criteria, and only manages to entrench exclusion in a systematic way, to the detriment of urban growth.

Findings from the 2009 UN-HABITAT survey point to a strong correlation in the three regions between economic exclusiveness on the one hand, and social, cultural and political equality on the other. Figure 2.3.6 illustrates the four aspects of inclusiveness along a spectrum ranging from "not inclusive at all" (0 on the X-axis) to "highly inclusive" (4 on the X-axis). While, as expected, no city was found to be fully inclusive (rating 5), none was totally exclusive either (rating 1). Most were concentrated between ratings of 2 (low inclusiveness) and 4 (high inclusiveness). As one would expect, a large number of the cities were given a rating of 3 (denoting partial inclusiveness) for most or all four dimensions of inclusiveness. It must be stressed here that the specific ratings for Chittagong, New Delhi, Abuja, Dakar, Mombasa, Oruro and Port-au-Prince indicate that the four dimensions are inter-related. Therefore, beyond a confirmation of the central role of economic inclusiveness, this goes to show its interrelations with other forms of equality – and the need for cities to provide opportunities for all types of inclusiveness.

END NOTES

1   Sen, 1999.
2   UNIFEM. (2008). Who answers to women? Progress of the world's women 2008/9. New York.
3   Barber, Bertiozzio & Gertler, 2005.
4   Government of Brazil, Institute for Applied Economic Research, 2007.
5   Under the Indian Constitution, Schedule Castes and Schedule Tribes are categorized as disadvantaged or marginalized groups. Each state also prepares its own list of castes and tribes that could be considered "backward" by their respective legislatures, thereby making them eligible for affirmative action programmes.
6   National Institute of Urban Affairs (India), 2008, information provided by Society of Development Studies to UN-HABITAT, as part of Jaipur City Background Report, 2009.
7   Ferreira, F. and Walton, M. (2006).
8   Ravallion, 1997.
9   Birdsall & Londoño, 1997.
10 R2 = 0.087; y = 0.6653x + 9.1114; t-Stat = 2.67 (significant). Regression results are for a group of 77 countries, primarily developing countries since the WID dataset does not include poverty data for developed countries.
11 R2 = 0.8855; y = 0.5799 -2.4493x; t-Stat = -5.57 (significant).
12 *World Development Indicators*, World Bank, 2007.

© Manoocher Deghati/IRIN

2.4
The Opportunity Divide
When the "Urban Advantage" eludes the poor

Quick Facts

1. Globalization can stimulate economic growth in cities and, with proper redistributive policies, help alleviate poverty. However, it can also exacerbate the urban divide.

2. About 85 per cent of all new employment opportunities around the world occur in the informal economy.

3. Young people in slums are more likely to work in the informal sector than their non-slum peers. Despite some advantages, informal employment ends up trapping slum-dwelling and other low-income young people in perpetual poverty.

4. Among people living in poverty in the developing world, employment opportunities, whether formal or informal, are skewed in favour of young men, who are twice as likely to find gainful employment as young women.

Policy Points

1. The particular ways cities are planned, designed and built says much about what is valued there, and the control of planning processes can help or hinder the development of opportunities for all.

2. "World class city" strategies are a legitimate way of taking advantage of globalization, but they should include a sustainable, inclusive dimension that also benefits the poor.

3. Large-scale, labour-intensive infrastructure and urban improvement works could provide gainful employment to the poor while granting them their fair share in the "urban advantage". These labour-intensive programmes are to be combined with vocational training and skill development activities.

4. Continued emphasis on expanding opportunities for girls and young women will be an essential requirement if the Millennium Development Goals are to be met in cities.

Weak institutions

In every country in the world, access to the "urban advantage" and distribution of the related benefits in terms of opportunities, employment, services, etc., is determined by various organizations and institutions – including, crucially, the formal land and labour markets as well as public utilities. The problem in developing countries is that most of these institutions are weak or dysfunctional, exposing them to undue influence from, or capture by, vested domestic or foreign interests. In some cities, necessary public institutions are lacking altogether, in which case essentially private vested interests fill the void and act as substitutes for institutions that would otherwise prioritize the interests of society at large. In both situations, the markets for land, basic services and labour are skewed in favour of private interests, enabling these to claim more than their fair share of the benefits of the "urban advantage". In this process, young slum dwellers, particularly women, are deprived of the formal, secure livelihoods that could lift them up and out of the dire socioeconomic outcomes associated with the informal, insecure conditions in which they are forced to live.

Inequitable and divisive land and planning policies

Institutional capture by interest group factions or other coalitions in the developing world results in the apportionment to only a select few of opportunities that should be shared by all. The particular ways cities are planned, designed and built says much about what is valued there, and the control of planning processes can help or hinder the development of opportunities for all. While urban planning has the potential to promote urban harmony and bridge the urban divide through an equitable distribution of city amenities, it has too often been used as an instrument of exclusion. Indeed, powerful members of society have used "master planning" to capture land and provide infrastructure, manipulating land use patterns in favour of the gentrification of entire areas in cities. In the process, massive displacement has taken place to make room for highways, skyscrapers, luxury compounds or shopping malls, to the detriment of the habitats and livelihoods of the poor. This is a worldwide phenomenon. The bulldozing of the vibrant slums of Maroko, Lagos, has led to the displacement of 300,000 residents; the government-led destruction of Harare and Bulawayo (known as "Operation *Murambatsvina*", or "drive out trash") has been associated with large numbers of arrests and killings, as well as ransacking and the dislocation of more than 700,000 people; and in Shanghai, deliberate gentrification of neighbourhoods between 1991 and 1997 led to the relocation of 1.5 million people, the same number as those displaced by Rangoon's tourism-oriented makeover.

On top of displacing the poor, these self-serving planning policies also fail to provide adequate low-cost housing alternatives, making them all the more inequitable. Such government- and market-induced actions force millions to live in unsuitable, insecure conditions, often characterized by a lack of basic services and serious health threats. Public authorities further exacerbate the housing crisis through failures on four major counts: (1) lack of land titles and other forms of secure tenure; (2) cutbacks in funds for social housing; (3) lack of land reserves earmarked for low-income housing; and (4) inability to intervene in the market to control land and property speculation. Furthermore, urban renewal and redevelopment efforts sometimes result in the demolition of homes and relocation of thousands to areas which, being far removed from livelihood opportunities, result in further impoverishment for those already on low incomes. Ironically, the very "renewal" that often comes associated with goals as "cities without slums" can contribute to the urban divide, with all sorts of inequalities in both opportunities and outcomes. In many cities around the world, renewal and redevelopment have caused a most visible burgeoning of slums and inadequately serviced informal settlements,

▲
In Dubai, many workers live in precarious conditions, and are subject to extensive working hours and heavy social control. ©**Paul Keller. This file is licensed under the Creative Commons Attribution 2.0 License**

including pockets of severe poverty. Such dispossession and housing distress also fuel the rise in homelessness as entire families find themselves forced to live on the streets for lack of better alternatives. These conditions deny poor people the benefits of the urban advantage and have serious implications particularly for women's safety, health and access to education and employment opportunities.

An especially divisive aspect of urbanization has been the recent rapid expansion of gated communities and other protected enclaves of wealth. As more and more tracts of land and civic services are monopolized by those with the most resources, urban amenities are systematically denied to residents with lower incomes. In Shanghai, for example, the advent of gated communities has given the better-off an opportunity to set up what are seen as "civilized" communities away from the perceived "uncivilized" and much-stigmatized underclass of rural immigrants.[1] In São Paulo, too, gated communities have increasingly given the upper class an opportunity to withdraw into their own enclaves, inevitably creating a contrast between the safe and familiar *inside* and a "threatening" and "unknown" *outside*.[2] This trend is particularly evident in Dubai, a *de facto* if overstretched gated community rooted in commercial interests, which was deliberately built as a "global city" in a bid to attract upper-class investors and residents from all over the world. Behind the facade of luxury, though, lies a dire day-to-day reality for thousands of Filipino, Indian and Pakistani immigrant workers who are barred from local citizenship (and related rights), housed in camps on the periphery in extremely precarious conditions, and subject to extensive working hours as well as tight and heavy social control.

On top of spatial segregation, gated communities and protected enclaves of wealth also result in social and economic segregation, and even outright social exclusion. In South Africa, for example, the persistence and even expansion of gated communities is seen as the continuation of "*apartheid geography*", which continues to separate the rich and poor from each other, creating an environment of exclusion that militates against the much-lauded post-apartheid goals of social mixing, integration and inclusion.[3] Exclusive developments create a barrier to interaction among people of different ethic groups, races, religions, cultures, and classes, inhibiting the construction of social networks that allow for social mobility and economic development.[4] It also happens frequently that gated communities interfere with efficient urban management and civic functions by limiting access to high-quality schools, health-care centres, libraries, parks and other amenities. In some cases – in Johannesburg and Pretoria, for instance – public facilities located in the vicinity of gated developments have also been enclosed, forcing non-residents to negotiate controlled access points in order to benefit from those collective services as part of their daily routines. Moreover, public transport to enclosed, exclusive communities may be limited or unavailable; this is all the more deplorable as businesses within these communities frequently rely upon low-wage workers who live elsewhere, and therefore force them to find alternative means of transport if any.

"Global" vs. local urban advantage

As reflected in the limited resources available for good schooling, health and other facilities, unequal opportunities create "minorities in the marketplace", whose individual members are automatically excluded from a wide range of the outcomes associated with economic growth and globalization – including demand for a skilled and healthy labour force. Moreover, markets are not as transparent as one would assume and benefits do not trickle down in any automatic way, if at all. In most cases, government intervention is required if opportunities and benefits are to be fairly apportioned across the population. In many cities of the developing world, globalization imposes an unfair pattern of dispensation, whereby those already well placed – such as government officials and the political and economic elites – benefit the most.

Privatization of basic services

Basic services make a significant contribution to the "urban advantage", and together with employment feature high among the aspirations of those who move to cities in search of a brighter future. Economic liberalization has added further momentum to an ongoing trend toward privatization of basic utilities, including water, electricity and sanitation. In developing countries, private interests have often filled the gap left by public authorities and their inability to provide affordable access to such basic commodities as water, often putting them out of financial reach of the most vulnerable and marginalized segments of society. Privatization of basic services (including through public-private partnerships) is questionable when it fails properly to consider specific criteria for access by the poor (such as preferential rates or subsidies). Globalization can stimulate economic growth in cities and, with proper redistributive policies, help alleviate poverty; however, globalization can also exacerbate the urban divide. Those at the bottom of the economic scale may actually end up poorer, because while their incomes may not have decreased, the gap between them and the rich has widened at the same time as prices of basic services and facilities are becoming more expensive with privatization. As stressed in Chapter 2.5, environmental equity is an essential determinant of health and mortality, especially for the urban poor. This is why access to basic services like water and sanitation plays a crucial role in poverty reduction and the improvement in slum-dwellers' living conditions, as mandated under the Millennium Development Goals.

From a human rights perspective, critical evaluations of the recent privatization of basic services have drawn three major lessons:

1. By its very nature, privatization is increasingly forcing public authorities (both central and local) to become more profit-oriented in the provision of essential services. Among developing nations, where a significant proportion of the population lives in poverty, many segments of society are in no position to guarantee sufficient or adequate rates of return to the shareholders of the private companies now providing basic services. Therefore, unless the rates charged by those utilities are subsidized in some way or another, already underprivileged people will likely be forced to forego basic services altogether.

2. Private corporate entities place strong emphasis on profit generation and cost recovery, which often has the effect of fragmenting service scope and delivery. If no potential or actual user can pay the full price for the new services, the project may become financially unsustainable.

3. Private operators are accountable to investors rather than to the communities they serve. Of particular concern are the growing incidences of unethical practices by private suppliers and other institutions that aggressively push for increased privatization. The need to strengthen participatory monitoring mechanisms could not be more acute, since privatization is extremely difficult to reverse once effective.[5]

Displacing the urban poor to create "world-class" cities

In the developing world, global economic forces have led to fierce competition among conurbations to become "world-class" cities, namely, cities that generate high rates of profitability through provision of high-quality international financial, professional and business services. Major cities are jockeying for "world-class" status at the same time that the demonstrated effects of global economic flows and international policy constraints appear to be rather mixed. Global economic investment creates new and unprecedented sources of wealth, offering the promise of reduced poverty and broader access to basic services; however, the fact remains that, within cities, extreme poverty persists in a significant way. The raw numbers of people enjoying better, more secure conditions, with access to potable water, improved sanitation and sustainable livelihoods have increased as a result of economic prosperity and redistributive policies; but some of the policy prescriptions that have been imposed on developing country governments to promote their integration into global economic flows are not necessarily oriented to redistribution. Instead, they tend to restrict government involvement in the provision of adequate resources and services that are often of critical importance to large majorities of their populations. Economic liberalization is one of the factors behind the continuing deterioration in the education, health, housing and related services on which a majority of the urban poor depend.

Against this background of persistent inequality, aspiring "world-class" cities take advantage of the improvements in global connectivity that have facilitated a dramatic expansion in cross-border networks and flows of goods, services and finance.[6] Some new world-class cities are emerging – or are scheduled to emerge – in the developing world in such specific areas as science, technology, financial management, and knowledge. These cities often find themselves at the core of new mega-regions, city-regions or urban corridors, attracting both capital expenditure and workers (see Chapter 1.1). As

The "Kuala Lumpur City Plan 2020" prioritizes not just economic prosperity and environmental quality, but also social equity. ©**Perfect Illusion/Shutterstock**

part of broader growth and development strategies, aiming for world-class status makes sense for cities: such efforts demonstrate entrepreneurial capacity, creativity, ambition and a political determination to enhance a city's potential. However, problems consistently arise when ambitious projects and policies are deployed at the expense or even to the detriment of the poor, without authentically engaging them in decisions that affect their lives.

This report argues that short of a sustainable vision, there can be no inclusive cities. A sustainable vision, almost by definition, combines optimism, ambition and innovation, but it must also be realistic and holistic, encompassing all segments of the city population. Some of the grand plans for "world-class" cities are exclusionary, tending to overlook poor and marginalized populations from the design stage through the final outcome. In other cases, though, planning has taken into account the whole urban population from inception, deliberately ushering in a more equitable, spatially integrated city. For instance, the "Kuala Lumpur City Plan 2020" prioritizes not just economic prosperity and environmental quality, but also social equity. The plan is shaped by social concerns and aims to make the city more inclusive.[7] Likewise, the "Joburg 2030 Vision" scheme that was first developed in 2001 has since been revisited, with the "Growth and Development Strategy 2006 ("Joburg GDS"), to integrate some dimensions of social and economic inclusiveness that had been overlooked early on. As it stands now, the Joburg GDS stresses the need for more extensive opportunities for all in the economic sector, in a bid to address any remaining inequalities that have been identified. The new city vision clearly states that "…the benefits of balanced economic growth will be shared in a way that enables all residents to gain access to the ladders of prosperity, and where the poor, vulnerable and excluded will be supported out of poverty to realize upward social mobility…"[8]

Laws and administrative policies

The persistence of discriminatory legislation, such as anti-vagrancy and anti-beggary laws, combines with other methods – interpretation of criminal law, anti-squatting laws, misuse of anti-terrorist laws, new surveillance strategies and "zero-tolerance" policies – to add to the marginalization of vulnerable groups, such as the homeless, and even openly turn them into declared targets. For example, India's Bombay Prevention of Beggary Act 1959 is routinely used to round up the homeless, even when they are gainfully employed. For municipal authorities, the problem also has to do with budget constraints and choices. In Buenos Aires, the Municipal Housing Institute had to cut its budgetary allocation by nearly four from 519 to 120 million pesos (US $137 to 32 million) in 2009; concomitantly, over the past five years, the city's municipal security (i.e., police) budget has undergone a tenfold increase.[9]

Today, various urban areas in developing countries suffer from unemployment rates that are similar to those experienced in the cities that were most severely affected by the Great Depression in the United States of America.[10] The only difference is that in the developing world, the prospects for cities to solve the unemployment issues they face in the short or medium terms are poor, making these problems chronic. For instance, Johannesburg reported unemployment rates of 33 per cent in 2005 and 30 per cent in 2007,[11] which are higher than those in Chicago when the city bore the brunt of the depression in the 1930s. Local and national governments together can design a number of programmes and schemes to open up opportunities for all. This can include cash transfers, support aid programmes and targeted social interventions or specific support to the labour market in order to generate jobs. In this section, we refer more specifically to employment creation, as opposed to the other redistribution alternatives that are addressed in Chapter 3.3 of this Report.

▲
Dhaka, Bangladesh. The few urban poor who find employment often work in hazardous environments. ©**Manoocher Deghati/IRIN**

Employment: A mis-shared urban advantage

In the dreams of all those who move there, cities foster the healthy development of children and young people, providing easier access to education, health care and employment than is available in rural areas. As they soon find out, though, not all who grow up in cities benefit from this other major component of the "urban advantage", because no city offers all children and young people a single, undivided urban condition.[12] Cities can generate and intensify the kind of social exclusion that denies most of the up-and-coming generation and other marginalized groups the benefits of urban life, particularly against a contrasted background of unprecedented urban growth and increasing poverty and inequality. Indeed, these two opposite trends can be found to coexist within the confines of a single city.

Developing and developed countries alike face an employment crisis, but the causes are different. While in developed countries, the scarcity of jobs is a consequence of the recent financial and economic crunch, in the developing world unemployment is endemic and the global financial crisis is only making it even worse. In most developing countries, the working-age population is growing much faster than new, gainful employment opportunities. Most of these countries are experiencing an "employment transition", with more and more people seeking non-agricultural work, and mainly in urban areas. This is part of the general industrial trends in Africa, Asia and Latin America as they move to manufacturing-based economies, while those countries that had already reached that stage are moving toward high technology and services. Some cities and regions (for instance, Bangalore and New Delhi in India) are moving straight from agriculture-based to high-technology and services provision without any significant manufacturing

transition to speak of, contrary to the established historical pattern. Unconventional or not, though, these economic transitions come as a major socio-economic challenge for urban areas, insofar as they have been unable to generate sufficient numbers of durable job opportunities in the manufacturing or service sectors that could provide gainful employment to people migrating from rural areas. In a sharp contrast to the North, urbanization in many developing countries has taken place without commensurate increases in productive employment or increases in agricultural productivity that could sustain rural areas while feeding cities at more affordable prices for all.

In addition to the endemic job crisis, most developing countries have had to deal with the consequences of the financial and economic crisis that since 2008 has caused significant labour market deterioration in all parts of the world. The risk is that this deterioration may, in turn, trigger serious social and political tension in a number of countries. In a recent analysis, the International Labour Organization (ILO) suggested that the crisis might be much deeper and broader, and might last much longer, than initially anticipated.[13] However, the pace and nature of its impact varies quite significantly across regions and countries depending on economic structure, policy constraints and other specificities. Some countries are more vulnerable than others, particularly those where people on low incomes are heavily dependent on remittances from abroad. From a more general point of view, the ongoing crisis is likely to reverse any modest gains many developing countries had been making lately in terms of growth, poverty reduction and job creation. The resulting significant effects may outlast the crisis.

Girls and young women living in poverty in cities consistently face steeper challenges than their male peers. ©**Jacob Silberberg/Panos Pictures**

Youth employment: The gender divide

Even before the global financial crisis began to affect the developing world, data on urban young people's access to education and livelihoods showed that against a general background of persistent deprivation and endemic unemployment, the benefits of the "urban advantage" eluded some specific groups, and women in particular. Girls and young women living in poverty in cities consistently face steeper challenges than their male peers when it comes to acquiring the knowledge and skills they need to live healthy, productive lives. Continued emphasis on expanded opportunities for girls and young women, therefore, will be an essential requirement if the Millennium Development Goals are to be met in cities.

Young slum dwellers are more likely to have a child, be married or head a household than their counterparts in non-slum areas – a phenomenon that acts as a further challenge to female access to the "urban advantage". The majority of young female slum dwellers tend to bear children at an earlier age than their non-slum counterparts: this is the case in Uganda, where six out 10 young women living in slums have a child or are married, or twice as many as in non-slum communities (by comparison, 34 per cent of young Ugandans in slum areas head a household, compared with 5 per cent of those in non-slum areas.) In many places, young women serve as unpaid carers of children or other family members.

All these situations combine to make young women particularly likely to stay out of the income-earning workforce and miss out on opportunities for decent, durable gainful employment. Those women who *do* work in developing countries tend to do so in the informal economy, owing to lack of formal job opportunities in many regions. For example, in Dhaka most of the jobs performed by women in garment and textile or food processing firms are of an informal nature, although many of them are the main bread-earners for their families. In the absence of organized labour markets, only small numbers of women have access to formal employment with the associated benefits (social security, paid and parental leave, retirement and unemployment money); instead, most women find themselves dependent upon the informal economy for their own and their family's survival.

In sub-Saharan Africa, 84 per cent of women's non-agricultural employment is informal. Few are employed in the formal economy, and those who do are frequently confined to "traditionally female", or "pink collar", jobs with the low status, poor job security and low pay typically shunned by men. In some areas, however, women and men are competing for low-status jobs in sales and other services. Women also fall victims to discriminatory stereotyping, or to the fact that family responsibilities make them less available for full-time employment.

As far as youth non-employment is concerned (an ingrained, endemic phenomenon), rates are also generally much higher for females than males. Non-employment refers to situations that are typical of countries with poor labour market structures, where a young working-age individual is neither at school nor employed or formally registered as a job-seeker. In most African countries, the female non-employment rate is around 40 per cent, or twice as much as for males. By comparison, in those countries where the labour market is formal and well-organized, the unemployment rates of both young women and men are quite similar; in less organized labour markets, unemployment tends to be under-reported and data collection is difficult. For instance, in Quito, the official rate of unemployment is around 7 per cent, but the experts surveyed reckon the actual figure to be some three times higher. They also estimate that in the Ecuadoran capital, under-employment affects 45 per cent of the working population.[14]

The informal sector: Gateway or trap for youth?

In developing countries, confinement of slum-dwelling women to largely informal jobs provides a stark illustration of a wider phenomenon whereby the formal, secure livelihoods that typically accompany the "urban advantage" elude too many among the urban population. In most developing countries, trends suggest that urban economies have become increasingly informal over the past 10 years, as the formal sector consistently fails to provide for both young people and adults seeking employment, even in the face of healthy economic growth. In India, for example, whose economy grew at a 5 per cent annual rate over the past 10 years, some 370 million people, or 9 out of 10 employees, are not affiliated with any formal social security scheme. Mexico, which grew an average 2.5 per cent per year in the past 10 years, extends social security to only 30 per cent of its workforce.

About 85 per cent of all new employment opportunities around the world occur in the informal economy, but this is not without some beneficial effects. For the young, these include opportunities for work experience and self-employment. Part-time, seasonal and contract work in both the formal and informal economies also counts as informal employment. Tracking the number of young people employed in the informal sector is a challenge for a number of reasons, though, and currently available data is inadequate.[15] UN-HABITAT analysis suggests that the majority of young people working in the urban informal sector live in slum areas. For example, in Benin, slum dwellers comprise 75 per cent of informal sector workers, while in Burkina Faso, the Central African Republic, Chad and Ethiopia, the proportion is as large as 90 per cent.

With its combination of job insecurity, low wages and dangerous work, the informal sector should provide no more than a short-term solution to urban unemployment. Formal job creation can be so scarce, though, that informal employment ends up trapping slum-dwelling and other low-income young people in perpetual poverty. With the financial and economic crisis, job losses are also pushing more people deeper into the informal economy or outright poverty. As construction projects are interrupted, for example, builders lose their jobs and the street vendors who served them lose customers. A slowdown in tourist and other leisure activities also has repercussions for the informal sector. These are the losses that unemployment statistics fail to capture – and that are likely to be overlooked in efforts to stimulate new employment.

Unemployment, the informal sector, slums and instability

The current economic downturn makes employment prospects for young urban dwellers all the more worrisome as the issues related to their specific segment of the labour market had never been addressed during previous, more prosperous years. The upcoming generations continue to suffer disproportionately from a scarcity of decent employment opportunities. This scarcity is the primary cause of poverty and social instability. In the developing world, the lack of decent, sustainable jobs promotes a sense of displacement among the young. This can lead to crime, under-development and a cycle of poverty, potentially feeding political and ideological unrest and inciting violence.[16] The risk is especially significant in those many countries where demographic patterns exhibit so-called "youth bulges", when young people comprise at least 40 per cent of the population. The majority of criminal offences around the world are committed by youth aged between 12 and 25. Young people's resentment of their own limited opportunities and their place in society can also give rise to public displays of frustration and violence: in 2005, the French riots over employment conditions for school leavers underscored the volatility of the up-and-coming generations when they feel marginalized.

The persistence of the urban informal sector and the expansion of urban slums point to the pressing need for well-adapted employment policies.[17] The 2009 UN-HABITAT survey suggests that what is happening is quite the opposite, though: in too many cities of the developing world, and regardless of the specific target set by the Millennium Development Goals, slum areas remain a "blind spot" when it comes to policy interventions, job creation and youth support. For many of the working poor, low incomes in the face of rising land prices virtually rule them out of access to land, in the process encouraging the persistence or expansion of slums. In the absence of effective institutions or policies, if any at all, cities are essentially being built "back to front",[18] as land development takes place *before* the formulation, enactment and implementation of planning strategies and control mechanisms: the urban poor lead this process whereby building comes first (admittedly, as a matter of emergency), with servicing and regularizing only at some later, undetermined stage.

Facing up to the global crisis: Youth employment in the development agenda

Unemployment is the one option that many of the urban poor cannot afford. They frequently have no savings and cannot fall back on social security. A large proportion of workers in developing economies have no alternative when economic conditions deteriorate and the cost of living increases: they must work even more, picking up any available job regardless of terms and conditions. Such circumstances are not captured in official statistics. Higher unemployment rates will continue to reflect the current crisis, though only to a point; at the same time, more and more people will be joining the ranks of the insecure working poor in developing economies.

Youth employment features high on the development agenda. The international community formally recognizes the importance of providing opportunities for income generation among young people: Millennium Development Goal 8, target 16, calls on rich nations to enter into partnerships with developing countries to devise and deploy strategies for decent and productive work for youth. For the purposes of these

BOX 2.4.1: **THE "URBAN ADVANTAGE"**

The "urban advantage" refers to the abundance and variety of goods, services, amenities and opportunities which cities make available compared with rural areas. Social connections – or "human capital" – are also part of that. The urban advantage is a function of the density and scale of public, business, education, health, cultural and other institutions a city manages to concentrate.

Although the phrase "urban advantage" belongs to urban economics, the notion refers to tangible as well as intangible benefits, from water, sanitation and transportation networks to employment and social opportunities to pursuits of a political, cultural or academic nature. In this sense, the urban advantage includes the four dimensions of inclusiveness – economic, social, political and cultural – which coincide with the basic components of individual and collective development and well-being.

The urban advantage makes a city attractive to both rich and poor, but it takes adequate policies if it is to be broadly shared across the whole pop-ulation. Rights-based policy approaches, such as the "right to the city", promote a more equitable distribution of the urban advantage among residents of a given city. As advocated in this Report, this type of approach looks to make effective the whole range of universally recognized fundamental rights, prominent among which are equality and non-discrimination. These rights largely overlap with the four dimensions of inclusiveness, which ultimately provide the foundations of what is known as civilization.

▲
In many developing countries, boys drop out of school and never find jobs outside the informal sector. ©**Socrates/Shutterstock**

BOX 2.4.2: MEASURING "INEQUALITY OF OPPORTUNITY"

Monetary measures of inequality – income and the consumption of various household goods and services – reveal little about the specific deprivations people experience in different places, and this recognition has prompted fresh thinking about the best ways of capturing the complexity of the forces behind inequality. Researchers are now looking beyond the Gini coefficient to focus on measures of *unequal opportunity*.

As developed recently by experts at the World Bank and institutions in several Latin American countries, the Human Opportunity Index (HOI) measures the likelihood that children from different backgrounds, or in different combinations of circumstances, will be able to access the basic services they need. By synthesizing measures of both the opportunities available to children, in the form of the general provision of various services in an area, and the equitable distribution of those services, the opportunity index provides a holistic picture of how level the playing field is for people from different social backgrounds. This type of measurement is of significant value to public authorities, as it points out precisely where policy interventions could be most effective; more generally, the index has the merit of highlighting the ways in which inequalities of opportunity affect peoples' life chances.

The HOI is a composite indicator that summarizes provision and accessibility of basic opportunities related to education and housing, based on measures such as timely completion of sixth grade, school attendance at ages 10 to 14, and access to clean water, sanitation and electricity. On top of other composite measures of well-being – first and foremost, the Human Development Index (HDI), which synthesizes average literacy, life expectancy and income – the really novel element the HOI introduces is a focus on *potential* opportunities. Together with government policies, labour markets, and myriad other factors such as trade union affiliation and political participation, these potential opportunities determine measurable effects, such as income and the way it is distributed. Ability to anticipate potential opportunities places researchers and policymakers alike in a better position to understand the forces at work that hinder the chances for some social groups to fulfil their potential.

In the first practical application of the Human Opportunity Index in 2005, researchers calculated the values based on household survey data for 19 countries in Latin America and the Caribbean. As noted earlier in this report, inequalities are more pronounced and pervasive in that region than anywhere else in the world. The results identified widespread differences across countries, both in terms of education and housing and in relation to the overall composite index summarizing all five variables. As shown in the table below, several countries, including Chile, Jamaica, Argentina and Mexico, were found to provide broad-based access to education opportunities, while others, such as Guatemala, Nicaragua and Honduras, were in need of substantial improvement. In terms of housing conditions, Costa Rica, Chile, Argentina and Venezuela were at the forefront, with Nicaragua, Honduras and Bolivia lagging behind. The overall composite index showed that in 2005, Chile was where equality of opportunity was at its best in the sample. This is hardly surprising, given the country's sustained efforts to target public services, including housing, to the poor and other vulnerable groups.

Unequal access to opportunities cannot be justified from a moral or ethical standpoint, but the fact remains that the bundle of opportunities available to any individual begins taking shape even before they are born. Whether a child will have access to clean water, education, medical care, let alone to life in the first place, is largely determined by circumstances that are beyond their control. A combination of race and ethnicity, the incomes and education of a child's parents, and the child's place of birth – whether a rural or an urban area, a slum or a wealthier neighbourhood – will largely determine not just the child's probability of surviving their first year, but also their future prospects. Given the rather deterministic nature of birth circumstances, it is hardly surprising that measurable outcomes, such as poverty, persist across generations for identifiable sub-sets of the population, insofar as they are rooted in racial or other types of discrimination, or in inequitable access to basic opportunities such as health and education.

However, family circumstances are only one part of the equation; exclusionary political systems (such as colonialism and apartheid) have also been shown severely to hamper equality of opportunity, even after these regimes were dismantled and after several years under less repressive governments. Many researchers have suggested that inequality persists in these countries because colonial or racist regimes handed power over to local elites who only extended the exclusionary systems and policies of their former oppressors.

TABLE 2.4.1: **SUMMARY, HUMAN OPPORTUNITY INDEX (HOI) - 2005**

Country	HOI for education variables	HOI for housing conditions	HDI Composite
Argentina	89	88	88
Bolivia	83	41	62
Brazil	67	77	72
Chile	90	93	91
Colombia	78	69	74
Costa Rica	79	94	86
Dominican Republic	77	65	71
Ecuador	80	69	74
El Salvador	65	46	55
Guatemala	51	50	50
Honduras	62	44	53
Jamaica	90	55	73
Mexico	88	75	82
Nicaragua	59	34	46
Panama	81	57	69
Paraguay	74	59	67
Peru	83	49	66
Uruguay	85	85	85
Venezuela	84	89	86
Average	**76**	**64**	**70**

Source: Barros et al., 2006.

partnerships, as for any other efforts to generate dignified and legitimate employment opportunities, two factors militate in favour of targeting urban youth living in poverty, as suggested by the recent UN-HABITAT survey data: (1) young people in slums are more likely to work in the informal sector than their non-slum peers, and (2) informal sector jobs provide little financial security, or chances to access well-paid employment in the future.

If youth employment is to be addressed in any effective way, four elements must be taken into consideration: young people's employability, equal opportunities for jobs, entrepreneurship opportunities, and employment creation strategies. Employability is an outgrowth of education and economic development; any efforts to promote equity should investigate whether young women and men benefit from the same opportunities; efforts to encourage youth-run enterprises can ensure that young people develop skills for the benefit of local communities. It is for public policies to pave the way for new employment opportunities for youth. Beyond enhanced skills, public and private sector partners must keep job creation as a central concern of their capital investment strategies. It is also high time to promote local economic development based on a participatory process that encourages partnerships between the main private and public stakeholders, as part of joint pro-poor and pro-employment urban development strategies; these should make use of local resources and competitive advantage in a global set-up, with the final objective of creating decent jobs and stimulating economic activity.[19]

Efforts to share the "urban advantage" more equitably with young job-seekers should go hand in hand with support for the informal sector, where most of the urban poor work in low-paid, low-productivity and low-security jobs. Local authorities should adjust laws and regulations to lower the costs and increase the benefits for those willing to formalize their businesses. Local authorities should also provide assistance to small enterprises, enabling them to upgrade

skills and improve access to both productive resources and market opportunities.

Jobs through state-built infrastructure for all

On top of the policy recommendations above, another broad type of initiative can generate both decent jobs and socially inclusive growth that benefits the vulnerable and the working poor. It is for individual governments to explore these avenues and build them into economic stimulus policies. The suggestion is to generate more formal employment through rehabilitation and construction of physical infrastructure, such as roads, bridges, schools and hospitals, including upgraded social care and community centres. Given the current scarcity of financial capital, these schemes should best be labour-based. Labour-intensive approaches have become an important element of job creation strategies in many low-wage developing countries, in the process taking advantage of substantial reserves of underused labour, and they are relevant in developed countries as well. While it takes time for major capital-intensive new infrastructure projects to result in additional employment, labour-based approaches can generate jobs and much-needed infrastructure in shorter timeframes.

Such massive mobilization of available local workforces could provide low-income and slum-dwelling women, young and other vulnerable people with a wide range of amenities and services, including clean and safe community centres, support for early childhood development programmes and eldercare, new uses of public spaces for cultural and educational programmes, repair of rural road networks, or irrigation networks, among others.

In the medium term, these labour-intensive programmes are to be combined with vocational training and skill development activities. After eluding them for so long, the "urban advantage" would finally become a tangible reality for many marginalized urban dwellers, and through their own efforts.

END NOTES

1. Pow Choon-Piew (2007), Securing the 'Civilised' Enclaves: Gated Communities and the Moral Geographies of Exclusion in (Post-)socialist Shanghai. Urban Studies, Vol. 44, No. 8, 1539–1558.
2. Caldeira, T. (2001) City of Walls: Crime, Segregation, and Citizenship in São Paulo. Berkeley, CA: University of California Press.
3. Lemanski, 2004.
4. Landman, K, & Schönteich, M, Urban Fortresses, *African Security Review Vol 11* No 4, 2002. Online at - http://www.iss.co.za/Pubs/ASR/11No4/Landman.html
5. For a detailed discussion of the negative implications for human rights of privatization see: Miloon Kothari "Privatising Human Rights – the impact of globalization on adequate housing, water and sanitation" in Social Watch Report 2003 at : http://www.socialwatch.org/en/informelmpreso/pdfs/privatisinghumanrights2003_eng.pdf
6. Gioc Ling Ooi, Yuen Belinda, *"World Cities: Achieving Liveability and Vibrancy"*, Civil Service Colleague,

Institute of Policy Studies, World Scientific, Singapore, 2010
7. Kuala Lumpur City Hall (2008) "KL City Plan 2020" webpage accessed online on 16/10/09 from http://klcityplan2020.dbkl.gov.my/eis/
8. City of Johannesburg (2009) "Growth and Development Strategy 2006" accessed online on 16/10/09 from http://www.joburg.org.za/content/view/139/114/
9. Reynals, 2009.
10. At the time of the Great Depression, New York was affected by unemployment rates of 25 per cent and Chicago, which was considered to be one of the worse hit by the crises, had unemployment rates as high as 30 per cent.
11. Awuor-Hayangah, (2009b).
12. Kruger & Chawla 2005.
13. ILO. 2009. Global Employment Trends Report 2009 (Geneva) (pdf 916 KB). See also, Remarks by José Manuel Salazar-Xirinachs, Executive Director, Employment Sector, ILO, at the Africa Group Meeting,

20 March 2009. The Impact of the Global Financial and Economic Crisis on Developing Countries, in particular Africa, and the prospects for attaining the MDGs. See also, Asia's suffering: Asia's sinking economies, in The Economist, 31 January 2009.
14. Vásconez Jaime, Centro Internacional de Gestión Urbana, UN-HABITAT, Background Report for Quito, 2009.
15. The ILO is currently working with national statistical offices to improve data collection on employment in the informal sector. See ILO 2004.
16. Commission for Africa, 2005 *Our Common Interest: Report of the Commission for Africa,* March
17. Arup Mitra, 1990. "Duality, Employment Structure and Poverty Incidence: The Slum Perspective," Indian Economic Review, Department of Economics, Delhi School of Economics, vol. 25(1), pages 57-73, January
18. Zetter, 2002.
19. ILO, 2001.

2.5
The Social Divide
Impact on Bodies and Minds

Quick Facts

Hunger in Cities

1. Hunger is endemic in many poor urban areas of the developing world and the food crisis can only compound the situation.

2. The food crisis is often not one of supply, but access.

3. The doubling of global food prices over the last three years could potentially push 100 million people in low-income countries deeper into poverty.

The Health Divide

1. In urban slums, shelter deprivations and environmental risks combine to hinder people's ability to escape hunger, and exposure to infectious illnesses creates a vicious cycle where children are constantly malnourished.

2. Indoor air pollution is a "quiet" and overlooked killer, and lack of global awareness is one of the primary obstacles to the widespread implementation of existing, proven responses.

Education: Opportunities and Inequalities

1. The education system perpetuates and reproduces social inequalities.

2. In the poor areas of many African cities, primary school enrolment is decreasing.

3. Efforts to improve the education of girls in some countries have resulted in significant increases and progress in female enrolment and narrowing the gender gap, but male enrolment is regressing in some cities in various regions.

Invalidated hopes

The economic divide does more than deprive the poor of the land tenure, proper shelter, basic utilities and dignified employment that are typically associated with the "urban advantage" and to which they are entitled. Beyond the functional goods and services that provide for decent living conditions, the repercussions of poverty can reach into life in its most physical and social dimensions. In urban areas, the endemic hunger and malnutrition caused by inequitable distribution of largely available food resources are so debilitating for the poor as to invalidate hopes for improved opportunities in the future. Inequitable distribution of basic services across urban areas has the same debilitating physical effect on low-income households, who are exposed to more health hazards than the better-off that can afford water, sanitation and waste disposal services.

Hunger and poor health feed on each other. Their physical repercussions are ingrained from infancy onwards, affecting the development and opportunities of the younger generations. Disease adds to economic pressures on the poor, and so do the costs of children's schooling – although education is known for improving general health and reducing poverty. This is how the physical and intellectual potential of millions of young urban dwellers is impaired, dilapidated or denied for lack of equitable distributive policies. This unfair dispensation is frequently more detrimental to girls, although they are the privileged vectors of healthy bodies and minds from one generation to another. The ongoing global economic crisis can only compound the hard choices urban poor families are left facing nowadays–food to survive the day, but no health care to survive tomorrow, and no school to pave the way for the future.

©Mike Jones

Poverty and hunger: The nutritional divide

Hunger has, for a long time, been considered a rural phenomenon, mostly related to the availability of produce depending on weather and other factors. The assumption that food security is much more tenuous for rural agriculturalists than city residents has been based primarily on the persistence of a rural/urban dichotomy, which holds that residents of one area live fundamentally different lives from those in the other. Many country reports and publications from international agencies indeed show higher rates of malnutrition in rural than in urban areas; however, various studies show that hunger can be found in urban areas, too. The relatively low prevalence of malnutrition in urban areas, as measured by the incidence of underweight children, conceals significant differences in food security across socioeconomic groups; this low prevalence also conceals the fact that poverty can have remarkably similar practical effects in urban and in rural areas.

In market economies, cities are characterized by "relative inequality", where poverty is not absolute but rather is measured by the gaps in opportunities and resources between the poor and the rich living in a segmented environment. In urban areas, disposable income and food prices largely determine the amounts and types of foods consumed by poor urban families, whereas in rural areas it is largely left to cropping patterns and the timing and quality of the harvest to determine food availability for subsistence farmers. The relative differences in income and wealth are much less stark among rural than urban residents. In urban areas, the higher purchasing power of the rich contributes to inflation of food and health care costs, making these unaffordable for the poor. For the urban poor, hunger originates with the sheer lack of money to purchase food that is adequate both in quantity and quality.[1] Even when a country produces enough food to sustain its whole population, hunger may remain a persistent problem among poor urban populations if the available food commands prices that they cannot afford. In urban areas, hunger, just as poverty, is only the outcome of an inequitable distribution of available resources.

Unequal access to food and other basic needs exposes poor populations to a host of diseases. The data presented here shows that hunger is endemic among both the urban poor and rural populations of many countries in Africa, Asia and Latin America and the Caribbean.[2] Ultimately, poverty afflicts populations in both urban and rural environments with ill health and limited life chances. However, those living in urban slums and squatter settlements frequently have to endure worse conditions than their rural relatives, with the children in the poorest urban income bracket experiencing malnutrition at more than twice the rate of those in the richest income category.[3]

Policy Points

Hunger in Cities

1. The structural food crises the urban poor experience on an ongoing basis call for fundamental policy remedies, including production, marketing, distribution, handling and control of food for the urban market.

2. The food crisis will be long-term and the worst is yet to come for the most vulnerable unless extraordinary measures are taken to help them.

The Health Divide

1. The fight against childhood ill-health must take in the modern environment of disease, namely, the local neighbourhood and the city as a whole.

2. Policymakers can help alleviate health inequalities in poor urban areas with comprehensive primary care and better access to healthy food.

3. Slum upgrading and the sustainability of health and nutrition programmes are linked and they should be part of integrated slum upgrading initiatives.

Education: Opportunities and Inequalities

1. If school enrolment and achievement are to be improved in underprivileged urban areas, a combination of incentives that stimulates both demand and supply is required.

2. Improvements in girls' enrolment have resulted from various interrelated strategies that may provide some insights into ways of keeping boys in school.

3. Most national and international literacy and education programmes so far have focused on reducing the urban/rural gap in education, overlooking the divide between rich and poor prevailing in urban areas.

▲
Delhi, India. India experiences a high rate of child malnutrition.
©**Paul Prescott/Shutterstock**

Lessons from countries in continuous and structural food crisis

For many developing countries, the current food crisis is not unprecedented. In many places food insecurity has affected the daily lives of urban poor and rural families for at least the past two decades, with hunger and both chronic and acute malnutrition remaining matters of serious concern. Children are often born into hunger, grow up in hunger and die in hunger. Malnutrition starts during pregnancy, when women suffering from anaemia and other complications do not receive proper antenatal care. In urban areas, children from deprived households are often severely malnourished, at times to the point where immune systems are suppressed and the risk of disease is high.

As part of its Monitoring Urban Inequities Programme (MUIP), UN-HABITAT has made a fresh review of Demographic and Health Survey data collected between 1990 and 2007 in various countries in Africa, Asia and Latin America and the Caribbean. Analysis reveals that serious malnutrition has been widespread in these regions' urban slums and rural areas since 1990, regardless of the local food crisis situation.[4] The data highlights serious malnutrition in the African countries of Burkina Faso, Benin, Chad, Central African Republic, Malawi, Mali, Mozambique, Niger, Nigeria, Rwanda, Tanzania, Uganda and Zambia, where more than four out of 10 children suffered from stunted development resulting from malnutrition throughout the survey years. For instance, Niger featured high proportions of children with stunted development in both poor urban and rural areas for the years 1992, 1998 and 2006. In Asia, these proportions were the highest in Bangladesh, India and Nepal, with more than four out of 10 children in Bangladesh malnourished in survey years 1996, 1999 and 2004. In India, similarly high proportions of malnourished children were observed in 1992, 1998 and 2005. In Latin America and the Caribbean, high rates of malnutrition were observed in Bolivia, Guatemala and Haiti, where stunted development affected three to five out of 10 children. The two Demographic and Health Surveys conducted in Guatemala in 1995 and 1998 show high, though decreasing, proportions of children with stunted development among the urban poor, at 61 per cent in 1995 and 49 per cent in 1998.

The data also shows that malnutrition in most poor urban and rural areas has remained serious over time, sometimes more than 20 times the 2.3 per cent rate expected in healthy, well-nourished children. These extremely high rates have occurred against a background of adverse longer-term trends and structural vulnerability associated with the living conditions in both slums and rural areas. This is why, for instance, several authors have suggested that the 2005 food crisis in Niger has been misinterpreted as a unique phenomenon resulting from a large shock, although the situation was exacerbated by relatively moderate production and price shocks.[5]

Poverty and hunger coexist across human settlement types

As mentioned earlier, children in the poorest income brackets are malnourished at twice the rate of their counterparts in the richest ones. Even in many countries with serious malnutrition, children from rich families are much less affected than those from lower-income households. Data from 2005 in Niger shows that while stunted development affected four or five out of 10 children from both poor urban and rural areas, the proportion in non-slum urban areas was only about one out of four (or 26 per cent). The highest differential in malnutrition rates was observed in Ethiopia in 2005, where only 11 per cent of children in non-slum urban areas were malnourished, or some four times fewer than their counterparts in both urban slum areas and rural settlements (48 per cent). Similar patterns were observed in the Democratic Republic of Congo in 2007, with 41 per cent of children from poor urban areas malnourished compared with 16 per cent in non-slum urban areas. In Bolivia, while high proportions of malnutrition have been observed in rural and poor urban areas (37 per cent and 32 per cent, respectively), in non-slum urban areas fewer than 15 per cent of children experienced chronic malnutrition. In India and Bangladesh, the incidence of malnutrition in poor urban areas is more than twice that in non-slum urban areas: for India, the figures are 54 per cent and 21 per cent, respectively, and for Bangladesh, 51.4 per cent and 24 per cent.

Several factors account for nutritional deprivation among slum dwellers, including extreme poverty, discrimination and geographic isolation. The multiple poverty-related factors leading to malnutrition include low incomes that limit access to food in terms of quantity, quality or both. Lack of access to land restricts access to credit and other resources, with repercussions on income.[6] The replacement of traditional crops with more profitable cash crops also tends to compound nutritional vulnerability among the urban poor, reducing the availability of staple foods and further inflating prices. Food purchases among the urban poor are heavily dependent on competing demands for unavoidable non-food expenditures, such as commuting to work, housing and remittances to relatives in the countryside. With limited transport options, the urban poor seldom have easy access to central markets, and therefore are compelled to buy food in small quantities from local shops at higher prices.[7] A recent survey conducted in Bangladesh in 2009 by the World Food Programme and UNICEF found that one in four households in Bangladesh is food-insecure, and 58 per cent of the households had had insufficient food during the previous 12 months.[8] The same survey showed that real household income in the country dropped by 12 per cent between 2005 and 2008. At the end of 2008, food expenditure represented 62 per cent of total household expenditures, or 10 percentage points more than the national average in 2005.

Dhaka, Bangladesh. Though there is plenty of produce, much is unaffordable to the urban poor. ©David Mckee/Shutterstock

Rising food prices worldwide are intensifying the crisis

The prices of many basic foods have increased over the past two years, leading to a major crisis that affects millions of poor people throughout the world. The price increases have involved virtually all major commodities. International Monetary Fund statistics show that prices of imported rice and local cereals have increased by 230 to 350 per cent since early 2008.[9] Prices of dairy products and many cereals more than doubled in 2007 and continued to climb throughout 2009. This rapid price increase has worsened already dire conditions for the urban poor and rural populations.[10] Before the current global food crisis, many countries experienced food supply changes that reflected their own specific vulnerabilities. For example in 2005, Niger underwent a food crisis as a result of severe droughts. Bangladesh also experienced a food crisis in the same year. In both countries, the poorest people suffered the most – those who before the crisis were already spending far higher proportions of their incomes on food than those better-off, and found it increasingly difficult to afford basic rations. For them, the food crisis meant smaller portions, fewer meals and foods with lower nutritional value, with the immediate effect of increasing rates of malnutrition. In Madhya Pradesh, India, where ongoing food crises have been compounded by a four-year drought, the rise in world food prices has stretched many families beyond breaking point.[11]

Rising food prices impact consumers in both rich and poor countries, where even the urban middle classes can be affected; this is particularly the case in developing countries.[12] During a severe food crisis, hunger spreads to almost all socioeconomic groups in a given place. In Zimbabwe, for example, where the ongoing food crisis has its own internal causes, food shortages and rising costs have affected all social segments, even the rich. For the first time, malnutrition became serious among the richest urban residents, affecting 25 per cent of that population, compared with 29 per cent among the poorest urban residents – a difference of only four percentage points.

BOX 2.5.1: SHELTER DEPRIVATIONS AND CHILDHOOD DISEASES

▲
Congo (D. R.) ©**Aubrey Graham/IRIN**

Hunger is not only an outcome of food deficiency – it is also an indication of the conditions in which families live. Besides food deficiency, malnutrition is influenced by living conditions that increase exposure to disease; this is the case with the overcrowding, inadequate housing and poor access to water and sanitation that are typical of slums. At the community level, lack of waste management and waste water treatment systems increases children's likelihood of contracting diseases such as diarrhoea, acute respiratory infections and malaria. Available information shows that approximately half of all nutritional problems occur in areas that are exposed to environmental risks. Exposure to infectious illnesses, mainly parasite-borne, creates a vicious cycle where children are constantly malnourished as a consequence of unhealthy living conditions.[17]

Data from Benin shows that where shelter deprivation is severe, child malnutrition is twice as prevalent as in areas with safe water, adequate sanitation and decent housing conditions. For slum households that lack access to improved water and sanitation, the prevalence of child malnutrition is often higher even than in rural areas. This is the case in the Democratic Republic of Congo, where 46 per cent of children living in non-durable urban housing are malnourished, compared with 16 per cent in rural areas. In Cameroon in 2004, the proportions were 50 per cent and 16 per cent respectively. Similarly, in India, 45 per cent of children from households without adequate sanitation are malnourished, according to recent Demographic and Health Survey data. Even in Jordan, where proportions of malnourished children are low overall, 2007 data show that 36 per cent of children without access to adequate sanitation in urban areas were malnourished, compared with 12 per cent among those in non-slum areas and 26 per cent among those in rural areas. High rates of malnutrition – as measured by the incidence of childhood diseases such as diarrhoea, malaria and acute respiratory infections – are clearly associated with lack of access to basic shelter amenities.

Crisis of access and tight budgets

Many countries have enough food for all of the population, but only the richest can have access, while the poorest struggle every day to secure one meal for their children. In places where child malnutrition rates are high among the poorest, the crisis is often not one of food *supply*, but rather of *access* – access not only to food of sufficient quality and quantity for the household, but also access to income with which to buy or barter for food while on top of this paying for basic public health services, education and other needed goods and services. This situation represents a "silent emergency", characterized by persistent high degrees of acute malnutrition in "non-emergency" times.[13] In Latin America and the Caribbean, for example, the greatest threat to food security is social inequality, since the region is the most unequal in the world.[14] High food prices have added another layer of instability for the poorest urban and rural residents in the region, who already found that affording the basic essentials for survival was a challenge. In these areas, it takes improved food distribution networks, better health facilities and access to improved drinking water to improve child nutrition.

During famines and droughts, rural populations can rely on domestic stores while those in urban slums often experience starvation, unable as they are to afford inflated food prices. Poor urban families often have to use up to 70 per cent of their income to purchase any food that is available, forcing them to reduce spending on education, childcare and other costs. In the most deeply affected countries, families eat fewer meals, sometimes even not eating for whole days, and children stop going to school as parents save on fees to pay for food.[15] Under such circumstances, poor households become poorer, suffering a significant loss in household well-being. The doubling of global food prices over the last three years could potentially push 100 million people in low-income countries deeper into poverty.[16]

After the food crisis: What is next for the urban poor?

To date, no adequate systematic effort has been made to alleviate hunger in poor urban areas. The focus tends to remain on rural areas, where prevailing responses are not relevant in urban settings, since supply-related malnutrition in cities is largely a consequence of household dependence on food prices and cash income. Since urban dwellers do not cope with vulnerability and risk in the same way as rural populations, unique policy responses are required to address their needs. Experts predict that the food crisis will be long-term, and that the worst is yet to come unless extraordinary measures are taken to help the most vulnerable. In hunger-struck developing countries, people have been consuming food stocks and selling off assets to purchase food, but they will not be able to do so indefinitely.[18] As recent Demographic and Health Survey data on child malnutrition reveals, hunger is endemic in many poor urban areas. The urban poor were living with hunger before the crisis, are still living with hunger

BOX 2.5.2: THE SURGE IN FOOD PRICES HURTS THE URBAN POOR

The surge in food prices since the end of 2006 has led to increasing hunger in the world's poorest countries and made urban food security more precarious. The Food and Agriculture Organization (FAO) estimated the number of hungry people at 923 million in 2007, a more than 80 million rise since 1992. The most rapid increases in chronic hunger occurred between 2003 and 2005, and in 2007 when high food prices drove millions of people into food insecurity. Chronic hunger and malnutrition became more prevalent among the urban poor, who had to spend more to purchase not just food but other household necessities as well.

Agencies monitoring food security in Kenya, for instance, have recorded deepening urban food insecurity caused by rising prices and further compounded by conflict, floods and drought. In March 2009, an estimated 4.1 million urban poor in the country were classified as "highly food-insecure". High prices caused slum-dwelling households to reduce food consumption; as many as 7.6 million slum-dwellers countrywide found themselves unable to meet daily food needs, with maize prices soaring by more than 130 per cent in the capital, Nairobi, and by 85 per cent in the coastal town of Mombasa, in 2008. The cost of non-food items also increased, leading to reduced overall household consumption. Prices of cooking fuels, particularly kerosene, rose by 30 to 50 per cent, and the cost of water more than doubled.

In neighbouring Burundi, the urban areas of Bujumbura, Gitenga and Ngozi saw a 20 per cent increase in local food prices between 2007 and 2008. The situation was exacerbated by the ongoing conflict that has hindered agricultural production in recent years. In the same period, wheat prices doubled in Senegal and quadrupled in Somalia. Zimbabwe's highly inflationary environment has reduced purchasing power, making nearly half the population food-insecure. In Zimbabwe as in other African countries, urban communities resort to a variety of coping strategies, including reduced frequency and contents of meals, which could lead to rising malnutrition.

Stabilization or decline in food prices have occurred in several countries, but the outlook for some African countries remains bleak: they have been unable to reduce prices to pre-2006 levels, which has increased both malnutrition and household food expenditures.

FIGURE 2.5.1: **AFRICAN CITIES – MAIZE – RETAIL PRICE FLUCTUATIONS (US$ PER KG)**

Accra   Maputo   Lilongwe   Harare   International

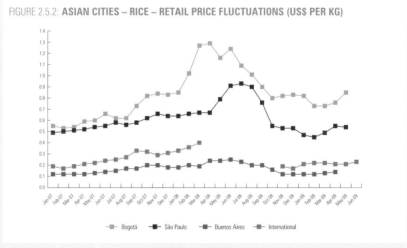

FIGURE 2.5.2: **ASIAN CITIES – RICE – RETAIL PRICE FLUCTUATIONS (US$ PER KG)**

Bogotá   São Paulo   Buenos Aires   International

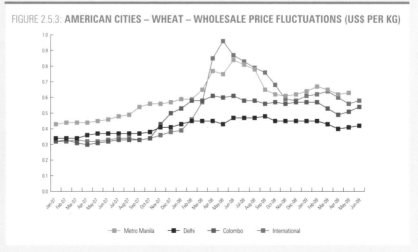

FIGURE 2.5.3: **AMERICAN CITIES – WHEAT – WHOLESALE PRICE FLUCTUATIONS (US$ PER KG)**

Metro Manila   Delhi   Colombo   International

Sources: World Food Programme, 2009; Gandure, 2008; United Nations Food and Agricultural Organization (FAO), 2008.

Source: FAO, Global Information and Early Warning Service - http://www.fao.org/giews/pricetool/

and will continue to live with hunger after the global food crisis ends. Indeed, they experience structural food crises on an ongoing basis. Consequently, it will take structural measures to tackle hunger among the urban poor.

Long-term solutions will depend on a variety of factors, such as provision of jobs and services and reduction of poverty and inequalities, which could take generations to achieve in many low-income countries. Policymakers can build on currently available knowledge and resources in order dramatically to reduce hunger among the urban poor, particularly in the production, marketing, distribution, handling and control of food for the urban market.[19] For example, in Sri Lanka in the 1970s, a successful food delivery system known as "fair price" (or "ration") shops distributed staples at subsidized prices in low-income urban areas. While many international agencies advise against the general use of food subsidies, research shows that it is possible to design targeted interventions for particular commodities or types of "ration" shops.[20] Local authorities must also pay attention to the potential of urban agriculture. Even in crowded areas, people can often find space to grow vegetables or raise animals to supplement their food purchases.[21]

Hunger alleviation goes beyond food availability

Eradicating hunger will require multiple interventions, and not only those related to food availability. Nutrition and good health depend on access to health care as well as adequate food, particularly for children. Use of safe water, improved sanitation and durable housing materials, together with provision of sufficient living areas to ease overcrowding, will improve the chances of better health and life conditions for slum dwellers and rural residents, with or without increases in food availability. This goes to show that slum upgrading and the sustainability of health and nutrition programmes are linked and should, together, become part of a comprehensive approach to improving the lives of the urban poor.[22]

More comprehensive provision of health services, including immunization campaigns, would also improve nutrition among the urban poor through prevention of gastrointestinal and infectious diseases. Along with primary health care, direct nutrition programmes are urgently needed, including food fortification and mass distribution of capsules and tablets to eliminate deficiencies of iodine, iron, folic acid and vitamin A. Adequate diet among pregnant and lactating women, together with community education in proper infant and child feeding, can also improve children's nutritional well being.[23]

▲
Kolkata, India. Eradicating hunger will require multiple interventions, and not only those related to food availability. ©**Maciej Dakowicz**

The health divide

In order to understand public health needs in urban areas, one must look beyond poverty rates and crude rates of morbidity or mortality, and focus on disparities in living conditions. Although poverty alleviation is often considered the most important step toward improving general health, in urban areas marginal increases in income for the poor do not ensure access to decent accommodation, safe water or adequate sanitation. The poor are typically driven to the least developed areas of a city, where dilapidated environments lead to worse health outcomes and greater risks of premature death than in improved, well-maintained areas. Child mortality rates remain highly associated with diarrhoeal diseases, malaria and acute respiratory infections related to overcrowding and air pollution, which in turn result from various environmental health hazards such as lack of sanitation and hygiene, lack of access to safe water, poor housing conditions, poor management of solid wastes, and many other hazardous conditions. Children in substandard environments are exposed to contaminated air, food, water, soil and conditions where parasite-carrying insects breed. Environmental equity is a more powerful determinant of health and mortality than the overall wealth of nations.[24]

Adequate shelter protects against exposure to environmental diseases

Poor sanitation, combined with unsafe water supply and lack of hygiene, claims the lives of many slum dwellers every year. Sanitation is the primary factor that protects water, air, soil and food from contamination, and thereby reduces the risk of disease.[25] When sanitation is combined with positive hygiene – hand washing with soap or other cleansing agents, and safe storage of water – its effectiveness is greatest, creating a safe environment and enhancing the health of the population. However, in densely populated urban areas, access to latrines does not significantly reduce the risk of faecal-oral diseases because the facilities may not be cleaned and maintained regularly. Indeed, short of sound hygiene practices, latrines alone have no positive influence on health. Recent data from Pakistan, for instance, indicates very little difference in the frequency of diarrhoeal episodes between households with latrines and those without.[26] Furthermore, in 2006, the prevalence of diarrhoea among children in Pakistan was 21.2 per cent for those living in non-slum urban households, compared with 23 per cent for those living in slum households. The only significant difference in the prevalence of diarrhoea among urban children emerges when severe shelter deprivations are present: in households lacking all four basic shelter services, the prevalence is 38 per cent. Similarly, there are differences between children of the poorest and the richest urban families, among whom the prevalence of diarrhoea is 26 per cent and 18 per cent, respectively.[27]

The link between sanitation and diarrhoeal diseases is not uniform across regions, countries or cities. For instance, in

▲
Kroo Bay slum, Freetown, Sierra Leone. Better housing conditions are essential to ensuring a healthy population. ©**Save the Children UK/IRIN**

Cameroon, children from households without improved water, improved sanitation and sufficient living area feature a much greater prevalence of diarrhoeal diseases – 33.3 per cent – than those living in non-slum urban households (9 per cent). In Democratic Republic of Congo (DRC), the mere lack of improved sanitation is enough for a child to be highly exposed to diarrhoeal diseases (18.3 per cent, compared with 13.9 per cent among children of households with all four basic shelter services). In DRC, when combined with lack of sanitation, lack of improved water causes the prevalence of diarrhoea to rise to 23.9 per cent.

Improving the quantity and quality of water available for domestic use can significantly reduce illness and death from diarrhoeal and waterborne illnesses. However, in some cases the source of water is safe, but contamination occurs through polluted containers or other environmental conditions before the water reaches the household for consumption. In many cities of the developing world, water supplies are undrinkable, contaminated as they are by bacteria, untreated or poorly treated sewage, heavy metals or silt from soil erosion, fertilizers and pesticides, mining tailings and industrial waste. According to 2007 data from Jordan, the sole lack of improved water is enough by itself to double (to 32.3 per cent, compared with 16 per cent) the risk of diarrhoeal diseases for children by comparison with the entire urban area. Even in Jordan's rural areas, only 16 per cent of children were affected by diarrhoeal diseases in 2007.

Better housing conditions are also essential to ensuring a healthy population. High-density accommodation in slums and squatter settlements, or poor-quality housing in general, intensifies the risk of disease transmission. Overcrowding increases exposure to droplet-spread infections, as poor ventilation inhibits the dispersion of contaminated air and lack of sunshine prevents natural air sterilization by sunlight.

Nairobi, Kenya. Flooding and pools of standing water can increase the incidence of malaria and other mosquito-borne diseases.
©**Nairobi River Basin Project/UNEP**

In an overcrowded slum area, pit latrines expose more children to diarrhoeal diseases compared with a non-overcrowded rural area.[28] In slums, where many households often share a single toilet between them, even the use of improved latrines is unsafe and exposes children to diarrhoeal diseases. The number of latrines may not be adequate, leading to unsanitary conditions that increase exposure to contaminated faecal matter and then to diarrhoea. The concentration of people living in small, poorly ventilated areas increases the risk of disease transmission and multiple infections.[29] In Nepal, lack of sanitation in overcrowded urban areas exposes children to diarrhoeal diseases at a higher rate (17.9 per cent) than in the country's rural areas (12.6 per cent) or its urban environments overall (10.3 per cent). Where all four basic shelter services are lacking, the prevalence of diarrhoea rises to 20.8 per cent. In India as well, children from households without improved water and sanitation in poor housing conditions are exposed to a high prevalence of diarrhoea (16.7 per cent); in Namibia and Niger, lack of sanitation and durable housing are also responsible for high rates of diarrhoeal diseases among children, with a prevalence of 17.6 per cent in Namibia and 29.9 per cent in Niger, compared with 11.6 per cent and 16.7 per cent, respectively, among children from non-slum households.

Poor solid waste management causes environmental diseases

Improperly managed solid waste can clog storm drains, cause flooding, result in garbage heaps and provide breeding and feeding grounds for mosquitoes, flies and rodents. The combination of environmental hazards surrounding solid waste can lead to injuries and easy transmission of bacterial diseases and parasitic infections. Occasional flooding and the presence of pools of standing water can lead to increased incidence of malaria and other mosquito-borne diseases, especially during rainy seasons, placing workers and local residents at risk. Public facilities often fall into disrepair for lack of maintenance, setting the stage for accidents and poor waste management. Living in a poor environment can also make it harder to access other shelter services. Any positive effects of improved sanitation facilities can be diluted and offset by ineffective management, collection, treatment and disposal of human excreta, household waste water, storm water, sewage effluents, industrial and other hazardous waste products.

In most African cities, households typically have no safe ways to dispose of solid waste. In Benin, for example, fewer than 50 per cent of urban households benefit from collection of household wastes by public or private systems; this proportion is particularly low in smaller cities (17 per cent, compared with 47 per cent in large cities). Associated health problems include high incidences of cholera, diarrhoea and dysentery, especially in children who tend to play where waste accumulates. Again, in Benin, recent data shows that the prevalence of diarrhoea among children under 5 years old is 18.5 per cent in those urban households dumping waste in the yard, compared with 7 per cent where waste is collected and taken away. In Kenya in 2003, one out of four children living in households where solid waste is dumped in the yard had diarrhoea, compared to fewer than one out of 10 living in households with regular garbage collection. In addition to lack of solid waste collection, it is recognized that lack of drainage, especially in areas of communal water supply, breeds mosquitoes and flies, which can be a nuisance and spread disease. Water lines flow next to storm drains, which frequently turn into open sewers.

Poor management of waste and waste water can also increase the spread of disease in many ways. Mosquito-related diseases, especially malaria and dengue fever, can be spread from breeding areas in standing water that collects in potholes, disposed-of construction materials and holes dug for sand and gravel. Demographic and Health Surveys in African urban areas show that the prevalence of fever remains high in many cities. In Benin in 2001, for example, more than two out of five children living in households where waste was not collected had fever. In contrast, only one out of four children living in households with regular collection had fever, according to the same survey. Lack of collection of household waste is also associated with the spread of respiratory infections. In Benin, the prevalence of acute respiratory infections is 17.1 per cent among children living in households where waste is dumped in the yard, compared with 13.6 per cent among children living in households with regular waste collection. In Ethiopia, the prevalence of acute respiratory infections is six times higher among children living in households where the waste is dumped in a nearby river than among children living in households with regular waste collection (18 per cent, compared with 3 per cent).

▲
Buying firewood in Addis Ababa, Ethiopia. Indoor air pollution is a "quiet" and overlooked killer. ©**Manoocher Deghati/IRIN**

Indoor air pollution and acute respiratory infections

It is estimated that indoor air pollution is responsible for some three million deaths every year.[30] Women who cook in enclosed quarters using biomass fuels and coal are at risk of chronic bronchitis and acute respiratory infections, as are their children, who are often exposed to significant indoor air pollution alongside their mothers on a daily basis.[31] Indoor air pollution is a "quiet" and overlooked killer, and lack of awareness is one of the primary obstacles to the widespread implementation of existing, proven responses.[32]

A majority of households in many sub-Saharan African cities are still primarily dependent on biomass fuels for cooking. For example, in Benin, 86 per cent of urban families use wood or charcoal for cooking, and the prevalence remains high even in non-slum areas (74 per cent). Wood and charcoal are predominant in the cities of 10 African countries reviewed in UN-HABITAT's analysis of Demographic and Health Survey data (Benin, Burkina Faso, Cameroon, Ghana, Ethiopia, Malawi, Mali, Rwanda, Uganda and Zambia). In these cities, the prevalence of acute respiratory infections among children under 5 is highest in households using wood, charcoal or dung. When burned, these solid fuels produce significant amounts

of pollutants, including suspended particulate matter and noxious gases, particularly in the absence of improved stoves or adequate ventilation.[33] In Burkina Faso, the prevalence of acute respiratory infections among urban children under 5 is almost two times higher in households cooking with solid fuels than in those using cleaner-burning liquid or gas fuels (9.2 per cent, compared with 5.1 per cent). Kigali, Rwanda, displays higher variations, with a 6 per cent prevalence of acute respiratory infections among children living in households cooking with non-solid fuels, compared with 15.6 per cent among those using solid fuels. The use of dung for fuel is rare in most African cities today, but as indicated in many studies, when burned, dung produces more pollutants than any other solid fuel. In the urban areas of Congo, the prevalence of acute respiratory infections is twice as high in households cooking with dung than in those using wood or charcoal (16.8 per cent *vs.* 8.8 per cent and 7.6 per cent, respectively). The urban areas of Ethiopia display the largest variation, with an acute respiratory infection prevalence of 28.7 per cent among households cooking with dung, compared with 8.3 per cent among those using charcoal and 4.8 per cent among those using kerosene.

Maputo, Mozambique. Environmental health hazards have become major contributors to the environmental diseases affecting Africa. ©**Africa 924/Shutterstock**

The modern environment of disease

Against a global background of urbanization and continuing industrialization, modern environmental health hazards have become major contributors to the environmental diseases affecting the African continent.[34] The major such hazards include water pollution from environmental degradation and industrial operations, urban air pollution from motor vehicles, radiation hazards, climate change, and emerging or re-emerging infectious diseases. Industrial pollution, in particular, is becoming highly concentrated in expanding urban areas, and as a result pollution intensity in Africa is among the highest in the world.[35] Such environmental health hazards affect many urban residents even in countries that have made significant progress in the provision of access to services, including improved water and sanitation, as well as durable housing with sufficient living area. In Dakar, for instance, and despite reduced numbers of slum-dwellers, the prevalence of diarrhoea among children remains high, even compared with rural areas: 28.1 per cent in the Senegalese capital, *vs.* 16.7 per cent in smaller cities and 22.4 per cent in rural areas. In Dakar, access to improved water and sanitation, durable housing, waste collection and sufficient living areas has been extended to many households, but even among these the prevalence of diarrhoea remains dramatically high (27.1 per cent, compared with 32.2 per cent in non-slum areas). It is clear that the fight against childhood diseases must transcend the traditional realm of the household, in order to encompass the modern environment of disease: the neighbourhood, and the city as a whole, with all the attendant risks and harms.

Environmental risks to children's health become particularly acute after the first few months of life, and again when they enter toddlerhood and begin to move around inside and outside the home. There is little difference between neonatal mortality rates in slum and non-slum urban areas; only after the first few months of life, when they start receiving external food and liquids, do more children die in slum than in non-slum areas. This can only further highlight the importance of proper homes and diets as children grow. For example in Egypt, antenatal and delivery health care is quasi-universal, resulting in relatively low neonatal mortality. However, a clear divide emerges early on in post-neonatal mortality, with deaths of children aged between one and 12 months two times higher in slums than in non-slum areas (27 deaths per thousand, compared with 13 per thousand). A similar order of magnitude has been recorded in Morocco: the post-neonatal mortality rate is 15 per thousand in slum areas, compared with 8 per thousand in non-slum areas, although in both types of settlements the neonatal mortality rate is an identical 24 per thousand. In urban Benin, the situation is alarming as the post-neonatal mortality rate is 46 deaths per thousand in slums, or three times higher than in non-slum urban areas (14 deaths per thousand), although, again, neonatal mortality rates are an identical 24 per thousand. This demonstrates that antenatal health care clearly benefits babies more in the immediate period after birth than after the first month of their lives, when different outcomes reflect different social conditions.[36]

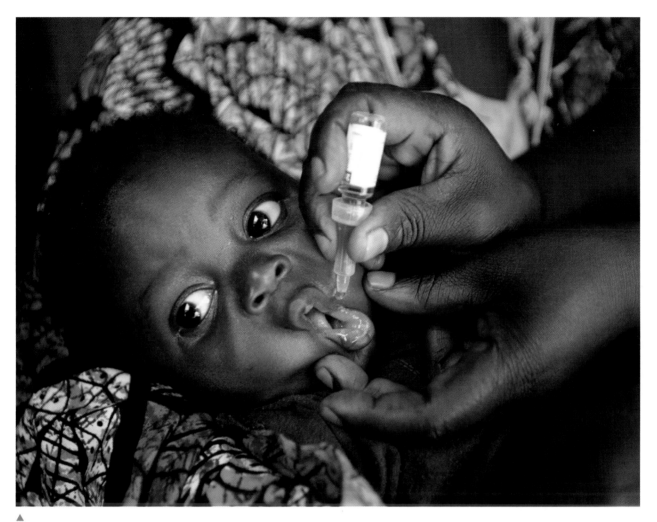

A child receives polio drops in Malawi. ©**Giacomo Pirozzi/Panos Pictures**

Cities provide better access to health services

In most countries, children born to the richest families have a high probability of access to health care, including antenatal and delivery, as well as immunization. Even in countries like Niger, where the overall proportion of children without any immunization is as high as 40 per cent, the majority of the better-off children are immunized, or slightly more than twice as many of the poorest children. Although access to health care and delivery is skewed in favour of the rich in Niger, all children in urban areas are still better off on this count than those in rural areas. The same is true in Malawi, where more than 80 per cent of children living in slums have been immunized against measles. In Malawi as in most countries, this particular type of immunization is widespread in cities, both in non-slum and slum areas. The effect of urbanization on access to health care services is undeniably positive; still, in some countries like Niger, Nigeria, India, Pakistan and Haiti, childhood diseases such as measles remain among the five main causes of child death in slum and rural areas where immunization is not widespread. In those countries, it will take substantial resources to curb the number of deaths related to measles and other diseases such as diarrhoea, pneumonia and malaria.

Improving urban living environments with thorough policymaking

Poor living environments clearly add to the health challenges slum dwellers keep facing. Inadequate sanitation, hygiene and water lead not only to more sickness and deaths, but also to higher health care costs, lower school enrolment and retention rates, and lower labour productivity among slum dwellers than their non-slum counterparts. Policymakers can alleviate health inequalities in cities through comprehensive primary health care, especially for the poor. Policymakers must at the same time address related issues like shelter deprivations and slum dwellers' lack of access to healthy food. Urban health inequalities must also be redressed with an adequate, functional network of services that reach out to all sections of the population. Finally, urban health policies must tackle social inequality in a proactive manner, since, as mentioned earlier, the urban poor will continue to depend on market vagaries for health care and all other aspects of daily life, including employment and sheer survival.

Primary School in Praia, Cape Verde. ©**Phuong Tran/IRIN**

Education: Opportunities and inequalities in cities

Education contributes to many important dimensions of well-being. It has a crucial role to play in poverty reduction, improved general health, halting the spread of HIV/AIDS and, more generally, enabling people to fulfil their potential. Basic education is a human right and is central to the Millennium Declaration, which in the year 2000 pledged that by 2015 boys and girls across the world would be able to complete a full course of primary education. Today, most national constitutions acknowledge the right to education, but effective access can remain a challenge, especially for those living in poverty. In countries where primary education is compulsory under law, governments deploy a nationwide education system with free primary school and social assistance towards indirect costs like transport and meals. However, effective attendance and access are rarely enforced in many countries. Parents are all-too frequently left free to decide whether or not to send their children to school, and do not face penalties when they fail to do so. Finally, social inequality in many countries influences and shapes the education system.

Access to education is greater in cities than in rural areas

Cities are hosts to more educational infrastructure than villages. They provide young people with opportunities to continue their education and access gainful employment in the formal sector, but not all cities are alike when it comes to young people's education and employment needs. Cities can also generate and intensify the kind of social exclusion that denies the benefits of the "urban advantage" to youth and other marginalized groups, particularly in conditions of unprecedented urban growth, increasing poverty and inequality, or inadequate policies. Even within one and the same city, some youth are able to succeed and prosper while others drop out of school, fail to find productive employment and sink into poverty.[37]

Available data indicates that enrolment rates are in general much higher in urban than in rural areas. In most of the countries reviewed here, more than 75 per cent of primary education age children in cities attend school, but in rural areas the proportion drops under 50 per cent. This pattern is most pronounced in Niger, where 73 per cent of children in the capital, Niamey, attend school, compared with 17 per cent in rural areas; in smaller cities and towns, 53 per cent of children of primary school age are enrolled. A similar pattern prevails in Burkina Faso, where the rural communities lag far behind their urban counterparts, with enrolment rates of 21 and 73 per cent respectively. In both Niger and Burkina Faso, as in many African countries, the "urban advantage" is quite clear for both rich and poor. Enrolment rates in rural areas are mainly dependent on the availability and accessibility of school facilities.

Generalization of basic education in some countries

In both Latin America and Asia, schooling is quasi-universal in urban and rural areas, with few exceptions. In some African countries, any disparities in enrolment rates remain small across cities and villages. This is the case in Cameroon, Congo, Kenya, Lesotho, Madagascar, Malawi, Namibia, Rwanda, South Africa, Tanzania, Togo, Uganda and Zambia, as well as in Egypt and Morocco, which also feature in the UN-HABITAT survey sample. In Egypt, school attendance rates remain consistent across various areas, with enrolment rates of 86 per cent in the capital and large cities, 89 per cent in smaller cities and towns and 84 per cent in rural areas. A broadly similar pattern is evident in Morocco, where school enrolment rates are 91 per cent in the capital and large cities, 92 per cent in smaller cities and towns, and 84 per cent in rural areas.

Cities also generate inequalities in education

Social and cultural barriers continue to deny slum dwellers the opportunity to complete basic education.[38] Children from slum communities are less likely to enroll in school, tend to complete fewer years and are less likely to complete primary or attend secondary school. Although large majorities of children in most cities are enrolled in school, the differential between slum and non-slum areas remains clear. This is particularly evident in the poorer areas of many African cities, where primary school enrolment is decreasing. In Eastern and Southern Africa, rural areas saw the most significant increases in school enrolment in the late 1990s, and many poor urban families were left behind. In Tanzania, for example, net enrolment ratios increased in both rural and non-slum urban areas, but actually decreased in slum areas. Similar patterns have been reported in Zambia and Zimbabwe, but are not confined to sub-Saharan Africa.

For instance in Guatemala, only 54 per cent of children living in slums were enrolled in primary education in 1999, compared with 73 per cent in non-slum urban areas and 61 per cent in rural areas. Brazil reported similar enrolment figures in the late 1990s, too. The educational gap associated with economic status can be quite substantial.[39] In Bangladesh, Nepal and Pakistan, for example, fewer than 40 per cent of children in the poorest socioeconomic quintile complete primary school, compared with 70 to 80 per cent in the richest quintile. In Sierra Leone, the figures are 20 per cent and 70 per cent, respectively. Among slum communities in Nigeria, children are 35 per cent less likely to attend school than those from non-slum areas. In Bolivia, only 10 per cent of children in the poorest quintile complete primary school, as compared with 40 per cent of those in non-slum areas, and 55 per cent of children in the richest quintile.[40]

Inequalities intensify at higher levels of education

In many countries in both the developing and developed world, the education system perpetuates and reproduces social inequalities. In China, for instance, research shows that government policies have fallen short of addressing inequitable practices: as schools perpetuate and reproduce inequities, a new system of social stratification emerges on the back of market forces rather than Socialist principles.[41] The American education system also comes under criticism for perpetuating the social inequalities of a class hierarchy, which is achieved through allocation of differential "educational capital" along class lines.

Secondary education, where the returns on knowledge and skill development are highest, has a particularly important role to play if children are to acquire the skills and abilities needed to enter the labour market and become economically empowered. This is the stage where slum and non-slum school enrolment rates are seen to diverge widely. Not only is enrolment of slum-dwelling children lower in secondary school, but many of those enrolled fail to succeed. As measured against learning achievement, the quality of educational services in most poor communities remains low. Research in both developed and developing countries also underscores the prime importance of educational quality (as measured by tests of cognitive achievement) for the level of earnings.[42] In the United States, for example, a one standard deviation increase in mathematics performance at the end of high school is associated with 12 per cent higher annual earnings.[43]

Education inequalities in both learning and earning outcomes persist in cities. Evidence from Ghana, for example, shows that although 37 per cent of pupils stay in school through ninth grade, only 5 per cent are fully literate. In Brazil, fewer than 22 per cent of pupils attend through ninth grade, and only 8 per cent are deemed literate. Therefore, better teaching standards are crucial if the performance of both boys and girls is to be improved, and equality in educational outcomes to become effective. Merely building schools and increasing enrolment without ensuring quality is unlikely to help countries meet their human capital objectives in an increasingly knowledge-based global economy. Recognizing that universal primary education cannot be achieved by expanding access at the expense of quality, policymakers are seeking to improve both simultaneously.

Education and gender inequality

The education of girls and young women generates powerful poverty-reducing synergies and yields enormous intergenerational gains. It is positively correlated with enhanced economic productivity, more robust labour markets, higher earnings and improved public health and well-being. Much has been done in favour of gender equity in education over the past 15 years. For instance, according to Demographic and Health Survey data, the rate of girls' enrolment at the primary level in low-income countries has grown from 87 per cent in 1990 to 94 per cent in 2004, signaling a significant narrowing of the gender gap. This progress was only

▲
Molo Town, Kenya. Girls' enrolment at primary level has increased in low-income countries. ©**Allan Gichigi/IRIN**

possible because policymakers clearly recognized the crucial importance of girls' education in development as well as the benefits derived from the "education for all" agenda. Various policy frameworks, including the "women in development", "gender and development", post-structural and rights-based approaches, have contributed to gender equality and quality education in their own way.[44] The "women in development" approach generates clear policy directives on issues such as the hiring of more female teachers, tracking the number of girls and women in and out of school, overcoming barriers to girls' education, and reaping the benefits of schooling. As for the "gender and development" approach, it encourages provision of complementary basic education programmes for socially excluded girls, as well as gender-sensitive and gender-equalizing curricula.

Estimates suggest that gender equality in education has made uneven progress within regions, though. In 2005, some 72 million children around the world remained out of school, with a majority (41 million) of girls from groups with multiple disadvantages and living mainly in sub-Saharan Africa and Southern Asia. Where girls are still at a disadvantage, resources and school facilities are limited and enrolment is altogether low. In many countries with low overall enrolment, fewer than 50 per cent of primary school-aged girls are involved. Female illiteracy rates remain high in these parts of the world, particularly in urban poor and rural areas, where many girls drop out of school too early to acquire the skills they need to function as literate individuals. Demographic and Health Survey data points to four main reasons why girls discontinue their education: lack of money, early marriage and pregnancy, domestic work responsibilities, and poor performance. Only a small proportion – fewer than 10 per cent – of girls and young women who had left school said it was because they had graduated. Gender gaps in education have historically been wider in Pakistan than the world average, with girls lagging behind boys in terms of access, school standards and outcomes: in primary education, for instance, the gap worsened by 30 per cent between 1985 and 1995.[45] A similar situation prevails in Yemen, where 60 per cent of women are illiterate, compared with a 45 per cent national rate.[46]

Boys' enrolment takes a downturn

Efforts to improve the education of girls in some countries have resulted in significant increases in their enrolment numbers, but today a slight regression in boys' enrolment and participation is becoming a cause for concern. In certain parts of Latin America and the Caribbean, the Middle East, and North and Southern Africa, many more girls than boys are now enrolled. In developed regions and Eastern Asia too, the gender disparity has reversed, with more girls than boys now enrolled at the primary level. In Bangladesh, boys are dropping out of school in much larger numbers than girls – a phenomenon that is now the country's most significant gender challenge – to the point where girls now account for 60 per cent of enrolment in some schools, especially in rural

Cambodia. Domestic work responsibilities force many girls to discontinue their education. ©**Irina Ovchinnikova/Shutterstock**

areas. Improvements in girls' enrolment have resulted from eight interrelated strategies, some of which may provide some insights into ways to keep boys in school, as well: (1) elimination of user fees; (2) conditional cash transfers; (3) increased focus on gender inequality; (4) recognition of cultural and social constraints to girls' education; (5) improvement in the economic returns to girls' education; (6) promotion of post-primary education for girls; (7) making primary education more gender-sensitive; and (8) developing and disseminating gender-sensitive school and pedagogical models. Obviously, none of these strategies can be implemented wholesale to tackle the regression in boys' enrolment, although they retain a general degree of relevance that deserves attention.

Education remains a luxury for the urban poor in the face of current crises

In those urban areas where income and social inequalities are significant, many urban families are so poor, or impoverished, that they cannot ensure basic education for their children. In urban areas, access to education is often determined by ability to pay fees more than by the physical proximity of schools, or by curricula. School fees, costs of uniforms, materials, exams and other educational expenses have been shown to affect the chances of children from poor families, and girls in particular, going to school, as they add to the already high opportunity costs of letting them leave home to benefit from

▲
Mopti, Mali. In times of crisis, school attendance always declines in developing countries; the tragedy is that some children may never return. **©Torsius/Shutterstock**

formal education. In Dhaka, parents spend around 10 per cent of household income on school costs for every child, but this proportion is twice as high (20 per cent) for the poorest households. UN-HABITAT's Urban Inequities Survey data indicates that in Lagos, Casablanca and São Paulo, families in the poorest income quintile spend more than 25 per cent of incomes on school costs.

These statistics highlight the economic dilemma poor urban families are facing, caught as they are between securing a better future for their children through education, on the one hand, and meeting their own and their children's needs for basic sustenance, housing, transportation and privatized basic services like water and sanitation, on the other hand. In slums, a majority of parents postpone sending their children, especially girls, to school, until they can take care of other expenses such as food, rent and transportation. In the meantime, children are expected to assist with domestic work and menial, low-earning jobs.

The direct effects of the financial and food crises are devastating for poor urban families who were already struggling to send at least one child to school. Today in many developing countries, the children of poor families face the most straightforward of dilemmas: food, or school. The immediate future is secured, if only barely, at the cost of forgoing opportunities for a better, longer-term future. For parents, postponing new enrolments and withdrawing enrolled children are the only options.[47] Girls are the typical first casualties of this hard choice,[48] as suggested by DHS data. In the urban areas of Uganda and Zambia, for instance, 74 per cent and 51 per cent, respectively, of young females between the ages of 15 and 24 mentioned inability to pay as the main reason they stopped going to school.

In Latin America, the impact of the financial crisis on education can be more visible in larger than in smaller cities. This is particularly the case in Bolivia, where 93 per cent of children in small cities and towns are enrolled in primary education, compared with 68 per cent in the capital and other large cities, and 72 per cent in rural areas. This disparity between large and smaller cities could be explained by the deep inequalities that characterize larger urban areas. A similar situation prevails in Colombia, though to a lesser degree, with 82 per cent of children in smaller cities attending school, compared with 73 per cent in large cities – the same as the percentage of rural children enrolled in school.

Among some impoverished urban communities in Africa, it is common practice for families to have boys educated in their village of origin, where schools are less expensive, while girls remain at home in the city to help with housework.[49] In 2007, girls already accounted for 54 per cent of the world's out-of-school population, a percentage that is only likely to increase. In times of crisis, school attendance always declines in developing countries; the tragedy is that some children may never return.

The combined social and cultural factors that make it difficult for girls to enroll and complete school also contribute to their dissatisfaction and poor performance regarding education. Combinations of domestic chores, marriage, motherhood and financial constraints seriously challenge girls' ability to maintain regular attendance, or to succeed when they do attend. Surveys show that poor performance is, in itself, the reason a significant proportion of urban young females give for dropping out of school before they complete their education or pass key national examinations.

Unsafe school environments

Another significant, though rarely mentioned factor behind low school enrolment in poor urban neighbourhoods is a perceived lack of safety, especially for girls. Schools in many slum areas are not child-friendly and in some cases, they are even hazardous for girls. Failure to provide adequate sanitary facilities and water services causes inconvenience for boys, but can make the situation disastrous for girls. During menstruation, girls will not attend school if basic toilet facilities are not available. Even where they are, servicing and maintenance are frequently poor. In many places, separate facilities for boys and girls are not available, which leaves girls at risk of sexual harassment. This is especially the case in those schools that become overcrowded, as they are too small or too few to serve expanding slum areas. The heightened risk of sexual violence in poor, overcrowded classrooms hinders educational prospects for girls. More or less unwillingly, girls often give in to unwanted sexual advances from boys or even teachers, leaving them exposed to unwanted pregnancies, unsafe abortions, HIV/AIDS and other sexually transmitted diseases.[50] The prevalence of such violence in schools hinders not only girls' educational performance, but also their achievements, self-esteem and physical and psychological health.

Against this background, Demographic and Health Survey data shows that a significant proportion of girls who drop out school do so because they "do not like it". This is the case for more than 30 per cent of the young women in urban slum communities in Mali and Guatemala who had left school, and for more than 20 per cent in Egypt, Nicaragua, Central African Republic and Burkina Faso. Lack of safety at school can also, on its own, be a reason for parents to withdraw their daughters. In Dhaka, many parents keep their daughters at home and away from the city's overcrowded schools, or marry them off at young ages, which, combined with motherhood, generally puts an end to any further schooling.[51] It is incumbent on policymakers to recognize the specific vulnerabilities of girls in schools and, through a set of minimum standards, mainstream gender equality and protection across all aspects of education.[52]

More incentives needed for a universal basic education

Most national and international literacy and education programmes so far have focused on reducing the *urban/rural* gap in education, overlooking the divide between rich and poor that prevails in urban areas. Although much remains to be done in rural areas, these have seen significant increases in enrolment over the past 10 years, and the simultaneous decreases in impoverished urban communities. In this regard, in Bangladesh as in many other countries, non-governmental organizations have traditionally maintained a rural focus; they have only recently begun to turn their attention to urban areas and to understand the particular educational challenges posed by slum populations.

If school enrolment and achievement are to be improved in poor urban areas, a combination of incentives that stimulates both demand and supply is required. On the demand side, incentives for poor families can include stipends, scholarships, free textbooks and learning materials, safe and affordable transportation schemes, and community awareness campaigns. On the supply side, it is for public authorities to build more secondary schools in poor urban areas or, alternatively, add boarding facilities to existing schools. Furthermore, direct linkages between secondary education and local work opportunities are required if graduates' employment prospects are to be enhanced. This type of scheme can boost both enrolment and achievement for all underprivileged groups, including girls and children from poor urban areas.

A comparison of the effects of eliminating school fees across several countries showed that enrolment rates rise dramatically wherever fees are abolished.[53] Elimination of fees in Malawi in 1994, for example, increased net enrolment from 68 to 99 per cent, and gross enrolment from 89 to 113 per cent in a single year. In Yemen, the government has launched cash and non-cash incentive programmes based on school attendance, on top of specific incentives such as exemption from fees for textbook costs, with the deliberate aim of increasing girls' enrolment and retention rates.[54] The Yemeni government has also hired more female teachers and established a Girls' Education Sector in the Ministry of Education, headed by a female deputy minister. During the same period, the gain in boys' enrolment was more modest, at only 14 per cent. Trends in secondary school enrolment over the same period were similarly lopsided, with increases of 162 per cent for girls and 60 per cent for boys. However, changes in enrolment patterns have been found to be potentially detrimental if schools do not receive financial compensation for the loss of much-needed resources such as fees. In Yemen, the combination of increased enrolment and loss of textbook fees has led schools to complain about budget shortages, as fees provide the resources for everyday tasks and programmes. In this regard, income targeting is an alternative to abolition of fees, as it allows cross-subsidization between those families that can afford higher fees and those on lower incomes who cannot. However, this alternative is only available when pupils are from a variety of backgrounds, which may be more unlikely in slum than in non-slum areas. The next best alternative is to help low-income families with the direct costs of education through conditional cash transfers and free transportation to school.

It is also important to consider the "geographical dimension of inclusive education", i.e., to pay more attention to inclusive education at the local and national levels. Highlighting social deprivation at the local level provides an incentive for policymakers and others to gain better understanding of the specific situation for students in each school, and create an opening for community participation in school improvement.[55]

In this second part of the report, the focus has gradually narrowed, from the characteristic dimensions of the urban divide and its current degree of prevalence across the world to its most tangible effects on those that have most to suffer from exclusion on a day-to-day basis. Overall, the evidence points to a continuum of deprivations on the wrong side of the urban divide, and they all call for redistributive change.

This and the four preceding chapters have highlighted various aspects of the paradox – some would say the scandal – that characterizes too many urban areas in this early 21st century. Cities concentrate what has become known as the "urban advantage", namely, a bundle of opportunities which, from basic and health services to education, amenities and gainful employment, have never been so favourable to human development. At the same time, in the developing world, cities also concentrate higher degrees of inequality than in rural areas – the urban divide. In fact, standards in slums and other low-income urban settlements can be as low as they remain in the countryside.

The other paradox – or scandal – of early 21st century cities is that not only do the benefits associated with urban life keep eluding the poorer segments of their populations, but these opportunities are more particularly denied to women and young people, who have such obvious vital roles to play in our collective future. This is why, as the continuum of urban deprivations described in each chapter has increasingly focused on the physical impact of slums and poverty on the bodies and minds of ordinary human beings, the number of recommendations for public authorities has also increased and gained in urgency in this Report.

Just as Part 2 identifies the failings and inadequacies in economic and social policies that lie behind the urban divide, Part 3 reintroduces the political and cultural dimensions of equality in order better to focus on remedies. The current state of urban inequality may represent only a transient phase in a broader, economics-driven dynamic; still, the ongoing waste of human capital and the attendant risks of social and political instability should act as incentives to make that transition as short as possible through redistributive change. As discussed in Part 3, bridging the urban divide calls for a more holistic vision–the "inclusive city". Whether or not a municipality formally endorses the concept of the "right to the city", a rights-based approach has two related benefits: it can put policymakers in a better position to identify the specific dynamics of integration at work locally, and to activate the various types of leverage that can bring about an "inclusive city".

END NOTES

1. Becker, 1991.
2. For a better understanding of hunger and food deprivation in urban areas, UN-HABITAT has analyzed Demographic and Health Survey and Multiple Indicator Cluster Survey data on child nutrition in Africa, Asia and Latin America and the Caribbean. Child malnutrition is assessed here as including both acute malnutrition (wasting) and chronic malnutrition (stunting). A child can be underweight for her or his age because s/he has suffered from "wasting", "stunting" or both. Wasting may be the result of inadequate food intake or recent episodes of illness causing loss of weight and the onset of malnutrition.
3. The wealth index measurement is used here to stratify the urban population into quintiles (poorest, second quintile, middle, fourth, and richest).
4. This analysis only includes countries with at least two sets of DHS data.
5. Grobler-Tanner, 2006.
6. Martinez & Fernandez, 2006.
7. United Nations Administrative Committee on Coordination, Subcommittee on Nutrition, 1988.
8. Helen Keller International, 2006.
9. International Monetary Fund, 2008.
10. Wahlberg, 2008.
11. Agarwal et al., 2002.
12. Recent research commissioned by UNICEF in 2009 in Bangladesh identified the same phenomena. See also The African Child Policy Forum, 2008.
13. Crowe, 2009.
14. Murillo, 2008.
15. As noted also by The African Child Policy Forum, 2008, poor households find they have to compromise on health care, education and other non-food household expenditures, or to sell key productive assets in order to cope with their worsened economic circumstances. See also UNICEF, 2008; Rashid, 2008.
16. The World Bank (2008) estimates that a doubling of food prices over the last three years could potentially push 100 million people in low-income countries deeper into poverty.
17. Martinez & Fernandez, 2006.
18. Catholic Relief Services, 2008.
19. Catholic Relief Services, 2008.
20. Catholic Relief Services, 2008.
21. As noted by Catholic Relief Services (2008), the Strategic Initiative on Urban and Peri-Urban Agriculture, an international research programme led by the International Potato Center, provides information on urban agriculture to local partners in a bid to help municipalities meet urban agricultural needs.
22. In Jordan in 1980, improvement of child nutrition was associated with the slum upgrading programme that expanded provision of and access to water and sanitation.
23. United Nations Administrative Committee on Coordination, Subcommittee on Nutrition, 1988.
24. Evans & Haller, 2005.
25. Proceedings from the South Asian Conference on Sanitation, 2006.
26. All data cited in this chapter is compiled from the most recent Demographic and Health Surveys available in the selected countries and analyzed by UN-HABITAT.
27. Where population density is low, and where soils can absorb water easily (e. g. sandy soils with a low groundwater level), some form of septic tank has been found to provide a safe and economic method of sewage disposal. The tank itself does not treat the sewage, and the water flowing out of it is highly contaminated; it is the soil into which the contaminated water flows that does the real 'filtering' of the sewage. However, where the water coming out of a septic tank system cannot be absorbed by the soil (and therefore runs along the ground), the system becomes a significant environmental health hazard and a septic tank is no longer appropriate. Septic tanks should not be located too close to drinking water supplies and pipes, as any leak is liable to contaminate drinking water.
28. Research on overcrowding in low-income settlements conducted by UN-HABITAT in 1995 confirmed that infectious diseases are likely to thrive in overcrowded and low-income areas due to lack of ventilation and hygiene as well as unhealthy environmental exposures. Supportive evidence has shown that diseases run rampant in crowded places.
29. Bruce, Perez-Padilla & Albalak, 2000; Smith, Samet, Romieu, & Bruce, 2000; Engle, Hurtado & Ruel, 1997.
30. Potential harm is the greatest for children under one year, since their lungs and immune system are not yet fully formed. Household use of biomass fuels has been found to significantly increase the risk of acute respiratory infections, which annually kill millions of children under age five (Smith, Samet, Romieu, & Bruce, 2000).
31. Raffensperger, 2007. Human exposure to these pollutants indoors is compounded in homes with close quarters and poor ventilation. Even low levels of indoor air pollution can negatively affect health because of the proportionally large amount of time families spend indoors. For that reason, researchers now take into account not only pollutant concentration but amount of time spent in each environment, calculating individual "time-activity patterns". Using this metric, the number of people exposed at unacceptable levels indoors is equivalent to or greater than the number exposed to unacceptable levels outdoors in all the world's cities combined (Smith, Samet, Romieu, & Bruce, 2000). Though no international standards for indoor air pollution exist, studies show that daily average levels of small particles in households that burn solid fuels are six to 60 times the World Health Organization air pollution guidelines (Rehfuess, Mehta & Prüss-Üstün, 2006).
32. See for example Ezzati & Kammen, 2002; Albalak, et al., 2001; Wafula, Kinyanjui, Nyabola, & Tenambergen, 2000.
33. World Bank, 2008a; Corvalán, Kjellstrom & Smith, 1999.
34. United Nations Industrial Development Organization (UNIDO), 2004.
35. Djagba, Mboup, Guedeme, & Nouatin, 1999; Mboup, 1997.
36. Inequalities in education and employment are assessed in this Report with data from Multiple Indicator Cluster Surveys administered by the United Nations Children's Fund (UNICEF) and Demographic and Health Surveys, funded by the U.S. Agency for International Development (USAID), collected between 1990 and 2007. These surveys include information on school attendance and literacy, youth employment and child labour that can be disaggregated by type of residence: urban and rural; slum and non-slum. UN-HABITAT has also used some data from Labour Force Surveys, funded by the International Labour Organization, and Living Standard Measurement Surveys, funded by the World Bank.
37. Filmer, 2000.
38. Lockheed, 2008.
39. Postiglione, 2006.
40. Hanushek, 2008.
41. Tembon & Fort, 2008.
42. As noted by Mannathoko, 2008.
43. Aslam, Kingdon & Söderbom, 2008.
44. Al-Mekhlafy, 2008.
45. Tembon & Fort, 2008.
46. Alberdi, 2009.
47. This is reflected in the age pyramid of slum areas, which shows that slum communities have more girls than boys between the ages of 5 and 14 years.
48. Akpo, 2008.
49. Rashid & Hossain, 2005; Lockheed, 2008. Parental concerns about the physical safety of their daughters may make community and non formal alternative schools, for example, more attractive than regular public schools. In Rajasthan, India, community schools employing paraprofessional teachers and part-time workers who escort girls from excluded groups to school have increased their enrollment, attendance, and test scores relative to those of regular public schools. Preschool programs in Bolivia, Brazil, and Turkey that involve both mothers and children from excluded groups have been effective in reducing children's subsequent dropout rates from primary school, as well as boosting their achievement (Lockheed, 2008).
50. Kirk, 2008. Fostering girl-friendly environments in education is one of the main objectives of UNICEF's "child-friendly schools" initiative, as deployed by 50 countries worldwide since its launch in the early 1990s. The "gender and development" framework promotes four specific types of initiatives: (1) a more gender-balanced make-up of teaching and non- teaching staff; (2) making school buildings and grounds physically and psychologically safe for girls; (3) providing adequate facilities for personal hygiene; and (4) policies to fight discrimination, harassment and abuse.
51. Barrera-Osorio, 2008.
52. Al-Mekhlafy, 2008.
53. Rambla, Ferrer, Tarabini, & Verger, 2008. See also Duru-Bellat, Kieffer & Reimer, 2008. The authors explore social selectivity in access to tertiary education in France and Germany in the period from 1980 to 2000. They show that access to different postsecondary institutions is characterized by marked social background effects in both countries.

THE SOCIAL DIVIDE – IMPACT ON BODIES AND MINDS

PART
03

Bridging the
Urban Divide

©Don Tran/Shutterstock

Quick Facts

1. The "right to the city" concept has been put to use to varying degrees of success over the past half-century, although some countries have ignored or spurned it altogether.

2. The "right to the city" must not be viewed as a new legal instrument, but instead subsumes a wide range of universally recognized human rights into a single claim for enforcement in urban areas.

3. Many cities in the developing world devise and enforce inclusive policies that abide by national and international commitments without any explicit reference to the "right to the city."

4. Whether they formally endorse the "right to the city" or not, many municipal authorities are institutionally ill-equipped to make this right effective, including when it comes to coordination with national and state/provincial government.

Policy Points

1. Individual or collective economic marginalization frequently extends to access to social services, cultural expression and political participation.

2. The "right to the city" can provide municipal authorities with the platform they need for a wide range of policies and initiatives that promote an "inclusive" urban environment.

3. A strong human rights-based approach upholds the dignity of all urban residents in the face of multiple rights violations, including the right to decent living conditions.

4. The right to the city calls for a holistic, balanced and multicultural type of urban development, including mixed neighbourhoods.

5. The basic principle behind the right to the city is that human rights are interdependent and indivisible, i.e., they are to be pursued simultaneously, if only achieved gradually over time.

6. Municipal rights-based approaches must be deployed in all policy areas, including land use, planning, management and reform, and in close cooperation with government bodies and civil society.

3.1
Taking forward the right to the city
The "urban advantage" for all

As described in Part 2, various lines of divide combine to deprive large numbers of residents from access to many of the opportunities cities have to offer - the "urban advantage". The often vital contribution of those in low-earning jobs to urban prosperity is not properly recognized not just in economic but also civic, political, cultural and other terms. They can neither fully realize their productive potential nor participate effectively in the decisions that impact on their lives. They are not socially integrated and often carry the stigma of the urban area where they reside. They are also denied opportunities to contribute to the city's cultural life and style.

How do cities close the urban divide? How do they become more inclusive, economically, politically, socially and culturally? What principles, platforms and strategies can public authorities deploy to bridge the current divide and make cities more inclusive? These are the questions virtually all the regions of the world are facing in this early 21st century, whether highly developed, emerging, in transition or post-conflict situations. They are as relevant to highly centralized nations and to those with devolved government, East, West, North and South.

The concept has been deployed differently in various regions, countries and cities of the world. Some places have applied the "Right to the City" as a theoretical, political, conceptual framework that refers to such aspects as enforcement, empowerment, participation, self-realization, self-determination, and different forms of protection of existing human rights at the city level. In other places, the concept is absent from the political discourse, either not used at all, or banned outright. Where the concept has been applied, it has not always achieved higher levels of inclusion; large numbers of people, particularly in the developing world, do not fully benefit from the "urban advantage", do not participate in decision-making and do not enjoy effective fundamental rights and liberties, while others do, live in

RAQUEL ROLNIK

In Latin America over the past few decades, an intense debate has enthralled civil society, political parties and governments—one over the role played by citizens in urban governance. Those years were also marked by the pursuit of a decentralized model and stronger local autonomy. Some significant legal breakthroughs are worthy of note in connection with the right to housing and the right to the city: several national constitutions and statute books (such as with the City Statute in Brazil) have come to include the principles of the social function of the city and property, the recognition of occupation rights for millions of slum dwellers, and the empowerment of citizens in urban decisionmaking. This rights-based approach has been advocated by social movements, non-government organizations, trade unions, and academic or research institutions, as part of campaigns in favour of democratic municipal management and the right to the city. This, in turn, came as a response to one of the fastest and most intense social and geographical phenomena ever witnessed: the massive reshaping of a typically rural into a predominantly urban population in fewer than 40 years (up until 1980). This was when urbanization in Latin America saw vast contingents of poor rural migrants run against a model of urban development that typically excluded the lower-income segments of the population, depriving them from any sense of citizenship or local belonging.

The "agenda of urban reform" has subsequently been endorsed over time by Brazil's political parties and governments. At the same time, though, Latin American cities, and large metropolitan areas in particular, came under the influence of the neoliberal macroeconomic reforms that burgeoned in the early 1990s, resulting in massive unemployment and the erosion of social institutions. The process only exacerbated already existing social and economic asymmetries, ultimately hindering the capacity of public authorities and social stakeholders to cope with them. These reforms extended to the whole government sector, including privatization of public utilities, plans to modernize and downsize government, introduction of entrepreneurial management, and a "participatory" rhetoric emphasizing the role of civil society. A kind of "perverse convergence" brought together—if only in a shared rhetoric—various political projects that pointed out to different directions. The participatory-democratic project has its origins in the challenge to authoritarian regimes, and ambitioned to build a new institutional reality to pave the way for a new social and cultural dispensation. Now collectively dubbed "the third sector" (alongside the government and market sectors), civil society was caught up in a movement that looked to downsize government in the name of "participation" and "citizenship".

The shared rhetoric conceals differences and minimizes antagonisms, emphasizing social, political and territorial fragmentation while diluting the promise of a full-fledged democratic endeavour in the form of full and universal access to civil, political, economic and social rights. As far as urban development models are more specifically concerned, the rhetoric of "participation" and "citizenship" implies that all citizens, regardless of income, ethnicity, race, creed or gender, are entitled to full access to the goods, services and opportunities that are locally available for the purposes of human development.

For about two decades now, urban reform across Latin America has had its ups and downs, hostage as it was to both this novel rhetoric and an enduring legacy of predatory territorial management by the more privileged. The "participatory" rhetoric has failed to pave the way for the dynamic relationship with mainstream political parties that could have boosted the quest for more cohesive, inclusive and sustainable cities. On the other hand, the rhetoric of "participation" and "citizenship" has continued to challenge urban policies in Latin America. As such, it has been a source of cultural innovation and civic rights promotion, and has expanded the spatial and political scope of Latin American democracy.

An architect and urban planner, Raquel Rolnik was appointed United Nations Special Rapporteur on the Right to Adequate Housing in 2008.

---

decent, healthy and environmentally friendly places with full exercise of their citizenship. Some other countries have made important efforts to close the urban divide without the overt use of the concept. Despite these ambiguities, the "Right to the City" remains a powerful vehicle for social change that warrants serious consideration.

What follows is a review of the "Right to the City" as it has been applied explicitly and implicitly in various regions, countries and cities. An effort is made to discern key principles that underlie the concept so that these might inform efforts by cities to promote inclusion and close the urban divide, even in regions where the historical, political and cultural conditions are not conducive to an explicit application of the "Right to the City" approach. The chapter reviews the factors that limit the ability of cities to translate policy into effective practice. These include poor coordination among tiers of government, absence of data for informed policy choices, influence of vested interests, weak adjustment to changing economic conditions, exclusion of marginalized groups and discrimination of minorities.

Evolution of the right to the city

The right to the city has evolved over the past 50 years under the influence of social groups and civil society organizations in response to the need for better opportunities for all, especially the more marginalized and underprivileged. In 2004, social movements and organizations from around the world together devised a *World Charter on the Right to the City*, with support from UNESCO and UN-HABITAT, among other agencies. This in turn led to the adoption of local charters in a number of cities.

The right to the city should not be viewed as a new legalistic instrument, but rather as an expression of the deep yearnings of urban dwellers to see their multiple human rights become more effective in urban areas.[1] In this perspective, the right to the city serves as a bulwark against the exclusionary types of development, the selective benefit-sharing and the marginalization and discrimination that are rampant in cities today. The right to the city provides an adequate platform for action as well as a framework for human rights enforcement.

So far, few countries or cities have given formal, explicit recognition to the right to the city in those of their policies, strategies or legislations that look to narrow the urban divide. Brazil was the first country to include in its Constitution (1988) a specific chapter on urban policy. Coming in response to years of dictatorship, this progressive body of law called on municipal authorities to deploy a range of instruments that could guarantee the right to the city, uphold the social function of cities and property, and make urban management more democratic.[2] At nationwide level, Brazil's *City Statute* (2001) is a groundbreaking body of legislation that redefines the concept of land ownership as it asserts the social value of urban land.[3] In São Paulo, the largest city in the country, experts surveyed by UN-HABITAT concurred that "talking about rights is talking about the right to the city".[4] One expert defined this right as "the equal enjoyment of cities within the principles of sustainability, democracy and social justice". Furthermore, "a city is a collective space, culturally rich and diversified, that belongs to all residents. The right to the city is an important entitlement to be claimed for by all those groups, both mainstream and marginalized, that live and interact in the city".[5]

Still in Latin America, in 2008 Ecuador recognized several housing-related rights in its new Constitution.[6] This pioneering, progressive statute simultaneously endorses: (1) the right to the city; (2) the right to adequate and dignified housing; (3) the right to a secure and healthy habitat; and (4) the right to water and sanitation.[7] Responding to the UN-HABITAT survey, an expert from Portoviejo, Ecuador, commented that "the right to the city [stood for] broad and unrestricted access to services, opinions, freedom of movement and access to space and economic opportunities". He added that "this right is, in its broader sense, endorsed by decisionmakers, as well as recognized and implemented by the community in everyday life through widespread practice."[8]

Many other cities in the developing world devise and deploy policies in compliance with national legal commitments to more inclusive communities, and although they fall short of explicit references to the right to the city *per se*, they endorse some particular aspects of the notion. For example, Rosario, Argentina's third largest city, has declared itself a *"Human Rights City"* with a formal commitment to openness, transparency and accountability. The municipality has opened itself up to scrutiny by a citizens' committee that monitors performance against international law on a continuing basis, making recommendations and organizing human rights training and awareness campaigns.[9] Another commendable example is the *Victoria Charter of Human Rights and Responsibilities* (2006) in Australia, which "recognizes that everyone is equally entitled to participate in, and contribute to, society and (the) community". The charter further sets out that "all individuals have equal rights to the provision of, and access to, Council services and facilities".[10] The purpose of the 20 rights that are recognized in the Victoria charter is to "assist

all people to live in freedom, respect, equality and dignity". The practical rationale is to secure effective rights recognition in all municipal planning and policymaking functions, anticipating on and preventing human rights infringements. This is why the Charter "requires all public authorities and their employees to act in compatibility with human rights in the delivery of services and when making decisions".[11]

Relevant urban policies and practices integrate aspects of democratic governance that are either explicitly or implicitly consistent with the "right to the city" concept. For instance in Dakar, municipal leaders and local authorities in 2003 endorsed a *"Civic and Citizens' Pact"* which sets out reciprocal responsibilities among signatories. The pact commits municipal authorities to acknowledge the diversity of cultures and beliefs among all residents; conversely, community-based organizations have agreed to act in a socially responsible way.[12] In India in 2001, a municipal authority has enacted a largely similar *"Citizens Charter"* that redefines its own functions in relation to residents' rights and expectations, with due regard for the need for reform and to hear public grievances.[13] This repositioning of municipal authorities was pioneered in the 1980s by the Brazilian city of Porto Alegre , with its participatory budgeting *(Orçamento Participativo)* on which over 70 cities around the world have since modeled their own procedures.[14] In 2004 came another improvement, known as the *Local Solidarity Governance Programme*; this scheme further entrenches participatory budgeting, with all Porto Alegre residents invited to sit in forums where projects for the next city budget are proposed and prioritized. The programme is implemented across the city's 17 municipal subdivisions, turning Porto Alegre into a "networked participatory city".[15]

A number of cities in India, Ghana, South Africa, Colombia, Brazil, Ecuador, Peru and other Latin American countries are also taking forward the right to the city concept in a variety of spheres (social, economic, political and cultural). However, progress is often rather slow and sometimes runs into continuous setbacks. This is the case in Mexico and Argentina, where various efforts keep stalling because the four dimensions of the inclusive city are not involved simultaneously. In some cities and countries, particularly in South-Eastern and Eastern Asia and North Africa, economic growth policies have gone hand in hand with positive social developments such as broad provision of basic services, improved literacy and life expectancy rates, and reductions in the prevalence of hunger and extreme poverty. These cities enjoy a decent quality of life; however, political rights and freedom are lagging behind. The Washington, D.C.-based non-governmental organization Freedom House (in its annual *Freedom in the World* report) rates some of those countries as "not free" (North Africa and East Asia) or "partly free" (Morocco and South-East Asia (except "free" Indonesia). Still, other cities and countries, mainly in sub-Saharan Africa and Western Asia, are looking to deploy legal and political frameworks based on equality and rights.

Rosario, Argentina. The country's third largest metropolis has declared itself a "human rights city". ©**Flavia Morlachetti /Shutterstock**

▲
Delhi, India. Rights-based urban policies pave the way for inclusiveness. ©**Galina Mikhalishina** /**Shutterstock**

Factors restricting the right to the city:
The disjuncture between policy aims and processes

For all their noteworthy efforts, those municipalities committed to a "right to the city" approach and those that have pursued other concepts of inclusion share a common feature, namely, a certain disjuncture between *policy* and *process*. Few have managed fully to turn policies aims into processes that actually bridge the urban divide and achieve more inclusiveness.

Part of the problem lies in a wide range of pressures, including urban expansion (or various forms of contraction, as the case may be), historical socioeconomic inequalities and grinding poverty, together with environmental degradation and natural disasters as compounded by the effects of climate change, among other threats. This is particularly the case with those cities in the developing world that experience serious resource constraints and lack the inclusive mechanisms and institutions required to bridge the urban divide. These cities have not yet devised proper programmes or initiatives to reduce inequality and tackle service shortfalls; they lack the mechanisms that would enable them to understand and anticipate some of the factors generating further inequalities (i.e., scarcity of land and concentration of ownership in very few hands; lack of redistributive policies; ineffective housing markets, etc.). Leaders in these cities have not demonstrated the strength of vision or political commitment needed to overcome the urban divide. Even cities with a stronger resource base are also struggling to implement more inclusive policies. They are typically hampered by five main factors: (1) weak institutions, often with outdated mandates and responsibilities; (2) multiple agencies, operating together with overlapping functions and poor results; (3) lack of adequate human and financial resources; (4) poor performance of fiscal and administrative systems; and (5) lack of harmony between political and technical interests, which results for instance in unethical planning practices or budget allocations to non-priority areas. Various other factors also hinder efforts to bridge the urban divide, contributing both to the cause and consequences of poor policies and ineffective urban governance.

In some cities, the disjuncture between policy aims and processes is not only the result of limited institutional and organizational capacities; it also has to do with rent-seeking groups that lobby for their vested interests to the detriment of other residents, as highlighted in the UN-HABITAT survey. Moreover, policy aims and processes often do not match because they fail to acknowledge the inter-linkages among the four spheres or dimensions of the inclusive city. This in turn has to do largely with the persistent view of development as synonymous with economic growth, with little attention paid to other dimensions of inclusiveness such as the need for distributive policies, more effective channels of social and political participation, and recognition of cultural diversity. The problem with development strategies has been that they view development as a technical problem requiring technical solutions,[16] instead of a systemic, organic process that includes all four critical dimensions of society. Any degree of recognition that is given to the four dimensions at the policymaking stage is often lost in the process of implementation. UN-HABITAT policy analysis found that cities frequently adopt new laws and regulations to address some exclusion-related issues, but these fail to turn into goalposts, sustained processes or tangible results that can be monitored. The reason for this disjuncture often lies in the institutional frameworks themselves: over time, they tend gradually to embed negative and rather inefficient attitudes, as well as informal social arrangements that are impervious to change. This is most evident in the lack of planning and coordination among central, regional and municipal institutions in Africa, Asia and Latin America.

Lack of coordination between national, provincial and local authorities

Table 3.1.1 shows that an overwhelming majority of cities surveyed across the three regions of the developing world feature very poor coordination for both planning and implementation on urban issues across national, provincial and municipal governments (first column left). Data in the table also confirms the weak linkage between coordination for planning and coordination for implementation (middle column), with fewer than 25 per cent of respondents from cities in Latin America and Asia reckoning that coordination was effective among the three tiers of government. This comes as a reminder that even where municipal authorities develop elaborate master plans with some kind of support from regional and central government, these are not matched by budget allocations or the organizational or technical skills that would ensure that implementation effectively involves the three tiers of government.

For instance, the master plan for Abuja, Nigeria's capital since 1991, was consciously designed in 1979 by various tiers of government with help from a foreign consultancy, and underwent further, multi-agency revisions after the year 2000. At the design stage, the master plan provided the platform needed to bridge the divide between rich and poor, making adequate provisions for inclusion in its different dimensions. Still, the process of turning the dream into reality is running into serious problems. As one of the local respondents to the UN-HABITAT survey commented, "implementation is not inclusive socially, politically or economically".[17] The high degree of institutional coordination among government agencies and various partners in the design stage has gone missing during the implementation phase.

Table 3.1.1 also shows that large majorities of experts in Asia and Latin America and the Caribbean reckon there is hardly any coordination for planning and implementation between the three tiers of government (third column right). On the other hand, and somewhat surprisingly, only 41 per cent of experts in Africa report a lack of such coordination in their respective cities. This relatively favourable return reflects the fact that the survey sample includes Accra, Dakar, Durban and Johannesburg – four cities where well-coordinated planning and implementation is supported by adequate efforts and resources.

Surveyed experts perceived coordination among government agencies to be more effective for the promotion of economic growth and inclusion than for cultural and political inclusion. Findings were that central governments tend to formulate and implement national policies and programmes with only some minor degree of involvement by local authorities as far as political and cultural inclusion is concerned. In some other cases, however, these initiatives originate with local authorities, but regional and central government shows little support or interest to collaborate. As a result, coordination is far from uniformly effective across the four dimensions that make up an inclusive city: some plans and actions related to economic and social development and inclusion tend to be better coordinated than those for cultural and political inclusion, which typically tend to attract only poor coordination. This is confirmed again by UN-HABITAT survey returns, which show that lack of policy focus (on all aspects of inclusion, as opposed to the mere promotion of economic opportunities) and absence of political will are two of the most critical factors hindering municipal inclusion policies in the three developing regions (see Table 3.1.2).

Making informed policy choices

In addition to lack of clear institutional coordination, ill-informed policymaking contributes substantially to municipal failure to integrate the four dimensions of equality in any "organic" manner. The UN-HABITAT survey sought to capture the extent to which informed policymaking was an essential part of slum upgrading policies in the 27 cities under review. The finding is that fewer than 50 per cent of survey respondents across Africa, Asia and Latin America and the Caribbean thought that slum upgrading policies were informed and based on sound local data. This result corroborates previous UN-HABITAT research as part of the Urban Indicators Programme, where 80 out of 120 cities surveyed admitted to lacking the institutional capabilities and human skills required to monitor urban growth. Municipalities' lack of technical skills is a reflection of a more general state of national underdevelopment. The 2009 UN-HABITAT survey found that Latin American cities were better equipped than those in Asia, which in turn outdid Africa. Even where some degree of institutional capacity can be found, institutional inertia in resource-poor environments leads to gradual erosion of any processes that promote coordination. Those institutions whose mandates involve urban planning and implementation are, more often than not, keener to preserve their respective turfs and assert their self-importance than to focus on proper planning and urban harmony.

Interest group influence

In the 27 cities surveyed by UN-HABITAT, powerful political and interest group influences were found to interfere with inclusive urban policies. These influences frequently take different forms that can be illustrated with two examples: (1) poor provision of public spaces and related services for all residents, and (2) arbitrary conversion or grabbing of public or reserved land by powerful interests. For example, religious groups in India are erecting temples in public parks; private interests in Bangladesh are constructing massive real estate developments along riverbanks; and developers and informal settlers in Nairobi, Kenya are constantly claiming riparian lands. Undue appropriation of critical public spaces by private entities often goes unnoticed, or is even promoted by municipal authorities. Similarly, changing the status of land from rural to urban on the periphery of expanding cities is typically associated with speculative investments by those better-off, and almost automatically excludes the poor and underprivileged.

In the city of Guadalajara, Mexico, recent research confirmed the findings of the UN-HABITAT survey. Because of relentless expansion of developments on the outskirts of the city, some 30 per cent of this new housing stock remains unoccupied, even as in the inner city a similar percentage goes underused.[18] This situation highlights the speculative patterns of investment at work, which are largely influenced by powerful interests. The experts responding to the UN-HABITAT survey pointed to the urban rich, political elites and civil servants as the interest groups that most benefit from urban expansion and reform. Table 3.1.3 shows that 59 per cent of Latin American, 69 per cent of Asian and 71 per cent of African respondents viewed urban reforms and changes as serving the interests of the rich. Similarly, politicians and bureaucrats are viewed as the second major group benefiting the most from the urbanization process, with the exception of Africa where they are considered to be the greatest beneficiaries (77 per cent). This goes to show that the urban poor in general stand to share only to a minimal extent, if at all, in any benefits accruing from urbanization and related reforms. The survey findings reflect the relatively more stable and accountable forms of democracy prevailing in Latin American as opposed to Asian and African cities. They also point to the extent of misallocation of scarce budget resources to non-priority areas as a result of interest group influences.

More generally, planning and policies appear to favour the empowered, mainly local and regional economic elites. In the developing world, this pattern is more often than not associated with historical and cultural hegemony, which adds to the inter-generational aspects of urban exclusion that lead to spatial partitioning and gentrification. Moreover, in

TABLE 3.1.1: **COORDINATION OF PLANNING AND IMPLEMENTATION, 27 CITIES** (percentage of respondents agreeing with each option)*

REGION	Effective coordination for both planning and implementation	Effective coordination for planning but not implementation	No coordination at all for planning or implementation
LAC	0.7	24	73
Asia	0.7	25	65
Africa	13	47	41

Source: UN-HABITAT, City Monitoring Branch, Policy analysis 2009
*Multiple responses not adding up to 100 per cent.

TABLE 3.1.2: **FACTORS HINDERING INCLUSION POLICIES, 27 CITIES** (percentage of respondents agreeing with each option)*

REGION	Lack of Policy Focus	Lack of Political Will	Lack of Human Resources	Inadequate Community Participation	Lack of Funding
LAC	42	48	23	38	26
Asia	44	36	25	23	17
Africa	41	46	13	33	21

Monitoring Branch, Policy analysis 2009
*Multiple responses not adding up to 100 per cent.

TABLE 3.1.3: **WHO BENEFITS MOST FROM URBAN REFORMS, 27 CITIES** (percentage of respondents agreeing with each option)*

REGION	The Urban Rich	The Urban Poor not living in Slums	The Urban Poor in Slums	Politicians and Bureaucrats (due to Corruption)	No particular interest group
LAC	59	23	19	39	11
ASIA	69	15	19	61	0.9
Africa	71	0.5	11	77	0.6

Source: UN-HABITAT, City Monitoring Branch, Policy analysis 2009
*Multiple responses not adding up to 100 per cent.

addition to gentrification, a number of other large projects and events have created urban environments that are of little benefit to the poor. These have included large infrastructure projects (water, sanitation and roads), "city beautification", riverfront development schemes and facilities for major global sports and cultural events.

Building facilities for *cultural mega-events* has on occasion led to the resettlement of underprivileged communities (Seville 1992, Shanghai 2010), as have *political mega-events* (Manila 1976, Seoul 1985), or *sporting mega-events* such as the Olympic Games, World Football Cup, Commonwealth Games and other regional events which, in some cases, can result in some

forms of discrimination and inequality, such as forced evictions of people living in slums and informal settlements to make way for infrastructure development (Beijing 2008, New Delhi 2010, Vancouver 2010). These sporting mega-events can also result in displacement of homeless people (Osaka 2002, Seoul 2002). Each of these events has more indirect consequences as well. For example, infrastructure improvements through redevelopment can lead to decreases in the public housing stock and an escalation in real estate prices, which makes housing unaffordable for many low-income residents and other marginalized groups. The desire to "show off" a city and make it an attractive tourist destination is often accompanied by a process of "sanitization", i.e., a "clean-up" of public areas that is facilitated by criminalization of the homeless and increased brutality by police forces. Rebuilding a city's image appears, from the examples of many mega-events, to mean making it more attractive for local, national and international elites (middle- and high-income earners), and as a result, less livable for those who fall outside these categories.[19]

The most excluded groups: A typology

A review of the various forms of exclusion and the layers of horizontal discrimination in selected cities shows that multiple forms of discrimination overlap at any given time. As one of the experts from Latin America commented as part of the UN-HABITAT survey, "when one is [economically] poor, one is also poor and excluded in a cultural, social and political sense".[20] Indeed, survey results have shown that when an individual or group is marginalized from economic opportunities, it is very likely that this condition extends to access to social services, expression of cultural identity and participation in political life. Exclusion in this sense "results from a complex and dynamic set of processes and relationships that prevent individuals and groups from accessing resources, participating in society and asserting their rights".[21]

Individuals and groups can find themselves excluded from the right to vote, the right to enter and enjoy all areas of the city, the right to use social and cultural facilities and venues, the right to access basic services, and various other rights which effectively restrict their full enjoyment of the right to the city. It is worthy of note that, from a list of categories or groups (women and children, the elderly, the disabled, uneducated people, migrants, ethnic groups and other minorities in terms of race or caste, people on low incomes and slum dwellers), three appear to be the most systematically excluded in various cities in Asia, Africa, Latin America and the Caribbean: the disabled, the elderly and slum dwellers, followed by the uneducated (for African cities, see Figure 3.1.1). In cities like Dakar, Mombasa, Abuja, Chittagong, Kathmandu, Dhaka, Port-au-Prince and Buenos Aires, slum dwellers are the most excluded from the various urban functions.

Exclusion is entrenched and rooted in the long history of marginalization and hierarchy that permeates the social patterns of individual cities. The urban poor, and slum dwellers in particular, go unnoticed and the places where they live are often not formally recognized by local or central authorities. However, in many parts of the world these "invisible" areas are growing faster than the "visible" ones.[22] Excluded groups in slum areas typically fall victim to a sort of *triple jeopardy*:

(1) they are poor and uneducated; (2) many are migrants or from ethnic minorities; and (3) many are female. As long as municipal authorities remain unaware of these groups and the underlying causes of their exclusion, they will remain unable to find effective ways to support them, and will fail them in a systematic way.

If city authorities are effectively to address the needs of these and other excluded groups, they must recognize that their systematic marginalization is unfair and avoidable – a wholesale denial of their "right to the city". This calls for informed discussions, negotiating support and proposing policies and actions that tackle the root causes and persistence of disadvantage, marginalization and exclusion. Municipal authorities must also devise a number of short- and long-term strategic responses to be delivered by all relevant organizations and institutions as part of anti-exclusion policies, with proper monitoring mechanisms. Otherwise, cities will persistently fail to acknowledge, uphold and fulfil the rights of all the individuals under their jurisdictions.

Co-evolution of policies with urban expansion and needs

Cities are constantly changing. They are built, rebuilt, transformed and inhabited by various groups, and used for various functions. In this sense, planning comes as an attempt to bring some order to this constant process of transformation. However, the evolution of cities in the developing world is under pressure from the multiple forces that make it difficult for planners and decision-makers to manage. As urban labour market structures steer away from manufacturing to services and high technology, it is important to provide the working poor with opportunities to retrain for jobs in the new growth sectors. The UN-HABITAT survey highlights a relative predominance of manufacturing and unskilled labour across the three regions under review. However, Asian cities feature far higher percentages of service and high-technology workers compared with Africa, Latin America and the Caribbean. Unskilled jobs, including in the services sector, are, by nature, less well-paid than high-technology jobs, and people in these categories tend to be economically underprivileged. Also needed are economic and fiscal incentives to support the economic transition process, particularly for small enterprises. However, in many cities these support schemes lag behind the economic transition process because of resource constraints, weak institutions and inadequate policies. This is how and why cities struggle to catch up with these structural changes, leaving large sections of the population behind and in the process exacerbating the urban divide.

Beijing, China. The risk with sporting and other "mega events" is that they can further maginalize the underprivileged. ©**Lee Prince/Shutterstock**

FIGURE 3.1.1: **PERCEIVED DEGREE OF EXCLUSION OF UNDERPRIVILEGED GROUPS (SEVEN AFRICAN CITIES)** *

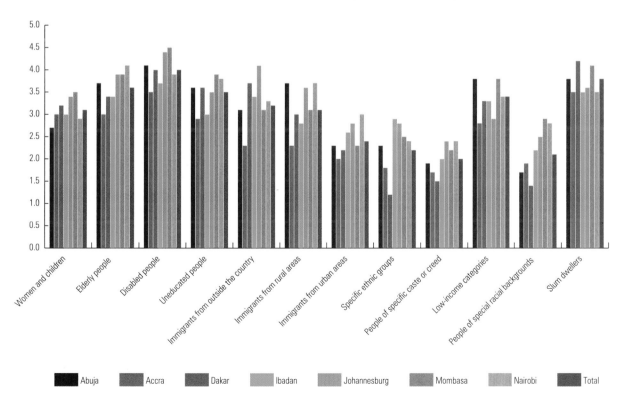

Source: UN-HABITAT, City Monitoring Branch, Policy analysis 2009
* Average of ratings (on a scale of 0 to 5) by local experts responding to the UN-HABITAT 2009 survey.

REGION	Vocational training	Simpler procedures for employment	New rules to promote equitable opportunities	State-created employment[1]*	Fiscal incentives	Micro-credit
LAC	0.8	0.6	0.9	13	10	15
Asia	14	11	0.9	18	11	21
Africa	23	0.7	14	24	11	28

Source: UN-HABITAT, City Monitoring Branch, Policy analysis 2009
For example, labour-intensive infrastructure development.

Table 3.1.4 shows that policies in support of urban economic change are lacking in Asia and Latin America. Local experts responding to the UN-HABITAT survey found that African cities provided relatively more vocational training (23 per cent), a perception that largely reflects tangible achievements in Accra and Ibadan. Elsewhere in Africa, though, vocational training clearly falls short of improving the labour market. Likewise, local experts reported that promotion of employment through simplified procedures was not happening in Latin American or African cities, and remained rather minimal in Asia. Deregulation, incentives and more favourable regulations were equally found lacking in Latin America and Asia, while Africa's relatively better ranking was entirely due to Johannesburg's strong individual performance. Another significant way of reducing inequalities of income and opportunities is state-created employment, a major source of labour-intensive jobs for unskilled or semi-skilled workers. UN-HABITAT survey respondents ranked state-created employment higher than other factors, though still relatively low. Although well-adapted to the needs of the urban poor (see Ch.3.3.), labour-intensive, state-created employment may not facilitate the adaptation of the local labour market to the novel types of jobs generated by new, growing economic sectors.

A comparison of employment trends with available job-generating factors makes the case for dedicated policy instruments at the city level in order better to distribute the benefits of prosperity. In close coordination with national government, dedicated municipal policies have the potential to provide targeted, context-specific solutions. Short of this, a city denies residents access to decent jobs and, indirectly, the right to adequate housing and other public goods and amenities, which together are fundamental aspects of the right to the city.

▲
Kathmandu, Nepal. The urban working poor need training into new skills.
©Dhoxax/Shutterstock

BOX 3.1.2: THE PRINCIPLES UNDERLYING THE "RIGHT TO THE CITY"

The right to the city calls for a holistic, balanced and multicultural type of development. This includes mixed neighbourhoods, as opposed to gated communities for the rich, "city beautification" or renewal schemes which all forcibly relocate the poor to the urban fringes. Urban working classes, who build cities and keep them operating smoothly, are entitled to adequate housing and basic services, too. Their living conditions must be gradually improved, *in situ* as far as possible, instead of being exposed to forced evictions and displacement. The contribution of the poor to a city's economy must be acknowledged and laws should not discriminate against them in favour of the rich.

The right to the city is a vision for an alternative, adequate and ideal city. It is not merely the right to any city, especially not to cities the way we know them today, but instead one where mutual respect, tolerance, democracy and social justice prevail. The right to the city incorporates four major principles.

Indivisibility of Human Rights. The basic principle of the right to city is that human rights are interdependent and indivisible, i.e., they are to be realized simultaneously. All human rights – civil, political, economic, social, cultural and environmental – must receive equal priority in urban governance, planning, management and implementation. The right to the city calls for acknowledgement and protection of all human rights such as self-determination, freedom of assembly and organization, and the right to personal and collective development.

Non-discrimination and Inclusion. Rights must be guaranteed to all those – including women, youth and children – who choose to make the city their home, irrespective of economic status, identity, caste, class, race, gender, religion, sexual inclination, occupation or civil status, and regardless of whether they are legal residents or formal "citizens." Cities must create enabling environments that provide equal access or entitlement to, and enjoyment of, basic and public services, public spaces and all kinds of benefits and opportunities for everyone. Cities must prevent social segregation, gentrification, social apartheid, criminalization of the poor and the homeless, as well as the increasing "ghettoization" of urban spaces that is becoming widespread across the world.

Priority to Vulnerable and Marginalized Groups. The principle of non-discrimination also calls for special protection of, and priority to, the rights of the more marginalized groups: women, the elderly and disabled, slum dwellers, the uneducated, migrants, etc. Cities must cater to the needs and rights of those belonging to historically discriminated groups, including through affirmative action where needed (with close monitoring of outcomes). The right to the city implies a strong commitment to poverty reduction and the removal of discriminatory legal and policy provisions.

Gender Equality. The right to the city is also the right to a "gendered city" ensuring equal protection and realization of women's human rights. Women's participation in city planning and governance is critical to any balanced, equitable urban development. Municipal authorities must develop and implement policies in close consultation with women to ensure they fully benefit from the "urban advantage" – including health, education, decent employment, adequate housing, equal access to both public and private spaces, public transport, streets, sidewalks, markets, parks, toilets (both public and private), workspaces, political spaces, and community spaces, all in a safe environment.

* Based on the background document "Taking the Right to the City Forward: Obstacles and Promises" prepared for UN-HABITAT by Miloon Kothari and Shivani Chaudhry, October 2009.

BOX 3.1.3: MAKING THE RIGHT TO THE CITY A REALITY: HOW TO COUNTER OBSTACLES

Taking the right to the city forward is not an easy task. The current reality is that this right is effective only for certain segments of society, with the economic and political power that affords those the full benefits of the "urban advantage". Cities all over the world, and particularly in developing countries, must take into account the following six critical aspects if they are to guarantee an effective right to the city for all.

Implementing international legal human rights commitments. This includes the enforcement of any human rights standards embedded in ratified legal instruments such as the International Covenant on Economic, Social and Cultural Rights, the International Covenant on Civil and Political Rights, the Convention on the Elimination of All Forms of Discrimination against Women, the Convention on the Elimination of All Forms of Racial Discrimination, the Convention on the Rights of the Child, and the Convention on the Rights of Persons with Disabilities. Outcomes of United Nations conferences, and other UN resolutions, guidelines and documents should also be adhered to. These include, *inter alia*, the Habitat Agenda, the UN Framework Convention on Climate Change and any successor to the Kyoto Protocol, the Vienna Declaration on human rights and fundamental freedoms, the Rio Declaration on the Environment and Development, the Beijing Declaration on women's advancement and Plan of Action, and the Plan of Implementation from the World Summit on Sustainable Development.

Harmonization of local and national laws with international human rights standards. Any local and national laws and policies such as those related to land acquisition, urban master plans, housing and resettlement must be consistent with the principles of international human rights law. On top of this, new legislation that guarantees adequate housing, protection against forced eviction, and rights to education, health, water and basic services, should be enacted where needed. International guidelines relevant to urban development and equitable distribution of resources should also be incorporated in laws and policies. Government action must be harmonized, integrating various tiers and municipal departments to ensure that public policies and decisions fully comply with recognized human rights.

Need for human rights-based urban reform. Short of a human rights-based reform of municipal policies, the urban divide cannot be bridged and the right to the city cannot become effective. A comprehensive urban land reform agenda must be developed with participation from government agencies and civil society. This agenda must detail the way land use rules, planning, decision making, budgeting, zoning, housing and equitable access to financial resources are to be reformed. Municipal authorities must also collect disaggregated data on key indicators, with a view to achieving higher human rights standards and monitoring their own performance in this respect.

Need for strong municipal political will to grant human rights and endorse the World Charter on the Right to the City. In close consultation with civil society, local and municipal authorities should endorse the Charter and all the human rights set out therein.

Plans and strategies for the simultaneous realization of rights for all groups, especially those marginalized. Urban planning should be participatory, inclusive and representative of a comprehensive cross-section of interests and social diversity, with special attention for economically weaker and marginalized groups.

Countering the excesses of market forces. The need here is to prevent or check any unsustainable or artificial inflation of real estate prices through speculation and the land cartels that make property and housing prices unaffordable to the majority. Municipalities must meet the needs of the economically weaker segments of the population, including through subsidies for access to basic services (particularly where privatized), housing and public transport.

* Based on the background document "Taking the Right to the City Forward: Obstacles and Promises" prepared for UN-HABITAT by Miloon Kothari and Shivani Chaudhry, October 2009.

BOX 3.1.4: HIDDEN IN THE CITY: DISPLACEMENT HAS BECOME AN URBAN PHENOMENON

Walking through the streets of Amman, Jordan, one is nearly as likely to pass by a person from Iraq or the Occupied Territories of Palestine as a Jordanian. At least 500,000 of Amman's 2 million residents (see Figure 3.1.2) have come to the city seeking refuge from conflicts and disasters in their own countries, making it the world's number one urban safe haven. No other city in the world is known to have taken in such a large number of refugees, yet many Iraqis and Palestinians sheltered there strive to keep a low profile to avoid detention or expulsion – risks faced by those who enter the country illegally, and by those perceived as threats by authorities striving to maintain security, economic stability and the provision of public services in an increasingly congested urban environment. Amman's education and health care systems have been particularly burdened by the huge numbers of refugees who have flocked to the city since 2003, and most of those also displaced there are jobless.

The issues refugees and city authorities are grappling with in Jordan's capital are becoming more and more commonplace around the world, as people displaced from their homes increasingly cross borders seeking personal security and access to services in cities. One out of every two refugees, like a significant proportion of internally displaced

persons (IDPs), now live in an urban area, according to the United Nations High Commissioner for Refugees (UNHCR). According to the agency an estimated 36 per cent of all known refugees, displaced people, asylum seekers and returnees combined, or more than 7 million people, resided in urban areas by the end of 2008.

While 16 per cent of all people displaced to cities have taken refuge in the developed world, more than 70 per cent, or 5.3 million, now reside in cities of the developing regions, particularly Western Asia, sub-Saharan Africa and Southern Asia. Strong economies are more capable of absorbing those in need of special assistance; yet the burden is disproportionately borne by the cities that can least afford it, often located in conflict-prone regions.

The ongoing conflicts in Southern and Western Asia have caused huge migration flows in the region. Baku, Azerbaijan, has become the second-largest receiver of displaced people after Amman, having taken in more than 180,000 people as of the end of 2008. Cairo, too, is a major haven for displaced persons in the region, with a population of more than 100,000 refuges and other people seeking assistance from UNHCR, while Kabul and Islamabad have become home to more than 30,000 displaced people each. Internal and external conflicts have

also displaced tens of thousands of people in Malaysia and Kenya, where Kuala Lumpur and Nairobi have become home to between 30,000 and 46,000 refugees and displaced people. The cities of Luanda, Kinshasa, Delhi, Panama City, Khartoum, Kampala and Sana'a all host between 15,000 and 26,000 people of concern to UNHCR.

When displaced people move to cities rather than to rural settlements or dedicated camps, they find better access to livelihood opportunities and other urban benefits, including the social networks of relatives already residing there. However, many displaced people find themselves facing the same challenges that already confront millions of poor urban residents, such as lack of secure tenure, overcrowded living quarters, and slum conditions, with poor access to basic services, high insecurity, unemployment, and significant health risks.

As "outsiders," refugees and displaced people tend to be more vulnerable to discrimination, violence and exploitation than their counterparts living in organized camps. Even inside urban IDP camps in cities such as Khartoum, however, life remains precarious. In 2004, more than 80 per cent of displaced families in the Sudanese capital lived in temporary shelters made out of plastic and paper, which were regularly flooded. That same year, the

FIGURE 3.1.2: **REFUGEES LIVING IN URBAN AREAS ACROSS THE WORLD*** (in absolute numbers - 2008)

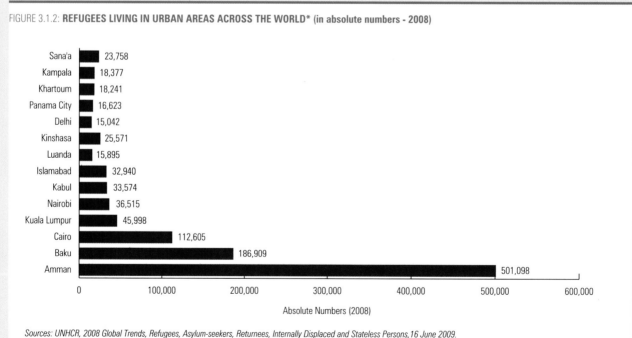

Sources: UNHCR, 2008 Global Trends, Refugees, Asylum-seekers, Returnees, Internally Displaced and Stateless Persons, 16 June 2009.
* UNHCR's population of concern is composed of various groups of people including refugees, asylum-seekers, internally displaced persons (IDPs) protected/assisted by UNHCR, stateless persons and returnees (returned refugees and IDPs).

Sources: Elhawary, 2007; Fielden, 2008; Lyytinen, 2009; Payanello & Pantuliano, 2009; Sweis, 2007; UNHCR, 2009a; UNHCRb.

government's urban planning strategy for Khartoum led to the demolition of more than 13,000 houses, schools and health facilities in IDP settlements, forcibly evicting thousands of families and creating a homelessness crisis in the city. Between 2003 and 2007, more than 300,000 displaced households in Khartoum became homeless after their houses were demolished for planning purposes. Forced relocations have resulted in violence, arrests and deaths of displaced people.

Urban displaced people's vulnerability is increased by the legal limbo in which they typically live, including absence of secure housing, land and property rights. In Colombian cities as in the Somali capital, Mogadishu, urban warfare forces frequent intra-urban displacement and contributes to slum growth.

For refugees in a foreign country, the situation can be even worse. Those without documents are vulnerable to exploitation by landlords, employers and others. Without legal status, access to the judiciary comes with the risk of expulsion. The urban displaced are also among those most likely to be affected by food crises.

Not all displaced people become part of the visible urban poor living in slums; a significant proportion is absorbed into the urban fabric, effectively becoming hidden in the host city. In several countries, the whereabouts of documented refugees are unknown altogether, making aid and service provision for them nearly impossible. Avoiding the attention of authorities comes at the cost of worse housing and health conditions.

UNHCR does not know the whereabouts of all people of concern displaced to cities. Some major host countries are able to report the urban proportion of displaced persons within their borders, but not the specific cities. In the Syrian Arab Republic, for example, UNHCR estimates that the total number of people of concern living in urban areas exceeds 1.1 million. The population of urban displaced people in Somalia's South Central region alone – including Mogadishu – also exceeds 1 million, though it is unknown whether all of the displaced people are living in the capital city. The absorption of refugees and displaced people into the urban fabric, their dispersal over large cities and their high mobility combine to inhibit not just service provision, but also policymaking and associated research.

▲
Kabul, Afghanistan. Economic marginalization often extends to the other spheres of life. ©**Manoocher Deghati/IRIN**

END NOTES

1 Brown & Kristiansen, 2009.
2 Instituto Polis, 2002.
3 Brown & Kristiansen, 2009.
4 Marx & Nobile, 2009.
5 Marx & Nobile, 2009.
6 Habitat International Coalition, 2008.
7 Habitat International Coalition, 2008.
8 Vásconez, 2009.
9 The People's Movement for Human Rights Education, 2007.
10 City of Stonnington, 2009.
11 City of Stonnington, 2009.
12 Brown & Kristiansen, 2009.
13 Municipal Corporation of Visakhapatnam.
14 Lavalle, Houtzager & Castello, 2005.
15 Brown & Kristiansen, 2009.
16 Stiglitz, 2003.
17 Babatunde Agbola, 2009a.
18 Fausto Brito, 2007.
19 COHRE, 2007.
20 Montezuma, 2009.
21 Nott & Meyer, 2009.
22 López Moreno, 2003.

©Allan Gichigi/IRIN

3.2
The regional dynamics of inclusion
Building on strengths

Quick Facts

1. Economic inclusion in cities is associated with different factors in every major developing region: planning and political will in Africa; government-induced jobs and legal certainty in Asia; and democratic institutions and freedom of the press in Latin America and the Caribbean.

2. Urban social inclusion is linked with freedom of expression in Asia; employment, political progress and free cultural expression in Latin America and the Caribbean; and multiparty elections and freedom of expression in Africa.

3. In Asian and African cities, improvements in social inclusiveness are closely associated with the political role of non-governmental organizations.

4. Beyond multiparty elections and freedom of the press and expression, political inclusion is driven by other factors in cities, including freedom of cultural expression and the empowerment associated with micro-credit.

5. In both Asian and African cities, poverty is an impediment to cultural participation, which in Latin American cities is favoured by equitable employment, fiscal incentives and micro-credit.

6. Government health care programmes appear to be an effective way of reducing marginalization and other types of urban inequality.

7. Social infrastructure, such as waste collection, recreational facilities, public parks and open spaces, benefits few people in most African cities, where public transport is a very effective way of reducing inequalities.

The previous chapter has analysed the "Right to the City", highlighting its potential as a general template for municipal efforts to bridge the urban divide and pave the way for more inclusive cities, and reviewing the challenges that face rights-based approaches in general. Such approaches take in the four dimensions of urban exclusion or inclusion, as well as their various linkages. This chapter highlights the diverse, specific dynamic interactions between these political, economic, social and cultural dimensions in the world's three major developing regions, as perceived by the local experts who participated in the UN-HABITAT policy analysis in 27 representative cities.

If planners, municipal officials and other stakeholders are to recognize the urban divide in all its four dimensions and facilitate a prompt and sustainable transition from a partially to a completely inclusive city, then they must build upon the existing strengths that together represent the specific "urban advantage" of their own cities. Just like the factors behind the urban divide, these specific strengths can be of a social, economic, cultural or political nature. It is for policymakers to identify those strengths in a comprehensive assessment of local assets in order to collect all the information they need to make progress toward broad-based inclusiveness. Such an assessment should include the operational and practical resources, both formal and informal, which the various stakeholders can contribute to achieve the redistributive change required to bridge the urban divide. At the same time, there can be no hiding that this endeavour is likely to run up against at least one of three major institutional and political challenges: (1) local authorities may not be committed to reducing inequality; (2) the three tiers of government (national, provincial and local) may be poorly coordinated, if at all; and (3) local and central authorities may lack an overall strategic vision, including on the best ways of closing the urban divide.

The four dimensions of the urban divide – social, economic, political and cultural – are frequently found to overlap. The linkages among the four dimensions are of a substantive though so far ill-defined nature. The findings of the UN-HABITAT survey of 27 cities featured here are significant because they make it possible to shed light on some of the inter-relationships at work in urban centres in the three major developing regions of the world. Among other findings, the survey shows that any government committed to promoting inclusiveness should act in a proactive way on all these dimensions, since they are linked together. Analysis of the survey results has identified a number of dynamic associations among them which municipal and other public authorities can use as guidelines in their own efforts to foster more inclusive cities.

Economic inclusion and its links to social and political inclusion

Regardless of the achievements of individual cities as hubs of prosperity, genuinely inclusive economic progress leading to an equitable allocation of opportunities and income is, to a very large extent, determined by the specific political, cultural and social equality parameters of any given city. As reviewed below, the findings from 27 cities in three developing regions surveyed – Africa, Asia and Latin America and the Caribbean – unanimously corroborate the dynamic inter-relationships between economic inclusion on the one hand, and political and cultural equality in cities on the other hand.

In the three subsections below, "Africa", "Asia", "Latin America and the Caribbean" refer to the relevant cities under review.

Africa: Economic inclusion is associated with planning and political will

The survey results from the seven African cities under review suggest that any economic inclusiveness they have to offer is associated with two elements: (1) the degree of coordination (where any) among the planning functions of local, provincial and national government, (2) the active involvement of non-governmental organizations calling for stronger political will and advocating freedom of expression and other human rights. Whereas in several Asian and Latin American cities, economic dynamism is under strong influence from recent structural changes such as the rise of banking and telecommunications services, this phenomenon is not so prevalent in the seven African cities included in the UN-HABITAT survey. Except for Mombasa and Ibadan, these cities are national capitals where government is a major provider of jobs. Though not a capital, Ibadan is a university town and, as such, to a large extent also relies on the public sector for formal job opportunities. Still, even in Ibadan, as in Accra and (at least partially) in Abuja, the predominant source of opportunities for formal employment has shifted from the civil service to the private sector, where (as in some Latin American and Asian cities) banks and telecommunications companies provide both skilled and semi-skilled jobs.[1]

In the African cities under review, the apparent association between civil society advocacy in favour of the poor and economic inclusiveness comes in response to the extensive rent-seeking and dominance of rich people and politicians in urban economies. On top of calling for government action and militating for human rights, non-governmental

© Ben Hubbard/IRIN

Policy Points

1. Africa's national, local and municipal authorities must improve coordination of their planning and implementation functions if the urban divide is to be narrowed across the continent.

2. A healthy, well-educated population is a major asset for any city, and knowledge is a prerequisite for enhanced civic participation in the social, political and cultural spheres.

3. Bridging the social divide in Asia will require greater collaboration between non-governmental organizations and poor communities, with advocacy organizations playing an even more proactive role in the political sphere, as is already the case in Latin American cities.

4. The empirical link between democratic governance and social inclusion highlights the need for institutions and enforcement mechanisms favouring participatory decision-making, while guaranteeing effective free speech and freedom of the press.

5. Cities should encourage anything that can foster multiple and complementary identities in order to reduce any polarization among groups, particularly in a multi-cultural, multi-linguistic, multi-ethnic type of society.

6. Recognition of cultural diversity entails the deployment of spaces and conditions that favour various forms of active participation, in accordance with the different societal, cultural and organizational forms that characterize any specific population.

BOX 3.2.1: MAIN FEATURES OF THE 27-CITY SURVEY

The concept of the "inclusive city" provided the rationale for the questionnaire at the core of the UN-HABITAT survey and policy analysis. As defined in this Report, an "inclusive city" is one that, regardless of race, ethnicity, gender or socio-economic status provides all residents with adequate housing and decent basic services, facilitating equal access to social amenities and public goods that are essential to promote the general and environmental well-being of everyone *(social inclusion)*. An inclusive city protects citizens' rights and freedom, and promotes social

and political participation that contributes to relevant and democratic decision-making *(political inclusion)*. An inclusive city fosters economic development by way of equal opportunities for business and access to employment, promoting pro-poor economic policies *(economic inclusion)*. An inclusive city promotes social integration and celebrates diversity. It values people's cultural rights, recognizing the human capital of all segments of society, and strives to enhance them by promoting creative expression in the arts and heritage activities *(cultural inclusion)*.

The questionnaire captured all these dimensions succinctly, along with the institutional and organizational issues that are critical to effective equality and equity in cities. The questionnaire submitted to some 400 experts on three continents covered the following:
(1) General information; (2) inclusion and inequality in the relevant city: general issues; (3) economic equality and inclusion; (4) social equality and inclusion; (5) political equality and access; (6) cultural equality and expression; (7) additional information.

TABLE 3.2.1: NUMBERS OF EXPERTS INTERVIEWED (BY CITY/REGION)

AFRICA		ASIA		LATIN AMERICA & THE CARIBBEAN	
CITY, COUNTRY	**No. of Experts**	**CITY, COUNTRY**	**No. of Experts**	**CITY, COUNTRY**	**No. of Experts**
Abuja, Nigeria	13	Chittagong, Bangladesh	17	Bogotá, Colombia	10
Ibadan, Nigeria	12	Dhaka, Bangladesh	15	Buenos Aires, Argentina	15
Accra, Ghana	15	Khulna, Bangladesh	22	Callao, Peru	12
Dakar, Senegal	14	Rajshahi, Bangladesh	24	Cartago, Costa Rica	13
Johannesburg, South Africa	8	Delhi, India	15	Curitiba, Brazil	12
Mombasa, Kenya	15	Jaipur, India	15	São Paulo, Brazil	12
Nairobi, Kenya	12	Mumbai, India	15	Oruro, Bolivia	12
		Colombo, Sri Lanka	14	Port-au-Prince, Haiti	10
		Jakarta, Indonesia	13	Portoviejo, Ecuador	13
		Kathmandu, Nepal	13	Quito, Ecuador	13
Total (7 Cities)*	**89**	**Total (10 cities)**	**163**	**Total (10 cities)**	**120**

* In Durban, South Africa, an expert provided background documents on inclusiveness that were largely used in this Report.

organizations look to mobilize urban communities in favour of accountability. In many African cities, the private sector is largely controlled by the political and economic elites, and human rights advocacy is to be interpreted as calls to democratize the business sector in order to open opportunities to all. Survey responses from a majority of African cities confirmed that the benefits of prosperity were unequally shared across various social segments. A large number of respondents felt that in the seven cities, current efforts to generate employment opportunities fell well short of providing hope to those who are economically marginalized.

Therefore, in the African cities under review, poor government management of the economic sphere seems to come as an outgrowth of weak institutions and inadequate regulatory frameworks; these, in turn, incite greater civil society involvement on behalf of the poorer and marginalized segments of the local population. This finding highlights the important (though hitherto largely ignored) role of *social* and *political* inclusiveness when it comes to fostering *economic* inclusiveness and harmony in cities. In such circumstances, civil society adds an economic function to its more conventional political and social roles; to put it in economic terms, transaction costs are reduced for local

communities when organized civil society steps in to enhance grassroots awareness of economic rights and opportunities, and to bypass formal institutional arrangements for easier delivery of services at relatively low cost.[2] However, in some circumstances, bypassing formal institutional arrangements can result in parallel structures that weaken the role of public authorities, which in turn can jeopardize government capacity for adaptation and delivery in the long run.

This apparent linkage between the economy on the one hand, and social and political activism on the other, provides much-needed evidence in support of the call for a more holistic, multi-dimensional approach to an inclusive city.

Asia: Economic inclusion is linked to government-induced jobs and legal certainty

In Asia, responses from the experts in the selected 10 cities suggest that government-induced employment (through infrastructure development, for example) is strongly associated with economic inclusiveness, together with fiscal incentives to business and sound contractual and legal frameworks. This supports the earlier findings by UN-HABITAT that urban growth is largely determined by macro-economic and industrial policies as well as by infrastructural development.[3] In Delhi, Jaipur and Mumbai, more than half the survey respondents concurred that government-induced employment was a very effective way of addressing inequalities of income and opportunities.

The survey also suggests that in the 10 Asian cities under review, freedom of expression is also strongly associated with economic inclusion. While this may seem surprising at first glance, Asia's changing employment patterns support this finding. A gradual transition from manufacturing to services and high technology (information and communication, pharmaceuticals, biotechnology, and electronics) has only been made possible through the availability of technically qualified and highly skilled workers. Subsequent economic prosperity has been characterized by increases in incomes and, concomitantly, an expanding middle class (especially in India). This socioeconomic transformation has been accompanied by greater demands not just for improved social and economic conditions, but also for transparency and accountability.[4]

The powerful apparent linkage between economic inclusiveness and freedom of expression corroborates the theory of cultural change, which poses that the more a society becomes industrialized and reliant on skilled work and technology, the more chances that the concomitant shift in values will in turn bring new societal changes, including more democratic politics.[5]

Latin America and the Caribbean: Economic inclusion is associated with democratic institutions and freedom of the press

In the 10 Latin American and Caribbean cities under review, multiparty democracy and freedom of the press seem to be strongly associated with economic inclusiveness. For all the significant strides democratic governance has been making in the region generally, the survey suggests that political institutions, rule of law and accountability do not always work properly; to put it another way, they still fall short of the expectations of urban populations.[6] Therefore, reform of government institutions, modernized public policies and novel forms of participation (particularly those related to freedom of the press and multiparty elections) are of crucial importance if poor economic performance is to be improved. In Latin America as in Africa, the strong association between economic inclusiveness and advocacy for democratic rights can be seen as an effort to tackle rent-seeking and curb the formation of interest group coalitions that could restrict economic benefits and opportunities to only a few specific segments of society. Political calls to amend dysfunctional social and economic institutions are echoed in survey respondents' perceptions that in Latin American cities, urban policies, reforms and decisions benefit the rich by up to three times as much as they do slum dwellers and the poor. In Bogotá, Callao, Cartago, Curitiba, Oruro and São Paulo, more than 90 per cent of the experts surveyed concurred that the economic prosperity

of their respective cities was not well apportioned among the various social segments. For all this quasi-unanimity, though, respondents could not agree on which particular groups were the main beneficiaries of formal income-generating activities and employment opportunities.

Furthermore, although a majority of respondents reckoned that their respective cities were addressing inequalities of income and opportunities through specific programmes and policy initiatives, they were of the view that only two types of policies – government-induced creation of specific forms of employment, and micro-credit – were the most effective mechanisms in this regard. Other measures such as vocational training to enable skills development, streamlined procedures for improved access to employment and new rules to promote jobs, were considered to be rather ineffective, as were fiscal incentives. The poor results of public authorities' efforts to curb inequality in Latin American and Caribbean cities can be largely explained by lack of political will among government officials, poorly focused programmes and, to a lesser extent, inadequate civic participation.

Social inclusiveness calls for a multidimensional approach

As mentioned earlier, Africa's national, local and municipal authorities must improve coordination of their planning and implementation functions if the urban divide is to be narrowed across the continent. Survey findings strongly suggest that the existing, rather moderate degree of planning coordination among the three tiers of government is not matched when it comes to implementation. This largely inhibits municipal authorities' ability to respond to the needs of the population. In resource-poor environments such as those prevalent in the three regions reviewed in the UN-HABITAT survey, local authorities rely on funding and technical support from state/provincial and central budgets to design and implement municipal programmes. In such circumstances, any lack of coordinated implementation signals a significant lapse in the way institutions operate, and one that must be rectified.

Coordination at all levels of government is critical to bridging the social divide

While most Latin American and, to some extent, Asian cities under review appear to enjoy better coordination among national, state and local authorities, most of the seven African cities were found lacking on this count. Still, the few exceptions identified by respondent experts are worth mentioning. In Johannesburg, for instance, city leaders have undertaken effectively to grant the specific social and economic rights detailed in South Africa's 1996 Bill of Rights, going beyond mere declarations of principles and establishing better coordination among national, regional and local authorities. The primary purpose was to address any backlogs in the provision of basic services, and to extend access to water, sanitation and electricity to the entire population. The Johannesburg municipality also launched an "Expanded Public Works Programme" to promote labour-intensive infrastructure construction funded by national and local budgets. The scheme enabled the city to create more than 1 million jobs in 2007 and 2008, an increase of no less than 546 per cent over the 2004/05 fiscal year.[7] Similarly, in Accra, effective coordination of efforts and resources between central and local authorities has made it possible to extend the benefits of Ghana's National Health Insurance Scheme to the bulk of the population, enabling local hospitals to extend treatment to the poor and vulnerable in the country's capital.

In contrast to Johannesburg and Accra, most of the other African cities under review were found deficient in terms of social inclusion mechanisms or proper integrated programmes and policies aimed at reducing inequality and service inadequacies. In addition to basic services such as water and sanitation, the types of social infrastructure most lacking in African cities include waste collection and recreational facilities, public parks and open spaces. Survey respondents concurred that such amenities did not benefit the large majority of the population in their respective cities. Waste collection is also a severely neglected agenda in a number of African cities. Here again, though, Accra stands out as a significant exception, with provision by private companies subject to scrutiny and supervision by public agencies. Improvements are also expected in Johannesburg, owing to substantial increases in budget allocations for waste removal in the 2009/10 municipal budget. Along with other cities under review, South Africa's economic capital clearly makes the case for city-specific or municipal approaches to resource mobilization that are based on improved coordination among all three tiers of government.

Health care is the most effective bridge over the social divide

The survey clearly suggests that government health care programmes are one of the most effective ways of reducing marginalization and other types of inequality that are detrimental to the more vulnerable urban dwellers. This is particularly the case in Ibadan, where municipal authorities are working closely with federal and state health care services to establish Primary Health Centres that include clinics, hospitals and dispensaries in various areas. The facilities provide prevention and treatment and are also involved in research and collection of statistics.[8] Likewise, in Accra, the three tiers of government are establishing clinics in most communities and suburbs in a concerted effort to extend provision of health services to all neighbourhoods. In both Ibadan and Accra, survey respondents concurred that health care programmes made a highly effective contribution to narrowing the urban divide. These findings also highlight a major policy dimension: the focus on health is necessary and important *per se* in African cities, but also comes in response to the Millennium Development Goals. It is worth

remembering here that some of these goals call for significant efforts with regard to education. As the signatories of the Millennium Declaration agreed in the year 2000, a healthy, well-educated population is a major asset for any city, and knowledge is a prerequisite for enhanced civic participation in the social, political and cultural spheres.

Public transport reduces social inequalities in African cities

Public transport features as the second most effective way of reducing inequalities in African cities, UN-HABITAT survey respondents suggest. This is important since nearly two-thirds of responses show that in Africa the average commute by public transport from residence to workplace exceeds one hour. Again, Johannesburg and Accra stand out for good, egalitarian practice. In Johannesburg, the municipality has upgraded the existing rail system and introduced a new Bus Rapid Transit service to improve access to the city's resources and services. The subsidized bus network does not just extend to poor peripheral residential areas that were inadequately served before: it also connects them, crucially, both to workplaces and vocational training centres.[9] In Accra, the Metro Mass Transit service has been improved with more connections both within the city and between the city and other urban centres, which facilitates affordable movement of people in various parts of the Ghanaian capital and the hinterland.

Asia: Social inclusiveness is linked with freedom of expression

In the 10 Asian cities under review, survey results suggest that improvements in social inclusiveness are closely associated with the political role of non-governmental organizations advocating stronger political commitment by government, along with freedom of expression and other human rights. This finding confirms the view that as non-governmental organizations extend their work to grassroots empowerment and capacity-building, the poor become more involved in politics.[10] For example, in India, health, education and other social welfare functions have been granted constitutional status (either as a fundamental right or as a "directive principle for state policy") largely as a result of civil society campaigns.

In Asia, non-governmental organizations have not just grown rapidly in numbers over the last 30 years. Their scope, in terms of sectors and population, has also expanded significantly. Today they are active in many areas including health, education, housing, basic service delivery, micro-credit, advocacy, empowerment and capacity-building. However, the strong link found between the degree of social inclusiveness and civil society's political activism in the Asian cities under review clearly suggests that these organizations should play an even more proactive role in the political sphere; they could, for instance, encourage the citizenry to regroup and put public authorities under more pressure, as is already the case in Latin American cities. Clearly, Asian non-governmental organizations must move beyond the conventional framework under which they have been operating so far. It is incumbent on them to explore new frontiers if they are to support the institutional strengthening required to promote equality, political rights and civil liberties.[11] This is essential for any bridging of the social divide.

Asian cities have experienced general improvements in housing and access to basic services, including electric power, telephone and cable facilities. Still, UN-HABITAT survey findings point to huge disparities in service provision between rich and poor. This is particularly true with regard to sewage disposal and waste collection, where the gap in access creates a visible distinction between the "haves" and the "have nots". In Bangladesh, more than 80 per cent of survey respondents in Dhaka, Khulna and Chittagong rated sewage disposal and waste collection as either "not provided at all" or "poorly provided". Dhaka, in particular, stands out for extensive land grabbing by a group of unscrupulous real estate companies and powerful local political leaders. As a result, the number of public spaces – parks, lakes, riversides, canals, playgrounds, graveyards and cremation grounds – has been decreasing. At the same time, development of private spaces such as country clubs, gymnasiums and amusement parks is booming, for the sole enjoyment of privileged groups. The net effect of these parallel developments is to reduce access to social amenities for the majority of the Dhaka population.[12]

Conditions in Asia are echoed in comments from survey respondents in African cities, where local experts were of the view that poor access, if any, to recreational facilities, public parks and free spaces for social activity ranked among the deficiencies in social infrastructure that contribute to the urban divide.

An analysis of the results across the 27 cities under review clearly suggests that lack of inclusive development policies is the main causal factor restricting the rights, opportunities and aspirations of the relatively weaker segments of society – the urban poor, women, children, the disabled, foreign immigrants, and some ethnic and religious minorities. Those who are also slum dwellers appear to be even more marginalized, with one-third of respondents rating them as specifically excluded and vulnerable (see Chapter 3.1).

▲
Senegal. Public transport is one of the most effective ways of reducing urban inequalities. ©**Kirsz Marcin/Shutterstock**

UN-HABITAT survey results point to the main fault in municipal social integration programmes, namely, their poor focus, or altogether absence thereof. Another, related deficiency is lack of monitoring and evaluation of city performance, with lack of political will ranking third among the causes of inefficiency.

This is where non-governmental organizations can play a complementary, supportive political role in social inclusion, as some are already demonstrating: they promote an inclusive concept of the public interest, advocate for monitoring of programmes and policies, as well as for improved decision-making and more focused policies that specifically target the underprivileged. In India, for instance, organized civil society and women's groups are pushing political parties into mainstreaming women's concerns in their platforms. In Thailand, civil society organizations call for the inculcation of trust in political and social institutions.[13] In India and Bangladesh, non-governmental organizations stand for the human rights of the Dalit community, one of the most politically, socially

and economically excluded groups in the two countries.[14] However, in some Asian centralized economic and political regimes, NGOs are likely to be operating in tandem with government interests, despite their rhetorical support of free expression of civil society and respect for human rights.

Latin America: Social inclusiveness through jobs, political progress and free cultural expression

In the 10 Latin American and Caribbean cities under review, survey results suggest that social inclusion is strongly associated with several policy variables, particularly in three areas: change in existing rules to promote employment, improvements in political governance, and freedom of cultural expression.

It comes as no surprise that employment promotion through regulatory changes should be strongly linked with social inclusiveness in a region characterized by high unemployment in the formal economy and poorly paid jobs in the informal

▲
Cité Soleil, Port-au-Prince. Civil rights favour the wealthy and powerful in many Latin American cities. © **Jacob Silberberg/Panos Pictures**

sector. Any rare new formal job is either for the highly skilled and well-paid, or the unskilled and low-paid, and a majority of the Latin American and Caribbean population falls in between these two categories. The experts answering the survey were of the view that an enabling, efficient legal framework would stimulate formal job creation and, as such, was an essential pre-requisite for social and economic inclusion. As suggested earlier in this Report, lack of income results in inadequate housing and minimum basic services, as well as poor access to the proper health, education and other social benefits that cities normally have to offer.

Against the background of the economic crisis and related massive layoffs, the UN Economic Commission for Latin America and the Caribbean and the International Labour Organization have estimated that over the course of 2009, some 2.5 million people would become unemployed, or a 1 per cent increase (to 8.5 per cent) in the unemployment rate worldwide.[15] Although this projection makes the general prospects for more social and economic inclusion rather more dubious, protecting the population from such shocks remains a government prerogative. As an expert from Quito remarked: "A poor job or lack thereof interferes with the possibility of a full exercise of the right to the city, as it results in an absence not just of economic, but also social inclusion".[16]

Further empirical evidence from previous UN-HABITAT surveys and background documents shows that advancements in political governance are significantly associated with social inclusion, and particularly legal assistance, freedom of expression, freedom of the press and multiparty elections.

Over the past three decades, Latin America and the Caribbean has made enormous progress in democratic governance, including in crucial areas like central government reform (decentralization, better use of institutions), social participation and democratic turnover of ruling parties and politicians. This is why, of all developing regions, Latin America today stands at the forefront for participatory process and female political representation.[17] In a number of cities, such progress has mainly come under the form of institutional strengthening and participatory budgeting. These have enhanced links between democratic governance and human rights in many cities and countries. Although civic rights appear to be secured in cities such as Bogotá, São Paulo, Callao and Quito, according to experts only three specific groups really seem to benefit from urban reforms, namely, civil servants, the wealthy and high-ranking officials. This is particularly true with regard to access to legal counsel and the courts. In Port-au-Prince, for instance, a single court is in charge of settling disputes and issuing birth, death and marriage certificates for 400,000 residents in one of the poorest neighborhoods, known as *"Cité Soleil"*.[18] Where cities fail to deploy institutions and procedures that are more responsive to the needs of ordinary people (including the poor), exclusion and social inequality will continue to interfere with effective basic rights and liberties for everyone – a phenomenon that can pose threats to social and political stability.

Democratic governance and social inclusion are inter-related

The empirical link between democratic governance and social inclusion highlights the need for institutions and enforcement mechanisms that can bring more inclusiveness in decision-making, while guaranteeing effective free speech and freedom of the press. These are the basic social and political conditions enabling communities to raise their voice, and to ensure that their demands are heard and mainstreamed both in legal frameworks and policy decisions. More institutional engagement from organized civil society seems to be an essential prerequisite for any pro-poor transformation and, more specifically, for effective social integration programmes. Failure to provide these, experts stress, reflects a "lack of political will" among governments, which, alongside "lack of appropriate focus of city programmes", is the main factor behind poor social inclusion in the 10 cities under review in Latin America and the Caribbean.

The UN-HABITAT survey also suggests that freedom of cultural expression is strongly associated with social inclusion. It is worth noting here that several cities promote culture as a means to achieve social inclusion. This is the case in Bogotá, where culture builds collective identity and conviviality as an antidote to violence (the dominant conflict resolution mechanism), illustrating its potential role in social transformation.[19] Uruguay is another case in point, with national and local authorities promoting cultural debate in a bid to instill a sense of democratic dignity, plurality, collective advancement and learning as a cornerstone of social inclusion.[20]

Political inclusiveness and democratic governance

In the two subsections below, "Africa" and "Latin America and the Caribbean" refer to the relevant cities under review.

Africa: Political inclusion through multiparty elections and freedom of expression

It comes as no surprise that freedom of expression and the press, multiparty elections and a constitutional guarantee of cultural expression were all found to be positively linked to political inclusiveness in the seven African cities under review – even though these components of democratic politics are at different stages of advancement across countries, and making relatively slow progress overall.

For all the formal recognition that civil and political rights are *constitutional* rights, implementation is poor on average, if not extremely scarce. In many African cities, though, some aspects of democracy such as proper election standards, viability of basic democratic institutions such as courts and legislatures, and social participation are becoming more dominant in the political discourse. It is also clear that over the past few decades,

▲
Ibadan, Nigeria. Inadequate empowerment hinders urban development. ©**UN-HABITAT**

demands for more local "voice" and involvement in decisions that affect living conditions have become more pressing. In general terms, though, urban residents remain sharply critical of municipal governance and management. Experts in cities as diverse as Nairobi, Ibadan, Dakar, Abuja and Mombasa concurred that local communities were neither coordinated nor sufficiently empowered to make effective demands on municipal institutions.[21] They were of the view that political guarantees like access to legal assistance and aid, along with civil society advocacy of political will, freedom of expression and human rights, were hardly or only moderately effective as they stood.

As an expert in Abuja stated, "the city is dominated by the politics of the rich and *godfatherism*", pointing to rampant political patronage.[22] In Ibadan, high-quality residential areas are host to the political class who enjoy what one of the local experts called the "dividends of democracy", such as proper infrastructure, employment opportunities and social services.[23] Another expert found that in Nairobi, "the municipal leadership does not generally promote civil participation or create accountability frameworks for overall municipal management".[24]

UN-HABITAT survey results suggest that those public administrations in charge of the welfare of urban populations lack both transparency and accountability. Experts rated as "very poor" the performance of these administrations. Even in Nairobi and Mombasa, and as in Ibadan, none of the experts reckoned that municipal officials were accountable or "transparent". They said corruption (as defined by lack or thorough, regular, independent audits and transparent accounting systems) was a major reason for these failures. The other factors behind poor municipal performance identified through the survey included inefficient and ineffective administrative systems and, to a lesser extent, discriminatory mechanisms that are particularly detrimental to the poor. In Africa, an overwhelming majority of expert opinion concurred that these practices were "facilitated" and exacerbated by lack of easy access to information, and whatever information available, even if limited, was typically found in the press.

Poor accountability and transparency allows some individuals, organizations and companies to secure significant economic gains without reciprocating any benefits back to society.[25] Experts have identified three special-interest groups as the beneficiaries of urbanization policies and related policy reforms: politicians, civil servants and the urban rich – whereas the urban poor and slum dwellers are systematically marginalized and rarely benefit from these policies.

Still, the UN-HABITAT survey has identified instances of more responsive public administrations. Ghana and Liberia have substantially enhanced civic participation in government selection, as well as freedom of expression, association and the media.[26] Rwanda has made progress in "strengthening local government structures as cornerstones of its post-conflict recovery strategy".[27] As far as individual cities are concerned, Durban and Johannesburg are worthy of note, with innovative governance mechanisms that facilitate participatory approaches. In eThekwini Metropolitan Municipality (which includes Durban), an efficient collective system of governance involves an executive mayor, sub-councils and wards. "Bridge City Thinking" is a pioneering programme that addresses residential differentiation and aims to link different communities across the whole municipal territory. Both Durban and Johannesburg have substantially enhanced public participation in municipal budgeting and accountability. In this respect, Johannesburg was rated as the most effective African city by the experts involved in the UN-HABITAT survey. This top regional rating remains relatively low by comparison with other regions; however, if Johannesburg were to adopt its proposed "City Accountability Programme", more indicators of city governance would become available with regard not just to budget revenues and expenditures, but also the tangible results of the city's efforts to promote democracy and freedom of expression. In the meantime, the Johannesburg municipality has already put in place an annual "satisfaction survey" enabling households and the business community to assess the effectiveness of city communication, performance of wards and community-based planning. Although the resulting "satisfaction index" has slightly fallen in the last two years, the municipality continues to compile the numbers and to disseminate the results.

Legend: ■ None at all ■ Fairly effective ■ Moderately effective ■ More effective ▨ Completely effective

Source: UN-HABITAT, City Monitoring Branch, Policy analysis 2009.

Latin America: Multiparty elections, free press and expression favour political inclusion

In the 10 Latin American and Caribbean cities under review, freedom of expression and of the press was, naturally enough, found to be associated with political inclusion, as were multiparty elections. National constitutions guarantee civil and political rights which in general can be exercised without any legal restrictions. In practice, however, poverty and exclusion act as restricting factors for some groups, so that civil and political freedoms for them often end up being more symbolic than effective.[28] Indeed, in Latin America and the Caribbean most cities included in the survey, if not all, are struggling against various forms of discrimination, and the factors behind inequalities remain as challenging as ever.

Political inclusiveness and democratic governance go hand in hand. In practice, though, any policies and actions focusing on vulnerable and excluded groups largely depend on the political participation of civil society organizations and, in particular, their degree of autonomy when it comes to advocating, upholding and fighting for the rights of these groups. However, UN-HABITAT policy analysis shows that most surveyed cities in Latin America and the Caribbean have no clear or reliable procedures for democratic governance or accountability. With the exceptions of Bogotá, Curitiba and Quito, which were granted relatively high ratings for social participation and accountability, experts took a critical view of the performance of the seven other cities on that count. They found public administrations to be generally inefficient

for lack of both adequate financial resources and properly trained staff.

In the majority of the 10 cities surveyed in Latin America and the Caribbean, it is clear again that according to local experts, two specific social groups are protected by city authorities and are disproportionately taking advantage of urbanization: the wealthy (owners of real estate and construction companies, developers and land speculators), and civil servants. Positive exceptions can be found, though, as in Quito, Portoviejo and Cartago where, in the words of an expert from Quito, "the actions of both national and local governments benefit society in general, and in recent years have ensured that these benefits were geared to the poor. However, in practice, the results are not so widespread or so positive, due to the shortcomings and deviations that occur when running urban programmes and implementing reforms".[29]

Under national constitutions, freedoms of association and expression are recognized civic rights, but survey respondents reckoned effective social participation was very poor. Most concurred that this dearth of participation results from a widespread belief among the citizenry that they are in no position to change or influence policy decisions. The other, by now familiar determinants behind poor participation have to do with policymakers: poorly focused programmes and lack of political will. In Bogotá, a survey of political culture conducted by the National Statistics Office in 2008 showed that lack of time and information were the main reasons behind poor participation in politics and municipal affairs, followed by mistrust of institutions.[30] Further factors behind poor social participation may also include the decreasing role played by conventional political parties and the weak legitimacy of the institutions in charge of elections.

For all these widespread shortcomings, though, the political process is looking very encouraging in a number of cities and countries in Latin America and the Caribbean, as it is beginning to usher in a more positive political and institutional environment. For instance, municipal officials and politicians have gained a deeper understanding of the conditions in informal neighbourhoods and are more committed to improve these, as illustrated by regional trends showing that more than 32 million people in the region are no longer considered "slum dwellers" (see Chapter 1.3).

Positive change is also making itself felt in areas like institutional strengthening, participatory budgeting and other participation procedures, along with greater efficiency in public capital investment, sounder administrative procedures and enhanced accountability. New forums for cross-sector coordination between social-oriented organizations and local and national governments have been created in many cities. Concerns for civic and human rights are more and more apparent in urban life. As an expert in São Paulo remarked, "social movements and organizations that support and guarantee the enforceability of rights consider that talk about "rights" effectively refers to the *right to the city*".[31]

Together with these more positive developments, municipal management and political participation in Latin America and the Caribbean have some instances of best practice to offer. In Curitiba, novel forms of civic participation are developed through the *Ruas da Cidadania* ("streets of citizenship") scheme. In these areas, residents contribute their views and practical ideas in a collective effort to improve access to municipal public services. In Oruro, a new "Dialogue Law" supports the political participation and inclusion of all citizens. In Port-au-Prince, the water supply and sanitation sector has been reformed by law, and network management has become participatory through so-called "Local Water Committees". In Quito, city authorities have established an autonomous commission (known as *"Quito Honesto"*) to fight corruption in municipalities. In Portoviejo, integral management of risks in slum settlements is a major project. In São Paulo as in other Brazilian and, more generally, Latin American cities, participatory democracy and budgeting are becoming integral to municipal management. If anything, these instances of best practice demonstrate the close links among political inclusiveness, democratic governance and the full exercise of civic and political rights.

Promoting cultural expression matters for political inclusion

The social and ethnic diversity that characterizes cities in both Africa and Latin America is probably behind the UN-HABITAT survey finding that when municipalities formally (i.e., by law) promote cultural expression, they also contribute to political inclusion. The survey has identified many municipal initiatives aimed at promoting cultural inclusion through specific events and facilities, including presentations, exhibitions and workshops in those areas where they would otherwise be unavailable. In this respect and as mentioned earlier, Bogotá has enacted its own "Declaration of Cultural Rights" in a bid to enhance equal opportunities for cultural expression by all segments of the population; this came as part of a broader-ranging effort to promote cultural diversity and more equitable appropriation of the city's cultural riches and heritage.

Micro-credit promotes political inclusion through knowledge and networking

In Latin America and the Caribbean, the UN-HABITAT survey has uncovered a positive, significant if rather indirect association between micro-credit and political inclusion. The causal link, which involves human capital, works as follows: on top of mobilizing the productive capacities of the poor, micro-credit also links those involved with other economic agents, disseminating local knowledge through networks – and contributing to the recognition of their associations as social, economic and political stakeholders to interact with. The Quito municipality supports micro-credit through a dedicated organization called AGRUPAR (for *Agricultura Urbana Participativa*), which promotes community urban agriculture and other forms of alternative business, in the process providing a degree of official recognition to all the beneficiaries. The municipality of São Paulo also provides micro-credit under its own entrepreneurship support programme, on top of facilitating access to loans for the poor through its "Solidarity Credit Programme".

Using culture as a tool for social, economic and political inclusion

A culturally inclusive city celebrates diversity while promoting the social integration of groups that are characterized by different cultural backgrounds and expressions, including ethnicity, language, religion, historic origins, values and beliefs. In most cities of the developing world, recognition and promotion of cultural inclusiveness are entrenched in municipal as well as fundamental and national legal frameworks. Still, as UNESCO stated in its *World Culture Report* (2000), "Cultural diversity [is] a descriptive feature of our contemporary world; [it] is a point of departure. Diversity fosters creativity, as demonstrated in the ability of human groups to adapt and transform their living conditions. (However,) as the developing world stands today, diversity and creativity are caught in the cage of inequality and injustice".[32]

Indeed, another finding of UN-HABITAT policy analysis is that cultural diversity and inclusiveness are challenged by similar factors in cities as diverse as Buenos Aires, Port-au-Prince, Chittagong, Abuja and Mombasa. In the developing world, cultural facilities in slums and low-income urban areas can be scarce (if at all available), underused or dilapidated,

Dhaka, Bangladesh. Bihari (Urdu speaking) woman and son. Bengali dominance hinders minorities' cultural rights. ©**David Swanson/IRIN**

and ill-adjusted to local demand. In contrast, most cultural facilities are located in more affluent neighbourhoods. This is not surprising, since those struggling day after day to secure tenure on their homes, livelihoods and other basic necessities are not in a position to participate in events and achieve their cultural potential. Inequitable distribution of amenities is only one aspect of cultural exclusion, though; another has to do with inequitable access to technology and information, which further undermines the capacities of the poor to take advantage of modern-day cultural and other opportunities for self-development. In many of the cities reviewed in the UN-HABITAT survey, cultural events are restricted to those with adequate purchasing power, even where such events are subsidized by public authorities. On the other hand, popular and alternative arts, musical and cultural events are often marginalized, or simply not promoted or funded by municipal authorities.

Cultural inclusiveness involves a dynamic process of engagement

UN-HABITAT survey results suggest that in a majority of the cities under review, the local ethnic group languages most spoken by the population are not used in official dealings, on signs or public information boards. Nevertheless, it must be recognized that cities enable some forms of cultural rights and expressions, and they do so through three main channels: (1) *ad hoc* provision of shared spaces for cultural events; (2) promotion of intercultural programmes; and (3) the protection and celebration of specific monuments and buildings that are part of the architectural heritage. In most cases, though, the rationale behind such cultural expression and heritage

preservation is to impose predetermined values and single, one-way meanings on places and narratives that reflect only the history of the country's or city's ethnic majorities and oligarchies. Consequently, these biased forms of cultural expression hardly have any relevance to the social, cultural and ethnic diversity that is a feature of the contemporary city; various groups fail to recognize themselves in that particular history or local identity, adding to their sense of systematic exclusion.[33] The cities of Dhaka, Chittagong and Rajshahi, in Bangladesh, are a case in point: the cultural dominance of Bengali Muslims (the majority demographic group) and, to a lesser extent, of Bengali Hindus, stands in the way of official recognition of the cultural rights of minority groups.[34] In India, some cities had at some point managed to become cohesive despite their diversity, but today are "facing a grave challenge to [the country's] constitutional commitment to multiple and complementary identities with the rise of groups that seek to impose a singular Hindu identity on the country".[35]

Freedom of expression is strongly linked with cultural inclusion

It may not be so surprising that those groups that find themselves systematically excluded when it comes to expressing their cultural identity or accessing opportunities for cultural integration are the same in Africa, Asia or Latin America and the Caribbean – namely the disabled, the elderly and young people, as well as, with some variations, either uneducated people or foreign immigrants. Somewhat more surprising is the fact that in all these regions, slum dwellers appear as the

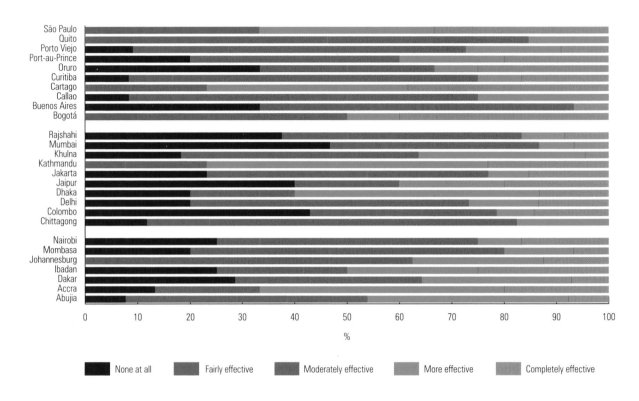

Source: UN-HABITAT, City Monitoring Branch, Policy analysis 2009.

third most excluded group. Comments from local experts are unambiguous, though:

- "A person that is poor economically will very often be poor socially and culturally, too" (Quito).[36]

- "Ethnic minorities rank, generally speaking, in the same category as the common poor and disempowered" (Dhaka).[37]

- "Cultural inclusion is linked to the economic well-being of a community, and since the poor are excluded economically, their degrees of social, political and cultural inclusion are low as well" (Rajshahi).[38]

These findings make it easier to understand why survey respondents, here again, perceived freedom of expression as strongly linked to the promotion of cultural inclusiveness, not just in Asia but in the African cities under review as well. These results call attention to a very important issue: in both Asian and African cities, poverty is the most significant impediment to cultural participation, which only very few institutions are in a position to promote. In contrast, in the Latin American and Caribbean cities under review, cultural inclusiveness is positively correlated with laws that promote equitable employment, as well as with fiscal incentives, micro-credit and formal municipal promotion of cultural inclusion.

Historically entrenched inequalities in regions affect cultural inclusion in cities

The Asian and, to a lesser extent, Latin American cities in the survey are located in countries with predominant cultures where minorities remain marginalized. This is why, in Asian cities, freedom of expression and promotion of cultural expression at the municipal level are strongly associated with cultural inclusiveness. This situation points to historically entrenched inequalities in the region and their persistence across generations. However, in Latin America dominance by a majority culture is mitigated by two types of factors: some are of a general kind, namely, economic incentives, which represent serious attempts to even out access to culture; other factors are more specific to the region, such as the greater emphasis on participatory approaches that characterizes the Latin American cities in the survey.

Those cities and countries that manage to mitigate cultural exclusion clearly demonstrate the need for multi-dimensional responses. These combine effective access to education, the judiciary and other public and private services, such as culture, sports and leisure activities and amenities.[39] Cities should also encourage anything that can foster multiple and complementary identities in order to reduce any polarization between groups, particularly in a multi-cultural, multi-linguistic, multi-ethnic type of society.[40] Recognition of cultural diversity entails the deployment of spaces and conditions that favour various forms of active participation, in accordance with the various societal, cultural and organizational forms that characterize any specific population.

It is becoming more and more accepted that recognition of cultural diversity is essential to the construction of citizenship, which in turn facilitates the transformation of customs, attitudes and practices for the purposes of an enhanced democratic culture. This broad-ranging effort is placed under the overarching principles of respect for the rights of others, including the right to be different, and the rights to solidarity and social inclusion, among others. In many cases, best practice seems to derive from close collaboration between national and local authorities, as most surveyed experts recognized. In Oruro, for instance, the new State Constitution (2009) recognizes the political rights of all segments of the Bolivian population, including the right of indigenous peoples to their own autonomy, customs and traditions in the political, economic, social and cultural spheres. In other cases, initiatives enabling cultural rights and expression are launched by municipalities themselves. In Bogotá, for instance, in the mid-1990s, mayor Antanas Mockus positioned culture as a cornerstone in the construction of citizenship. As mentioned earlier, Bogotá's own declaration of cultural rights promotes cultural freedom, pluralistic values and autonomy of individuals regardless of cultural, social or ethnic background. In Johannesburg, cultural inclusiveness is enshrined in the 1996 Bill of Rights, which, as also mentioned earlier, formally grants residents the right to use their language and to participate in the cultural life of their choice. In eThekwini, under the 2008/09 Integrated Development Plan, the municipality recognizes and supports cultural diversity, providing the opportunities (in the areas of sports and recreation, arts, culture and heritage) the population needs for individual development, community solidarity and economic advantage.

Other cities also take tangible steps to promote cultural equity beyond formal declarations. In Curitiba, municipal policies enhance the roles of urban planning and the environment, providing green areas, parks and forests that link the functions of environmental protection, sanitation, sports, leisure, social and cultural life. São Paulo has opened more than 40 "Unified Education Centres" providing much-needed venues for cultural activities in otherwise deprived areas. In Quito, best practice includes the defense of public spaces and recovery of areas and buildings of cultural significance, and for the enjoyment of the whole population.

BOX 3.2.2: **HOW THE FOUR DIMENSIONS OF URBAN EQUALITY ARE INTER-LINKED**

The 2009 UN-HABITAT policy analysis on the inclusive city suggests that the four dimensions of urban inclusion are each associated with a set of well-defined if diverse factors which municipal and other public authorities can activate simultaneously in order to bridge the urban divide.

Economic inclusiveness was found to be positively linked with (in descending order) (1) coordination and planning at all levels of government; (2) promotion of political will, free expression and other human rights by organized civil society; (3) government-induced employment; (4) fiscal incentives for business as well as contractual and legal certainty in the general business environment; and (5) freedom of the press and multi-party elections.

Social inclusiveness was found to be positively linked with (1) coordination and planning at all levels of government; (2) promotion of political will, free expression and other human rights; (3) new rules that promote equitable creation of formal employment; (4) access to legally enforceable rights, and freedom of the press; (5) multiparty elections, and (6) municipal laws that promote freedom of cultural expression.

Political inclusiveness was found to be positively linked with (1) freedom of expression and of the press; (2) multiparty elections; (3) a constitutional guarantee on cultural expression; and (4) micro-credit.

Cultural inclusiveness was found to be positively linked with (1) freedom of expression; (2) municipal laws that promote cultural expression; (3) laws that promote equitable employment opportunities; (4) fiscal incentives; and (5) micro-credit.

Source: UN-HABITAT Policy Analysis on the Inclusive City, 2009.

END NOTES

1 Agbola, 2009b
2 Xueyong, n.d.
3 UN-HABITAT, 2008.
4 This change is largely only for those categories of people who have been in a position to capitalize on the economic opportunities.
5 Refer to Inglehart, 1997.
6 Refer for instance to National Intelligence Council, 2004
7 Awuor-Hayangah, 2009b.
8 Olatubara, Omirin & Kasim, 2009.
9 Awuor-Hayangah, 2009b.
10 UN-HABITAT, 2003, p. 154.
11 UN-HABITAT, 2003, p. 154.
12 Taher & Islam Nazem, 2009.
13 Albritton & Bureekul, 2002.

14 Nagorik Uddyog & the International Dalit Solidarity Network, 2009.
15 ECLAC & ILO, 2009.
16 Vásconez, 2009.
17 UNDP, 2009.
18 Mathon, 2009.
19 Montezuma, 2009.
20 UNESCO, 2008.
21 Agbola, 2009b.
22 Agbola, 2009a.
23 Olatubara, C. O., Omirin O. J., Kasim, 2009.
24 Agevi (2009).
25 Investopedia, n.d.
26 World Bank, 2008.
27 United Nations, 2008.

28 Montezuma, 2009.
29 Vásconez, 2009.
30 Departamento Administrativo Nacional de Estadística, 2008.
31 Marx & Nobile, 2009.
32 UNESCO, 2000.
33 UN-HABITAT, 2008.
34 Taher & Islam Nazem, 2009; Taher & Chowdhury, 2009; Taher & Islam, 2009.
35 UNDP, 2004..
36 Vásconez, 2009.
37 Taher & Islam Nazem, 2009.
38 Taher & Islam, 2009.
39 Malloy & Gazzola, 2006.
40 UNDP, 2004.

©Silvia Antunes/Shutterstock

3.3 The Five Steps to an Inclusive City

Making rights effective

Quick Facts

1. The benefits of an inclusive city extend to the less tangible aspects of urban and community life, such as sense of belonging, identity and place. The concepts of human relationships, citizenship and civic rights are all inseparable from urban inclusiveness.
2. The rights recognized in constitutional or national laws remain largely notional, and it is for municipal authorities to make them effective with central and local government support. This is especially the case with cultural and political rights.
3. Institutions are now seen at the centre of efforts to promote sustainable development and reduce poverty and inequality. For the moment, existing rules and institutions are too often perceived as favouring the rich and powerful.
4. Information technologies can turn the relationship between municipal authorities and the community from a one-way into a two-way process, streamlining procedures and enhancing transparency.

An inclusive city can be defined and personally experienced in many different ways by its residents. Still, as suggested in this Report, inclusive cities share a number of basic features that take different shapes in various conditions. Any inclusive city provides the opportunities and supportive mechanisms that enable all residents to develop their full potential and gain their fair shares of the "urban advantage".[1] As suggested in Part 2, this "advantage" includes access to all aspects of basic, decent living conditions such as housing, transportation, education, recreation, communication, culture, religion, employment and the judiciary, among others. These benefits also extend to the less tangible aspects of urban or community life, such as experiencing a sense of belonging, identity and place. In an inclusive city, residents perceive themselves as important contributors to decision-making, ranging from political issues to the more mundane routines of daily lives. Active participation guarantees all residents a stake in the benefits of urban development. The concepts of human relations, citizenship and civic rights are all inseparable from urban inclusiveness.

Rights: From paper to reality

The local experts who participated in the 2009 UN-HABITAT Policy Analysis on the Inclusive City concurred that if municipal authorities are to foster inclusiveness in their cities, they must look beyond constitutional or national laws and the associated perfunctory lists of recognized rights and duties. Municipal authorities must also lay down the specific conditions that will make all declared rights effective. As an expert in Quito made quite clear, "*Las ciudades deben pasar del papel a la realidad*" (cities must move from paper to reality).[2] This said, however, the policy analysis also reveals a substantial degree of confusion with regard not only to the meaning and scope of declared rights, but also to the way these rights are to become effective on a day-to-day basis.

As noted in Chapter 3.2, the process of turning rights into tangible improvements in economic, social, political, and cultural inclusion begins with the recognition that the four dimensions of inclusion are inter-related. Municipal authorities make significant progress in bridging the urban divide when they integrate all dimensions of inclusion into policies. This is especially so where cities enhance each dimension of inclusion simultaneously, granting each equal priority in city governance, planning, management and implementation. Still, how can cities make multi-dimensional inclusion a tangible reality? What are the elements of success? What are the steps and catalysts that can bring or trigger change?

Based on UN-HABITAT survey returns, this final chapter lays down a series of practical steps and catalytic levers which municipal authorities can make and activate to bridge the urban divide.

Five steps to an inclusive city

UN-HABITAT policy analysis identifies five major steps to an inclusive city:

1. assessing the past and measuring progress;
2. establishing new, more effective institutions, or strengthening existing ones as needed;
3. building new linkages and alliances across tiers of government;
4. developing a sustained, comprehensive vision to promote inclusiveness; and
5. ensuring an equitable redistribution of opportunities.

Some additional factors may be needed, the specific nature of which will vary from one city to the other. In this endeavour, and given the many dimensions of inclusiveness, effective coordination of municipal authorities with local and central government has a pivotal role to play.

Assessing the past and measuring progress

The beauty and the challenge of urban space is that no two cities are alike. Each has its own history, economy, politics, social dynamics, cultural style and, above all, human potential. Understanding how these have come together over time in a particular city is a crucial step for any municipal authority committed to promoting inclusion. This comprehensive assessment will determine what the next four steps must involve, and what they require from the various stakeholders, with regard to institutional strengthening, coordination between various tiers of government, building and projecting a vision, and distribution of opportunities. This assessment will also provide the benchmark against which policies and practices can be measured, enabling municipal authorities to monitor progress and evaluate performance.

Policy Points

1. The way municipalities perform their duties is just as important as the nature of what they achieve.

2. It takes four steps to close the urban divide: new or strengthened, more effective institutions; new linkages and alliances across the three tiers of government; a sustained, comprehensive vision to promote inclusiveness; and ensuring an equitable redistribution of opportunities.

3. A city "vision" is not a fiction. It is based on a realistic assessment of current assets and comparative advantage, building on this potential to take advantage of future opportunities to fulfill the aspirations of a whole community.

4. It takes five levers to integrate the poor and marginalized into mainstream urban life: improved quality of life, investment in human capital formation, sustained economic opportunities, enhanced political inclusion, and cultural inclusion.

5. Cash transfers linked to health- or education-related conditions are increasingly found to be the best way of enhancing both incomes in the short run and capabilities in the longer term.

▲
Johannesburg. South Africa's economic capital provides a particularly good instance of proper coordination between central and municipal government. ©**MikeE/Shutterstock**

Confronting the past is a difficult but necessary exercise. As stressed throughout this Report, exclusion builds and perpetuates over time. Cities do not divide overnight. They are the product of contested development over generations, often fierce competition for land, labour and capital, for political representation and identity, and for basic human dignity. In Brazil, for instance, the end of military dictatorship in 1988 gave way to democratic practices both at national and local scales. The "right to the city" became a municipal expression of the broader opening at the national level (see Chapter 3.1). But then it would take many years, and a succession of leaders both national and municipal, just to begin to address the root causes of exclusion, and a decade to align policy and public capital investment with constitutional prerogative.

If the direction of change is to be realistically determined, and the political, social, institutional and financial requirements of reform to be accurately anticipated, understanding the evolution of a city is an essential prerequisite. Equally crucial is the process through which such an assessment is undertaken. Just like its intended outcome, a situation analysis of a city should be inclusive, i.e., involve municipal authorities, the business, utility and financial sectors, social movements, micro-finance institutions, private developers, investors and any relevant central government departments. The various local stakeholders each bring with them a distinct perspective and set of interests. As they help assess where the city has come from, they will also feel more committed to its future pathway.

A desired by-product of inclusive analysis is a monitoring framework with well-determined baseline conditions. In addition to demographic and health indicators, this framework can also capture the current condition and potential of municipal institutions. Since bridging the urban divide involves complex challenges and long-term solutions, it is important that any performance indicators can measure all aspects of inclusion, both the desired outcomes and the processes that can lead to them.

More effective, stronger institutions

Most of the experts participating in the UN-HABITAT urban policy analysis in the developing world agreed that existing rules and institutions are creations of the rich and powerful, and frequently cater solely to their interests with little regard for those of other social groups, particularly the poor. However, this negative perception is not held by all of the respondents; some have identified a new development paradigm that places institutions at the centre of efforts to promote sustainable development and reduce poverty and inequality – in the process recognizing the specific moral leverage of institutions and their power of social transformation.

Today, evidence from successful cities shows that *the way* municipalities perform their duties is just as important as *the nature* of what they achieve.[3] Inclusive cities conduct in-depth reviews of their systems, structures and institutional mechanisms; beyond enhancing the performance of development-related institutions, these cities look to improve methods and procedures to pave the way for genuine institutional change. The UN-HABITAT policy analysis identified many best practices with regard to municipal evaluation and adaptation. Almost all the cities surveyed are governed by some form of municipal statute and administrative bodies in charge of enforcement; but some perform better than others when it comes to evaluating and amending municipal mandates and enlarging the scope of governance to pressing issues of social, political and cultural inclusiveness. São Paulo, for instance, revised its municipal charter in 2003 to place "inclusive" issues like health, education, the environment, food security, the needs of elderly people and social welfare, among others, at the top of its agenda.[4] Establishing new institutions and strengthening existing ones is, in itself, a societal transformation process that requires national and local ownership. In this respect, Johannesburg provides a particularly good instance of proper coordination between central and municipal government: local implementation of the 1996 national "Growth, Employment and Redistribution Policy" required a restructuring of public sector institutions in the city and deployment of new policy frameworks for the delivery of social services, in order to match the mandates set out by central government.

In any city, institutional change requires periodic reviews of and amendments to municipal mandates, together with critical monitoring of institutional effectiveness to make sure policies keep adjusting to urban change. Previous research by the Asian Development Bank identified Quezon City in the Philippines as an apt example of a new urban development strategy, complete with a well-adjusted legal framework that has the potential to facilitate locally owned organizational change.[5] Similarly, the government of West Bengal in India has established a "Change Management Unit" to supervise the implementation of programmes that reduce poverty, enhance quality of life and improve access to basic services in Kolkata – a recognized best practice. This innovation is one of the Kolkata municipality's systemic efforts to deploy innovative strategies and structures for the sake of better accountability of local resource management.[6]

Nobel economics laureate Joseph Stiglitz has established that if socioeconomic development is to happen, it must involve an active role for government. This in turn requires strong institutions that guarantee systems efficiency, along with the procedures needed to evolve consensus around societal values and the new codes of conduct that enable any society to function well.[7] In Rwanda, for instance, the *Imihigo* ("challenging oneself") programme focuses on performance management of local authorities across the country, in the process enabling communities and local leaders to develop a culture of cooperation in pursuit of common goals.[8]

Laws and policies require enforcement institutions. However, the UN-HABITAT policy analysis shows that a number of cities fail to establish such institutions (owing to limited institutional or organizational capacities, or lack of

interest or focus), and as a result laws and policies do not achieve intended goals. For example, cultural prejudice and social bias are major factors behind exclusive access to the social venues and other amenities enjoyed by certain social groups, although national constitutions and other legal instruments may guarantee freedom of access. Fewer than 25 per cent of all respondents to the UN-HABITAT survey felt their city's institutional and organizational capacities were apt to address pervasive prejudice and bias; as far as urban populations are concerned, this situation can only cause disillusionment with the capacity of the system to respond to their needs, especially among marginalized and vulnerable groups.

New institutions or new channels

Those cities and countries that have effectively brought about institutional change and reforms have resorted to two main types of strategies. The more widespread one involves the creation of dedicated agencies to oversee public efforts to advance the rights and interests of the public (whether those of the citizenry at large or of specific, excluded groups). An alternative strategy has municipal authorities establish new institutional channels and allocate resources to specific issues within existing institutions. The first strategic option entails the creation of new organizations (ministries or departments) with new sets of rules, such as dedicated mechanisms for women's inclusion and empowerment. Brazil provides the most prominent example of a new ministry created (in 2003) to take care of racial issues related to the country's majority Afro-descendant population.[9] The second strategic option (i.e., new, dedicated institutional channels within existing public bodies) has seen the government of Australia improve social inclusion through reinforced coordination of public institutions, in a bid more directly to address the needs of jobless families and children at risk in deeply underprivileged communities. Since inception in 2007, this initiative has mainstreamed the social inclusion agenda into the work of all relevant government departments.[10]

Effective institutional change also requires appropriate indicators and metrics of evaluation. These can play two complementary roles: acting as "engines of learning", and as permanent mechanisms whereby institutions, programmes and systems are revised, improved and adapted. In South Africa, for instance, the municipality of Tshwane (which includes Pretoria) has set up a monitoring and evaluation unit; on top of reviewing and amending the city's "vision" and monitoring overall progress towards targets and benchmarks, the unit promotes stakeholder engagement and transparency. The unit assesses structures, processes and outcomes of existing and newly created institutions against clearly defined indicators. These combine with knowledge systems that keep a record of the process and facilitate the sharing of experiences and practices.[11]

In other cases, information technologies have done more than improve data processing: they have provided advanced decision support systems that strengthen institutions. In São

▲
Accra, Ghana. In a bid to promote education and social inclusiveness, the municipality
has abolished all forms of levies and school fees in government-run schools.
©Justin Moresco/IRIN

Paulo, for instance, the social housing department in 2005 deployed a dedicated information system which, on top of providing information on the main housing indicators, also operates as a set of rules that automatically signal which aspects of each programme call for priority attention at any one time. This set-up facilitates both institutional efficiency and acceptance of resource deployment rules by the relevant communities.[12]

Building new relations and alliances across tiers of government

Today in many countries, decentralization gives sub-national authorities ample autonomous powers for policymaking and public spending, at least notionally. In practice, however, it appears that lower tiers of government remain well short of the human and financial resources they need, especially when it comes to reducing structural forms of inequality. In other countries, local authorities lack the institutional autonomy, the resources and the mandates to address any of the four dimensions of inequality. Consequently, in both groups of countries, municipal authorities often depend on the policies, programmes and fiscal/budget initiatives of central governments.

Routine links for results

Some cities have managed to mobilize capacities to develop innovative programmes and actions, deploying both greater "entrepreneurship" and more resources to maximize comparative advantage and geographic endowment. It cannot be stressed too strongly, though, that even such dynamic municipalities can achieve little if they fail to develop strategic alliances that combine policies and resources with other tiers of government as well as the private and public sectors. The crux of their success is their understanding that local innovation mostly relies on national institutions and central budget allocations, particularly in the implementation phase. Efficient linkages among different tiers of government and civil society also ensure greater sustainability of local programmes, as findings of the UN-HABITAT Policy Analysis on the Inclusive City suggest. The analysis identifies several innovative instances where institutional inter-linkages routinely reduce urban inequalities. In Cartago, Costa Rica, for example, public-private collaboration in the issuance of so-called "municipal bonds" has raised much-needed resources for local development. Under this scheme, mortgage banks sell bonds to the central government (instead of individual or institutional investors) and transfer the proceeds to municipal authorities in support of local infrastructure improvements.[13] Ghana's capital, Accra, provides another noteworthy example. Thanks to financial backing from central government and in a bid to promote education and social inclusiveness, the municipality has abolished all forms of levies and school fees in government-run schools. These have been replaced by a capitation grant which, combined with free school buses, has led to an increase in enrolments.[14]

The UN-HABITAT policy analysis identifies many other instances where this type of coordination has narrowed the urban divide, including in Peru and Argentina. The fact that Latin America stands out in this respect is not surprising: the region concentrates an overwhelming majority of the programmes that involve cooperation among the three tiers of government. In contrast, the Asian cities under review are characterized by a predominance of national (as opposed to municipal) planning strategies and programmes, including for promotion of social, economic and political equality. In Asia, the intermediate (state/provincial) tier of government enjoys some degree of autonomy, but the policy analysis found that when it came to implementation, the involvement of, and coordination with local authorities were relatively weak. In the African cities under review, and apart from Johannesburg and Accra, lack of coordination among the three tiers of government seems to be one of the major determinants of the high degrees of inequality highlighted in Chapter 2.2.

The experts participating in the UN-HABITAT policy analysis concluded that it took no less than the three tiers of government to make a city inclusive, and even a fourth one – metropolitan-area coordinating bodies – depending on local circumstances. In the developing world, reality is all-too often at odds with this recommendation, as government coordination remains patchy, poor and informal. Persistent inability by various bodies at the three echelons of government to develop collaborative arrangements can only restrict their capacity to act together in one and the same urban space. In other words, poor coordination generally tends to reinforce under-development and exclusion. It is incumbent, therefore, on municipal authorities to display the "entrepreneurship" (i.e., a combination of initiative and dynamism) that will earn them the recognition they need from the intermediate and central tiers of government. Such recognition will result in a greater degree of involvement in regional and national development strategies, paving the way for the day-to-day coordination that will put municipal authorities in a position to tackle the urban divide in a more effective and sustainable way.

Bridging the political gaps: Share and collaborate

Experience shows that at the root of successful collaboration lies an institutional and managerial capacity to share resources such as staff, skills, funding, information and knowledge for mutual benefit. This capacity, in turn, derives from constant dialogue and interactions among public authorities. This is particularly the case in democratic societies, exposed as they are to the endless succession of breakdowns, negotiations and alliances that characterize day-to-day relationships among the three tiers of government, and against a background of political differences and shifts in ruling parties, ideologies and policies. Bogotá provides an apt example of effective collaboration that has not allowed the political ebb and flow to interfere with major innovations of an inclusive nature. The

city's innovative programmes and policies involve a universal, comprehensive health care programme that includes schemes known as "Health at home" and "Health at school" and is funded by the central government budget. The programmes achieve universal health care provision through due regard for local conditions. "Bogotá without Hunger" is another initiative that meshes the local with the national, providing food to local children free of charge thanks to central government funding.[15]

Another lesson from successful cities is that inequalities emphasize the need for interventions that are sensitive to local requirements and circumstances. Central government policies must fully take these particular conditions into account, while at the same time proposing solutions that are replicable and can be scaled up nationwide. In a number of cases, two-way collaboration between local and central authorities has resulted in a gradual expansion of functions and capacities that were traditionally assigned to local governments (basic infrastructure, urban transport, management of public spaces) to include more complex areas (resource management, environmental protection, promotion of competitiveness, capital investment, financing and other productive functions). In some cases, municipalities have also gained control over provision and regulation of health services, housing and education. Admittedly, these changes are occurring with variable intensities in a number of cities across the developing world.[16]

Adjusting national mandates

As part of the two-way local-national coordination process, central governments are also adjusting their own mandates and responsibilities – developing macro-economic and industrial policies, implementing nation-wide reforms, deciding on regional choices and allocations of resources, mobilizing public and private investments, and supervising and monitoring the implementation of a variety of decisions. These new configurations provide opportunities to develop various forms of coordination and synergies, testing new methods or solutions on an ongoing basis. This is where free political expression and freedom of association and participation have essential roles to play, ensuring accountability and transparency as improved coordination among public authorities results in enhanced effectiveness on the ground. Accountability also encourages collaboration over rights-based policies with institutions and stakeholders at national and intermediate levels; it also helps mobilize resources and support. Two avenues are available here: accountability can be secured either through institutionalized channels, or through social participatory movements. A good example of the latter is the *Forum Centro Vivo* in São Paulo, which acts as a relay for residents' demands for the right to live in the centre of the city, as part of a broader campaign for democracy and inclusiveness and against exclusionary types of urban renewal.

Demonstrating a sustained vision to promote inclusiveness

Cities need a clear "vision" of their future – a long-term plan that combines creativity, realism and inspiration and provides a framework for strategic planning. The building of a city's future starts today, and this can only be a future to be shared between present and future generations. This is why municipal authorities must address the major factors behind the current urban divide – social inequalities, poverty and exclusion. Municipal authorities must also take into account those factors on which communities build present and future opportunities, including competitiveness, economic development, good governance and sustainability.[17]

A city's "vision" builds upon its specific identity, comparative advantage and geographic endowments as well as defining historical and cultural dimensions. It is not just a city's function, structure and form that its vision projects into the future, but also a community's dreams and aspirations.[18] For this reason, any city "vision" should always be context-driven and developed with the participation of all segments of the population.

Too many cities in the developing world, however, lack both vision and long-term urban development plans. Outdated master plans are increasingly at odds with today's realities. Some cities have developed new plans deriving from unrealistic visions. Many others have no shortage of good plans or ideas, but lack the well-defined roadmaps and adequate resources required for implementation; this leaves them in a quandary with regard to costs and funding.

The practical import of these various shortcomings is the same: today, in a majority of cities, urban planning practice seems to be divorced from any long-term city vision. Many urban dwellers wonder who is in charge of planning nowadays: the public, developers, or politicians. This comes with a perception that many major decisions are not guided by any long-term community plan (see Box 3.3.1), but rather by here-and-now pressures from individual stakeholders[19]; this holds even where urban plans have been devised and the municipality is supposed to implement them through participatory mechanisms. There is a general sentiment that implementation rests not on resident participation, but rather on some vested interests, preventing expected benefits from trickling down to poor communities.[20] Dhaka's newly developed "Detailed Area Plan" is a case in point: this highly exclusive scheme allocates 34 per cent of available space to 4.4 million middle- and upper-income people in outer Dhaka, and only 0.3 per cent of space to 4.5 million low-income residents.[21] In other cities, though, the "vision" involves adequate plans for social inclusion. This is the case with the Abuja Master Plan (see Chapter 3.1), which has the potential to promote inclusiveness and reduce inequalities – if properly implemented. However, as one expert in Nigeria's capital remarked, "It is the process of implementing the dream of Abuja that is not inclusive socially, politically or economically, not the plan itself".[22] This resonates with experts in other locations, such as Jaipur: "It is not the Master Plan that is flawed, but the implementation".[23]

Evolving a vision, together

The remarks of respondents to the survey component of UN-HABITAT's policy analysis and the experiences of others suggest that it is not enough for a city's vision to reflect the shared aspirations of its whole population. Implementation should also take on a collective dimension, since any progress towards a more inclusive city is a collective endeavour. This entails collaboration among all tiers of government and civil society (business, trade unions, community groups and the citizenry), which should prevent some interest groups from dominating the whole process and dictating "what is best for the city". As noted in Chapter 3.2, the problem is that (according to nearly half of survey respondents) residents are not really interested in participating in the political process that shapes a city's future; this comes as a direct reflection of their dissatisfaction with current participatory approaches, which they perceive as biased or ineffective.

Considering the high degrees of complexity and abstraction involved in the development of a vision for a city, it is advisable to start with a preliminary general plan on which other stakeholders can build. As Stiglitz remarks, "A development strategy is a living document. It needs to set forth how it is to be created, revised, and adopted; the process of participation; the means by which ownership and consensus is to be obtained; how the details will be fleshed out. Such a development strategy would fulfill several functions as it sets forth its vision for the future".[24]

An open, transparent process that integrates various kinds of urban stakeholders is in a better position to address entrenched problems of exclusion and to propose solutions that are appropriate both culturally and politically. Such inclusive development of a vision and planning in turn enhances the potential for collective ownership, as the proposed action plan is endorsed by everyone. This two-way, locally driven and collective process has the further benefit of opening up viable alternatives which, here again, offer a more widely accepted course of action. This is why adequate conditions must be provided and enough time allocated to revise and change initiatives, or redirect them, depending on proper assessments of both the process and the results. For example, and as mentioned in Chapter 3.2, the Johannesburg municipality uses a survey to monitor satisfaction with ward committees and other municipal bodies among households and businesses.[25]

A city's vision must be optimistic and ambitious, and at the same time realistic. It should be laid out in concise format for ease of communication. Above all, a city's vision of its own future must be comprehensive and inclusive in both statement and purpose. For instance, the Dakar Master Plan 2025 (*Plan Directeur d'Urbanisme de Dakar à l'horizon 2025*) "aims to stop the anarchic occupation of the urban space, to address the urban transport problem and to tackle the challenge of slums".[26] Likewise, in Callao, Peru, the *Plan de Ordenamiento Territorial* proposes to reduce social and spatial polarization with proper land management over the next 15 years.[27]

Any vision should be innovative if it is to break with the inertia of the past and bring about a qualitative leap towards the future.[28] The rationale behind Melbourne's "Plan 2001" was to transform the city into "one of the commercial, industrial, intellectual, and cultural capitals of the world, while retaining a global leadership as a livable city". A vision should also be attractive and focused. With its "Plan 1995", Rio de Janeiro aimed "to become a metropolis with increasing quality of life, socially integrated, respectful of public life, and confirming its vocation for culture and *joie de vivre*".[29] The Colombo "Corporate Plan" envisions the Sri Lankan capital as "a model city in Asia, a caring organization looking after the interests of citizens and users with an efficient, quality service for creation of safe, healthy and wealthy living conditions".[30]

A vision, not a fiction

For all its innovative features and focus on the longer term, any "vision" must be realistic and feasible. Short of detailing how it is to deliver on clear goals, a vision will sound like little else but a catchphrase. Nairobi Metropolitan's "Vision 2030", for example, "is to be a world-class metropolis, first and foremost in Africa ... for which it will create a sustainable world-class living and working environment".[31] Any "vision" must be accountable, and therefore come complete with (a) deliverable milestones, (b) mechanisms for review, monitoring and civil society feedback, and (c) capacity for revision and amendment based on built-up experience.

A vision is not only a broad statement. It must give a clear sense of direction: where the city is heading, and the key steps that will take it in that direction, including the first, second and last ones. In this sense, far from being a fiction, a "vision" is a plan, a roadmap, and a commitment that is made by city authorities (who are the leaders, custodians and promoters of the vision) and the other tiers of government and civil society (who are major stakeholders in the process). The strength of the commitment will be a function of some of the elements outlined above: effective coordination with intermediate and central tiers of government, and participatory formulation of the "vision" and how it is to become a reality. For instance, in South Africa, the eThekwini Municipality's "Integrated Development Plan 2010 and Beyond" is based on eight distinct sub-plans, each of which comes complete with specific goals, strategic focus areas and associated programmes, major projects, budget allocations for desired outcomes, and performance indicators.[32] Indeed, turning a vision into a workable plan requires not just activities, projects and monitoring mechanisms, but also budgets with clearly defined funding sources. In Dakar, the above-mentioned *Plan Directeur d'Urbanisme* is now halfway through implementation, having secured permanent funding (including contributions from individual municipalities in the conurbation and several other national sector-specific projects).[33]

BOX 3.3.1: PLANNERS CAN BUILD BRIDGES TO AN INCLUSIVE FUTURE

PABLO VAGGIONE, FRANCISCO PEREZ ARRELANO*

As builders of bridges between present and future, urban planners are in a good position to help define and implement "visions" for inclusive cities – if only they would revisit the dynamics of the profession. Combining the broad perspective of the generalist and the focused expertise of the specialist, planners can better understand the interdependencies among various urban functions like land use policy and unemployment, transportation and poverty, economic development and education. Proactive, agile and plain-talking planners can provide both leadership and coordination to multi-disciplinary, participatory municipal teams.

The planning function must reclaim public space and improve urban conditions *for all*. Spatial planning can facilitate access to equal opportunities for everyone's development. Planners can work with communities and civil society, assessing grassroots demands and requirements, jointly devising community-based projects, facilitating public participation, mediating in negotiations and providing technical assistance in project implementation. In Cato Manor, eThekwini, South Africa, an integrated, participatory urban planning process has evolved a broad consensus on a development model that has since enabled the community to overcome long-standing social divides and spatial fragmentation.

With regard to infrastructure and services, planners can benchmark alternatives, assess scenarios and deliver neutral opinions on feasibility. They can also help source innovative financial alternatives; in this respect, Shanghai owes its success to its ability to strengthen institutional, legal and financial frameworks to attract funding which, combined with a proper master plan, has increased municipal revenue by a multiple of 14 since 1990.

In the perspective of sustainable, inclusive cities with participatory decision-making, planners' assistance with master-planning and comprehensive, long-term strategies are critical for public authorities. Planners are also well-placed to help develop the policies, programmes and capacity-building that link such strategies with the shorter term, as is happening in Bangladesh. In Bogotá and Medellín, Colombia, the social integration and civic transformation at the core of municipal policies involve planners along with politicians and multidisciplinary teams.

Planning also has a most natural role to play with regard to environmental threats, and more specifically climate change. Holistic, integrated planning is in order both for the development of new urban areas and the renewal and upgrading of the existing city. In Curitiba, Brazil, an innovative approach has been linking the upgrading of environmental conditions with public transport and land use planning.

As a group of eminent planning experts recognized in the *Global Report on Human Settlements 2009*[1], "Among the most significant challenges that urban planning has to address in the next few decades, especially in developing countries, are increasing poverty and inequality, as well as the rapidly expanding urban informal sector." The planning profession is determined to meet this challenge.

*Respectively, Secretary General and Vice President for Urban Planning Advisory Teams, International Society of City and Regional Planners (ISOCARP)
[1]UN-HABITAT, 2009b.

In conclusion, a sustained vision requires a high dose of imagination and creativity, along with a good many arguments and counter-arguments, which together combine into a comprehensive, final, shared solution, including the nuts of bolts of the implementation process and the funding required to turn the vision into action. Any city "vision" can only be rooted in common, solid ground.

Ensuring the redistribution of opportunities

Cities are places of opportunity. They act as engines of national economies through which wealth creation, enhanced social development and employment can grow. The urban environment also is the primary locus for innovation, industrial and technological progress, entrepreneurship and creativity.[34] Strong empirical evidence confirms that the concentration of people and productive activities in cities provides economies of scale and network effects that can dramatically reduce the costs of production and stimulate growth. Cities also produce economies of proximity, a phenomenon that involves a wide range of occupations such as "crafts; social and personal services such as doctors, teachers; administrative activities, such as government and justice; and finally, consumer-support activities, such as after-sales service and customization [which together] provide value-added close to the end-user".[35] Together with economies of scale, economies of proximity greatly reduce unit costs for collective basic services like piped water, sewers and drains, electricity, solid waste collection, public transport, health care, schools and many other social amenities and services.[36]

Springboard, or quagmire?

As a concentration of people and productive activities, a city can become a problem if it is inadequately planned or poorly governed, or when distributional policies are lacking or dysfunctional. The distribution of opportunities across the population can become skewed or inequitable, with large numbers hardly able to meet their basic needs, not to mention reaping the benefits of the "urban advantage". A springboard for the few, the city can become a quagmire for the many – often literally.

Many cities face the intense social and economic problems that come with divided societies: partitioned spaces, social, inter-generational and cultural divides, and poor political integration, among others. On top of this by now all-too-familiar predicament, many cities also face emerging risks in connection with climate change, diseases on pandemic scales and shortages of food and water. And they do so as they already find themselves in no position to deliver health, safety and security for all. However, all these challenges are outnumbered by opportunities: cities will continue to stand at the crossroads of an interdependent world, producing the bulk of ideas, trade, innovation and creativity, together with the necessary institutions and other forms of financial and intellectual capital that can be used to overcome, or exacerbate, the urban divide.[37]

Proactive cities can redistribute opportunities in many different ways. For instance, the municipality of Medellín has made massive investments in education in a bid to break the cycle of violence and narrow the urban divide. The challenge for the Colombian city lay not so much with access but rather the quality of schooling in the poorer *barrios* or slums. The response took the form of a variety of educational and nutritional programmes, especially for children under 6 years old.[38] Some cities opt to focus on transportation, with vast infrastructure plans spread out over many years to improve connections for poor communities, in the process expanding social and economic opportunities. In Johannesburg, for instance, 95 per cent of the infrastructure in the township of Alexandra has been upgraded, on top of massive capital investment in public transport and improved housing. The benefits combine additional affordable housing, job creation and a more dynamic local economy through better connections between slums and employment opportunities in the wider area.[39]

Creating or opening up opportunities: The five levers of inclusiveness

The five steps recommended above provide municipal authorities with the strategic framework they need to map out progress towards an inclusive city. Once they have reviewed the factors, including historical and cultural, that are specific to their city and adjusted the institutional and policy frameworks as required, the next step for municipal officials is to build a vision. Having laid out the foundations, policymakers can undertake over time to bridge the urban divide through a more equitable distribution of opportunities.

Since this is an open-ended phase, some sort of template is in order. UN-HABITAT has identified five levers which any city must activate if it is to bridge the urban divide and integrate excluded or marginalized groups. The first one is of a general nature (granting the right to lead a decent life), but the other four overlap with social, economic, political and cultural rights and inclusion. Together, the five levers are apt to create fresh opportunities for the underprivileged, allowing them to move away from the wrong side of the urban divide and to turn into fully empowered citizens, responsible parents, professionals, entrepreneurs, or otherwise full members of society.

The five levers of inclusiveness are as follows:

1. improve the quality of life, especially for the urban poor;
2. invest in human capital formation;
3. foster sustained economic opportunities;
4. enhance political inclusion; and
5. promote cultural inclusion.

Of course, cities are not combating exclusion all by themselves. New opportunities in urban areas come as the result of combined efforts by the three tiers of government, civil society (the private sector, non-governmental and community-based organizations) and participating communities.

As suggested in the previous chapter, economic, social, cultural and political opportunities tend to reinforce each other. This can only emphasize the importance of a rights-based approach to development, and one that is holistic (including the right to live a decent life) with decent employment and civil and political rights (including the right to cultural difference).

1. Improve quality of life, especially for the urban poor.

If a large segment of the city's population lacks adequate shelter, water and sanitation, and lives in overcrowded conditions without access to minimum health care and education, it is highly unlikely that this social group benefits from the other advantages that cities have to offer. Creating the conditions for improved access to safe and healthy shelter, basic services and social amenities such as health and education is essential to any individual's physical, psychological, social and economic well-being.[40] This is the starting point not just for better individual lives, but also for collective sustainable development, as the urban poor come to make the best of their individual and collective rights and potentials.

Successful urban schemes or policies integrate various sector-specific components as part of holistic social policies. For instance, in Brazil, the federal government has increased the budget for housing and expanded the supply side of the market through changes to home loan regulations. Concomitantly, the government has increased capital investment in urban infrastructure in *favelas*, or slum areas, through the so-called "Growth Acceleration Programme" *(Programa de Aceleração do Crescimento)*. More recently, the Brazilian government launched the "My Home, My Life" *(Minha Casa, Minha Vida)* programme, providing substantial support to the housing sector in a bid to build one million homes in five years.[41] This housing programme is associated with vigorous steps in the areas of education, cash transfers and job creation for the poor. The rationale behind these combined efforts is to make the right to housing and the right to the city more effective, beyond their nominal recognition in Brazil's Constitution and Statute of Municipalities (see Chapter 3.1).

In South Africa too, a similar combination of the Constitution and the legislation on municipal authorities makes provision of basic services to the poor mandatory. Accordingly, the Johannesburg City Council provides free-of-charge water (6kl), electricity (50kw), sanitation, and solid waste removal, together with an exemption of assessment rates on properties (valued under ZAR20,001, or US$2,650). In Viet Nam since 1992, Ho Chi Minh City has been deploying the so-called "Hunger Eradication and Poverty Reduction Fund", a scheme that has helped reduce the proportion of poor people in the city over the past 15 years. The scheme has funded the construction of thousands of free homes for the poor, as well as infrastructure in underprivileged and remote areas and various welfare programmes (education, health care and employment).[42]

▲
Rio de Janeiro, Brazil. The federal government has increased the budget for housing and expanded the supply side of the market through changes to home loan regulations.
©AND Inc./Shutterstock

2. Invest in human capital formation.

Current literature provides abundant evidence that human capital formation is a prerequisite for urban development and a more equitable distribution of benefits. Experts believe that regions and cities are the more appropriate scales for the interface between the formation and use of human capital. In this regard, cities must remain well aware that they do not operate in isolation. Municipal authorities must fully take into account their various interactions with the national (e.g., education, the labour market) and supranational spheres (e.g., globalization and demand-driven policies). Cities and regions are well-placed to ensure strategic coordination between the institutions and various stakeholders involved in human capital formation, and to design policies that are well-adjusted to local needs. Cities can also offer improved communication mechanisms to strengthen the internal and external partnerships that are required to create and reinforce learning communities.[43]

▲
Fnideq, Morocco. Proper planning and land policies are major factors of inclusiveness. ©**UN-HABITAT/Alessandro Scotti**

In order to encourage human capital formation, municipal authorities can also deploy dedicated programmes to enhance the individual knowledge, skills and abilities that in turn pave the way for personal, social and economic well-being. Human capital development should not be measured only in terms of skills, outputs and related economic benefits, though; it also contributes to the non-economic aspects of development, such as character building, civic awareness, appreciation of the arts and humanities, etc.[44]

3. Foster sustained economic opportunities.[45]

A number of cities develop specific initiatives to address systemic failures in economic inclusion, but some of these responses are not necessarily of an economic nature. For instance, a regulatory framework can be adjusted to facilitate the creation of pro-poor policies, some of which can also favour overall economic growth, if only over time.[46] Participatory decision-making mechanisms can also be designed to facilitate the engagement of the urban poor, since "they have the ability to influence those local decisions and policies that greatly determine the 'pro-poorness' of local strategic planning, priority setting and capital investments".[47] The 2009 UN-HABITAT survey found that participatory planning and expression of political will, legal certainty and democratic institutions were perceived as key determinants of urban economic inclusion (see Chapter 3.2). Granting secure tenure (though not necessarily property titles) to the urban poor has also been identified as another effective long-term solution, since this security, an appreciating asset, provides an adequate base for business activities.[48]

Cities can also stimulate sustained economic growth for poor and underprivileged populations through promotion of labour-intensive work methods, principally in the public works and construction industry, as well as support for small-scale enterprises and the informal sector. Survey results (see Chapter 3.1) showed that in Latin America, policies and schemes favouring government-induced creation of specific forms of employment ranked, along with micro-credit, as the most effective ways of reducing inequalities of income and opportunities. According to several studies, savings and credit schemes are more appropriately organized at community level, where they can benefit from the support of civil society organizations.[49]

The power of conditional cash transfers

In close cooperation with national governments, a number of cities in the developing world are implementing various forms of social security or protection schemes in a bid to expand access to economic opportunities for those traditionally excluded from mainstream wealth creation and economic development. In this respect, conditional cash transfers (CCTs) stand out as the most efficient poverty reduction mechanism. These

schemes enhance incomes in the short run and capabilities in the long term.[50] They consist in direct subsidies (a small amount every month) to poor households that meet certain conditions in the areas of health and education, such as enrolling children in government-run schools, getting regular medical check-ups and vaccinations, etc.

Brazil runs the largest such scheme in the world, known as *Bolsa Familia* ("family stipend"), with more than 11 million poor families as beneficiaries (or 46 million individuals in the country's 5,563 municipalities). As part of the "Hunger Zero" initiative, this scheme has contributed to a 50 per cent reduction in poverty between 2003 and 2008.[51] In Mexico, the "*Oportunidades*" ("opportunities") scheme launched in 1997 has resulted in such a substantial reduction in the poverty gap that in 2009 it was introduced in urban areas. Cash transfer schemes have by now become widespread in Latin America and the Caribbean: "*Familias en Acción*" in Colombia, "*Red de Protección Social*" ("social protection network", 2000) in Nicaragua, and "*Bonos de Desarrollo Humano*" ("human development bonds", 2006) in Ecuador are the most representative in the region. Another pioneering experience, in Bangladesh, is the "Female Secondary School Assistance Programme" (1997), which aims to close the gender gap after primary education.

The success of these schemes – in terms of inequality and poverty reduction, together with their beneficial effects on schooling, health, infant mortality and child labour, among other issues – has facilitated replication in other parts of the world. Today, conditional cash transfer schemes operate in more than 12 countries, including the United States ("Opportunity New York City"), Indonesia ("*Jaring Pengamanan Sosial*", or safety net programme), Ghana ("Livelihood Empowerment Against Poverty") and Kenya ("Cash Transfers for Orphans and Vulnerable Children"). Regardless of scope (some involve only a few thousand families), such programmes look to balance social assistance with human capital formation.[52] A word of caution is in order here, though: as cash transfer initiatives continue to multiply in urban areas, more rigorous monitoring and evaluation systems are needed; more particularly, sharper focus must be brought to bear on the real beneficiaries of these schemes, as well as on any potential additional costs that can take the form of disincentive costs, stigma costs and political economy costs.[53]

4. Enhance political inclusion.

Over the past few years, the concepts of political inclusion and participation have gained considerable currency in the cities of many developing countries. Today, more and more municipal and national authorities share the same basic philosophy: bringing government within the reach of ordinary people through enhanced mutual engagement.

Regrettably, in many places these concepts are no more than that – they have no bearing on reality. The old order of things – centralized, top-down, rigid methods – remains the norm, ensconced behind supposedly participatory mechanisms that are not only ineffective, but also lack political or institutional legitimacy. However, other cities resort to a variety of participatory channels and other inclusive tools to engage civil society, residents' associations and local communities in decision-making and implementation. Some of these municipalities are constantly trying out new modes of political participation, creating permanent fora for dialogue and negotiation. Opportunities for extended participation can give certain groups and individuals (the elderly, the disabled, women, and those on low incomes) effective access to the benefits of basic rights which otherwise could be systematically denied to them.

Voice and improved conditions

Cities that are politically inclusive recognize that on top of building trust and legitimacy, continuous interaction between civil society and public authorities improves quality of life. In this sense, participation is both a consequence and a cause of improved material conditions. Additionally, when urban areas offer enough material resources to everyone and when residents perceive cities as places of opportunity, effective participation can really take place. Otherwise, poverty and dispossession become serious barriers to political inclusion, as the poor and marginalized can easily fall victims to manipulation by their well-to-do peers and civic leaders.[54]

Cities can only become inclusive if all residents enjoy the possibility of being heard by the authorities. This does not require constant participation by all in all decisions; what it does require, instead, is a right for all to be heard and taken seriously in matters that concern them.[55] The possibility of being heard also requires that channels for individual or collective participation are always open for debate over political or more technical issues that affect their interests and those of the city at large. Such local participation has become one of the cornerstones of modern-day democracy, and the only way of guaranteeing full, effective exercise of the right to the city.

Cities must promote local democracy. Recognizing diversity and specific socio-spatial identities, and allowing all residents the political space they need to express themselves, is a cornerstone of any promotion of democracy and the right to the city. It is clear that space matters in the creation of systems of political representation and local participation structures.[56] The recent demarcation of wards with elected councilors in South African cities came as an attempt to organize communities and local politics as part of a democratization process that promotes civic rights, and particularly those of previously marginalized groups.[57] In Argentina, the civic forums join with local authorities and organizations to run the "Citizens' Audit Programme". Since inception in 2003, the scheme has established 37 active forums in 65 municipalities and 17 provinces. These forums give access to information,

political debate and negotiation, including participatory budgeting.[58] In the Philippines, the Local Government Code does more than redefine the mandates, roles and responsibilities of local government; it also establishes a clear connection among provincial, city, municipal and *barangay* (the smallest political unit) authorities for the delivery of basic services and various other sector-specific issues (education, tourism, telecommunications, housing and capital investment). Thanks to the code, innovative mechanisms have increased local financial resources and made their management more efficient and participatory.[59]

Two-way communication for more accountability and transparency

Municipal authorities are increasingly resorting to information and communication technologies to foster participation and interaction. These go beyond improved information sharing, as they also transform the traditional relationships between local authorities and citizens – and what used to be one-way communication becomes two-way.

Today in many cities, the Internet and the World Wide Web enable communities both to influence policy decisions and provide feedback on implementation of government projects. This can only enhance the accountability, transparency and effectiveness of municipal and other local authorities.

In Morocco, the municipality of Fès gives the public access to records through an online portal. Municipal information kiosks make administrative procedures more transparent, reducing and eliminating bureaucratic delays. This scheme, which is supported by the International Development Research Centre, is now replicated in northern Ghana, where information technology improves local governance and a climate of transparency and cooperation encourages civic participation.

Ultimately, of course, it is for every city to decide which political mechanisms, participation tools and implementation methods will make it more inclusive. Whatever their preferred option, though, municipal authorities must establish local information systems to evaluate the effectiveness of their political inclusion policies; for instance, they will need to assess whether these policies effectively enhance the political representation of traditionally marginalized groups. Municipalities will also want to know whether such enhanced representation in governance systems improves the political integration of marginalized people, such as ethnic minorities. In other words, a municipality should not assess participation based on such superficial indicators as numbers of consultative meetings or participants. Since inclusiveness is less of a notional than a substantive outcome, municipal authorities must keep in mind that a participatory process is a transformational tool, the effectiveness of which is measured in the progress achieved on the way to a more equal, inclusive city.

Kharkov, Ukraine. Local participation has become one of the cornerstones of modern-day democracy. ©**Lurii Osadchi/Shutterstock**

5. Promote cultural inclusion.

Culture has historically been left out of the conventional international development agenda, or relegated to its fringes. Today, more and more scholars and experts have come to recognize that past development strategies (such as those associated with the "Washington Consensus" on economic reform) have failed because they "saw development as a technical problem requiring technical solutions … [with] little attention paid to institutional constraints or cross-cultural value differences".[60]

Against this background, some cities in the South have opted for a more comprehensive perspective on development – one where culture features as one of the levers of success. Accordingly, their development policies integrate cultural values, social capital, tradition and other related factors.[61] At the same time, these municipalities are well aware that, conversely, culture can easily lead to social exclusion if aspects such as the right to diversity or free cultural expression are not properly addressed and turned into a force for the greater good.

As more and more municipal authorities are finding now, the success of development policies also relies on a broader scope – including for implementation – which takes into account the diversity and the specific needs of communities. More specifically, inclusive municipalities pay greater attention to the symbolism and meanings residents attach to local space, the sense of belonging and territoriality among people, and optimal and sustainable use of resources by local groups.[62] This makes it possible for participatory processes to speak to various communities' own sense of identity and ways of thinking, which can only encourage trust and debate. This sense of empowerment and influence secures community adherence and support to development projects they perceive as promoting their own interests and values. Bridging the cultural gap, therefore, plays a fundamental role in forging citizenship – shaping local identities and facilitating various forms of expression and participation.

Indeed, as Steven Friedman put it, "Cities cannot be inclusive if people are expected to deny who they are or where they come from, or if they are expected to relinquish their own values and traditions, in order for them to be part of the urban *polis.*·On the other hand, an urban community built purely on respect for difference cannot endure, let alone include all who live in it because a significant degree of agreed commonality is crucial if people are to live with one another."[63] In this sense, culture itself must be a focus of development policies, or, as noted by Mark Brennan, "it can be seen as presenting both the means and ends for development".[64] A number of cities today are using culture as a transformational tool to integrate ethnic minorities, preserve regional values, protect the heritage in the built environment and safeguard the linguistic and religious diversity of the city. Beyond the sole cultural sphere, these policies together can go a long way towards bridging the urban divide in its other – social, political and economic – dimensions.

Cultural rights through government coordination

It is worth noting here that in urban areas, progress on the way to more effective cultural rights is often one of the outcomes of close collaboration among national, regional and local authorities. In Brazil, for instance, the three tiers of government are implementing the National Cultural Plan (adopted in 2008), which uses the social and civic dimensions of culture in various programmes and initiatives that are implemented at the municipal level; these include the National Museum Policy, the *Monumenta* programme, the "Live Culture Programme" and others.[65] In South Africa, in the aftermath of xenophobic attacks in 2008, a number of programmes have been launched in Johannesburg and other cities to promote cultural tolerance and cohesion with foreigners. Under these schemes, "Migrant Help Desks" have been established and "Anti-xenophobic Awareness Campaigns" launched in partnership with the Department of Home Affairs and other national agencies.[66] In such cooperative efforts, local authorities focus on specifically local issues, concentrating on rehabilitation of historic neighbourhoods, laying out public spaces and facilities in the least favoured urban areas, or allowing different land use patterns and diversified social land and housing schemes for people from different origins or social or economic backgrounds. As far as urban planning is concerned, some municipalities eliminate building codes and zoning standards that act as "architectural lines of divide", isolating and unfavourably differentiating some neighbourhoods from others; instead, new standards take into account gender, ethnic as well as socio-cultural and linguistic differences, turning them into inclusionary factors rather than allowing them to generate further exclusion.[67]

Many cities are making efforts to democratize access to culture. The South African city-region of eThekwini (which includes Durban) is upgrading and expanding cultural venues and increasing capital investment in cultural centers. Bogotá, Curitiba and Quito, among various other cities in Latin America, are extending cultural policies to marginal suburbs. In São Paulo, the "Library Bus Project" extends access to cultural goods to children, youth and the elderly in underprivileged neighbourhoods.[68] Medellín in Colombia is building five large public parks, each with a library or a museum as symbols of cultural expression, social encounter and peace in the poorest areas.[69]

Cities are coming to realize that cultural activities are a significant source of growth and employment, too, with great potential to contribute to poverty reduction. This is why they often engage in urban renewal and rehabilitation programmes in decaying historic neighbourhoods and traditional urban cores, rehabilitating historic buildings as part of heritage preservation policies. The overall rationale is to create business opportunities for local communities and develop specific local senses of identity.

Other cities deploy cultural initiatives to develop a sense of space and belonging and to promote cultural diversity within communities. Some are developing appropriate policies and actions to foster multiple and complementary identities as part of broader-ranging policies that reinforce citizenship through cultural development. Cultural activities have also contributed to building or maintaining peace and stability within cities and regions, particularly in multi-ethnic settings. This has been the case in Bogotá, as part of a conflict resolution and prevention programme. In Guatemala, formal recognition of Mayan customary law became an important factor both of genuine reform and internal peace agreements. These and other initiatives strengthen the role of culture in development, recognizing it as a positive force for the transformation of society.

Steps, levers and the inclusive city

The review of practical steps and catalytic levers suggests that cities can, in fact, bridge the urban divide. By assessing their past, identifying ways to strengthen their institutions, working through relations among tiers of government, projecting a realistic vision, and dedicating resources equitably to redistribute opportunities, municipal authorities demonstrate that they can foster greater inclusion. Similarly, cities that concentrate systematically on support to the urban poor and make long-term investment in human capital can reduce the urban divide, just as cities that introduce levers (CCTs, land tenure systems, etc.) to remove market barriers can achieve far more sustainable economic opportunities. And cities that successfully implement transparent budgeting and two-way accountability enhance political inclusion, just as cities that involve ethnic minorities foster cultural inclusion. Taken together, these steps and levers constitute a formidable set of instruments with which cities can at once address the economic, social, political, and cultural dimensions of inclusion.

Two cross-cutting factors implicit in the review, and which underlie much of this Report, are political will and human agency. In virtually all examples, successful efforts to bridge the urban divide were produced through consensus among diverse, often competing interests. The necessity of political will and human agency highlights again the relevance of the right to the city. As noted above, the concept resonates deeply in many cities. It speaks directly to the issue of human dignity and, as such, provides a vehicle to rally political will and build consensus. Simply put, it is what drives the debate. Not all cities can deploy this concept. As discussed earlier in this Report, context is important. Many cities have not experienced the political and cultural history that makes the right to the city a viable instrument for social change. Importantly, these cities are also pursuing inclusion, but elect to bridge the urban divide by other means. Theirs is an equally tough challenge. This is a search for politically and culturally appropriate methods that will disrupt complacency and create incentives for protagonists to break the *status quo* that too often perpetuates inequality and exclusion.

In all cities, whether they do or do not endorse the right to the city, the challenge is to deliver on the promise achieved through consensus. All-too frequently, the social contract is vulnerable to the next election or cycle of violence and fails to translate into education, employment, citizenship, respect, and dignity. The sheer extent of exclusion and the strength of vested interests warrant *sustained* political will and human agency over the long term.

As the results of UN-HABITAT's policy analysis show, closing the urban divide is not a one-off engagement. It is a commitment among successive leaders of cities, social movements, organized labour, businesses and the general public to implement practical steps and catalytic levers so that the city, in fact, becomes more inclusive over time.

END NOTES

1 Adapted from the definition proposed by the Social Planning Council of Ottawa, 2003
2 Vásconez, 2009.
3 European Centre for Development Policy Management (ECDPM), (2004).
4 Marx & Nobile, 2009.
5 Asian Development Bank, 2004.
6 UN-HABITAT Best Practice Database, 2008a.
7 Stiglitz, 2009.
8 UN-HABITAT Best Practice Database, 2008b.
9 Inter-American Development Bank, 2007.
10 Australian Government, 2009.
11 Ethekwini Municipality, 2007.
12 UN-HABITAT Best Practice Database, 2008c.
13 Baldares Martínez, August 2009.
14 Nunoo, 2009.
15 Vásconez, 2009.
16 López Moreno, 2009.
17 Borja, 2003.
18 López Moreno, 1997.
19 City of Portland, 2007.
20 City of Portland, 2007.
21 Taher & Islam Nazem, 2009.
22 Agbola, 2009a.
23 Society for Development Studies, 2009a.
24 Stiglitz, 2009.

25 A "ward committee" is an advisory and supervisory body at urban sub-district level. Awuor-Hayangah, 2009b.
26 Diop, 2009.
27 Santandreu & Price, 2009.
28 Fernández Güell, 2006.
29 Quoted by Fernández Güell, 2006.
30 Warnakula, 2009.
31 Ministry of Nairobi Metropolitan Development, 2009.
32 eThekwini Municipality, 2007.
33 Diop, 2009.
34 UN-HABITAT, 2008.
35 Garelli, 2002.
36 Satterthwaite, 2000.
37 Pricewaterhouse Coopers, 2008.
38 UN-HABITAT, Best Practice Database, 2009.
39 UN-HABITAT, Best Practice Database, 2009a.
40 UN-HABITAT, 1996.
41 IPEA, 2009.
42 HCM City People's Committee, 2009.
43 Van Damme, 2009.
44 Tan, 1999.
45 Sustainable economic opportunity is one of the four pillars of governance quality. The Ibrahim Index aims to be Africa's leading assessment of governance that informs and empowers citizens to hold their

governments and public institutions to account. Refer to: http://www.moibrahimfoundation.org/en/section/the-ibrahim-index
46 Abbott, 2008.
47 UN-HABITAT, 2003.
48 Rakodi, 2001.
49 Satterthwaite, 2000.
50 Hyun, 2008.
51 Soares, Ribas & Soares, 2009.
52 World Bank, 2009.
53 Sumarto & Suryahadi, 2001.
54 Friedman, n.d.
55 Friedman, n.d.
56 Gervais-Lambony, 2008
57 Gervais-Lambony, 2008.
58 UN-HABITAT, 2005.
59 UN-HABITAT, 2005.
60 Stiglitz, 2009.
61 Brennan, 2005.
62 Brennan, 2005.
63 Friedman, n.d.
64 Brennan, 2005.
65 United Nations Economic and Social Council, 2009.
66 Marx & Nobile, 2009.
67 UCLG, 2008.
68 Marx & Nobile, 2009.
69 UN-HABITAT, 2004.

City population and city population growth rate of urban agglomerations with 750,000 inhabitants or more in 2007

Country	City	City Population of Urban Agglomerations								City Population Growth Rate of Urban Agglomerations						
		1990	1995	2000	2005	2010	2015	2020	2025	1990-1995	1995-2000	2000-2005	2005-2010	2010-2015	2015-2020	2020-2025
Afghanistan	Kabul	1,306	1,616	1,963	2,994	3,768	4,730	5,836	7,175	4.26	3.90	8.44	4.60	4.55	4.20	4.13
Algeria	El Djazaïr (Algiers)	1,908	2,295	2,754	3,199	3,574	3,922	4,235	4,499	3.69	3.65	2.99	2.22	1.86	1.54	1.21
Algeria	Wahran (Oran)	647	675	706	765	852	944	1,030	1,105	0.86	0.91	1.59	2.15	2.05	1.74	1.41
Angola	Huambo	326	444	578	775	1,035	1,310	1,567	1,824	6.17	5.25	5.87	5.79	4.71	3.59	3.04
Angola	Luanda	1,568	1,953	2,591	3,533	4,775	6,036	7,153	8,236	4.39	5.66	6.20	6.02	4.69	3.40	2.82
Argentina	Buenos Aires	10,513	11,154	11,847	12,553	13,089	13,432	13,653	13,768	1.18	1.21	1.16	0.84	0.52	0.33	0.17
Argentina	Córdoba	1,200	1,275	1,348	1,423	1,494	1,556	1,606	1,645	1.21	1.11	1.09	0.98	0.81	0.63	0.48
Argentina	Mendoza	759	802	838	876	918	959	993	1,020	1.11	0.88	0.89	0.93	0.86	0.70	0.54
Argentina	Rosario	1,084	1,121	1,152	1,186	1,233	1,283	1,326	1,360	0.68	0.55	0.58	0.77	0.80	0.66	0.50
Argentina	San Miguel de Tucumán	611	666	722	781	832	871	902	928	1.71	1.63	1.58	1.24	0.92	0.72	0.56
Armenia	Yerevan	1,175	1,142	1,111	1,103	1,102	1,102	1,102	1,102	-0.55	-0.55	-0.15	-0.01	-0.00	-0.00	—
Australia	Adelaide	1,046	1,074	1,102	1,133	1,167	1,212	1,258	1,300	0.53	0.51	0.55	0.60	0.75	0.75	0.65
Australia	Brisbane	1,329	1,471	1,603	1,780	1,970	2,092	2,170	2,233	2.04	1.71	2.10	2.02	1.21	0.73	0.57
Australia	Melbourne	3,117	3,257	3,433	3,641	3,851	4,013	4,137	4,238	0.88	1.05	1.17	1.12	0.83	0.61	0.48
Australia	Perth	1,160	1,273	1,373	1,484	1,598	1,683	1,746	1,800	1.87	1.51	1.56	1.48	1.03	0.74	0.61
Australia	Sydney	3,632	3,839	4,078	4,260	4,427	4,582	4,716	4,826	1.11	1.21	0.87	0.77	0.69	0.57	0.46
Austria	Wien (Vienna)	2,096	2,127	2,158	2,264	2,385	2,451	2,476	2,496	0.29	0.29	0.96	1.04	0.54	0.20	0.16
Azerbaijan	Baku	1,733	1,766	1,806	1,867	1,931	2,006	2,097	2,187	0.37	0.45	0.67	0.67	0.76	0.89	0.84
Bangladesh	Chittagong	2,023	2,578	3,308	4,187	5,012	5,814	6,688	7,639	4.85	4.99	4.71	3.60	2.97	2.80	2.66
Bangladesh	Dhaka	6,621	8,332	10,285	12,576	14,796	17,015	19,422	22,015	4.60	4.21	4.02	3.25	2.80	2.65	2.51
Bangladesh	Khulna	985	1,133	1,285	1,466	1,699	1,979	2,294	2,640	2.79	2.53	2.63	2.95	3.05	2.95	2.81
Bangladesh	Rajshahi	521	606	678	766	887	1,037	1,208	1,396	3.02	2.27	2.42	2.94	3.13	3.05	2.91
Belarus	Minsk	1,607	1,649	1,700	1,775	1,846	1,879	1,883	1,883	0.52	0.61	0.85	0.79	0.35	0.05	0.00
Belgium	Antwerpen	893	906	912	918	920	920	920	920	0.28	0.13	0.14	0.05	0.00	—	—
Belgium	Bruxelles-Brussels	1,680	1,715	1,733	1,742	1,744	1,744	1,744	1,744	0.41	0.21	0.10	0.02	0.00	—	—
Benin	Cotonou	504	577	642	720	841	1,004	1,196	1,411	2.73	2.13	2.27	3.11	3.56	3.49	3.31
Bolivia	La Paz	1,062	1,267	1,390	1,527	1,692	1,864	2,027	2,178	3.53	1.85	1.89	2.05	1.94	1.68	1.43
Bolivia	Santa Cruz	616	833	1,054	1,320	1,551	1,724	1,876	2,016	6.04	4.69	4.51	3.22	2.11	1.70	1.44
Brazil	Baixada Santista	1,184	1,319	1,468	1,638	1,810	1,941	2,031	2,095	2.15	2.14	2.18	2.00	1.40	0.90	0.62
Brazil	Belém	1,129	1,393	1,748	2,043	2,335	2,525	2,639	2,717	4.20	4.54	3.11	2.68	1.56	0.88	0.58
Brazil	Belo Horizonte	3,548	4,093	4,659	5,304	5,941	6,356	6,597	6,748	2.86	2.59	2.59	2.27	1.35	0.74	0.45
Brazil	Brasília	1,863	2,257	2,746	3,341	3,938	4,284	4,463	4,578	3.84	3.92	3.92	3.29	1.68	0.82	0.51
Brazil	Campinas	1,693	1,975	2,264	2,634	3,003	3,241	3,380	3,474	3.08	2.74	3.02	2.62	1.52	0.85	0.55
Brazil	Campo Grande	486	574	654	741	830	896	943	978	3.31	2.63	2.49	2.26	1.55	1.02	0.73
Brazil	Cuiabá	510	606	686	770	857	924	972	1,008	3.43	2.49	2.31	2.12	1.51	1.01	0.73
Brazil	Curitiba	1,829	2,138	2,494	2,908	3,320	3,582	3,735	3,836	3.12	3.07	3.07	2.65	1.52	0.83	0.53
Brazil	Florianópolis	503	609	734	934	1,142	1,263	1,328	1,374	3.85	3.72	4.81	4.03	2.02	1.01	0.68
Brazil	Fortaleza	2,226	2,554	2,875	3,237	3,599	3,852	4,011	4,117	2.75	2.37	2.37	2.12	1.36	0.81	0.52
Brazil	Goiânia	1,132	1,356	1,608	1,898	2,189	2,373	2,482	2,556	3.61	3.41	3.31	2.85	1.62	0.89	0.59
Brazil	Grande São Luís	672	775	876	990	1,106	1,192	1,252	1,296	2.83	2.45	2.45	2.22	1.51	0.98	0.69
Brazil	Grande Vitória	1,052	1,221	1,398	1,613	1,829	1,975	2,067	2,132	2.97	2.72	2.85	2.51	1.54	0.91	0.62
Brazil	João Pessoa	652	741	827	918	1,012	1,088	1,142	1,183	2.54	2.21	2.09	1.95	1.44	0.98	0.70
Brazil	Maceió	660	798	952	1,116	1,281	1,391	1,460	1,510	3.77	3.55	3.17	2.76	1.65	0.97	0.67
Brazil	Manaus	955	1,159	1,392	1,645	1,898	2,060	2,156	2,223	3.87	3.68	3.33	2.87	1.64	0.91	0.61
Brazil	Natal	692	800	910	1,035	1,161	1,254	1,316	1,362	2.89	2.58	2.58	2.31	1.53	0.97	0.68
Brazil	Norte/Nordeste Catarinense	603	709	815	936	1,059	1,146	1,205	1,247	3.22	2.78	2.78	2.47	1.59	0.99	0.70
Brazil	Pôrto Alegre	2,934	3,236	3,505	3,795	4,096	4,344	4,517	4,633	1.96	1.59	1.59	1.52	1.18	0.78	0.51
Brazil	Recife	2,690	2,958	3,230	3,527	3,831	4,072	4,236	4,347	1.90	1.76	1.76	1.65	1.22	0.79	0.52
Brazil	Rio de Janeiro	9,595	10,174	10,803	11,469	12,171	12,775	13,179	13,413	1.17	1.20	1.20	1.19	0.97	0.62	0.35
Brazil	Salvador	2,331	2,644	2,968	3,331	3,695	3,951	4,114	4,222	2.53	2.31	2.31	2.07	1.34	0.81	0.52
Brazil	São Paulo	14,776	15,948	17,099	18,333	19,582	20,544	21,124	21,428	1.53	1.39	1.39	1.32	0.96	0.56	0.29
Brazil	Teresina	614	706	789	872	958	1,029	1,082	1,121	2.77	2.24	2.00	1.88	1.43	0.99	0.71
Bulgaria	Sofia	1,191	1,168	1,128	1,166	1,212	1,233	1,236	1,236	-0.38	-0.70	0.65	0.78	0.35	0.05	0.00

Country	City	1990	1995	2000	2005	2010	2015	2020	2025	1990-1995	1995-2000	2000-2005	2005-2010	2010-2015	2015-2020	2020-2025
Burkina Faso	Ouagadougou	537	667	828	1,044	1,324	1,676	2,111	2,632	4.32	4.33	4.63	4.75	4.71	4.62	4.41
Cambodia	Phnum Pénh (Phnom Penh)	615	836	1,160	1,363	1,651	2,028	2,457	2,911	6.14	6.55	3.23	3.84	4.11	3.84	3.39
Cameroon	Douala	931	1,155	1,432	1,766	2,108	2,425	2,721	2,996	4.30	4.30	4.20	3.54	2.80	2.30	1.93
Cameroon	Yaoundé	754	948	1,192	1,489	1,787	2,058	2,312	2,549	4.59	4.59	4.44	3.65	2.83	2.33	1.95
Canada	Calgary	738	809	953	1,056	1,182	1,258	1,304	1,345	1.84	3.26	2.06	2.26	1.25	0.72	0.62
Canada	Edmonton	831	859	924	1,017	1,112	1,174	1,217	1,256	0.67	1.47	1.92	1.79	1.08	0.71	0.63
Canada	Montréal	3,154	3,305	3,471	3,603	3,781	3,912	4,014	4,108	0.94	0.98	0.74	0.97	0.68	0.52	0.46
Canada	Ottawa-Gatineau	918	988	1,079	1,119	1,182	1,232	1,274	1,315	1.48	1.74	0.75	1.08	0.83	0.68	0.63
Canada	Toronto	3,807	4,197	4,607	5,035	5,447	5,687	5,827	5,946	1.95	1.86	1.78	1.57	0.86	0.49	0.41
Canada	Vancouver	1,559	1,789	1,959	2,093	2,219	2,310	2,380	2,444	2.75	1.81	1.33	1.17	0.80	0.60	0.54
Chad	N'Djaména	477	579	711	902	1,127	1,405	1,753	2,172	3.88	4.11	4.75	4.46	4.41	4.42	4.28
Chile	Santiago	4,616	4,964	5,275	5,599	5,879	6,084	6,224	6,310	1.46	1.21	1.19	0.98	0.68	0.46	0.28
Chile	Valparaíso	733	771	803	838	880	922	956	982	1.02	0.83	0.85	0.98	0.92	0.73	0.54
China	Anshan, Liaoning	1,442	1,496	1,552	1,611	1,703	1,863	2,029	2,167	0.74	0.74	0.74	1.12	1.79	1.71	1.32
China	Anshun	658	709	763	822	896	992	1,085	1,164	1.49	1.49	1.49	1.71	2.03	1.81	1.41
China	Anyang	617	686	763	849	948	1,056	1,156	1,240	2.13	2.13	2.13	2.20	2.16	1.81	1.40
China	Baoding	595	728	890	1,042	1,206	1,355	1,482	1,586	4.03	4.03	3.15	2.92	2.34	1.79	1.36
China	Baotou	1,229	1,426	1,655	1,920	2,209	2,472	2,691	2,869	2.97	2.98	2.97	2.81	2.24	1.70	1.28
China	Beijing	7,362	8,486	9,782	10,717	11,741	12,842	13,807	14,545	2.84	2.84	1.83	1.82	1.79	1.45	1.04
China	Bengbu	695	748	805	867	944	1,044	1,142	1,225	1.47	1.47	1.47	1.70	2.02	1.80	1.40
China	Benxi	938	958	979	1,000	1,046	1,143	1,249	1,339	0.43	0.43	0.43	0.90	1.78	1.77	1.39
China	Changchun	2,192	2,446	2,730	3,046	3,400	3,763	4,082	4,338	2.19	2.19	2.19	2.20	2.03	1.63	1.22
China	Changde	1,180	1,258	1,341	1,429	1,543	1,699	1,852	1,979	1.28	1.28	1.28	1.54	1.92	1.73	1.33
China	Changsha, Hunan	1,329	1,667	2,091	2,451	2,832	3,167	3,443	3,663	4.53	4.53	3.18	2.89	2.24	1.67	1.24
China	Changzhou, Jiangsu	730	883	1,068	1,249	1,445	1,622	1,772	1,894	3.81	3.81	3.13	2.91	2.32	1.76	1.34
China	Chengdu	2,955	3,403	3,919	4,065	4,266	4,634	5,014	5,320	2.82	2.82	0.73	0.97	1.65	1.57	1.19
China	Chifeng	987	1,065	1,148	1,238	1,348	1,489	1,625	1,739	1.51	1.51	1.51	1.71	1.98	1.75	1.35
China	Chongqing	3,123	4,342	6,037	6,363	6,690	7,254	7,823	8,275	6.59	6.59	1.05	1.00	1.62	1.51	1.12
China	Dalian	2,472	2,658	2,858	3,073	3,335	3,662	3,971	4,221	1.45	1.45	1.45	1.64	1.87	1.62	1.22
China	Dandong	661	716	776	841	921	1,020	1,117	1,198	1.61	1.61	1.61	1.81	2.05	1.81	1.40
China	Daqing	997	1,167	1,366	1,594	1,842	2,066	2,252	2,404	3.15	3.15	3.09	2.90	2.29	1.73	1.30
China	Datong, Shanxi	1,277	1,392	1,518	1,763	2,038	2,283	2,488	2,653	1.73	1.73	2.99	2.90	2.28	1.71	1.29
China	Dongguan, Guangdong	1,737	2,559	3,770	4,320	4,850	5,366	5,808	6,157	7.75	7.75	2.72	2.32	2.02	1.58	1.17
China	Foshan	429	569	754	888	1,027	1,155	1,265	1,356	5.63	5.63	3.26	2.92	2.35	1.81	1.38
China	Fushun, Liaoning	1,388	1,410	1,433	1,456	1,516	1,652	1,800	1,924	0.32	0.32	0.32	0.81	1.72	1.72	1.33
China	Fuxin	743	685	631	725	839	945	1,036	1,112	-1.63	-1.63	2.77	2.93	2.38	1.84	1.41
China	Fuyang	232	376	609	726	840	946	1,038	1,114	9.63	9.63	3.52	2.93	2.38	1.84	1.41
China	Fuzhou, Fujian	1,396	1,710	2,096	2,453	2,834	3,170	3,445	3,666	4.06	4.06	3.15	2.89	2.24	1.67	1.24
China	Guangzhou, Guangdong	3,918	5,380	7,388	8,425	9,447	10,414	11,218	11,835	6.34	6.34	2.62	2.29	1.95	1.49	1.07
China	Guilin	557	666	795	929	1,075	1,209	1,323	1,418	3.55	3.55	3.12	2.92	2.35	1.80	1.38
China	Guiyang	1,665	2,208	2,929	3,447	3,980	4,443	4,818	5,114	5.65	5.65	3.26	2.87	2.20	1.62	1.19
China	Haerbin	2,991	3,209	3,444	3,566	3,753	4,083	4,421	4,696	1.41	1.41	0.70	1.02	1.68	1.59	1.20
China	Handan	1,092	1,201	1,321	1,535	1,775	1,991	2,171	2,318	1.90	1.90	3.00	2.90	2.29	1.73	1.31
China	Hangzhou	1,476	1,887	2,411	2,831	3,269	3,654	3,967	4,217	4.91	4.91	3.21	2.88	2.22	1.65	1.22
China	Hefei	1,100	1,342	1,637	1,916	2,214	2,480	2,700	2,878	3.98	3.98	3.14	2.89	2.27	1.70	1.28
China	Hengyang	702	783	873	973	1,087	1,210	1,324	1,418	2.17	2.17	2.17	2.22	2.15	1.79	1.38
China	Heze	1,200	1,238	1,277	1,318	1,388	1,518	1,655	1,771	0.62	0.62	0.62	1.04	1.79	1.73	1.35
China	Hohhot	938	1,142	1,389	1,625	1,878	2,106	2,295	2,449	3.92	3.92	3.14	2.90	2.29	1.73	1.30
China	Huai'an	1,113	1,154	1,198	1,243	1,315	1,440	1,571	1,681	0.74	0.74	0.73	1.13	1.82	1.74	1.35
China	Huaibei	536	627	733	858	995	1,120	1,227	1,315	3.14	3.14	3.14	2.96	2.37	1.82	1.39
China	Huainan	1,228	1,289	1,353	1,420	1,515	1,663	1,812	1,937	0.97	0.97	0.97	1.30	1.86	1.73	1.33
China	Huzhou	1,028	1,083	1,141	1,203	1,288	1,416	1,545	1,654	1.05	1.05	1.05	1.37	1.89	1.75	1.36
China	Jiamusi	660	750	853	969	1,099	1,229	1,345	1,441	2.56	2.56	2.56	2.52	2.23	1.79	1.38
China	Jiaozuo	605	670	742	822	915	1,019	1,115	1,196	2.05	2.05	2.05	2.14	2.15	1.81	1.40
China	Jiaxing	741	806	877	954	1,047	1,160	1,268	1,359	1.68	1.68	1.68	1.86	2.05	1.79	1.38
China	Jilin	1,320	1,596	1,928	2,255	2,606	2,916	3,171	3,376	3.79	3.79	3.13	2.89	2.25	1.68	1.25
China	Jinan, Shandong	2,404	2,512	2,625	2,743	2,914	3,182	3,453	3,674	0.88	0.88	0.88	1.21	1.76	1.63	1.24
China	Jining, Shandong	871	954	1,044	1,143	1,260	1,396	1,525	1,632	1.81	1.81	1.81	1.95	2.06	1.76	1.36
China	Jinxi, Liaoning	1,350	1,605	1,908	2,268	2,658	2,986	3,248	3,457	3.46	3.46	3.46	3.17	2.33	1.68	1.25
China	Jinzhou	736	795	858	925	1,009	1,117	1,221	1,309	1.52	1.53	1.52	1.74	2.02	1.79	1.39
China	Jixi, Heilongjiang	835	871	908	947	1,006	1,105	1,208	1,295	0.83	0.83	0.83	1.21	1.87	1.78	1.39
China	Kaifeng	693	741	793	848	918	1,014	1,110	1,191	1.34	1.34	1.34	1.60	1.99	1.80	1.40

		City Population of Urban Agglomerations								City Population Growth Rate of Urban Agglomerations						
Country	City	1990	1995	2000	2005	2010	2015	2020	2025	1990-1995	1995-2000	2000-2005	2005-2010	2010-2015	2015-2020	2020-2025
China	Kaohsiung	1,380	1,424	1,469	1,515	1,595	1,743	1,899	2,029	0.62	0.62	0.62	1.03	1.77	1.71	1.33
China	Kunming	1,612	2,045	2,594	2,837	3,095	3,404	3,694	3,928	4.75	4.76	1.79	1.74	1.91	1.63	1.23
China	Langfang	591	648	711	780	861	957	1,048	1,124	1.84	1.85	1.84	1.99	2.11	1.82	1.41
China	Lanzhou	1,618	1,830	2,071	2,411	2,785	3,115	3,387	3,604	2.47	2.47	3.04	2.89	2.24	1.67	1.24
China	Leshan	1,070	1,094	1,118	1,143	1,197	1,307	1,427	1,528	0.44	0.44	0.44	0.91	1.77	1.75	1.37
China	Lianyungang	537	605	682	768	865	967	1,060	1,137	2.38	2.38	2.38	2.39	2.22	1.82	1.41
China	Liaoyang	640	681	725	773	835	922	1,009	1,083	1.26	1.26	1.26	1.54	1.99	1.81	1.42
China	Linfen	583	647	719	799	891	993	1,087	1,167	2.11	2.11	2.11	2.18	2.16	1.82	1.41
China	Linyi, Shandong	1,740	1,834	1,932	2,035	2,177	2,385	2,594	2,765	1.04	1.04	1.04	1.34	1.83	1.68	1.28
China	Liuan	1,380	1,464	1,553	1,647	1,771	1,946	2,120	2,263	1.18	1.18	1.18	1.46	1.88	1.71	1.31
China	Liupanshui	827	905	989	1,149	1,329	1,493	1,632	1,745	1.79	1.79	3.00	2.91	2.33	1.77	1.35
China	Liuzhou	751	950	1,201	1,409	1,629	1,828	1,995	2,131	4.69	4.69	3.19	2.90	2.30	1.75	1.32
China	Luoyang	1,202	1,334	1,481	1,644	1,830	2,030	2,212	2,361	2.09	2.09	2.09	2.14	2.07	1.72	1.30
China	Luzhou	412	706	1,208	1,447	1,673	1,877	2,047	2,187	10.75	10.76	3.60	2.90	2.30	1.74	1.32
China	Mianyang, Sichuan	876	1,004	1,152	1,322	1,509	1,688	1,842	1,969	2.75	2.75	2.75	2.65	2.24	1.75	1.33
China	Mudanjiang	751	868	1,004	1,171	1,355	1,521	1,662	1,778	2.91	2.91	3.07	2.91	2.32	1.77	1.35
China	Nanchang	1,262	1,516	1,822	2,188	2,585	2,911	3,168	3,373	3.67	3.67	3.67	3.33	2.38	1.69	1.25
China	Nanchong	619	1,029	1,712	2,046	2,364	2,647	2,881	3,070	10.18	10.18	3.56	2.89	2.26	1.69	1.27
China	Nanjing, Jiangsu	2,611	3,013	3,477	3,621	3,813	4,149	4,492	4,771	2.87	2.87	0.81	1.04	1.69	1.59	1.20
China	Nanning	1,159	1,421	1,743	2,040	2,357	2,640	2,873	3,061	4.08	4.08	3.15	2.89	2.26	1.69	1.27
China	Nantong	470	597	759	891	1,031	1,160	1,269	1,360	4.79	4.80	3.20	2.92	2.35	1.81	1.38
China	Nanyang, Henan	375	753	1,512	1,830	2,115	2,370	2,581	2,752	13.95	13.96	3.81	2.90	2.27	1.71	1.28
China	Neijiang	1,289	1,338	1,388	1,441	1,525	1,669	1,819	1,944	0.74	0.74	0.74	1.13	1.81	1.72	1.33
China	Ningbo	1,142	1,331	1,551	1,810	2,092	2,344	2,553	2,723	3.06	3.06	3.08	2.90	2.27	1.71	1.28
China	Pingdingshan, Henan	997	949	904	861	854	921	1,006	1,080	-0.98	-0.98	-0.98	-0.16	1.50	1.78	1.42
China	Pingxiang, Jiangxi	569	664	775	905	1,047	1,178	1,289	1,381	3.09	3.09	3.08	2.92	2.35	1.81	1.38
China	Qingdao	2,102	2,381	2,698	2,817	2,977	3,246	3,521	3,746	2.50	2.50	0.86	1.11	1.73	1.63	1.24
China	Qinhuangdao	519	646	805	944	1,092	1,228	1,344	1,440	4.40	4.40	3.17	2.92	2.35	1.80	1.38
China	Qiqihaer	1,401	1,466	1,535	1,607	1,712	1,876	2,043	2,182	0.92	0.92	0.92	1.26	1.83	1.71	1.32
China	Quanzhou	480	745	1,158	1,377	1,592	1,787	1,950	2,083	8.81	8.81	3.47	2.91	2.31	1.75	1.32
China	Shanghai	8,205	10,423	13,243	14,503	15,789	17,214	18,466	19,412	4.79	4.79	1.82	1.70	1.73	1.41	1.00
China	Shangqiu	245	574	1,349	1,650	1,907	2,138	2,331	2,487	17.08	17.08	4.02	2.90	2.28	1.72	1.30
China	Shantou	885	1,054	1,255	1,495	1,756	1,978	2,158	2,304	3.50	3.50	3.50	3.22	2.38	1.74	1.31
China	Shaoxing	293	426	617	731	846	953	1,045	1,121	7.44	7.44	3.38	2.93	2.38	1.84	1.41
China	Shenyang	4,655	4,627	4,599	4,720	4,952	5,374	5,808	6,156	-0.12	-0.12	0.52	0.96	1.64	1.55	1.17
China	Shenzhen	875	2,304	6,069	7,233	8,114	8,952	9,654	10,196	19.36	19.37	3.51	2.30	1.97	1.51	1.09
China	Shijiazhuang	1,372	1,634	1,947	2,275	2,628	2,941	3,198	3,405	3.50	3.50	3.11	2.89	2.25	1.68	1.25
China	Suining, Sichuan	1,260	1,305	1,352	1,401	1,481	1,620	1,766	1,888	0.71	0.71	0.71	1.11	1.80	1.73	1.34
China	Suzhou, Anhui	258	623	1,509	1,849	2,137	2,394	2,607	2,780	17.67	17.68	4.06	2.90	2.27	1.71	1.28
China	Suzhou, Jiangsu	875	1,077	1,326	1,553	1,795	2,013	2,195	2,343	4.16	4.16	3.16	2.90	2.29	1.73	1.31
China	Taian, Shandong	1,413	1,472	1,534	1,598	1,696	1,857	2,022	2,160	0.82	0.82	0.82	1.19	1.81	1.71	1.32
China	Taichung	754	838	930	1,033	1,151	1,280	1,400	1,499	2.10	2.10	2.10	2.17	2.13	1.78	1.37
China	Tainan	679	702	725	750	791	869	951	1,021	0.65	0.65	0.65	1.09	1.86	1.81	1.42
China	Taipei	2,711	2,676	2,640	2,606	2,651	2,862	3,104	3,305	-0.26	-0.26	-0.26	0.35	1.53	1.63	1.25
China	Taiyuan, Shanxi	2,225	2,274	2,521	2,794	3,104	3,432	3,725	3,962	0.44	2.06	2.06	2.10	2.01	1.64	1.23
China	Tangshan, Hebei	1,485	1,590	1,703	1,825	1,977	2,175	2,367	2,526	1.38	1.38	1.37	1.60	1.91	1.69	1.29
China	Tianjin	5,804	6,246	6,722	7,040	7,468	8,113	8,745	9,243	1.47	1.47	0.92	1.18	1.66	1.50	1.11
China	Tianmen	1,484	1,545	1,609	1,676	1,777	1,945	2,118	2,261	0.81	0.81	0.81	1.18	1.80	1.70	1.31
China	Tianshui	1,040	1,090	1,143	1,199	1,279	1,404	1,533	1,640	0.95	0.95	0.95	1.29	1.87	1.75	1.36
China	Tongliao	674	729	790	855	935	1,036	1,133	1,215	1.59	1.59	1.59	1.79	2.04	1.80	1.40
China	Ürümqi (Wulumqi)	1,161	1,417	1,730	2,025	2,340	2,620	2,851	3,038	3.99	3.99	3.15	2.89	2.26	1.70	1.27
China	Weifang	1,152	1,257	1,372	1,498	1,646	1,821	1,985	2,120	1.75	1.75	1.75	1.89	2.01	1.73	1.32
China	Wenzhou	604	1,056	1,845	2,212	2,556	2,860	3,111	3,313	11.16	11.16	3.63	2.89	2.25	1.68	1.26
China	Wuhan	3,833	5,053	6,662	7,093	7,542	8,199	8,837	9,339	5.53	5.53	1.26	1.23	1.67	1.50	1.10
China	Wuhu, Anhui	553	619	692	774	868	968	1,061	1,138	2.24	2.24	2.24	2.29	2.19	1.82	1.41
China	Wuxi, Jiangsu	1,009	1,192	1,410	1,646	1,903	2,134	2,326	2,481	3.35	3.35	3.10	2.90	2.28	1.72	1.30
China	Xiamen	639	1,124	1,977	2,371	2,739	3,064	3,331	3,545	11.28	11.29	3.64	2.89	2.24	1.67	1.25
China	Xi'an, Shaanxi	2,873	3,271	3,725	3,926	4,178	4,556	4,931	5,233	2.60	2.60	1.05	1.24	1.74	1.58	1.19
China	Xiangfan, Hubei	492	649	855	1,006	1,164	1,309	1,431	1,533	5.53	5.53	3.25	2.92	2.34	1.79	1.37
China	Xiantao	1,361	1,415	1,470	1,528	1,618	1,771	1,930	2,062	0.77	0.77	0.77	1.15	1.81	1.71	1.32
China	Xianyang, Shaanxi	737	835	946	1,072	1,212	1,354	1,480	1,584	2.50	2.50	2.50	2.47	2.21	1.78	1.36
China	Xingyi, Guizhou	593	651	715	785	868	964	1,056	1,133	1.86	1.87	1.86	2.00	2.11	1.82	1.41
China	Xining	698	770	849	987	1,142	1,283	1,404	1,504	1.96	1.96	3.01	2.92	2.34	1.80	1.37
China	Xinxiang	613	687	770	863	968	1,080	1,182	1,268	2.27	2.28	2.27	2.31	2.19	1.81	1.39
China	Xinyang	273	571	1,195	1,450	1,677	1,881	2,052	2,192	14.76	14.76	3.87	2.90	2.30	1.74	1.31

Country	City	\multicolumn{8}{c}{City Population of Urban Agglomerations}	\multicolumn{7}{c}{City Population Growth Rate of Urban Agglomerations}
		1990	1995	2000	2005	2010	2015	2020	2025	1990-1995	1995-2000	2000-2005	2005-2010	2010-2015	2015-2020	2020-2025
China	Xinyu	608	685	772	870	981	1,095	1,199	1,285	2.39	2.39	2.39	2.39	2.21	1.81	1.39
China	Xuanzhou	769	795	823	851	899	987	1,079	1,158	0.68	0.68	0.68	1.10	1.85	1.79	1.41
China	Xuzhou	944	1,247	1,648	1,960	2,284	2,564	2,792	2,975	5.58	5.58	3.46	3.06	2.31	1.70	1.27
China	Yancheng, Jiangsu	497	580	677	789	914	1,029	1,127	1,209	3.09	3.09	3.08	2.92	2.37	1.83	1.40
China	Yantai	838	1,188	1,684	1,991	2,301	2,577	2,805	2,989	6.98	6.98	3.35	2.89	2.26	1.70	1.27
China	Yibin	685	743	805	872	954	1,057	1,157	1,240	1.61	1.61	1.61	1.80	2.05	1.80	1.40
China	Yichang	492	589	704	823	953	1,072	1,174	1,259	3.58	3.58	3.12	2.92	2.36	1.82	1.40
China	Yichun, Heilongjiang	882	849	816	785	785	848	928	997	-0.78	-0.78	-0.78	-0.00	1.55	1.79	1.43
China	Yichun, Jiangxi	836	876	917	961	1,025	1,127	1,231	1,320	0.93	0.93	0.93	1.28	1.89	1.78	1.39
China	Yinchuan	502	632	795	932	1,079	1,213	1,328	1,423	4.60	4.60	3.19	2.92	2.35	1.80	1.38
China	Yingkou	572	630	694	764	847	942	1,032	1,107	1.93	1.94	1.93	2.05	2.13	1.82	1.41
China	Yiyang, Hunan	1,062	1,140	1,223	1,313	1,425	1,571	1,714	1,833	1.41	1.41	1.41	1.64	1.96	1.74	1.34
China	Yongzhou	946	960	976	991	1,032	1,127	1,231	1,320	0.31	0.31	0.31	0.82	1.76	1.77	1.39
China	Yuci	467	555	660	785	921	1,041	1,141	1,224	3.46	3.46	3.46	3.21	2.45	1.83	1.40
China	Yueyang	1,078	995	918	847	821	879	961	1,032	-1.60	-1.61	-1.60	-0.63	1.37	1.77	1.42
China	Yulin, Guangxi	667	779	909	1,060	1,227	1,379	1,507	1,613	3.09	3.09	3.08	2.91	2.33	1.79	1.36
China	Zaozhuang	1,793	1,889	1,990	2,096	2,242	2,456	2,670	2,846	1.04	1.04	1.04	1.34	1.83	1.67	1.28
China	Zhangjiakou	720	803	897	1,001	1,120	1,247	1,364	1,461	2.20	2.20	2.20	2.25	2.15	1.79	1.37
China	Zhanjiang	1,049	1,185	1,340	1,514	1,709	1,903	2,076	2,216	2.45	2.45	2.45	2.42	2.16	1.73	1.31
China	Zhaotong	620	670	724	783	855	948	1,038	1,113	1.56	1.56	1.56	1.77	2.05	1.81	1.41
China	Zhengzhou	1,752	2,081	2,472	2,590	2,738	2,987	3,243	3,452	3.44	3.44	0.93	1.11	1.74	1.64	1.25
China	Zhenjiang, Jiangsu	490	581	688	803	930	1,047	1,147	1,230	3.39	3.39	3.10	2.92	2.37	1.83	1.40
China	Zhuhai	331	518	809	963	1,114	1,253	1,371	1,468	8.94	8.94	3.48	2.92	2.35	1.80	1.37
China	Zhuzhou	585	713	868	1,016	1,176	1,322	1,445	1,548	3.95	3.95	3.14	2.92	2.34	1.79	1.37
China	Zibo	2,484	2,640	2,806	2,982	3,209	3,515	3,812	4,053	1.22	1.22	1.22	1.46	1.82	1.62	1.23
China	Zigong	977	1,012	1,049	1,087	1,149	1,259	1,375	1,473	0.71	0.71	0.71	1.11	1.83	1.76	1.37
China	Zunyi	392	516	679	799	924	1,041	1,140	1,223	5.50	5.50	3.25	2.92	2.37	1.83	1.40
China, Hong Kong SAR	Hong Kong	5,677	6,206	6,662	7,057	7,419	7,744	8,040	8,305	1.78	1.42	1.15	1.00	0.86	0.75	0.65
Colombia	Barranquilla	1,229	1,363	1,531	1,719	1,907	2,048	2,157	2,251	2.06	2.32	2.32	2.07	1.42	1.04	0.85
Colombia	Bogotá	4,740	5,494	6,356	7,353	8,320	8,916	9,299	9,600	2.95	2.92	2.91	2.47	1.38	0.84	0.64
Colombia	Bucaramanga	650	759	855	964	1,073	1,157	1,223	1,282	3.08	2.39	2.39	2.14	1.50	1.12	0.93
Colombia	Cali	1,552	1,757	1,950	2,164	2,378	2,544	2,675	2,786	2.48	2.08	2.08	1.88	1.35	1.01	0.82
Colombia	Cartagena	561	645	737	842	948	1,026	1,086	1,139	2.77	2.68	2.67	2.36	1.58	1.14	0.95
Colombia	Medellín	2,135	2,372	2,724	3,127	3,524	3,789	3,975	4,129	2.11	2.76	2.76	2.39	1.45	0.96	0.76
Congo	Brazzaville	704	830	986	1,216	1,505	1,729	1,938	2,150	3.31	3.44	4.19	4.26	2.78	2.28	2.07
Costa Rica	San José	737	867	1,032	1,217	1,374	1,506	1,627	1,737	3.25	3.48	3.29	2.43	1.84	1.53	1.32
Côte d'Ivoire	Abidjan	2,102	2,535	3,032	3,564	4,175	4,810	5,432	6,031	3.74	3.58	3.24	3.16	2.83	2.43	2.09
Cuba	La Habana (Havana)	2,108	2,183	2,187	2,189	2,159	2,151	2,150	2,150	0.69	0.04	0.02	-0.27	-0.08	-0.01	-0.00
Czech Republic	Praha (Prague)	1,212	1,194	1,172	1,164	1,160	1,159	1,159	1,159	-0.29	-0.38	-0.14	-0.07	-0.02	-0.00	—
Dem. People's Republic of Korea	Hamhung	705	712	732	762	788	818	851	882	0.20	0.56	0.80	0.68	0.73	0.80	0.72
Dem. People's Republic of Korea	N'ampo	580	806	1,020	1,110	1,148	1,187	1,232	1,274	6.58	4.71	1.69	0.67	0.68	0.74	0.67
Dem. People's Republic of Korea	P'yongyang	2,526	2,838	3,117	3,265	3,346	3,434	3,537	3,630	2.33	1.88	0.93	0.49	0.52	0.59	0.52
Democratic Republic of the Congo	Kananga	372	466	557	700	879	1,109	1,383	1,698	4.47	3.57	4.57	4.55	4.66	4.41	4.11
Democratic Republic of the Congo	Kinshasa	3,448	4,447	5,485	7,108	9,052	11,313	13,875	16,762	5.09	4.19	5.18	4.84	4.46	4.08	3.78
Democratic Republic of the Congo	Lubumbashi	692	852	1,004	1,243	1,544	1,938	2,406	2,943	4.17	3.28	4.28	4.33	4.54	4.33	4.03
Democratic Republic of the Congo	Mbuji-Mayi	613	773	932	1,181	1,489	1,876	2,330	2,851	4.64	3.75	4.74	4.64	4.62	4.33	4.04
Denmark	København (Copenhagen)	1,035	1,048	1,077	1,085	1,087	1,092	1,095	1,096	0.25	0.54	0.14	0.04	0.09	0.06	0.02
Dominican Republic	Santo Domingo	1,522	1,670	1,854	2,062	2,298	2,525	2,722	2,885	1.86	2.09	2.12	2.17	1.88	1.50	1.16
Ecuador	Guayaquil	1,572	1,808	2,077	2,386	2,690	2,941	3,154	3,328	2.80	2.78	2.77	2.40	1.79	1.39	1.08
Ecuador	Quito	1,088	1,217	1,357	1,593	1,846	2,035	2,189	2,316	2.25	2.18	3.20	2.95	1.95	1.45	1.13
Egypt	Al-Iskandariyah (Alexandria)	3,063	3,277	3,600	3,995	4,421	4,817	5,210	5,652	1.35	1.88	2.08	2.03	1.71	1.57	1.63
Egypt	Al-Qahirah (Cairo)	9,061	9,707	10,534	11,487	12,503	13,465	14,451	15,561	1.38	1.64	1.73	1.70	1.48	1.41	1.48
El Salvador	San Salvador	970	1,107	1,233	1,374	1,520	1,649	1,776	1,902	2.65	2.16	2.16	2.01	1.63	1.48	1.37
Ethiopia	Addis Ababa	1,791	2,157	2,493	2,902	3,453	4,184	5,083	6,156	3.72	2.90	3.03	3.48	3.84	3.89	3.83
Finland	Helsinki	872	943	1,019	1,094	1,139	1,169	1,195	1,220	1.57	1.56	1.42	0.81	0.51	0.46	0.41

		City Population of Urban Agglomerations								City Population Growth Rate of Urban Agglomerations						
Country	City	1990	1995	2000	2005	2010	2015	2020	2025	1990-1995	1995-2000	2000-2005	2005-2010	2010-2015	2015-2020	2020-2025
France	Bordeaux	698	730	763	793	817	836	853	869	0.88	0.88	0.78	0.60	0.46	0.40	0.36
France	Lille	961	984	1,007	1,033	1,059	1,081	1,102	1,120	0.47	0.47	0.50	0.50	0.42	0.37	0.33
France	Lyon	1,265	1,313	1,362	1,407	1,443	1,471	1,495	1,516	0.74	0.73	0.66	0.50	0.38	0.32	0.28
France	Marseille-Aix-en-Provence	1,305	1,331	1,357	1,386	1,418	1,445	1,469	1,490	0.39	0.39	0.43	0.46	0.38	0.33	0.28
France	Nice-Cannes	854	874	894	917	941	962	980	997	0.46	0.46	0.50	0.52	0.44	0.38	0.34
France	Paris	9,330	9,510	9,692	9,852	9,958	10,007	10,031	10,036	0.38	0.38	0.33	0.21	0.10	0.05	0.01
France	Toulouse	654	714	778	832	863	883	900	916	1.75	1.74	1.34	0.72	0.46	0.40	0.35
Georgia	Tbilisi	1,224	1,160	1,100	1,093	1,108	1,113	1,114	1,114	-1.07	-1.07	-0.12	0.26	0.09	0.01	0.00
Germany	Berlin	3,422	3,471	3,384	3,391	3,423	3,434	3,436	3,436	0.29	-0.51	0.04	0.19	0.07	0.01	0.00
Germany	Hamburg	1,639	1,707	1,710	1,739	1,777	1,791	1,792	1,792	0.81	0.04	0.34	0.43	0.15	0.02	0.00
Germany	Köln (Cologne)	950	965	963	976	1,037	1,059	1,061	1,061	0.31	-0.04	0.28	1.19	0.43	0.04	0.00
Germany	München (Munich)	1,218	1,241	1,202	1,254	1,300	1,317	1,318	1,318	0.37	-0.62	0.85	0.72	0.26	0.03	0.00
Ghana	Accra	1,197	1,415	1,674	1,984	2,332	2,688	3,041	3,382	3.35	3.35	3.40	3.23	2.84	2.47	2.13
Ghana	Kumasi	696	909	1,187	1,518	1,826	2,112	2,393	2,667	5.34	5.34	4.92	3.69	2.91	2.50	2.16
Greece	Athínai (Athens)	3,070	3,122	3,179	3,230	3,256	3,278	3,300	3,326	0.34	0.37	0.31	0.17	0.13	0.13	0.16
Greece	Thessaloniki	746	771	797	821	837	851	865	880	0.66	0.67	0.59	0.39	0.33	0.33	0.35
Guatemala	Ciudad de Guatemala (Guatemala City)	803	839	908	984	1,104	1,281	1,481	1,690	0.89	1.57	1.62	2.30	2.97	2.90	2.64
Guinea	Conakry	895	1,045	1,219	1,409	1,645	1,984	2,393	2,856	3.11	3.08	2.90	3.09	3.75	3.75	3.54
Haiti	Port-au-Prince	1,134	1,427	1,653	1,885	2,209	2,621	3,012	3,346	4.60	2.94	2.62	3.17	3.42	2.78	2.10
Honduras	Tegucigalpa	578	677	793	901	1,022	1,165	1,317	1,472	3.16	3.16	2.56	2.52	2.62	2.46	2.22
Hungary	Budapest	2,005	1,893	1,787	1,693	1,664	1,655	1,655	1,655	-1.15	-1.15	-1.08	-0.35	-0.10	-0.01	-0.00
India	Agra	933	1,095	1,293	1,511	1,705	1,899	2,118	2,364	3.20	3.32	3.12	2.42	2.15	2.18	2.20
India	Ahmadabad	3,255	3,790	4,427	5,122	5,726	6,320	6,989	7,735	3.04	3.11	2.92	2.23	1.97	2.01	2.03
India	Aligarh	468	554	653	763	864	966	1,083	1,215	3.39	3.29	3.11	2.48	2.24	2.28	2.30
India	Allahabad	830	928	1,035	1,152	1,279	1,425	1,592	1,781	2.23	2.17	2.15	2.10	2.15	2.22	2.24
India	Amritsar	726	844	990	1,152	1,299	1,449	1,619	1,811	3.00	3.20	3.02	2.41	2.18	2.22	2.24
India	Asansol	727	891	1,065	1,258	1,425	1,590	1,776	1,985	4.06	3.56	3.33	2.51	2.18	2.21	2.23
India	Aurangabad	568	708	868	1,049	1,200	1,341	1,499	1,678	4.38	4.09	3.78	2.69	2.22	2.23	2.25
India	Bangalore	4,036	4,744	5,567	6,465	7,229	7,967	8,795	9,719	3.23	3.20	2.99	2.24	1.94	1.98	2.00
India	Bareilly	604	664	722	787	869	970	1,087	1,219	1.87	1.67	1.73	1.98	2.19	2.28	2.30
India	Bhiwandi	362	479	603	745	860	964	1,081	1,212	5.62	4.60	4.23	2.88	2.28	2.28	2.30
India	Bhopal	1,046	1,228	1,426	1,644	1,845	2,053	2,288	2,553	3.21	3.00	2.84	2.31	2.13	2.17	2.19
India	Bhubaneswar	395	504	637	790	913	1,024	1,147	1,286	4.90	4.69	4.30	2.90	2.28	2.27	2.29
India	Chandigarh	564	667	791	928	1,051	1,174	1,314	1,472	3.36	3.40	3.20	2.49	2.22	2.25	2.27
India	Chennai (Madras)	5,338	5,836	6,353	6,918	7,559	8,309	9,170	10,129	1.78	1.70	1.71	1.77	1.89	1.97	1.99
India	Coimbatore	1,088	1,239	1,420	1,619	1,810	2,012	2,243	2,503	2.60	2.73	2.62	2.23	2.12	2.18	2.19
India	Delhi	8,206	10,092	12,441	15,053	17,015	18,669	20,484	22,498	4.14	4.18	3.81	2.45	1.86	1.86	1.88
India	Dhanbad	805	915	1,046	1,189	1,330	1,482	1,656	1,852	2.56	2.67	2.57	2.24	2.16	2.22	2.24
India	Durg-Bhilainagar	670	780	905	1,044	1,174	1,310	1,465	1,640	3.03	2.98	2.84	2.35	2.19	2.24	2.25
India	Faridabad	593	779	1,018	1,298	1,512	1,691	1,887	2,109	5.47	5.35	4.86	3.05	2.23	2.20	2.22
India	Ghaziabad	492	675	928	1,237	1,464	1,639	1,830	2,046	6.30	6.38	5.74	3.37	2.26	2.21	2.22
India	Guwahati (Gauhati)	564	675	797	932	1,054	1,178	1,318	1,477	3.60	3.32	3.13	2.47	2.22	2.25	2.27
India	Gwalior	706	779	855	940	1,040	1,160	1,298	1,455	1.97	1.88	1.90	2.03	2.17	2.25	2.27
India	Hubli-Dharwad	639	705	776	855	948	1,057	1,184	1,327	1.95	1.93	1.94	2.05	2.19	2.27	2.28
India	Hyderabad	4,193	4,825	5,445	6,117	6,761	7,446	8,224	9,092	2.81	2.42	2.32	2.00	1.93	1.99	2.01
India	Indore	1,088	1,314	1,597	1,914	2,176	2,421	2,696	3,005	3.77	3.91	3.62	2.57	2.13	2.15	2.17
India	Jabalpur	879	981	1,100	1,231	1,369	1,524	1,703	1,904	2.19	2.29	2.24	2.12	2.15	2.21	2.23
India	Jaipur	1,478	1,826	2,259	2,748	3,136	3,482	3,867	4,298	4.23	4.26	3.91	2.64	2.09	2.10	2.11
India	Jalandhar	502	588	694	811	918	1,027	1,150	1,290	3.16	3.31	3.13	2.48	2.24	2.27	2.29
India	Jammu	356	458	588	739	859	963	1,079	1,211	5.00	5.01	4.58	3.00	2.30	2.28	2.30
India	Jamshedpur	817	938	1,081	1,239	1,389	1,548	1,729	1,933	2.75	2.84	2.72	2.29	2.16	2.21	2.23
India	Jodhpur	654	743	842	951	1,062	1,185	1,327	1,486	2.54	2.51	2.44	2.22	2.19	2.25	2.27
India	Kanpur	2,001	2,294	2,641	3,019	3,369	3,731	4,141	4,601	2.73	2.82	2.68	2.20	2.04	2.09	2.11
India	Kochi (Cochin)	1,103	1,229	1,340	1,463	1,612	1,791	1,999	2,232	2.17	1.73	1.76	1.94	2.11	2.19	2.21
India	Kolkata (Calcutta)	10,890	11,924	13,058	14,282	15,577	17,039	18,707	20,560	1.82	1.82	1.79	1.74	1.80	1.87	1.89
India	Kota	523	604	692	789	885	989	1,108	1,243	2.89	2.71	2.62	2.30	2.22	2.28	2.29
India	Kozhikode (Calicut)	781	835	875	924	1,008	1,123	1,257	1,409	1.33	0.94	1.10	1.74	2.15	2.26	2.28
India	Lucknow	1,614	1,906	2,221	2,567	2,877	3,191	3,546	3,944	3.33	3.06	2.89	2.29	2.07	2.11	2.13
India	Ludhiana	1,006	1,183	1,368	1,572	1,762	1,961	2,186	2,440	3.24	2.91	2.77	2.29	2.13	2.18	2.20
India	Madurai	1,073	1,132	1,187	1,255	1,367	1,519	1,697	1,897	1.07	0.95	1.11	1.72	2.11	2.21	2.23
India	Meerut	824	975	1,143	1,328	1,496	1,667	1,862	2,080	3.36	3.18	3.00	2.39	2.16	2.20	2.22
India	Moradabad	436	520	626	743	847	948	1,062	1,192	3.53	3.68	3.45	2.60	2.26	2.28	2.30
India	Mumbai (Bombay)	12,308	14,111	16,086	18,202	20,072	21,946	24,051	26,385	2.73	2.62	2.47	1.96	1.78	1.83	1.85

		City Population of Urban Agglomerations								City Population Growth Rate of Urban Agglomerations						
Country	City	1990	1995	2000	2005	2010	2015	2020	2025	1990-1995	1995-2000	2000-2005	2005-2010	2010-2015	2015-2020	2020-2025
India	Mysore	640	708	776	853	943	1,053	1,179	1,322	2.01	1.85	1.88	2.03	2.19	2.27	2.29
India	Nagpur	1,637	1,849	2,089	2,350	2,611	2,895	3,219	3,583	2.44	2.44	2.36	2.10	2.06	2.12	2.14
India	Nashik	700	886	1,117	1,381	1,590	1,775	1,981	2,213	4.71	4.63	4.24	2.82	2.20	2.19	2.21
India	Patna	1,087	1,331	1,658	2,029	2,325	2,587	2,879	3,207	4.05	4.40	4.04	2.72	2.14	2.14	2.16
India	Pune (Poona)	2,430	2,978	3,655	4,411	5,010	5,543	6,135	6,797	4.07	4.09	3.76	2.55	2.02	2.03	2.05
India	Raipur	453	553	680	824	944	1,057	1,184	1,327	4.00	4.13	3.83	2.72	2.26	2.27	2.28
India	Rajkot	638	787	974	1,186	1,359	1,518	1,696	1,896	4.21	4.26	3.93	2.73	2.21	2.22	2.23
India	Ranchi	607	712	844	990	1,120	1,251	1,400	1,567	3.21	3.39	3.19	2.48	2.21	2.24	2.26
India	Salem	574	647	736	834	933	1,042	1,168	1,309	2.38	2.58	2.50	2.25	2.21	2.27	2.29
India	Solapur	613	720	853	1,002	1,135	1,267	1,417	1,587	3.20	3.41	3.21	2.49	2.21	2.24	2.26
India	Srinagar	730	833	954	1,087	1,218	1,358	1,518	1,699	2.62	2.72	2.62	2.27	2.18	2.23	2.25
India	Surat	1,468	1,984	2,699	3,558	4,174	4,639	5,142	5,703	6.01	6.16	5.53	3.19	2.11	2.06	2.07
India	Thiruvananthapuram	801	853	885	927	1,008	1,122	1,256	1,408	1.25	0.73	0.93	1.68	2.14	2.26	2.28
India	Tiruchirappalli	705	768	837	916	1,011	1,127	1,262	1,414	1.71	1.74	1.78	1.99	2.17	2.26	2.28
India	Vadodara	1,096	1,273	1,465	1,675	1,875	2,085	2,324	2,592	2.99	2.81	2.69	2.25	2.12	2.17	2.19
India	Varanasi (Benares)	1,013	1,106	1,199	1,303	1,434	1,595	1,781	1,991	1.75	1.62	1.67	1.91	2.12	2.21	2.23
India	Vijayawada	821	914	999	1,094	1,209	1,346	1,505	1,684	2.14	1.79	1.82	1.98	2.15	2.23	2.25
India	Visakhapatnam	1,018	1,168	1,309	1,465	1,628	1,810	2,020	2,256	2.73	2.29	2.25	2.11	2.12	2.19	2.21
Indonesia	Bandar Lampung	454	578	743	824	937	1,064	1,172	1,260	4.84	5.01	2.08	2.57	2.53	1.93	1.45
Indonesia	Bandung	2,035	2,097	2,138	2,303	2,568	2,887	3,156	3,370	0.59	0.39	1.48	2.18	2.34	1.79	1.31
Indonesia	Bogor	596	668	751	865	1,003	1,142	1,257	1,351	2.26	2.36	2.82	2.97	2.59	1.92	1.44
Indonesia	Jakarta	8,175	8,322	8,390	8,843	9,703	10,792	11,689	12,363	0.36	0.16	1.05	1.86	2.13	1.60	1.12
Indonesia	Malang	689	725	757	783	857	967	1,065	1,146	1.03	0.88	0.67	1.81	2.41	1.94	1.47
Indonesia	Medan	1,718	1,816	1,912	2,040	2,264	2,545	2,786	2,977	1.11	1.03	1.30	2.08	2.34	1.80	1.33
Indonesia	Padang	626	671	716	810	931	1,059	1,166	1,254	1.40	1.30	2.46	2.78	2.57	1.93	1.45
Indonesia	Palembang	1,130	1,287	1,459	1,656	1,903	2,154	2,361	2,526	2.59	2.51	2.54	2.78	2.48	1.83	1.35
Indonesia	Pekan Baru	389	481	588	735	891	1,023	1,128	1,213	4.26	4.02	4.45	3.87	2.76	1.95	1.46
Indonesia	Semarang	1,243	1,333	1,427	1,385	1,462	1,633	1,792	1,921	1.40	1.36	-0.60	1.08	2.22	1.86	1.39
Indonesia	Surabaya	2,467	2,544	2,611	2,754	3,035	3,402	3,715	3,962	0.62	0.51	1.07	1.94	2.28	1.76	1.29
Indonesia	Ujung Pandang	816	926	1,051	1,194	1,374	1,559	1,713	1,837	2.53	2.53	2.56	2.81	2.53	1.88	1.40
Iran (Islamic Republic of)	Ahvaz	685	784	867	957	1,056	1,158	1,252	1,326	2.69	2.01	1.98	1.97	1.84	1.56	1.14
Iran (Islamic Republic of)	Esfahan	1,094	1,230	1,382	1,553	1,743	1,920	2,071	2,185	2.33	2.34	2.34	2.30	1.94	1.51	1.07
Iran (Islamic Republic of)	Karaj	693	903	1,087	1,318	1,585	1,802	1,952	2,061	5.30	3.70	3.85	3.69	2.57	1.60	1.08
Iran (Islamic Republic of)	Kermanshah	608	675	729	781	837	907	981	1,041	2.11	1.55	1.36	1.40	1.60	1.56	1.18
Iran (Islamic Republic of)	Mashhad	1,680	1,854	2,073	2,349	2,654	2,929	3,151	3,315	1.97	2.23	2.50	2.44	1.97	1.46	1.01
Iran (Islamic Republic of)	Qom	622	744	841	933	1,035	1,137	1,230	1,302	3.56	2.45	2.08	2.07	1.88	1.57	1.15
Iran (Islamic Republic of)	Shiraz	946	1,030	1,115	1,203	1,300	1,410	1,521	1,608	1.70	1.58	1.52	1.55	1.63	1.51	1.11
Iran (Islamic Republic of)	Tabriz	1,058	1,165	1,264	1,369	1,484	1,611	1,736	1,834	1.91	1.64	1.59	1.61	1.65	1.50	1.10
Iran (Islamic Republic of)	Tehran	6,365	6,687	7,128	7,653	8,221	8,832	9,404	9,814	0.99	1.28	1.42	1.43	1.43	1.26	0.85
Iraq	Al-Basrah (Basra)	474	631	759	837	923	1,024	1,143	1,270	5.71	3.68	1.96	1.96	2.07	2.20	2.11
Iraq	Al-Mawsil (Mosul)	736	889	1,056	1,236	1,447	1,677	1,891	2,097	3.78	3.44	3.15	3.15	2.95	2.40	2.06
Iraq	Baghdad	4,092	4,598	5,200	5,327	5,891	6,618	7,345	8,060	2.34	2.46	0.48	2.01	2.33	2.08	1.86
Iraq	Irbil (Erbil)	536	644	757	874	1,009	1,158	1,305	1,450	3.65	3.23	2.88	2.88	2.76	2.38	2.11
Ireland	Dublin	916	946	989	1,037	1,098	1,177	1,257	1,332	0.65	0.87	0.96	1.14	1.38	1.31	1.17
Israel	Hefa (Haifa)	582	775	888	992	1,043	1,104	1,159	1,210	5.74	2.73	2.22	0.99	1.13	0.98	0.85
Israel	Tel Aviv-Yafo (Tel Aviv-Jaffa)	2,026	2,442	2,752	3,012	3,256	3,453	3,600	3,726	3.73	2.39	1.81	1.56	1.18	0.83	0.69
Italy	Milano (Milan)	3,063	3,020	2,985	2,953	2,940	2,938	2,938	2,938	-0.28	-0.23	-0.21	-0.09	-0.01	-0.00	—
Italy	Napoli (Naples)	2,208	2,218	2,232	2,246	2,253	2,254	2,254	2,254	0.09	0.13	0.12	0.06	0.01	0.00	0.00
Italy	Palermo	844	850	855	860	865	868	869	871	0.14	0.12	0.12	0.12	0.06	0.02	0.05
Italy	Roma (Rome)	3,450	3,425	3,385	3,348	3,333	3,330	3,330	3,330	-0.14	-0.24	-0.22	-0.10	-0.01	-0.00	—
Italy	Torino (Turin)	1,775	1,733	1,694	1,660	1,647	1,645	1,645	1,645	-0.48	-0.45	-0.40	-0.16	-0.02	-0.00	—
Japan	Fukuoka-Kitakyushu	2,487	2,619	2,716	2,771	2,816	2,833	2,834	2,834	1.04	0.73	0.40	0.33	0.12	0.01	0.00
Japan	Hiroshima	1,986	2,040	2,044	2,045	2,045	2,046	2,046	2,046	0.54	0.04	0.01	0.01	0.00	0.00	0.00
Japan	Kyoto	1,760	1,804	1,806	1,805	1,804	1,804	1,804	1,804	0.49	0.02	-0.01	-0.01	-0.00	-0.00	—
Japan	Nagoya	2,947	3,055	3,122	3,199	3,267	3,292	3,295	3,295	0.71	0.44	0.49	0.42	0.15	0.02	0.00
Japan	Osaka-Kobe	11,035	11,052	11,165	11,258	11,337	11,365	11,368	11,368	0.03	0.20	0.17	0.14	0.05	0.01	0.00
Japan	Sapporo	2,319	2,476	2,508	2,534	2,556	2,564	2,565	2,565	1.31	0.26	0.20	0.17	0.06	0.01	0.00

| Country | City | \multicolumn{8}{c}{City Population of Urban Agglomerations} | \multicolumn{7}{c}{City Population Growth Rate of Urban Agglomerations} |
		1990	1995	2000	2005	2010	2015	2020	2025	1990-1995	1995-2000	2000-2005	2005-2010	2010-2015	2015-2020	2020-2025
Japan	Sendai	2,021	2,135	2,184	2,231	2,272	2,287	2,288	2,288	1.09	0.46	0.43	0.36	0.13	0.01	0.00
Japan	Tokyo	32,530	33,587	34,450	35,327	36,094	36,371	36,399	36,400	0.64	0.51	0.50	0.43	0.15	0.02	0.00
Jordan	Amman	851	973	1,007	1,042	1,106	1,185	1,268	1,359	2.67	0.68	0.68	1.19	1.39	1.35	1.38
Kazakhstan	Almaty	1,080	1,108	1,142	1,190	1,240	1,298	1,355	1,404	0.52	0.60	0.82	0.83	0.90	0.87	0.70
Kenya	Mombasa	476	572	686	821	985	1,196	1,453	1,763	3.65	3.65	3.59	3.65	3.88	3.90	3.87
Kenya	Nairobi	1,380	1,755	2,233	2,787	3,363	4,052	4,881	5,871	4.81	4.81	4.43	3.76	3.73	3.72	3.69
Kuwait	Al Kuwayt (Kuwait City)	1,392	1,190	1,499	1,888	2,305	2,592	2,790	2,956	-3.13	4.62	4.61	3.99	2.35	1.47	1.16
Kyrgyzstan	Bishkek	635	703	770	817	869	934	1,011	1,096	2.03	1.82	1.20	1.23	1.43	1.58	1.62
Lebanon	Bayrut (Beirut)	1,293	1,268	1,487	1,777	1,941	2,051	2,119	2,173	-0.39	3.19	3.57	1.76	1.10	0.66	0.50
Liberia	Monrovia	1,042	464	836	1,140	1,185	1,457	1,753	2,083	-16.18	11.76	6.22	0.77	4.14	3.70	3.45
Libyan Arab Jamahiriya	Banghazi	612	799	945	1,113	1,271	1,398	1,505	1,590	5.34	3.36	3.27	2.65	1.91	1.47	1.10
Libyan Arab Jamahiriya	Tarabulus (Tripoli)	1,500	1,678	1,877	2,098	2,322	2,532	2,713	2,855	2.24	2.24	2.23	2.04	1.73	1.38	1.01
Madagascar	Antananarivo	948	1,169	1,361	1,590	1,877	2,229	2,642	3,118	4.20	3.04	3.10	3.33	3.44	3.39	3.32
Malaysia	Johore Bharu	417	516	630	797	999	1,175	1,294	1,382	4.28	4.01	4.68	4.53	3.24	1.94	1.31
Malaysia	Klang	345	466	631	849	1,128	1,360	1,503	1,603	6.01	6.07	5.93	5.68	3.75	1.99	1.29
Malaysia	Kuala Lumpur	1,120	1,213	1,306	1,405	1,519	1,670	1,820	1,938	1.58	1.47	1.47	1.56	1.89	1.72	1.26
Mali	Bamako	746	910	1,110	1,368	1,708	2,130	2,633	3,214	3.96	3.97	4.18	4.44	4.41	4.24	3.99
Mexico	Aguascalientes	552	631	734	829	927	1,000	1,050	1,089	2.69	3.02	2.42	2.25	1.51	0.96	0.73
Mexico	Chihuahua	539	625	683	760	841	904	949	985	2.94	1.77	2.15	2.03	1.44	0.97	0.74
Mexico	Ciudad de México (Mexico City)	15,312	16,811	18,022	18,735	19,485	20,189	20,695	21,009	1.87	1.39	0.78	0.79	0.71	0.50	0.30
Mexico	Ciudad Juárez	809	997	1,225	1,308	1,396	1,478	1,544	1,597	4.19	4.11	1.32	1.30	1.14	0.88	0.67
Mexico	Culiacán	606	690	749	791	837	886	928	964	2.60	1.63	1.10	1.13	1.12	0.94	0.75
Mexico	Guadalajara	3,011	3,431	3,703	4,051	4,408	4,673	4,847	4,973	2.61	1.53	1.80	1.69	1.17	0.73	0.51
Mexico	León de los Aldamas	961	1,127	1,290	1,429	1,573	1,682	1,758	1,817	3.19	2.70	2.04	1.92	1.35	0.88	0.66
Mexico	Mérida	664	765	848	931	1,017	1,087	1,139	1,180	2.83	2.06	1.85	1.77	1.33	0.94	0.72
Mexico	Mexicali	607	690	770	851	935	1,002	1,051	1,090	2.57	2.21	1.99	1.89	1.38	0.95	0.73
Mexico	Monterrey	2,594	2,961	3,266	3,579	3,901	4,140	4,298	4,413	2.65	1.96	1.83	1.72	1.19	0.75	0.53
Mexico	Puebla	1,686	1,692	1,907	2,109	2,318	2,474	2,578	2,657	0.07	2.40	2.02	1.89	1.30	0.83	0.60
Mexico	Querétaro	561	671	795	911	1,032	1,118	1,172	1,215	3.58	3.39	2.71	2.50	1.59	0.96	0.71
Mexico	Saltillo	491	577	643	720	802	864	907	942	3.21	2.16	2.28	2.14	1.49	0.98	0.75
Mexico	San Luis Potosí	665	774	858	952	1,050	1,126	1,181	1,223	3.04	2.06	2.09	1.97	1.40	0.94	0.71
Mexico	Tijuana	760	1,017	1,287	1,472	1,666	1,799	1,881	1,943	5.82	4.71	2.69	2.47	1.54	0.89	0.65
Mexico	Toluca de Lerdo	835	981	1,417	1,498	1,584	1,671	1,743	1,802	3.22	7.35	1.11	1.12	1.06	0.85	0.66
Mexico	Torreón	882	954	1,014	1,105	1,201	1,280	1,339	1,387	1.55	1.22	1.73	1.66	1.28	0.91	0.69
Mongolia	Ulaanbaatar	572	661	763	856	919	978	1,044	1,112	2.90	2.89	2.30	1.41	1.25	1.31	1.25
Morocco	Dar-el-Beida (Casablanca)	2,682	2,951	3,043	3,138	3,267	3,475	3,716	3,949	1.91	0.62	0.62	0.80	1.24	1.34	1.21
Morocco	Fès	685	785	870	963	1,060	1,152	1,243	1,332	2.72	2.04	2.04	1.92	1.67	1.52	1.37
Morocco	Marrakech	578	681	755	837	923	1,005	1,085	1,163	3.26	2.07	2.07	1.95	1.69	1.54	1.39
Morocco	Rabat	1,174	1,379	1,507	1,647	1,793	1,938	2,083	2,222	3.22	1.77	1.77	1.70	1.55	1.44	1.30
Mozambique	Maputo	776	921	1,096	1,334	1,621	1,921	2,235	2,560	3.43	3.47	3.94	3.90	3.40	3.03	2.71
Myanmar	Mandalay	636	718	810	915	1,034	1,168	1,308	1,446	2.43	2.43	2.43	2.44	2.44	2.26	2.01
Myanmar	Nay Pyi Taw	—	—	—	57	1,024	1,177	1,321	1,461	—	—	—	57.77	2.79	2.30	2.01
Myanmar	Yangon	2,907	3,213	3,553	3,928	4,348	4,841	5,361	5,869	2.01	2.01	2.01	2.04	2.15	2.04	1.81
Nepal	Kathmandu	398	509	644	815	1,029	1,284	1,578	1,907	4.92	4.70	4.71	4.67	4.43	4.12	3.78
Netherlands	Amsterdam	936	988	1,005	1,023	1,044	1,064	1,078	1,089	1.09	0.34	0.36	0.41	0.39	0.26	0.21
Netherlands	Rotterdam	951	981	991	1,000	1,014	1,033	1,046	1,057	0.62	0.19	0.19	0.28	0.35	0.26	0.22
New Zealand	Auckland	870	976	1,063	1,189	1,321	1,398	1,441	1,475	2.30	1.71	2.24	2.10	1.14	0.60	0.47
Nicaragua	Managua	735	865	887	909	944	1,015	1,104	1,193	3.26	0.50	0.50	0.75	1.46	1.68	1.54
Niger	Niamey	432	542	680	846	1,027	1,258	1,580	2,028	4.54	4.55	4.36	3.88	4.06	4.56	5.00
Nigeria	Abuja	330	526	832	1,315	1,994	2,558	2,971	3,358	9.31	9.16	9.16	8.32	4.98	3.00	2.45
Nigeria	Benin City	689	845	975	1,124	1,302	1,520	1,755	1,991	4.08	2.85	2.85	2.94	3.10	2.88	2.52
Nigeria	Ibadan	1,739	1,993	2,236	2,509	2,835	3,270	3,752	4,234	2.73	2.30	2.30	2.45	2.85	2.75	2.41
Nigeria	Ilorin	515	580	653	735	835	970	1,123	1,277	2.38	2.38	2.38	2.54	3.00	2.92	2.59
Nigeria	Kaduna	961	1,083	1,220	1,375	1,560	1,807	2,083	2,360	2.39	2.39	2.39	2.53	2.94	2.84	2.50
Nigeria	Kano	2,095	2,360	2,658	2,993	3,393	3,914	4,487	5,056	2.38	2.38	2.38	2.51	2.86	2.73	2.39
Nigeria	Lagos	4,764	5,966	7,233	8,767	10,572	12,403	14,134	15,796	4.50	3.85	3.85	3.74	3.19	2.61	2.22
Nigeria	Maiduguri	598	673	758	854	969	1,125	1,301	1,479	2.37	2.37	2.37	2.53	2.98	2.90	2.57
Nigeria	Ogbomosho	622	704	798	904	1,031	1,199	1,386	1,575	2.49	2.49	2.49	2.64	3.01	2.90	2.56
Nigeria	Port Harcourt	680	766	863	972	1,104	1,280	1,479	1,680	2.38	2.38	2.38	2.54	2.97	2.88	2.55
Nigeria	Zaria	592	667	752	847	963	1,118	1,293	1,470	2.39	2.39	2.39	2.55	2.99	2.90	2.57

Country	City	1990	1995	2000	2005	2010	2015	2020	2025	1990-1995	1995-2000	2000-2005	2005-2010	2010-2015	2015-2020	2020-2025
Norway	Oslo	684	729	774	816	858	885	909	936	1.28	1.19	1.07	0.99	0.63	0.54	0.57
Pakistan	Faisalabad	1,520	1,804	2,140	2,482	2,833	3,260	3,755	4,283	3.43	3.41	2.97	2.64	2.81	2.82	2.63
Pakistan	Gujranwala	848	1,019	1,224	1,433	1,643	1,898	2,195	2,513	3.69	3.66	3.15	2.74	2.89	2.90	2.71
Pakistan	Hyderabad	950	1,077	1,221	1,386	1,581	1,827	2,112	2,420	2.51	2.52	2.53	2.64	2.89	2.91	2.71
Pakistan	Islamabad	343	452	594	732	851	988	1,148	1,320	5.54	5.46	4.17	3.00	2.99	2.99	2.80
Pakistan	Karachi	7,147	8,467	10,019	11,553	13,052	14,855	16,922	19,095	3.39	3.36	2.85	2.44	2.59	2.61	2.42
Pakistan	Lahore	3,970	4,653	5,448	6,259	7,092	8,107	9,275	10,512	3.17	3.16	2.78	2.50	2.68	2.69	2.50
Pakistan	Multan	953	1,097	1,263	1,445	1,650	1,906	2,203	2,523	2.82	2.82	2.69	2.66	2.88	2.90	2.71
Pakistan	Peshawar	769	905	1,066	1,235	1,415	1,636	1,893	2,170	3.27	3.26	2.94	2.72	2.91	2.92	2.73
Pakistan	Quetta	414	504	614	725	836	971	1,128	1,298	3.96	3.93	3.34	2.85	2.98	3.00	2.80
Pakistan	Rawalpindi	1,087	1,286	1,519	1,762	2,015	2,324	2,683	3,067	3.36	3.34	2.96	2.68	2.86	2.87	2.68
Panama	Ciudad de Panamá (Panama City)	847	953	1,072	1,216	1,379	1,527	1,653	1,759	2.36	2.36	2.51	2.52	2.04	1.59	1.24
Paraguay	Asunción	1,091	1,287	1,507	1,762	2,030	2,277	2,506	2,715	3.32	3.15	3.13	2.83	2.30	1.91	1.61
Peru	Arequipa	564	635	705	782	862	927	984	1,038	2.39	2.08	2.08	1.93	1.46	1.20	1.06
Peru	Lima	5,837	6,537	7,116	7,747	8,375	8,857	9,251	9,600	2.27	1.70	1.70	1.56	1.12	0.87	0.74
Philippines	Cebu	612	661	721	787	862	960	1,062	1,153	1.53	1.75	1.76	1.83	2.14	2.02	1.65
Philippines	Davao	854	1,001	1,152	1,325	1,523	1,728	1,910	2,065	3.17	2.81	2.80	2.78	2.52	2.00	1.56
Philippines	Manila	7,973	9,401	9,958	10,761	11,662	12,786	13,892	14,808	3.30	1.15	1.55	1.61	1.84	1.66	1.28
Philippines	Zamboanga	444	509	605	721	856	988	1,098	1,192	2.71	3.47	3.50	3.44	2.86	2.11	1.64
Poland	Kraków (Cracow)	735	748	756	757	755	755	755	755	0.35	0.21	0.04	-0.05	-0.02	-0.00	-0.00
Poland	Lódz	836	825	799	770	745	736	735	735	-0.26	-0.64	-0.73	-0.67	-0.24	-0.02	-0.00
Poland	Warszawa (Warsaw)	1,628	1,652	1,666	1,693	1,724	1,735	1,736	1,736	0.29	0.17	0.33	0.36	0.13	0.01	0.00
Portugal	Lisboa (Lisbon)	2,537	2,600	2,672	2,762	2,890	2,996	3,058	3,086	0.49	0.55	0.66	0.91	0.72	0.41	0.18
Portugal	Porto	1,164	1,206	1,254	1,309	1,380	1,438	1,476	1,497	0.72	0.77	0.86	1.05	0.83	0.52	0.29
Puerto Rico	San Juan	1,539	1,855	2,237	2,604	2,758	2,795	2,803	2,803	3.74	3.74	3.03	1.15	0.27	0.06	0.00
Republic of Korea	Bucheon	651	771	763	833	907	942	948	948	3.39	-0.23	1.77	1.70	0.74	0.13	0.00
Republic of Korea	Busan	3,778	3,813	3,673	3,533	3,421	3,386	3,383	3,383	0.18	-0.75	-0.78	-0.64	-0.21	-0.02	-0.00
Republic of Korea	Daegu	2,215	2,434	2,478	2,466	2,455	2,458	2,458	2,458	1.88	0.36	-0.10	-0.08	0.02	0.00	0.00
Republic of Korea	Daejon	1,036	1,256	1,362	1,438	1,507	1,540	1,544	1,544	3.85	1.62	1.09	0.95	0.43	0.06	0.00
Republic of Korea	Goyang	241	493	744	859	960	1,005	1,012	1,012	14.28	8.25	2.88	2.21	0.92	0.14	0.00
Republic of Korea	Gwangju	1,122	1,249	1,346	1,413	1,474	1,503	1,507	1,507	2.16	1.49	0.97	0.84	0.39	0.05	0.00
Republic of Korea	Incheon	1,785	2,271	2,464	2,527	2,580	2,604	2,607	2,607	4.82	1.62	0.51	0.41	0.19	0.02	0.00
Republic of Korea	Seongnam	534	842	911	934	954	967	971	971	9.10	1.59	0.48	0.42	0.28	0.08	0.00
Republic of Korea	Seoul	10,544	10,256	9,917	9,825	9,762	9,740	9,738	9,738	-0.55	-0.67	-0.19	-0.13	-0.05	-0.00	-0.00
Republic of Korea	Suweon	628	748	932	1,037	1,130	1,172	1,178	1,179	3.50	4.42	2.13	1.72	0.73	0.10	0.00
Republic of Korea	Ulsan	673	945	1,011	1,047	1,080	1,098	1,102	1,102	6.80	1.36	0.69	0.62	0.34	0.07	0.00
Romania	Bucuresti (Bucharest)	2,040	2,018	1,949	1,936	1,947	1,949	1,949	1,949	-0.21	-0.69	-0.13	0.10	0.02	0.00	0.00
Russian Federation	Chelyabinsk	1,129	1,104	1,082	1,094	1,088	1,086	1,085	1,085	-0.45	-0.40	0.21	-0.11	-0.04	-0.00	-0.00
Russian Federation	Kazan	1,092	1,092	1,096	1,112	1,119	1,122	1,122	1,122	-0.01	0.07	0.29	0.14	0.05	0.00	0.00
Russian Federation	Krasnoyarsk	910	911	911	920	930	934	935	935	0.02	0.02	0.18	0.23	0.08	0.01	0.00
Russian Federation	Moskva (Moscow)	8,987	9,201	10,016	10,416	10,495	10,524	10,526	10,526	0.47	1.70	0.78	0.15	0.05	0.01	0.00
Russian Federation	Nizhniy Novgorod	1,420	1,375	1,331	1,286	1,269	1,263	1,262	1,262	-0.65	-0.65	-0.69	-0.26	-0.09	-0.01	-0.00
Russian Federation	Novosibirsk	1,430	1,428	1,426	1,400	1,376	1,367	1,366	1,366	-0.03	-0.03	-0.38	-0.35	-0.12	-0.01	-0.00
Russian Federation	Omsk	1,144	1,140	1,136	1,140	1,129	1,125	1,125	1,125	-0.07	-0.07	0.08	-0.20	-0.07	-0.01	-0.00
Russian Federation	Perm	1,076	1,044	1,014	992	1,003	1,007	1,007	1,007	-0.59	-0.59	-0.43	0.22	0.08	0.01	0.00
Russian Federation	Rostov-na-Donu (Rostov-on-Don)	1,022	1,041	1,061	1,056	1,047	1,044	1,044	1,044	0.38	0.38	-0.10	-0.17	-0.06	-0.01	-0.00
Russian Federation	Samara	1,244	1,208	1,173	1,146	1,126	1,120	1,119	1,119	-0.58	-0.58	-0.48	-0.34	-0.12	-0.01	-0.00
Russian Federation	Sankt Peterburg (Saint Petersburg)	4,989	4,836	4,729	4,590	4,508	4,479	4,477	4,476	-0.62	-0.45	-0.59	-0.36	-0.13	-0.01	-0.00
Russian Federation	Saratov	901	890	878	853	831	823	822	822	-0.25	-0.25	-0.60	-0.52	-0.19	-0.02	-0.00
Russian Federation	Ufa	1,078	1,063	1,049	1,034	1,000	988	987	986	-0.27	-0.27	-0.29	-0.67	-0.24	-0.02	-0.00
Russian Federation	Volgograd	999	1,005	1,010	994	973	966	965	965	0.11	0.11	-0.32	-0.43	-0.15	-0.02	-0.00
Russian Federation	Voronezh	880	867	854	847	840	838	838	838	-0.30	-0.30	-0.17	-0.16	-0.06	-0.01	-0.00
Russian Federation	Yekaterinburg	1,350	1,326	1,303	1,307	1,319	1,323	1,324	1,324	-0.35	-0.35	0.06	0.18	0.07	0.01	0.00
Rwanda	Kigali	219	289	497	775	947	1,152	1,413	1,715	5.50	10.89	8.86	4.01	3.93	4.08	3.87
Saudi Arabia	Ad-Dammam	409	533	639	766	903	1,019	1,119	1,212	5.30	3.63	3.62	3.29	2.42	1.88	1.58
Saudi Arabia	Al-Madinah (Medina)	529	669	795	944	1,105	1,243	1,364	1,474	4.69	3.45	3.45	3.15	2.36	1.85	1.56
Saudi Arabia	Ar-Riyadh (Riyadh)	2,325	3,035	3,567	4,193	4,856	5,405	5,866	6,275	5.33	3.23	3.23	2.93	2.14	1.64	1.35
Saudi Arabia	Jiddah	1,742	2,200	2,509	2,860	3,239	3,590	3,906	4,190	4.66	2.63	2.62	2.49	2.06	1.69	1.40
Saudi Arabia	Makkah (Mecca)	856	1,033	1,168	1,319	1,486	1,651	1,806	1,948	3.76	2.45	2.45	2.38	2.11	1.79	1.52
Senegal	Dakar	1,405	1,688	2,029	2,434	2,856	3,275	3,726	4,225	3.67	3.68	3.64	3.20	2.74	2.58	2.52

Country	City	1990	1995	2000	2005	2010	2015	2020	2025	1990-1995	1995-2000	2000-2005	2005-2010	2010-2015	2015-2020	2020-2025
Serbia	Beograd (Belgrade)	1,162	1,149	1,127	1,106	1,096	1,108	1,132	1,163	-0.22	-0.39	-0.38	-0.18	0.22	0.43	0.54
Sierra Leone	Freetown	529	603	688	785	894	1,029	1,200	1,406	2.62	2.63	2.62	2.60	2.82	3.08	3.16
Singapore	Singapore	3,016	3,478	4,017	4,327	4,592	4,809	4,965	5,104	2.85	2.88	1.49	1.19	0.92	0.64	0.55
Somalia	Muqdisho (Mogadishu)	1,035	1,147	1,201	1,415	1,500	1,794	2,142	2,529	2.04	0.92	3.28	1.17	3.58	3.55	3.33
South Africa	Cape Town	2,155	2,394	2,715	3,087	3,357	3,504	3,627	3,744	2.10	2.52	2.57	1.68	0.86	0.69	0.64
South Africa	Durban	1,723	2,081	2,370	2,635	2,839	2,962	3,070	3,173	3.77	2.60	2.12	1.49	0.85	0.71	0.66
South Africa	Ekurhuleni (East Rand)	1,531	1,894	2,326	2,820	3,157	3,309	3,427	3,539	4.26	4.11	3.85	2.26	0.94	0.70	0.65
South Africa	Johannesburg	1,898	2,265	2,732	3,258	3,618	3,785	3,916	4,041	3.53	3.75	3.52	2.10	0.90	0.68	0.63
South Africa	Port Elizabeth	828	911	958	1,001	1,053	1,102	1,150	1,197	1.93	1.00	0.87	1.02	0.91	0.85	0.80
South Africa	Pretoria	911	951	1,084	1,273	1,409	1,482	1,544	1,604	0.85	2.61	3.22	2.04	1.01	0.81	0.76
South Africa	Vereeniging	743	800	897	1,028	1,127	1,185	1,236	1,286	1.48	2.30	2.72	1.83	1.01	0.84	0.79
Spain	Barcelona	4,101	4,318	4,560	4,815	5,057	5,169	5,182	5,183	1.03	1.09	1.09	0.98	0.44	0.05	0.00
Spain	Madrid	4,414	4,701	5,045	5,414	5,764	5,918	5,934	5,935	1.26	1.41	1.41	1.25	0.52	0.06	0.00
Spain	Valencia	776	785	795	804	816	831	841	847	0.25	0.24	0.24	0.29	0.36	0.24	0.14
Sudan	Al-Khartum (Khartoum)	2,360	3,242	3,949	4,518	5,185	6,077	7,017	7,937	6.35	3.95	2.69	2.75	3.17	2.88	2.46
Sweden	Stockholm	1,038	1,138	1,206	1,248	1,285	1,308	1,326	1,343	1.83	1.16	0.69	0.58	0.35	0.27	0.26
Switzerland	Zürich (Zurich)	1,006	1,048	1,078	1,100	1,119	1,134	1,150	1,172	0.83	0.56	0.39	0.35	0.26	0.29	0.37
Syrian Arab Republic	Dimashq (Damascus)	1,691	1,849	2,044	2,330	2,675	2,981	3,293	3,605	1.79	2.00	2.62	2.76	2.17	1.99	1.81
Syrian Arab Republic	Halab (Aleppo)	1,554	1,870	2,222	2,584	2,968	3,306	3,649	3,993	3.70	3.45	3.02	2.77	2.15	1.98	1.80
Syrian Arab Republic	Hims (Homs)	565	680	809	946	1,095	1,228	1,365	1,504	3.70	3.48	3.14	2.91	2.30	2.12	1.94
Thailand	Krung Thep (Bangkok)	5,888	6,106	6,332	6,582	6,918	7,332	7,807	8,332	0.73	0.73	0.78	0.99	1.16	1.26	1.30
Togo	Lomé	619	796	1,023	1,315	1,669	2,038	2,410	2,791	5.02	5.02	5.02	4.77	3.99	3.36	2.93
Turkey	Adana	907	1,011	1,123	1,245	1,362	1,466	1,557	1,635	2.18	2.10	2.06	1.80	1.47	1.20	0.97
Turkey	Ankara	2,561	2,842	3,179	3,572	3,908	4,178	4,403	4,589	2.08	2.25	2.33	1.80	1.34	1.05	0.82
Turkey	Antalya	370	471	595	735	839	910	969	1,021	4.83	4.67	4.25	2.63	1.62	1.27	1.04
Turkey	Bursa	819	981	1,180	1,413	1,589	1,713	1,817	1,906	3.62	3.69	3.60	2.34	1.51	1.18	0.95
Turkey	Gaziantep	595	710	844	992	1,109	1,199	1,274	1,340	3.54	3.47	3.22	2.24	1.54	1.23	1.00
Turkey	Istanbul	6,552	7,665	8,744	9,709	10,530	11,177	11,695	12,102	3.14	2.63	2.09	1.62	1.19	0.91	0.68
Turkey	Izmir	1,741	1,966	2,216	2,487	2,724	2,920	3,085	3,223	2.43	2.39	2.31	1.82	1.39	1.10	0.88
Turkey	Konya	508	610	734	871	978	1,058	1,126	1,185	3.66	3.69	3.42	2.32	1.57	1.25	1.02
Uganda	Kampala	755	912	1,097	1,318	1,597	1,979	2,506	3,198	3.79	3.68	3.68	3.84	4.29	4.72	4.88
Ukraine	Dnipropetrovs'k	1,162	1,119	1,077	1,055	1,045	1,042	1,042	1,042	-0.77	-0.77	-0.40	-0.20	-0.06	-0.00	-0.00
Ukraine	Donets'k	1,097	1,061	1,026	997	978	973	972	972	-0.67	-0.67	-0.56	-0.39	-0.11	-0.01	-0.00
Ukraine	Kharkiv	1,586	1,534	1,484	1,464	1,457	1,456	1,455	1,455	-0.66	-0.66	-0.27	-0.09	-0.03	-0.00	-0.00
Ukraine	Kyiv (Kiev)	2,574	2,590	2,606	2,672	2,748	2,770	2,772	2,772	0.13	0.13	0.50	0.56	0.16	0.01	0.00
Ukraine	Odesa	1,092	1,064	1,037	1,004	977	970	970	970	-0.52	-0.52	-0.65	-0.53	-0.15	-0.01	-0.00
Ukraine	Zaporizhzhya	873	847	822	797	778	773	772	772	-0.60	-0.60	-0.62	-0.48	-0.14	-0.01	-0.00
United Arab Emirates	Dubayy (Dubai)	473	650	938	1,272	1,516	1,709	1,894	2,077	6.36	7.35	6.08	3.51	2.40	2.05	1.85
United Kingdom	Birmingham	2,301	2,291	2,285	2,283	2,291	2,303	2,315	2,323	-0.09	-0.05	-0.02	0.07	0.11	0.10	0.07
United Kingdom	Glasgow	1,217	1,186	1,171	1,160	1,164	1,175	1,187	1,197	-0.52	-0.26	-0.19	0.07	0.19	0.20	0.17
United Kingdom	Liverpool	831	829	818	811	815	825	836	845	-0.05	-0.26	-0.18	0.11	0.24	0.25	0.22
United Kingdom	London	7,654	7,908	8,225	8,505	8,607	8,618	8,618	8,618	0.65	0.79	0.67	0.24	0.02	0.00	—
United Kingdom	Manchester	2,282	2,262	2,243	2,230	2,235	2,246	2,258	2,267	-0.18	-0.16	-0.12	0.04	0.11	0.11	0.08
United Kingdom	Newcastle upon Tyne	877	883	880	880	887	898	908	918	0.14	-0.07	-0.01	0.16	0.24	0.24	0.21
United Kingdom	West Yorkshire	1,449	1,468	1,495	1,521	1,539	1,552	1,565	1,575	0.27	0.36	0.34	0.24	0.17	0.16	0.13
United Republic of Tanzania	Dar es Salaam	1,316	1,668	2,116	2,679	3,319	4,020	4,804	5,688	4.75	4.75	4.72	4.29	3.83	3.56	3.38
United States of America	Atlanta	2,184	2,781	3,542	4,307	4,695	4,888	5,035	5,151	4.84	4.84	3.91	1.73	0.80	0.60	0.45
United States of America	Austin	569	720	913	1,108	1,216	1,277	1,329	1,372	4.73	4.73	3.88	1.86	0.99	0.79	0.64
United States of America	Baltimore	1,849	1,962	2,083	2,207	2,322	2,422	2,508	2,578	1.19	1.19	1.16	1.02	0.84	0.70	0.55
United States of America	Boston	3,428	3,726	4,049	4,364	4,597	4,774	4,919	5,032	1.66	1.66	1.50	1.04	0.76	0.60	0.46
United States of America	Bridgeport-Stamford	714	799	894	987	1,056	1,108	1,154	1,193	2.25	2.25	1.99	1.34	0.97	0.81	0.66
United States of America	Buffalo	955	966	977	1,000	1,046	1,096	1,142	1,180	0.23	0.23	0.46	0.90	0.94	0.81	0.67
United States of America	Charlotte	461	596	769	947	1,044	1,098	1,144	1,183	5.10	5.10	4.16	1.96	1.02	0.81	0.67

Country	City	City Population of Urban Agglomerations								City Population Growth Rate of Urban Agglomerations						
		1990	1995	2000	2005	2010	2015	2020	2025	1990-1995	1995-2000	2000-2005	2005-2010	2010-2015	2015-2020	2020-2025
United States of America	Chicago	7,374	7,839	8,333	8,820	9,211	9,516	9,756	9,932	1.22	1.22	1.14	0.87	0.65	0.50	0.36
United States of America	Cincinnati	1,335	1,419	1,508	1,600	1,687	1,764	1,831	1,886	1.22	1.22	1.19	1.06	0.89	0.74	0.60
United States of America	Cleveland	1,680	1,734	1,789	1,857	1,944	2,029	2,104	2,165	0.63	0.63	0.74	0.92	0.86	0.72	0.58
United States of America	Columbus, Ohio	950	1,040	1,138	1,236	1,314	1,377	1,431	1,477	1.81	1.81	1.65	1.22	0.93	0.78	0.63
United States of America	Dallas-Fort Worth	3,219	3,665	4,172	4,658	4,955	5,146	5,300	5,419	2.59	2.59	2.20	1.24	0.76	0.59	0.45
United States of America	Dayton	616	659	706	754	800	841	878	909	1.37	1.37	1.33	1.18	1.00	0.85	0.70
United States of America	Denver-Aurora	1,528	1,747	1,998	2,241	2,396	2,502	2,590	2,661	2.68	2.68	2.29	1.34	0.86	0.69	0.55
United States of America	Detroit	3,703	3,804	3,909	4,037	4,203	4,364	4,499	4,606	0.54	0.54	0.64	0.81	0.75	0.61	0.47
United States of America	El Paso	573	623	678	733	780	820	856	886	1.67	1.67	1.56	1.24	1.01	0.85	0.71
United States of America	Hartford	783	818	853	894	942	989	1,031	1,066	0.86	0.86	0.94	1.05	0.97	0.82	0.68
United States of America	Honolulu	635	676	720	767	813	854	891	923	1.27	1.27	1.26	1.15	0.99	0.85	0.70
United States of America	Houston	2,922	3,353	3,849	4,324	4,609	4,790	4,936	5,049	2.76	2.76	2.33	1.28	0.77	0.60	0.46
United States of America	Indianapolis	921	1,063	1,228	1,388	1,491	1,562	1,623	1,673	2.87	2.87	2.45	1.43	0.93	0.76	0.62
United States of America	Jacksonville, Florida	742	811	886	962	1,023	1,074	1,119	1,157	1.78	1.78	1.64	1.24	0.97	0.81	0.67
United States of America	Kansas City	1,233	1,297	1,365	1,438	1,514	1,584	1,645	1,696	1.02	1.02	1.04	1.03	0.90	0.76	0.61
United States of America	Las Vegas	708	973	1,335	1,722	1,917	2,011	2,085	2,146	6.34	6.34	5.08	2.15	0.95	0.72	0.58
United States of America	Los Angeles-Long Beach-Santa Ana	10,883	11,339	11,814	12,307	12,773	13,160	13,461	13,672	0.82	0.82	0.82	0.74	0.60	0.45	0.31
United States of America	Louisville	757	810	866	925	980	1,028	1,071	1,108	1.34	1.34	1.31	1.15	0.97	0.82	0.67
United States of America	Memphis	829	899	976	1,053	1,118	1,173	1,221	1,262	1.64	1.64	1.53	1.20	0.95	0.80	0.66
United States of America	Miami	3,969	4,431	4,946	5,438	5,755	5,969	6,141	6,272	2.20	2.20	1.90	1.13	0.73	0.57	0.42
United States of America	Milwaukee	1,228	1,269	1,311	1,362	1,429	1,495	1,553	1,602	0.65	0.65	0.77	0.96	0.90	0.76	0.62
United States of America	Minneapolis-St. Paul	2,087	2,236	2,397	2,558	2,695	2,809	2,905	2,983	1.38	1.39	1.30	1.04	0.83	0.67	0.53
United States of America	Nashville-Davidson	577	660	755	848	912	959	999	1,034	2.69	2.69	2.33	1.45	1.00	0.83	0.68
United States of America	New Orleans	1,039	1,024	1,009	996	982	977	1,002	1,037	-0.30	-0.30	-0.26	-0.27	-0.10	0.50	0.68
United States of America	New York-Newark	16,086	16,943	17,846	18,732	19,441	19,974	20,370	20,628	1.04	1.04	0.97	0.74	0.54	0.39	0.25
United States of America	Oklahoma City	711	729	748	774	813	854	891	922	0.51	0.51	0.68	0.99	0.98	0.85	0.70
United States of America	Orlando	893	1,020	1,165	1,307	1,401	1,468	1,526	1,574	2.66	2.66	2.30	1.39	0.94	0.77	0.62
United States of America	Philadelphia	4,725	4,938	5,160	5,396	5,630	5,835	6,003	6,133	0.88	0.88	0.89	0.85	0.71	0.57	0.43
United States of America	Phoenix-Mesa	2,025	2,437	2,934	3,419	3,687	3,841	3,964	4,062	3.71	3.71	3.06	1.51	0.82	0.63	0.49
United States of America	Pittsburgh	1,681	1,717	1,755	1,808	1,889	1,972	2,044	2,105	0.43	0.43	0.59	0.88	0.86	0.72	0.58
United States of America	Portland	1,181	1,372	1,595	1,812	1,946	2,035	2,110	2,172	3.01	3.01	2.55	1.43	0.90	0.72	0.58
United States of America	Providence	1,047	1,111	1,178	1,249	1,318	1,380	1,435	1,481	1.18	1.18	1.17	1.08	0.92	0.78	0.63
United States of America	Richmond	696	757	822	888	944	992	1,033	1,069	1.66	1.66	1.55	1.22	0.98	0.82	0.68
United States of America	Riverside-San Bernardino	1,178	1,336	1,516	1,691	1,808	1,892	1,962	2,021	2.53	2.53	2.19	1.34	0.90	0.73	0.59
United States of America	Rochester	621	658	696	738	781	821	856	887	1.14	1.14	1.16	1.13	1.00	0.85	0.71

		City Population of Urban Agglomerations								City Population Growth Rate of Urban Agglomerations						
Country	City	1990	1995	2000	2005	2010	2015	2020	2025	1990-1995	1995-2000	2000-2005	2005-2010	2010-2015	2015-2020	2020-2025
United States of America	Sacramento	1,104	1,244	1,402	1,556	1,662	1,739	1,805	1,860	2.39	2.39	2.09	1.32	0.91	0.74	0.60
United States of America	Salt Lake City	792	840	890	944	998	1,047	1,091	1,128	1.17	1.17	1.18	1.11	0.96	0.82	0.67
United States of America	San Antonio	1,134	1,229	1,333	1,437	1,522	1,593	1,655	1,706	1.62	1.62	1.50	1.16	0.91	0.76	0.61
United States of America	San Diego	2,356	2,514	2,683	2,854	3,002	3,126	3,231	3,315	1.30	1.30	1.23	1.01	0.81	0.66	0.52
United States of America	San Francisco-Oakland	2,961	3,095	3,236	3,387	3,544	3,684	3,803	3,898	0.89	0.89	0.91	0.90	0.78	0.64	0.49
United States of America	San Jose	1,376	1,457	1,543	1,632	1,720	1,798	1,865	1,921	1.14	1.14	1.13	1.04	0.89	0.74	0.60
United States of America	Seattle	2,206	2,453	2,727	2,991	3,174	3,305	3,415	3,503	2.12	2.12	1.85	1.18	0.81	0.65	0.51
United States of America	St. Louis	1,950	2,014	2,081	2,161	2,260	2,357	2,441	2,510	0.65	0.65	0.75	0.90	0.84	0.70	0.56
United States of America	Tampa-St. Petersburg	1,717	1,886	2,072	2,254	2,389	2,493	2,581	2,652	1.88	1.88	1.68	1.16	0.85	0.69	0.55
United States of America	Tucson	582	649	724	798	854	898	936	969	2.18	2.18	1.95	1.35	1.00	0.84	0.69
United States of America	Virginia Beach	1,286	1,341	1,397	1,461	1,535	1,606	1,667	1,719	0.83	0.83	0.90	0.99	0.90	0.75	0.61
United States of America	Washington, D.C.	3,376	3,651	3,949	4,241	4,464	4,636	4,778	4,889	1.57	1.57	1.42	1.02	0.76	0.60	0.46
Uruguay	Montevideo	1,546	1,584	1,561	1,525	1,504	1,506	1,515	1,520	0.49	-0.30	-0.47	-0.28	0.03	0.12	0.06
Uzbekistan	Tashkent	2,100	2,116	2,135	2,158	2,247	2,416	2,636	2,892	0.15	0.17	0.22	0.80	1.46	1.74	1.85
Venezuela (Bolivarian Republic of)	Barquisimeto	742	838	947	1,068	1,184	1,279	1,356	1,420	2.42	2.44	2.41	2.06	1.54	1.18	0.91
Venezuela (Bolivarian Republic of)	Caracas	2,767	2,816	2,864	2,930	3,098	3,306	3,482	3,619	0.35	0.34	0.46	1.11	1.30	1.04	0.77
Venezuela (Bolivarian Republic of)	Maracaibo	1,303	1,501	1,725	1,976	2,200	2,369	2,501	2,606	2.82	2.78	2.72	2.15	1.48	1.09	0.82
Venezuela (Bolivarian Republic of)	Maracay	760	831	899	973	1,060	1,144	1,214	1,271	1.78	1.56	1.60	1.71	1.51	1.19	0.93
Venezuela (Bolivarian Republic of)	Valencia	1,053	1,183	1,370	1,662	1,900	2,055	2,172	2,266	2.31	2.94	3.87	2.67	1.57	1.11	0.84
Viet Nam	Hà Noi	3,126	3,424	3,752	4,170	4,723	5,357	6,036	6,754	1.82	1.83	2.11	2.49	2.52	2.39	2.25
Viet Nam	Hai Phòng	1,474	1,585	1,704	1,876	2,129	2,428	2,752	3,096	1.45	1.46	1.91	2.53	2.63	2.50	2.36
Viet Nam	Thành Pho Ho Chí Minh (Ho Chi Minh City)	3,996	4,296	4,621	5,072	5,723	6,480	7,293	8,149	1.45	1.46	1.86	2.41	2.49	2.36	2.22
Yemen	Al-Hudaydah	212	311	457	672	951	1,232	1,528	1,854	7.70	7.70	7.70	6.95	5.19	4.30	3.86
Yemen	Sana'a'	653	1,034	1,365	1,801	2,345	2,955	3,636	4,382	9.18	5.55	5.54	5.28	4.62	4.14	3.73
Yemen	Ta'izz	234	330	465	657	902	1,159	1,437	1,743	6.89	6.89	6.89	6.34	5.02	4.30	3.87
Zambia	Lusaka	757	902	1,073	1,261	1,421	1,587	1,797	2,047	3.49	3.49	3.23	2.39	2.20	2.49	2.60
Zimbabwe	Harare	1,047	1,255	1,379	1,515	1,663	1,839	2,037	2,247	3.62	1.89	1.88	1.87	2.01	2.05	1.97

Data Source: UNPD-WUP2007

Urban population, proportion of urban population living in slum area and urban slum population

Major area, region, country or area	URBAN POPULATION AT MID-YEAR BY MAJOR AREA, REGION AND COUNTRY (THOUSANDS)[a]					PROPORTION OF URBAN POPULATION LIVING IN SLUM AREA[b]					URBAN SLUM POPULATION AT MID-YEAR BY MAJOR AREA, REGION AND COUNTRY (THOUSANDS)				
	1990	1995	2000	2005	2007	1990	1995	2000	2005	2007	1990	1995	2000	2005	2007
AFRICA															
Angola	3,913	5,418	6,824	8,684	9,505				86.5					7512	
Benin	1,786	2,282	2,770	3,397	3,684	79.3	76.8	74.3	71.8	70.8	1416	1753	2058	2439	2608
Burkina Faso	1,226	1,554	1,971	2,555	2,827	78.8	72.4	65.9	59.5	59.5	966	1125	1300	1520	1682
Burundi	357	450	552	749	858				64.3		230	289	355	481	552
Cameroon	4,983	6,372	7,908	9,657	10,381	50.8	49.6	48.4	47.4	46.6	2534	3161	3825	4578	4841
Central African Republic	1,108	1,284	1,454	1,596	1,665	87.5	89.7	91.9	94.1	95.0	969	1152	1337	1502	1582
Chad	1,272	1,568	1,979	2,563	2,819	98.9	96.4	93.9	91.3	90.3	1259	1512	1858	2341	2546
Comoros	147	172	196	223	234	65.4	65.4	65.4	68.9	68.9	96	112	128	153	162
Congo	1,316	1,576	1,868	2,172	2,296				53.4					1160	
Côte d'Ivoire	5,079	6,200	7,423	8,704	9,277	53.4	54.3	55.3	56.2	56.6	2710	3367	4102	4892	5249
Democratic Republic of the Congo	10,556	12,892	15,126	18,860	20,841				76.4					14409	
Egypt	23,972	25,966	28,364	31,062	32,193	50.2	39.2	28.1	17.1	17.1	12029	10166	7978	5312	5505
Equatorial Guinea	118	148	167	188	199				66.3					125	
Ethiopia	6,455	8,381	10,339	12,687	13,813	95.5	95.5	88.6	81.8	79.1	6163	8001	9164	10380	10923
Gabon	635	796	948	1,079	1,127				38.7					418	
Gambia	369	508	680	872	951				45.4					396	
Ghana	5,677	7,180	8,856	10,763	11,566	65.5	58.8	52.1	45.4	42.8	3717	4221	4615	4890	4945
Guinea	1,691	2,159	2,547	2,970	3,176	80.4	68.8	57.3	45.7	45.7	1359	1485	1458	1358	1451
Guinea-Bissau	286	355	407	473	503				83.1					393	
Kenya	4,273	5,193	6,167	7,384	7,982	54.9	54.8	54.8	54.8	54.8	2345	2848	3379	4044	4370
Lesotho	224	292	377	461	496				35.1					162	
Madagascar	2,836	3,598	4,390	5,313	5,733	93.0	88.6	84.1	80.6	78.0	2636	3186	3694	4283	4470
Malawi	1,092	1,338	1,764	2,293	2,545	66.4	66.4	66.4	66.4	67.7	725	889	1171	1522	1722
Mali	1,789	2,229	2,787	3,537	3,896	94.2	84.8	75.4	65.9	65.9	1685	1890	2101	2332	2569
Morocco	12,005	13,931	15,375	16,763	17,377	37.4	35.2	24.2	13.1	13.1	4490	4904	3713	2196	2276
Mozambique	2,857	4,180	5,584	7,084	7,718	75.6	76.9	78.2	79.5	80.0	2161	3216	4368	5632	6175
Namibia	392	494	608	708	751	34.4	34.1	33.9	33.9	33.6	135	169	206	240	252
Niger	1,202	1,465	1,801	2,161	2,331	83.6	83.1	82.6	82.1	81.9	1005	1217	1487	1774	1909
Nigeria	33,325	42,372	53,048	65,270	70,539	77.3	73.5	69.6	65.8	64.2	25763	31127	36930	42928	45309
Rwanda	395	468	1,126	1,619	1,753	96.0	87.9	79.7	71.6	68.3	379	411	898	1160	1198
Senegal	3,075	3,603	4,200	4,891	5,203	70.6	59.8	48.9	38.1	38.1	2172	2154	2055	1863	1982
Sierra Leone	1,346	1,417	1,605	2,057	2,194				97.0					1995	
Somalia	1,992	1,962	2,346	2,884	3,136				73.5					2120	
South Africa	19,034	22,614	25,827	28,419	29,266	46.2	39.7	33.2	28.7	28.7	8794	8978	8575	8156	8399
Sudan	6,903	9,233	12,034	15,043	16,420				94.2		6502	8697	11336	14170	15468
Togo	1,192	1,501	1,974	2,492	2,722				62.1					1548	
Uganda	1,976	2,477	2,983	3,632	3,955	75.0	75.0	75.0	66.7	63.4	1482	1858	2238	2423	2507
United Republic of Tanzania	4,814	6,143	7,551	9,313	10,128	77.4	73.7	70.1	66.4	65.0	3725	4528	5291	6186	6580
Zambia	3,201	3,436	3,637	4,017	4,198	57.0	57.1	57.2	57.2	57.3	1826	1962	2080	2298	2404
Zimbabwe	3,040	3,742	4,273	4,706	4,911	4.0	3.7	3.3	17.9	17.9	122	138	142	842	879

Major area, region, country or area	URBAN POPULATION AT MID-YEAR BY MAJOR AREA, REGION AND COUNTRY (THOUSANDS)[a]					PROPORTION OF URBAN POPULATION LIVING IN SLUM AREA[b]					URBAN SLUM POPULATION AT MID-YEAR BY MAJOR AREA, REGION AND COUNTRY (THOUSANDS)				
	1990	1995	2000	2005	2007	1990	1995	2000	2005	2007	1990	1995	2000	2005	2007
ASIA															
China	314,845	380,553	454,362	530,659	561,251	43.6	40.5	37.3	32.9	31.0	137,272	153,985	169,600	174,587	173,988
Mongolia	1,264	1,357	1,397	1,464	1,497	68.5	66.7	64.9	57.9	57.9	865.8	905.3	906.8	847.5	866.7
Bangladesh	22,396	27,398	32,893	39,351	42,191	87.3	84.7	77.8	70.8	70.8	19,552	23,206	25,574	27,860	29,871
India	219,758	253,774	289,438	325,563	341,247	54.9	48.2	41.5	34.8	32.1	120,746	122,376	120,117	113,223	109,501
Nepal	1,692	2,361	3,280	4,269	4,712	70.6	67.3	64.0	60.7	59.4	1,194	1,589	2,099	2,591	2,798
Pakistan	34,548	40,676	47,884	55,135	58,487	51.0	49.8	48.7	47.5	47.0	17,620	20,271	23,304	26,189	27,508
Cambodia	1,222	1,613	2,161	2,753	3,022				78.9		964	1,273	1,705	2,172	2,385
Indonesia	55,922	70,188	88,918	108,828	116,832	50.8	42.6	34.4	26.3	23.0	28,407	29,912	30,620	28,574	26,852
Lao People's Democratic Republic	629	815	1,148	1,551	1,740				79.3					1230	
Myanmar	9,986	11,270	12,860	14,700	15,575				45.6					6703	
Philippines	29,863	37,053	44,621	53,032	56,503	54.3	50.8	47.2	43.7	42.3	16,224	18,817	21,080	23,175	23,891
Thailand	15,974	17,416	18,893	20,352	21,021				26.0					5,291	
Viet Nam	13,403	16,284	19,204	22,454	23,888	60.5	54.6	48.8	41.3	38.3	8,109	8,897	9,366	9,274	9,137
Iraq	12,906	14,878	16,993	18,729	19,316	16.9	16.9	16.9	52.8	52.8	2,182	2,516	2,873	9,889	10,199
Jordan	2,350	3,366	3,755	4,341	4,642				15.8					686	
Lebanon	2,472	2,961	3,244	3,473	3,560				53.1					1,844	
Saudi Arabia	12,449	14,358	16,614	19,120	20,138				18.0					3,442	
Syrian Arab Republic	6,224	7,314	8,524	10,049	10,726				10.5					1,055	
Turkey	33,949	38,974	44,126	49,097	51,101	23.4	20.7	17.9	15.5	14.1	7,947	8,055	7,911	7,610	7,202
Yemen	2,577	3,688	4,776	6,104	6,729				67.2					4,102	
LATIN AMERICA AND THE CARIBBEAN															
Argentina	28,340	30,883	33,252	35,411	36,298	30.5	31.7	32.9	26.2	23.5	8,644	9,790	10,940	9,278	8,530
Belize	88	102	117	138	147				47.3					65	
Bolivia	3,706	4,444	5,143	5,896	6,205	62.2	58.2	54.3	50.4	48.8	2,304	2,589	2,794	2,972	3,030
Brazil	111,851	125,685	141,404	157,369	163,462	36.7	34.1	31.5	29.0	28.0	40,998	42,856	44,601	45,613	45,708
Chile	10,974	12,145	13,246	14,280	14,675				9.0					1,285	
Colombia	23,811	26,979	30,043	33,071	34,237	31.2	26.8	22.3	17.9	16.1	7,433	7,224	6,711	5,920	5,520
Costa Rica	1,559	1,939	2,318	2,670	2,804				10.9					291	
Dominican Republic	4,029	4,630	5,459	6,322	6,668	27.9	24.4	21.0	17.6	16.2	1,123	1,131	1,146	1,110	1,079
Ecuador	5,659	6,583	7,420	8,308	8,670				21.5					1,786	
El Salvador	2,516	3,039	3,618	3,985	4,138				28.9					1,152	
French Guiana	87	104	124	145	153				10.5					15	
Grenada	31	31	31	32	32				6.0					2	
Guadeloupe	385	400	414	431	437				5.4					23	
Guatemala	3,663	4,313	5,067	5,997	6,419	58.6	53.3	48.1	42.9	40.8	2,145	2,300	2,438	2,572	2,619
Guyana	216	215	210	209	208				33.7					70	
Haiti	2,027	2,554	3,052	3,974	4,373	93.4	93.4	93.4	70.1	70.1	1,893	2,385	2,851	2,786	3,065
Honduras	1,970	2,356	2,748	3,177	3,368				34.9					1,109	
Jamaica	1,171	1,258	1,342	1,413	1,439				60.5					855	
Mexico	59,994	67,368	74,524	79,564	81,951	23.1	21.5	19.9	14.4	14.4	13,859	14,484	14,830	11,457	11,801
Nicaragua	2,167	2,497	2,796	3,055	3,163	89.1	74.5	60.0	45.5	45.5	1,931	1,861	1,678	1,390	1,439
Panama	1,299	1,602	1,941	2,288	2,424				23.0					526	
Paraguay	2,068	2,502	2,960	3,453	3,658				17.6					608	
Peru	14,994	16,764	18,141	19,394	19,890	66.4	56.3	46.2	36.1	36.1	9,958	9,439	8,382	7,001	7,180
Saint Lucia	40	43	43	45	46				11.9					5	
Suriname	275	292	315	334	342				3.9					13	
Trinidad and Tobago	104	122	141	162	171				24.7					40	
Venezuela (Bolivarian Republic of)	16,630	19,161	21,891	24,675	25,749				32.0					7,896	

Source:

a. World Urbanization Prospects: The 2007 Revision

b. Computed from country household data using the four components of slum (improved water, improved sanitation, durable housing and sufficient living area

Proportion of urban population living in slums 1990-2010

Major region or area	Urban Population at Mid-Year by Major Area, Region (Thousands)[a]						Urban Slum Population at Mid-Year by Region (Thousands)[b]					
	1990	1995	2000	2005	2007	2010	1990	1995	2000	2005	2007	2010
Developing Regions	1,424,631	1,676,635	1,949,244	2,231,883	2,350,358	2,534,978	656,739	718,114	766,762	795,739	806,910	827,690
Northern Africa	57,402	65,141	72,397.5	80,145.8	83,435	88,666	19,731	18,417	14,729	10,708	11,142	11,836
Sub-Saharan Africa	146,564	182,383	222,733	269,246	289,938	323,525	102,588	123,210	144,683	169,515	181,030	199,540
Latin America and the Caribbean	313,852	353,457	394,099	432,554	448,006	471,177	105,740	111,246	115,192	110,105	110,554	110,763
Eastern Asia	365,574	436,582	513,919	592,873	624,430	671,795	159,754	177,063	192,265	195,463	194,020	189,621
Southern	315,726	368,423	423,518.3	479,718.3	504,697	545,766	180,449	190,276	194,009	192,041	191,735	190,748
South-eastern Asia	139,355	169,980	206,682.6	245,895.5	262,101	286,579	69,029	76,079	81,942	84,013	83,726	88,912
Western Asia	84,584	98,922	113,979.9	129,355.1	135,576	145,164	19,068	21,402	23,481	33,388	34,179	35,713
Oceania	1,572	1,748	1,914.8	2,095.6	2,176	2,306	379	421	462	505	524	556

Major region or area	Proportion of Urban Population						Proportion of Urban Population Living in Slum Areas					
	1990	1995	2000	2005	2007	2010	1990	1995	2000	2005	2007	2010
Developing Regions	34.9	37.5	40.1	42.7	43.7	45.3	46.1	42.8	39.3	35.7	34.3	32.7
Northern Africa	48.6	50.1	51.3	52.5	53.0	53.7	34.4	28.3	20.3	13.4	13.4	13.3
Sub-Saharan Africa	28.2	30.6	32.8	35.0	35.9	37.3	70.0	67.6	65.0	63.0	62.4	61.7
Latin America and the Caribbean	70.6	73.0	75.3	77.5	78.3	79.4	33.7	31.5	29.2	25.5	24.7	23.5
Eastern Asia	30.0	33.9	38.1	42.5	44.3	46.8	43.7	40.6	37.4	33.0	31.1	28.2
Southern	26.5	27.7	29.0	30.2	30.8	31.8	57.2	51.6	45.8	40.0	38.0	35.0
South-eastern Asia	31.6	35.3	39.7	44.1	45.8	48.2	49.5	44.8	39.6	34.2	31.9	31.0
Western Asia	61.5	63.1	64.6	65.9	66.4	67.1	22.5	21.6	20.6	25.8	25.2	24.6
Oceania[c]	24.4	24.1	23.6	23.3	23.3	23.4	24.1	24.1	24.1	24.1	24.1	24.1

(a): United Nations Population Division, World Urbanization Prospects: The 2007 Revision
(b): Population living in household that lack either improved water, improved sanitation, sufficient living area (more than three persons per room), or durable housing
(c): Trends data are not available for Oceania. A constant figure does not mean there is no change

Distribution of households by shelter deprivation, country 2005

MDG region and country name	All Types of Slums	One Shelter Deprivation	Two Shelter Deprivations	Three Shelter Deprivations	Four Shelter Deprivations
AFRICA					
Angola	86.5	24.6	36.1	20.5	5.3
Benin	71.8	38.6	20.3	11.9	1.0
Burkina Faso	59.5	43.2	10.0	2.7	3.7
Burundi	64.3	30.9	23.8	9.3	0.4
Cameroon	47.4	29.6	13.0	4.3	0.5
Central African Republic	94.1	23.2	59.8	9.2	1.8
Chad	91.3	26.1	38.0	22.5	4.6
Comoros	68.9	43.9	20.8	4.3	0.0
Congo	53.4	37.5	13.4	2.4	0.1
Côte d'Ivoire	56.2	38.7	16.5	0.9	0.0
Democratic Republic of the Congo	76.4	31.1	29.5	14.1	1.8
Egypt	17.1	14.9	2.0	0.1	0.0
Ethiopia	81.8	36.2	30.7	12.6	2.3
Equatorial Guinea	66.3	37.7	26.8	1.7	0.1
Gambia	45.4	32.6	10.4	2.2	0.1
Gabon	38.7	28.7	8.1	1.7	0.1
Ghana	45.4	29.9	9.9	5.8	0.0
Guinea	45.7	32.3	9.4	2.6	1.4
Guinea-Bissau	83.1	38.5	30.4	12.6	1.7
Kenya	54.8	31.2	15.1	6.9	1.6
Lesotho	35.1	29.4	5.0	0.6	N/A
Madagascar	80.6	29.6	25.0	13.2	12.8
Malawi	66.4	36.4	21.0	7.8	1.2
Mali	65.9	36.0	22.7	7.3	0.0
Morocco	13.1	11.9	1.0	0.1	0.0
Mozambique	79.5	31.3	25.5	19.6	3.1
Namibia	33.9	20.9	9.9	2.9	0.2
Niger	82.1	30.6	31.6	17.1	2.7
Nigeria	65.8	38.2	20.5	6.5	0.6
Rwanda	71.6				
Senegal	38.1	22.3	12.0	3.8	0.0
Sierra Leone	97.0	47.2	34.2	13.9	1.7
Somalia	73.5				
South Africa	28.7	21.8	6.0	0.8	0.1
Sudan	94.2	17.8	35.8	31.0	9.6
Swaziland	39.8	29.3	8.8	1.7	0.1
Togo	62.1	43.2	15.6	2.8	0.5
United Republic of Tanzania	66.4	35.4	22.0	8.3	0.6
Uganda	66.7	47.6	10.6	2.9	5.7
Zambia	57.2	36.9	15.2	4.3	0.9
Zimbabwe	17.9	17.9	0.0	0.0	0.0
LATIN AMERICA & THE CARIBBEAN					
Argentina	26.2				
Belize	47.3				
Bolivia	50.4	29.2	14.4	5.7	1.2
Brazil	29.0	24.2	4.8	0.0	0.0
Chile	9.0				
Colombia	17.9	15.0	2.4	0.4	0.0
Costa Rica	10.9				
Dominican Republic	17.6	15.0	1.9	0.6	0.0
Ecuador	21.5				
El Salvador	28.9				
French Guiana	10.5				
Grenada	6.0				
Guadeloupe	5.4				
Guatemala	42.9	23.9	10.0	6.6	2.4
Guyana	33.7	27.6	6.1	0.1	N/A
Haiti	69.5	43.9	17.5	5.3	2.8
Honduras	34.9	24.6	7.2	2.6	0.5
Jamaica	60.5	49.5	11.0	N/A	N/A
Mexico	14.4				
Nicaragua	45.5	26.7	16.0	2.8	0.0
Panama	23.0				
Paraguay	17.6				
Peru	36.1	22.6	9.2	3.4	0.9
Saint Lucia	11.9				
Suriname	3.9	3.6	0.4	0.0	0.0
Trinidad and Tobago	24.7				
Venezuela	32.0				
ASIA					
Bangladesh	70.8	27.5	29.7	13.4	0.2
Cambodia	78.9				
China	32.9				
India	34.8	27.8	6.9	0.0	N/A
Indonesia	26.3	22.4	3.1	0.8	N/A
Iran (Islamic Republic of)	30.3				
Iraq	52.8				
Jordan	15.8				
Lao People's Dem Republic	79.3	30.9	35.2	13.2	N/A
Lebanon	53.1				
Mongolia	57.9	36.1	18.8	2.9	0.0
Myanmar	45.6	36.6	7.9	1.0	0.0
Nepal	60.7	34.4	12.3	14.0	0.0
Pakistan	47.5				
Philippines	43.7	30.1	10.4	3.3	0.0
Saudi Arabia	18.0				
Syrian Arab Republic	10.5				
Thailand	26.0				
Turkey	15.5	13.5	2.0	0.0	0.0
Viet Nam	40.5	28.0	9.8	2.6	0.9
Yemen	67.2	39.9	18.1	7.9	1.4

Distribution of households by type of residence, country 2000-2005

COUNTRY	TYPE OF HOUSEHOLD	DISTRIBUTION OF URBAN HOUSEHOLDS BY TYPE OF RESIDENCE			
		Area with 25% or less slum households	Area with 26-50% slum households	Area with 51-75% slum households	Area with 75+% of slum households
AFRICA					
Benin	Non-slum household	66.5	7.4	18.0	8.1
Benin	Slum household	3.9	2.1	18.0	76.0
Burkina Faso	Non-slum household		35.1	39.4	25.4
Burkina Faso	Slum household		7.6	21.6	70.8
Cameroon	Non-slum household	21.8	43.8	27.9	6.5
Cameroon	Slum household	4.6	21.0	32.5	41.8
Central African Republic	Non-slum household	40.0			60.0
Central African Republic	Slum household	0.7			99.3
Chad	Non-slum household			11.8	88.2
Chad	Slum household			1.0	99.0
Comoros	Non-slum household	11.8	13.7	45.3	29.2
Comoros	Slum household	2.5	3.5	28.8	65.2
Côte d'Ivoire	Non-slum household	27.4	27.8	32.4	12.4
Côte d'Ivoire	Slum household	3.4	8.9	29.5	58.2
Egypt	Non-slum household	76.0	13.9	8.3	1.8
Egypt	Slum household	18.0	17.4	27.3	37.4
Ethiopia	Non-slum household			9.1	90.9
Ethiopia	Slum household			0.4	99.6
Gabon	Non-slum household	26.9	41.5	26.7	5.0
Gabon	Slum household	5.9	23.1	38.2	32.7
Ghana	Non-slum household	41.5	35.3	18.9	4.4
Ghana	Slum household	6.6	23.9	31.4	38.1
Guinea	Non-slum household	3.4	9.2	27.6	59.8
Guinea	Slum household	0.6	0.2	3.7	95.5
Kenya	Non-slum household	44.6	26.6	17.2	11.6
Kenya	Slum household	4.5	8.5	20.0	67.0
Madagascar	Non-slum household	7.8	8.6	15.5	68.1
Madagascar	Slum household	0.1	0.3	2.4	97.3
Malawi	Non-slum household	60.9	12.7	6.5	19.8
Malawi	Slum household	0.2	2.1	3.5	94.2
Mali	Non-slum household	26.2	27.7	30.1	16.1
Mali	Slum household	1.3	5.4	12.7	80.5
Morocco	Non-slum household	78.3	20.2	1.5	0.0
Morocco	Slum household	40.9	43.2	8.8	7.1
Mozambique	Non-slum household	34.1	16.4	9.1	40.5
Mozambique	Slum household	0.4	0.7	1.1	97.8
Namibia	Non-slum household	74.6	18.9	4.0	2.5
Namibia	Slum household	16.5	16.9	14.1	52.4
Niger	Non-slum household			36.1	63.9
Niger	Slum household			2.0	98.0
Nigeria	Non-slum household	27.8	19.8	28.3	24.1
Nigeria	Slum household	1.7	3.1	12.8	82.4
Rwanda	Non-slum household	12.0	25.7	43.6	18.7
Rwanda	Slum household	0.9	8.7	35.8	54.6
Senegal	Non-slum household	48.8	17.0	8.0	26.3
Senegal	Slum household	1.4	2.0	3.8	92.8
South Africa	Non-slum household	81.7	13.6	3.8	0.9
South Africa	Slum household	15.3	15.1	12.2	57.4
Tanzania	Non-slum household	12.6	30.5	15.3	41.7

COUNTRY	TYPE OF HOUSEHOLD	Area with 25% or less slum households	Area with 26-50% slum households	Area with 51-75% slum households	Area with 75+% of slum households
Tanzania	Slum household	1.5	3.6	4.9	90.1
Togo	Non-slum household	8.3		11.8	79.9
Togo	Slum household	1.6		1.1	97.3
Uganda	Non-slum household	27.0	9.0	25.3	38.8
Uganda	Slum household	1.3	0.8	9.3	88.6
Zambia	Non-slum household	74.5	9.5	10.5	5.5
Zambia	Slum household	3.7	3.8	10.5	82.0
Zimbabwe	Non-slum household	93.4	5.1	1.5	
Zimbabwe	Slum household	38.1	35.6	26.3	

LATIN AMERICA AND THE CARIBBEAN

Bolivia	Non-slum household	49.9	23.1	19.5	7.5
Bolivia	Slum household	8.8	10.5	26.3	54.4
Brazil	Non-slum household	51.3	35.8	8.4	4.6
Brazil	Slum household	11.9	22.3	15.2	50.5
Colombia	Non-slum household	84.0	13.4	2.4	0.2
Colombia	Slum household	28.8	31.4	13.9	25.8
Dominican Republic	Non-slum household	77.9	19.5	2.5	0.1
Dominican Republic	Slum household	39.6	42.2	14.5	3.6
Guatemala	Non-slum household	38.8	40.0	16.3	4.8
Guatemala	Slum household	7.5	23.6	20.3	48.6
Haiti	Non-slum household	61.1	20.7	16.5	1.8
Haiti	Slum household	14.7	20.2	45.5	19.6
Nicaragua	Non-slum household	43.1	22.5	24.3	10.1
Nicaragua	Slum household	6.0	8.2	24.6	61.2
Peru	Non-slum household	60.3	25.7	10.6	3.4
Peru	Slum household	10.7	18.7	21.7	48.9

ASIA

Bangladesh	Non-slum household	31.5	23.8	28.2	16.4
Bangladesh	Slum household	0.7	2.8	7.3	89.2
India	Non-slum household	14.9	54.4	28.1	2.6
India	Slum household	3.3	36.8	43.3	16.5
Indonesia	Non-slum household	38.6	36.0	19.7	5.6
Indonesia	Slum household	6.3	19.7	33.1	40.8
Nepal	Non-slum household	62.0	14.6	14.2	9.2
Nepal	Slum household	7.0	8.9	17.5	66.7
Pakistan	Non-slum household	15.3	19.5	46.7	18.5
Pakistan	Slum household	5.1	5.8	36.7	52.4
Philippines	Non-slum household	63.1	30.5	5.6	0.7
Philippines	Slum household	24.9	40.7	22.0	12.4
Viet Nam	Non-slum household	52.2	35.5	9.3	3.0
Viet Nam	Slum household	17.0	23.9	18.9	40.1
Armenia	Non-slum household	73.5	11.7	9.1	5.7
Armenia	Slum household	9.8	11.4	25.6	53.3
Turkey	Non-slum household	49.1	34.1	14.8	2.0
Turkey	Slum household	11.9	31.2	36.8	20.1
Yemen	Non-slum household	4.1	37.4	50.2	8.3
Yemen	Slum household	0.2	10.6	33.0	56.1
Kazakhstan	Non-slum household	43.9	30.3	18.4	7.4
Kazakhstan	Slum household	5.0	14.5	24.4	56.1
Kyrgyzstan	Non-slum household	68.9	14.0	10.5	6.7
Kyrgyzstan	Slum household	4.6	2.9	7.4	85.1
Uzbekistan	Non-slum household	42.8	23.7	19.8	13.8
Uzbekistan	Slum household	1.5	2.8	6.2	89.5

Solid waste disposal by shelter deprivation, country 2000-2005

COUNTRY	YEAR OF SURVEY	TYPE OF SOLID WASTE DISPOSAL	URBAN	NON SLUM HOUSEHOLD	SLUM HOUSEHOLD	ONE SHELTER DEPRIVATION	TWO SHELTER DEPRIVATIONS
AFRICA							
Benin	2001	Public removal	2.5	4.0	1.2	2.3	
Benin	2001	Private removal	24.8	44.9	8.5	13.9	2.7
Benin	2001	Bury it	1.8	1.5	1.9	1.4	2.5
Benin	2001	Burn it	4.7	4.6	4.7	5.5	3.9
Benin	2001	In the yard	1.9	1.4	2.2	2.6	1.9
Benin	2001	In the bush/fields	63.2	42.4	80.1	73.3	87.5
Benin	2001	Other	1.2	1.1	1.3	1.1	1.6
Benin	2001	**Collected by public/private services**	**27.3**	**48.9**	**9.7**	**16.1**	**2.7**
Egypt	2005	Collected from home	53.7	55.6	44.2	44.6	41.6
Egypt	2005	Collected from container in street	32.8	34.7	23.8	25.2	13.5
Egypt	2005	Dumped into street/empty plot	9.9	7.7	21.3	21.3	21.4
Egypt	2005	Dumped into canal/drainage	1.3	0.9	3.3	3.0	5.4
Egypt	2005	Burned	1.9	1.0	6.5	5.1	16.1
Egypt	2005	Fed to animals	0.3	0.1	1.0	0.8	2.1
Egypt	2005	**Collected by public/private services**	**86.6**	**90.3**	**68.0**	**69.8**	**55.1**
Kenya	2003	Regular collection by Govt.	2.5	3.0	2.1	2.8	1.1
Kenya	2003	Infrequent collection by Govt.	2.4	2.8	2.0	2.6	1.4
Kenya	2003	Pays for private collection	23.7	39.1	11.2	17.5	2.8
Kenya	2003	Composted	12.3	8.9	15.1	15.3	14.9
Kenya	2003	Dump, bury, burn in compound	29.3	22.4	34.8	31.2	39.5
Kenya	2003	Dump in street, empty plot	25.0	20.4	28.7	26.1	32.2
Kenya	2003	Other	4.9	3.4	6.1	4.5	8.2
Kenya	2003	**Collected by public/private services**	**28.5**	**44.9**	**15.3**	**22.8**	**5.3**
Senegal	1997	Collection	62.6	77.9	52.6	59.9	39.9
Senegal	1997	Buried in ground	2.5	0.6	3.7	3.0	4.8
Senegal	1997	Official tip	10.2	8.6	11.3	11.2	11.4
Senegal	1997	Unofficial tip	13.1	8.2	16.3	14.5	19.4
Senegal	1997	Incineration	7.6	2.6	10.9	6.8	17.9
Senegal	1997	Other	3.9	2.0	5.2	4.5	6.4
Senegal	1997	**Collected by public/private services**	**86.0**	**94.8**	**80.2**	**85.6**	**70.8**
LATIN AMERICA AND THE CARIBBEAN							
Dominican Republic	2002	Government	75.0	77.9	63.1	66.3	45.1
Dominican Republic	2002	Government's private contractors	2.3	2.4	1.7	1.9	0.6
Dominican Republic	2002	Other private companies	6.3	6.8	4.5	4.8	2.8
Dominican Republic	2002	Burn	7.1	5.6	13.2	10.8	26.2
Dominican Republic	2002	Throw in the yard	4.5	3.5	8.6	7.6	13.9
Dominican Republic	2002	Throw in the gully	3.5	2.7	6.8	6.6	8.0
Dominican Republic	2002	Other	1.3	1.1	2.2	1.9	3.5
Dominican Republic	2002	**Collected by public/private services**	**83.6**	**87.1**	**69.2**	**72.9**	**48.5**
Guatemala	1998	Public collection	14.7	17.3	11.6	14.7	7.0
Guatemala	1998	Private collection	41.5	56.0	24.1	36.0	6.7
Guatemala	1998	Throw in the backyard	12.6	5.7	21.0	13.2	32.3
Guatemala	1998	Throw in the street	1.9	1.4	2.5	2.4	2.6
Guatemala	1998	Bury underground	2.8	1.5	4.3	2.8	6.5
Guatemala	1998	Does not have any means	0.2	0.1	0.4	0.6	0.0
Guatemala	1998	Burn	17.6	9.7	26.9	20.3	36.6
Guatemala	1998	Throw in trash dump	6.6	5.5	8.0	8.8	6.9
Guatemala	1998	Other	2.0	2.6	1.2	1.1	1.5
Guatemala	1998	**Collected by public/private services**	**62.9**	**78.9**	**43.7**	**59.5**	**20.6**
Nicaragua	2001	Truck garbage collector	61.1	80.1	46.9	56.9	36.9
Nicaragua	2001	Burn it	24.8	11.3	34.8	28.3	41.3
Nicaragua	2001	Bury it	2.8	1.0	4.2	3.1	5.3
Nicaragua	2001	Cleaning cart	0.8	0.6	0.9	1.1	0.6
Nicaragua	2001	Pay for disposal	2.8	2.9	2.8	3.4	2.1
Nicaragua	2001	Authorized garbage dump	2.2	1.8	2.5	1.8	3.3
Nicaragua	2001	Throw in the yard	5.5	2.3	7.9	5.4	10.5
Nicaragua	2001	**Collected by public/private services**	**66.9**	**85.4**	**53.1**	**63.2**	**42.9**

Type of fuel for cooking type of household

COUNTRY	YEAR	TYPE OF COOKING OIL	URBAN	NON SLUM HOUSEHOLD	SLUM HOUSEHOLD	ONE SHELTER DEPRIVATION	TWO SHELTER DEPRIVATIONS
AFRICA							
Benin	2006	Electricity	0.1	0.2			
Benin	2006	Natural gas	9.0	17.8	4.3	7.2	0.7
Benin	2006	Kerosene	3.2	5.3	2.2	3.2	0.9
Benin	2006	Charcoal	43.1	53.7	37.4	50.3	22.0
Benin	2006	Straw / shrubs / grass	43.4	21.3	55.3	37.9	76.1
Benin	2006	Other	1.2	1.7	0.9	1.4	0.2
Benin	2006	**Solid fuel**	**86.5**	**75.1**	**92.7**	**88.2**	**98.1**
Burkina Faso	2003	LPG, natural gas	17.6	29.0	14.5	16.2	0.8
Burkina Faso	2003	Biogas	0.3		0.4	0.5	
Burkina Faso	2003	Kerosene	0.7	1.3	0.5	0.5	0.7
Burkina Faso	2003	Coal, lignite	1.2	0.9	1.2	1.4	
Burkina Faso	2003	Charcoal	15.4	17.3	14.9	15.8	7.1
Burkina Faso	2003	Firewood, straw	59.9	49.7	62.7	59.6	87.3
Burkina Faso	2003	Dung	0.1		0.2	0.1	0.4
Burkina Faso	2003	Does not cook	4.6	1.9	5.4	5.6	3.3
Burkina Faso	2003	Other	0.2		0.3	0.2	0.4
Burkina Faso	2003	**Solid fuel**	**76.6**	**67.9**	**78.9**	**77.0**	**94.7**
Cameroon	2004	LPG, natural gas	25.5	36.7	13.3	19.2	3.4
Cameroon	2004	Kerosene	13.5	16.4	10.3	12.8	6.1
Cameroon	2004	Charcoal	4.6	3.8	5.5	5.3	5.8
Cameroon	2004	Firewood, straw	52.1	38.1	67.3	59.1	81.3
Cameroon	2004	Other	4.3	5.0	3.6	3.6	3.5
Cameroon	2004	**Solid fuel**	**56.7**	**41.9**	**72.8**	**64.4**	**87.0**
Congo	2005	Electricity	4.9	5.3	3.6	5.3	1.6
Congo	2005	LPG, natural gas	15.7	17.9	8.0	11.8	3.6
Congo	2005	Kerosene	8.9	9.6	6.6	7.1	6.0
Congo	2005	Charcoal	49.9	47.6	57.7	58.7	56.7
Congo	2005	Firewood, straw	18.8	17.9	21.9	15.4	29.3
Congo	2005	Dung	1.2	1.0	2.0	1.8	2.3
Congo	2005	Other	0.6	0.7	0.2		0.5
Congo	2005	**Solid fuel**	**69.9**	**66.4**	**81.7**	**75.8**	**88.3**
Egypt	2005	Electricity	0.2	0.2	0.3	0.3	
Egypt	2005	LPG, natural gas	98.6	99.3	94.8	95.8	88.0
Egypt	2005	Biogas					
Egypt	2005	Kerosene	1.0	0.4	4.3	3.3	11.4
Egypt	2005	Firewood, straw			0.2	0.1	0.7
Egypt	2005	Other	0.1	0.1	0.3	0.4	
Egypt	2005	**Solid fuel**	**0.2**	**0.1**	**0.5**	**0.5**	**0.7**
Ethiopia	2005	Electricity	1.0	2.5	0.5	0.8	0.3
Ethiopia	2005	LPG, natural gas	0.9	2.1	0.5	0.9	0.3
Ethiopia	2005	Biogas	0.3	0.8	0.2	0.5	0.0
Ethiopia	2005	Kerosene	25.9	45.6	19.1	34.1	10.2
Ethiopia	2005	Charcoal	18.1	20.5	17.2	22.6	14.0
Ethiopia	2005	Firewood, straw	48.7	21.2	58.2	36.9	70.9
Ethiopia	2005	Dung	2.1	2.4	2.0	1.8	2.2
Ethiopia	2005	Do not cook	1.9	3.8	1.2	1.3	1.1
Ethiopia	2005	Other	1.1	1.2	1.1	1.1	1.1
Ethiopia	2005	**Solid fuel**	**68.9**	**44.1**	**77.5**	**61.3**	**87.0**
Gabon	2000	Electricity	0.8	1.4	0.3	0.2	0.4
Gabon	2000	Gas cylinder/Butane cylinder	75.7	85.3	66.7	76.5	44.6
Gabon	2000	Oil/kerosene	4.4	3.4	5.3	6.3	3.2
Gabon	2000	Coal/charcoal	2.7	1.5	3.9	2.6	6.6
Gabon	2000	Wood/straw	11.4	2.6	19.7	9.0	43.8
Gabon	2000	Other	4.9	5.8	4.1	5.4	1.4
Gabon	2000	**Solid fuel**	**14.1**	**4.1**	**23.5**	**11.6**	**50.4**
Ghana	2003	Electricity	0.6	0.8	0.1	0.1	
Ghana	2003	LPG, natural gas	14.6	18.5	8.2	9.5	2.8
Ghana	2003	Biogas	0.7	0.8	0.6	0.7	

COUNTRY	YEAR	TYPE OF COOKING OIL	URBAN	NON SLUM HOUSEHOLD	SLUM HOUSEHOLD	ONE SHELTER DEPRIVATION	TWO SHELTER DEPRIVATIONS
Ghana	2003	Kerosene	1.3	1.4	1.0	1.3	
Ghana	2003	Coal, lignite	0.7	0.9	0.5	0.6	
Ghana	2003	Charcoal	54.1	56.1	50.9	54.5	36.0
Ghana	2003	Firewood, straw	25.6	19.0	36.6	30.5	61.2
Ghana	2003	Dung		0.1			
Ghana	2003	Other	2.3	2.3	2.3	2.8	
Ghana	2003	**Solid fuel**	**80.5**	**76.1**	**87.9**	**85.6**	**97.2**
Guinea	2005	Electricity	1.2	1.3	0.9	1.2	
Guinea	2005	LPG, natural gas	0.3	0.4	0.1	0.2	
Guinea	2005	Biogas		0.1			
Guinea	2005	Kerosene	0.2	0.2	0.3	0.3	
Guinea	2005	Coal, lignite	59.9	68.1	43.3	50.7	20.2
Guinea	2005	Charcoal	34.0	25.1	51.8	44.0	76.2
Guinea	2005	Firewood, straw	0.8	1.0	0.6	0.8	
Guinea	2005	Other	3.5	3.8	3.0	2.8	3.6
Guinea	2005	**Solid fuel**	**94.7**	**94.2**	**95.7**	**95.4**	**96.4**
Kenya	2003	Electricity	1.0	2.0	0.3	0.5	
Kenya	2003	LPG, natural gas	10.8	19.8	3.5	5.7	0.6
Kenya	2003	Biogas	0.3	0.6	0.1	0.2	
Kenya	2003	Kerosene	50.8	56.0	46.6	53.8	37.1
Kenya	2003	Coal, lignite	0.2	0.1	0.2	0.1	0.4
Kenya	2003	Charcoal	25.9	17.7	32.6	31.0	34.8
Kenya	2003	Firewood, straw	9.4	2.4	15.0	7.2	25.4
Kenya	2003	Dung		0.1			
Kenya	2003	Other	1.5	1.4	1.7	1.6	1.7
Kenya	2003	**Solid fuel**	**35.5**	**20.2**	**47.9**	**38.3**	**60.6**
Lesotho	2004	Electricity	7.0	9.8	2.0	2.5	
Lesotho	2004	LPG, natural gas	58.3	65.3	45.3	52.9	11.1
Lesotho	2004	Coal, lignite	0.0		0.1	0.1	
Lesotho	2004	Firewood, straw	6.6	3.3	12.6	8.9	29.3
Lesotho	2004	Dung	0.5	0.0	1.2	1.1	1.8
Lesotho	2004	Paraffin	27.4	21.5	38.3	34.2	56.9
Lesotho	2004	Crop Waste	0.1	0.1	0.3	0.1	0.9
Lesotho	2004	Other	0.0		0.1	0.2	
Lesotho	2004	**Solid fuel**	**7.2**	**3.4**	**14.2**	**10.2**	**32.0**
Madagascar	2004	Electricity	0.9	1.9	0.5	0.9	0.1
Madagascar	2004	LPG, natural gas	2.7	7.1	0.8	1.4	0.3
Madagascar	2004	Biogas	0.3	0.6	0.1	0.3	
Madagascar	2004	Kerosene	0.2	0.5	0.1	0.2	
Madagascar	2004	Coal, lignite	0.7	0.8	0.7	1.1	0.3
Madagascar	2004	Charcoal	59.4	81.9	50.0	74.6	26.4
Madagascar	2004	Firewood, straw	35.6	7.2	47.4	21.0	72.8
Madagascar	2004	Dung	0.1	0.0	0.2	0.3	0.1
Madagascar	2004	Other	0.1		0.1	0.2	0.1
Madagascar	2004	**Solid fuel**	**95.8**	**90.0**	**98.3**	**97.0**	**99.5**
Malawi	2004	Electricity	10.7	26.9	2.3	3.9	0.5
Malawi	2004	LPG, natural gas	0.1	0.4			
Malawi	2004	Biogas	0.1	0.2			
Malawi	2004	Kerosene	0.2	0.1	0.3	0.3	0.3
Malawi	2004	Coal, lignite			0.1		0.2
Malawi	2004	Charcoal	41.5	43.9	40.2	51.7	26.5
Malawi	2004	Firewood, straw	47.2	28.5	56.8	43.6	72.5
Malawi	2004	Dung	0.0		0.0		0.1
Malawi	2004	Other	0.2		0.3	0.5	
Malawi	2004	**Solid fuel**	**88.8**	**72.5**	**97.1**	**95.3**	**99.2**
Mali	2001	Electricity	0.1	0.2			
Mali	2001	LPG, natural gas	2.1	3.6	1.3	2.0	0.7
Mali	2001	Biogas	0.1	0.2			
Mali	2001	Kerosene	0.1		0.2	0.1	0.2
Mali	2001	Coal, lignite	0.7	1.3	0.4	0.3	0.5
Mali	2001	Charcoal	31.4	46.6	24.0	31.7	15.8
Mali	2001	Firewood, straw	62.3	45.8	70.3	63.3	77.7
Mali	2001	Dung	1.4	0.5	1.8	0.8	2.7
Mali	2001	Other	1.9	1.6	2.1	1.9	2.3
Mali	2001	**Solid fuel**	**95.7**	**94.3**	**96.4**	**96.1**	**96.8**
Mauritania	2001	Other	2.9	2.9	2.9	3.4	2.2
Mauritania	2001	Gas	48.5	64.7	39.7	50.8	25.8
Mauritania	2001	Charcoal	41.2	29.8	47.4	42.2	53.9

COUNTRY	YEAR	TYPE OF COOKING OIL	URBAN	NON SLUM HOUSEHOLD	SLUM HOUSEHOLD	ONE SHELTER DEPRIVATION	TWO SHELTER DEPRIVATIONS
Mauritania	2001	Straw	7.4	2.5	10.0	3.6	18.1
Mauritania	2001	**Solid fuel**	**48.7**	**32.4**	**57.4**	**45.8**	**72.0**
Morocco	2004	Firewood	0.3	0.2	1.0	0.5	6.6
Morocco	2004	Coal		0.1			
Morocco	2004	Electricity	0.1	0.2			
Morocco	2004	Gas liquid	0.1	0.1	0.1	0.2	
Morocco	2004	Gas	99.3	99.4	98.8	99.3	93.4
Morocco	2004	Other	0.1	0.0	0.1	0.1	
Morocco	2004	**Solid fuel**	**0.4**	**0.2**	**1.0**	**0.5**	**6.6**
Mozambique	2003	Electricity	2.1	5.9	1.1	2.2	0.4
Mozambique	2003	LPG, natural gas	4.9	14.9	2.2	4.7	0.6
Mozambique	2003	Kerosene	1.6	2.6	1.3	2.4	0.5
Mozambique	2003	Coal, lignite	40.9	55.7	37.0	54.9	25.0
Mozambique	2003	Charcoal	1.0	0.9	1.1	1.5	0.8
Mozambique	2003	Firewood, straw	49.3	20.0	57.0	33.8	72.6
Mozambique	2003	Dung		0.1			0.1
Mozambique	2003	Other	0.2		0.2	0.4	0.1
Mozambique	2003	**Solid fuel**	**91.3**	**76.6**	**95.1**	**90.3**	**98.4**
Namibia	2000	Electricity	59.6	76.7	26.0	40.6	3.2
Namibia	2000	LPG, natural gas	15.4	14.2	17.9	21.7	11.9
Namibia	2000	Kerosene	9.8	3.3	22.6	16.4	32.2
Namibia	2000	Charcoal	1.1	0.5	2.3	2.2	2.5
Namibia	2000	Firewood, straw	14.0	5.3	31.1	19.0	50.1
Namibia	2000	Other	0.1	0.1			0.1
Namibia	2000	**Solid fuel**	**15.1**	**5.8**	**33.4**	**21.2**	**52.6**
Niger	2006	Electricity	0.6	1.3	0.3	0.8	
Niger	2006	LPG, natural gas	3.4	8.1	1.3	1.9	0.8
Niger	2006	Charcoal	10.4	14.8	8.4	10.0	7.1
Niger	2006	Firewood, straw	85.0	75.1	89.4	86.5	91.8
Niger	2006	Dung	0.5	0.6	0.4	0.6	0.3
Niger	2006	Other	0.1		0.1	0.2	
Niger	2006	**Solid fuel**	**95.9**	**90.6**	**98.3**	**97.1**	**99.2**
Nigeria	2003	Electricity	0.5	0.8	0.3	0.5	
Nigeria	2003	LPG, natural gas	1.5	3.5	0.5	0.9	0.2
Nigeria	2003	Biogas	0.6	1.3	0.2	0.4	
Nigeria	2003	Kerosene	53.6	70.6	45.0	56.0	31.8
Nigeria	2003	Coal, lignite	0.2	0.2	0.2		0.3
Nigeria	2003	Charcoal	0.7	0.5	0.8	0.6	1.0
Nigeria	2003	Firewood, straw	41.2	20.8	51.4	39.8	65.2
Nigeria	2003	Dung	0.1	0.2	0.0		0.1
Nigeria	2003	Do not cook	1.7	1.9	1.6	1.7	1.4
Nigeria	2003	Other	0.1	0.2	0.0		0.1
Nigeria	2003	**Solid fuel**	**42.1**	**21.7**	**52.4**	**40.4**	**66.5**
Rwanda	2005	Electricity	0.3	0.9			0.1
Rwanda	2005	LPG, natural gas	0.1	0.4			
Rwanda	2005	Biogas	0.1	0.2			
Rwanda	2005	Kerosene	0.4	0.5	0.3	0.6	
Rwanda	2005	Coal, lignite	1.6	3.7	0.5	1.2	
Rwanda	2005	Charcoal	37.1	70.4	20.3	35.6	9.5
Rwanda	2005	Firewood, straw	58.3	19.7	77.7	61.1	89.3
Rwanda	2005	Other	2.2	4.1	1.2	1.4	1.1
Rwanda	2005	**Solid fuel**	**96.9**	**93.9**	**98.5**	**98.0**	**98.8**
Senegal	2005	Electricity	0.4	0.5	0.1	0.1	
Senegal	2005	LPG, natural gas	76.1	84.9	49.9	60.8	17.1
Senegal	2005	Charcoal	8.9	6.8	15.3	13.5	20.8
Senegal	2005	Firewood, straw	11.5	5.2	30.2	22.0	54.9
Senegal	2005	Dung	0.1	0.0	0.4	0.2	0.9
Senegal	2005	Other	3.0	2.6	4.1	3.4	6.3
Senegal	2005	**Solid fuel**	**20.6**	**12.0**	**45.9**	**35.8**	**76.6**
Sierra Leone	2006	Electricity	0.1		0.1	0.1	
Sierra Leone	2006	Natural gas					
Sierra Leone	2006	Biogas	0.1			0.1	
Sierra Leone	2006	Kerosene	1.4	0.3	0.4	1.1	0.1
Sierra Leone	2006	Coal/lignite	0.1		0.0	0.1	
Sierra Leone	2006	Charcoal	27.0	2.7	8.5	15.2	5.5

COUNTRY	YEAR	TYPE OF COOKING OIL	URBAN	NON SLUM HOUSEHOLD	SLUM HOUSEHOLD	ONE SHELTER DEPRIVATION	TWO SHELTER DEPRIVATIONS
Sierra Leone	2006	Wood	70.5	95.9	90.6	82.8	94.0
Sierra Leone	2006	Straw/shrubs/grass	0.1		0.1		0.1
Sierra Leone	2006	Agricultural crop residue					
Sierra Leone	2006	Other	0.5	1.1	0.2	0.3	0.2
Sierra Leone	2006	Solid fuel	97.7	98.6	99.2	98.2	99.6
Somalia	2006	Electricity	0.2	0.4		0.3	0.0
Somalia	2006	Liquid propane gas (LPG)	0.1	0.3			
Somalia	2006	Kerosene	0.3	0.5	0.1	0.5	0.1
Somalia	2006	Charcoal	79.1	89.1	26.3	80.9	16.6
Somalia	2006	Wood	19.3	9.0	69.7	17.4	79.0
Somalia	2006	Straw/shrubs/grass	0.8	0.3	3.6	0.9	4.1
Somalia	2006	Agricultural crop residue			0.1		0.1
Somalia	2006	Other		0.1			
Somalia	2006	Missing	0.1	0.4	0.1		0.1
Somalia	2006	Solid fuel	99.3	98.4	99.7	99.2	99.8
South Africa	1998	Electricity	54.3	65.1	27.4	33.0	9.6
South Africa	1998	Gas	6.9	7.5	5.6	6.3	3.4
South Africa	1998	Paraffin	25.7	16.9	47.7	43.6	60.5
South Africa	1998	Wood	2.6	1.5	5.5	4.0	10.3
South Africa	1998	Coal	8.8	7.7	11.6	12.1	10.0
South Africa	1998	Animal dung	0.1	0.1	0.3	0.1	0.9
South Africa	1998	Other	0.8	0.9	0.6	0.7	0.1
South Africa	1998	Missing	0.8	0.5	1.4	0.2	5.2
South Africa	1998	Solid fuel	11.6	9.2	17.4	16.2	21.3
Swaziland	2006	Electricity	41.0	51.4	20.6	23.0	9.4
Swaziland	2006	Natural gas	29.8	27.1	35.1	37.7	23.1
Swaziland	2006	Coal, lignite	0.8	1.1	0.3	0.4	
Swaziland	2006	Charcoal	0.9	1.3	0.1	0.2	
Swaziland	2006	Wood	11.4	8.3	17.7	13.8	35.3
Swaziland	2006	Paraffin	14.7	9.3	25.4	24.2	30.9
Swaziland	2006	No food cooked in HH	1.2	1.5	0.5	0.2	1.4
Swaziland	2006	Other	0.1		0.3	0.4	
Swaziland	2006	Solid fuel	13.2	10.6	18.1	14.4	35.3
Tanzania	2004	Electricity	0.9	2.1	0.3	0.4	0.3
Tanzania	2004	Bottled gas	0.4	1.1			
Tanzania	2004	Paraffin/Kerosene	9.7	13.9	7.5	9.4	5.4
Tanzania	2004	Charcoal	59.2	68.7	54.5	66.2	41.2
Tanzania	2004	Firewood, straw	27.8	12.3	35.6	21.6	51.5
Tanzania	2004	Dung					0.1
Tanzania	2004	Other	2.0	1.9	2.0	2.5	1.5
Tanzania	2004	Solid fuel	87.1	81.0	90.1	87.8	92.8
Uganda	2001	Electricity	4.8	9.4	1.5	2.1	0.2
Uganda	2001	LPG, natural gas	0.2	0.2	0.1	0.2	
Uganda	2001	Biogas	0.3	0.7	0.1	0.1	
Uganda	2001	Kerosene	9.8	9.4	10.1	11.6	6.7
Uganda	2001	Charcoal	66.8	71.5	63.5	69.3	51.0
Uganda	2001	Firewood, straw	15.6	6.6	21.9	13.8	39.4
Uganda	2001	Other	2.5	2.1	2.8	2.9	2.6
Uganda	2001	Solid fuel	82.4	78.1	85.4	83.1	90.4
Zambia	2002	Electricity	37.5	55.1	13.4	19.0	1.1
Zambia	2002	LPG, natural gas	0.1	0.1	0.1	0.2	
Zambia	2002	Coal, lignite	0.3	0.4	0.2	0.1	0.2
Zambia	2002	Charcoal	52.1	41.2	67.0	67.8	65.4
Zambia	2002	Firewood, straw	9.9	3.1	19.1	12.7	33.0
Zambia	2002	Dung	0.0		0.1	0.1	
Zambia	2002	Other	0.1	0.0	0.1		0.3
Zambia	2002	Solid fuel	62.3	44.8	86.4	80.8	98.6
Zimbabwe	2005	Electricity	88.0	90.1	78.0	79.2	48.7
Zimbabwe	2005	Biogas					
Zimbabwe	2005	Paraffin/Kerosine	0.6	0.7	0.3	0.3	
Zimbabwe	2005	Coal, lignite					
Zimbabwe	2005	Wood	11.2	8.9	21.4	20.2	51.3
Zimbabwe	2005	Straw/shrubs/grass	0.1	0.1	0.3	0.3	
Zimbabwe	2005	Animal dung	0.0	0.1			
Zimbabwe	2005	Do not cook	0.0	0.1			
Zimbabwe	2005	Solid fuel	11.4	9.1	21.7	20.5	51.3

COUNTRY	YEAR	TYPE OF COOKING OIL	URBAN	NON SLUM HOUSEHOLD	SLUM HOUSEHOLD	ONE SHELTER DEPRIVATION	TWO SHELTER DEPRIVATIONS
LATIN AMERICA AND THE CARIBBEAN							
Bolivia	2004	Electricity	0.8	1.5	0.1	0.1	0.0
Bolivia	2004	LPG, natural gas	88.2	92.4	84.1	90.2	75.3
Bolivia	2004	Kerosene	0.4	0.1	0.7	0.5	0.9
Bolivia	2004	Firewood, straw	7.4	1.9	12.7	6.5	21.3
Bolivia	2004	Dung	0.2	0.1	0.3	0.0	0.6
Bolivia	2004	Don't cook	3.1	3.9	2.3	2.6	1.8
Bolivia	2004	Other					
Bolivia	2004	**Solid fuel**	**7.5**	**2.0**	**12.9**	**6.6**	**21.9**
Colombia	2005	Natural gas	49.0	51.4	38.2	40.7	25.3
Colombia	2005	Propane gas	36.6	35.7	41.0	42.0	35.6
Colombia	2005	Kerosene, oil, cocinol, diesel, gasoline, alcohol	1.0	0.5	3.1	2.7	5.5
Colombia	2005	Electricity	8.3	8.5	7.0	6.5	9.7
Colombia	2005	Firewood, charcoal	2.5	1.3	7.8	5.4	20.7
Colombia	2005	Mineral coal	0.2	0.1	0.4	0.3	0.5
Colombia	2005	Disposable material					0.1
Colombia	2005	Do not cook	2.4	2.4	2.4	2.4	2.6
Colombia	2005	**Solid fuel**	**2.7**	**1.5**	**8.2**	**5.7**	**21.3**
Dominica Republic	2002	Electricity	0.1	0.1			0.1
Dominica Republic	2002	LPG, natural gas	92.5	93.7	87.9	90.2	74.9
Dominica Republic	2002	Charcoal	1.4	0.8	3.8	2.9	8.6
Dominica Republic	2002	Firewood, straw	1.3	0.7	4.0	2.7	11.0
Dominica Republic	2002	Do not cook	4.7	4.7	4.3	4.1	5.4
Dominica Republic	2002	Other	0.1	0.0	0.1	0.1	0.0
Dominica Republic	2002	Solid fuel	2.7	1.5	7.7	5.6	19.6
Guatemala	1998	Wood /coal	31.6	11.7	55.3	34.4	84.7
Guatemala	1998	Natural gas (Kerosene)	1.0	1.4	0.4	0.5	0.2
Guatemala	1998	Propane gas	65.4	84.2	43.2	64.3	13.4
Guatemala	1998	Electricity	1.1	1.3	0.8	0.1	1.7
Guatemala	1998	Other	0.9	1.4	0.4	0.7	0.0
Guatemala	1998	**Solid fuel**	**31.6**	**11.7**	**55.3**	**34.4**	**84.7**
Guyana	2000	Electricity	5.5	3.4	0.5	0.6	0.5
Guyana	2000	Gas	44.3	45.6	15.7	21.3	5.0
Guyana	2000	Kerosene	38.5	46.2	55.8	66.4	35.9
Guyana	2000	Goals	0.5	0.3	0.6	0.6	0.5
Guyana	2000	Woods	0.9	4.3	15.9	11.1	25.1
Guyana	2000	Others	0.4	0.3	0.2	0.1	0.3
Guyana	2000	Missing	9.9		11.4		32.7
Guyana	2000	**Solid fuel**	**1.3**	**4.6**	**16.1**	**11.1**	**25.4**
Haiti	2006	Electricity	0.1	0.1	0.1		0.3
Haiti	2006	LPG, natural gas	4.6	5.8	3.8	4.9	1.1
Haiti	2006	Biogas	2.0	3.3	1.1	1.4	0.3
Haiti	2006	Kerosene	6.0	8.6	4.5	5.1	2.8
Haiti	2006	Coal, lignite	0.3	0.3	0.3	0.4	0.1
Haiti	2006	Charcoal	76.5	77.4	76.0	78.8	69.2
Haiti	2006	Firewood, straw	10.0	4.3	13.5	8.7	25.3
Haiti	2006	Other	0.5	0.2	0.7	0.6	0.9
Haiti	2006	**Solid fuel**	**86.9**	**82.0**	**89.8**	**87.9**	**94.5**
Honduras	2005	Electricity	33.6	38.6	24.3	26.4	19.6
Honduras	2005	LPG	32.6	38.5	21.6	27.5	8.2
Honduras	2005	Kerosene	10.4	7.5	15.7	15.6	15.7
Honduras	2005	Coal, lignite	0.1		0.2	0.2	0.1
Honduras	2005	Wood	20.1	11.8	35.7	27.6	54.3
Honduras	2005	No food cooked in HH	3.2	3.5	2.5	2.7	2.1
Honduras	2005	**Solid fuel**	**20.2**	**11.8**	**35.8**	**27.8**	**54.4**
Nicaragua	2001	Electricity	1.4	1.5	1.4	1.5	1.3
Nicaragua	2001	LPG, natural gas	57.5	81.6	39.5	52.2	26.8
Nicaragua	2001	Gas & Kerosene	1.2	0.9	1.4	0.8	2.1
Nicaragua	2001	Charcoal	0.7	0.4	0.9	1.3	0.6
Nicaragua	2001	Firewood, straw	38.2	15.0	55.6	42.6	68.6
Nicaragua	2001	No cooking	0.9	0.7	1.1	1.6	0.6
Nicaragua	2001	Other					
Nicaragua	2001	**Solid fuel**	**38.9**	**15.4**	**56.6**	**43.8**	**69.2**
Peru	2004	Electricity	1.3	1.7	0.6	0.7	0.5
Peru	2004	LPG, natural gas	73.1	83.2	55.5	62.7	43.2

COUNTRY	YEAR	TYPE OF COOKING OIL	URBAN	NON SLUM HOUSEHOLD	SLUM HOUSEHOLD	ONE SHELTER DEPRIVATION	TWO SHELTER DEPRIVATIONS
Peru	2004	Kerosene	11.6	8.3	17.4	18.2	16.0
Peru	2004	Coal, lignite	1.8	0.8	3.6	2.6	5.3
Peru	2004	Firewood, straw	8.4	2.6	18.5	12.2	29.4
Peru	2004	Dung	0.9	0.3	1.9	1.2	3.1
Peru	2004	Don't cook	2.6	2.8	2.3	2.3	2.3
Peru	2004	Other	0.2	0.3	0.1	0.1	0.1
Peru	2004	**Solid fuel**	**11.1**	**3.7**	**24.0**	**16.0**	**37.9**

ASIA

COUNTRY	YEAR	TYPE OF COOKING OIL	URBAN	NON SLUM HOUSEHOLD	SLUM HOUSEHOLD	ONE SHELTER DEPRIVATION	TWO SHELTER DEPRIVATIONS
Bangladesh	2006	Electricity	0.5	1.0	0.1	0.3	0.1
Bangladesh	2006	Liquid propane gas (LPG)	3.8	7.2	0.2	0.7	0.0
Bangladesh	2006	Natural gas	15.5	37.6	4.2	10.3	2.1
Bangladesh	2006	Biogas	0.1	0.3			
Bangladesh	2006	Kerosene	0.6	1.0	0.1	0.3	0.1
Bangladesh	2006	Wood	55.0	42.9	49.3	56.2	46.9
Bangladesh	2006	Straw/shrubs/grass	2.4	1.9	1.5	1.8	1.4
Bangladesh	2006	Animal dung	6.0	2.4	9.2	7.0	10.0
Bangladesh	2006	Agricultural crop residue	14.6	4.8	33.4	21.8	37.3
Bangladesh	2006	Other	1.6	0.8	1.9	1.6	2.0
Bangladesh	2006	Missing	0.0	0.1			
Bangladesh	2006	**Solid fuel**	**77.9**	**52.0**	**93.4**	**86.8**	**95.7**
India	2006	Electricity	0.9	1.0	0.9	1.0	0.6
India	2006	LPG/Natural gas	58.7	78.0	43.7	56.7	23.2
India	2006	Biogas	0.5	0.6	0.4	0.5	0.2
India	2006	Kerosene	8.2	6.3	9.7	11.2	7.4
India	2006	Coal, lignite	4.3	3.0	5.3	4.8	6.1
India	2006	Charcoal	0.5	0.4	0.6	0.6	0.6
India	2006	Wood	22.0	8.1	32.8	21.1	51.4
India	2006	Straw/shrubs/grass	0.5	0.1	0.9	0.3	1.8
India	2006	Agricultural crop	0.8	0.6	0.9	0.7	1.3
India	2006	Animal dung	2.8	0.8	4.3	2.5	7.1
India	2006	Other	0.8	1.1	0.5	0.6	0.3
India	2006	**Solid fuel**	**30.9**	**13.0**	**44.8**	**30.0**	**68.3**
Indonesia	2002	Electricity	0.7	0.8	0.6	0.8	0.1
Indonesia	2002	LPG, natural gas	18.6	25.6	7.6	9.5	1.9
Indonesia	2002	Kerosene	63.9	65.3	61.6	65.8	49.1
Indonesia	2002	Coal, lignite	0.1	0.1			
Indonesia	2002	Charcoal	0.1	0.1	0.1	0.1	0.1
Indonesia	2002	Firewood, straw	15.9	7.1	29.8	23.5	48.6
Indonesia	2002	Other	0.8	1.0	0.3	0.4	0.2
Indonesia	2002	**Solid fuel**	**16.0**	**7.2**	**29.9**	**23.6**	**48.7**
Iraq	2006	Electricity	0.2	0.2	0.2	0.2	0.3
Iraq	2006	Liquid propane gas (LPG)	92.2	91.2	82.4	88.0	67.0
Iraq	2006	Kerosene	7.0	7.4	10.1	8.6	14.3
Iraq	2006	Coal/lignite			0.1		0.4
Iraq	2006	Wood	0.3	0.9	3.1	2.1	5.8
Iraq	2006	Straw/shrubs/grass	0.2	0.2	2.8	0.8	8.5
Iraq	2006	Animal dung		0.0	1.0	0.2	3.2
Iraq	2006	Agricultural crop residue		0.1	0.2	0.1	0.5
Iraq	2006	Other					0.1
Iraq	2006	Missing					
Iraq	2006	**Solid fuel**	**0.6**	**1.2**	**7.1**	**3.2**	**18.0**
Kazakhstan	2006	Electricity	20.5	21.1	9.7	10.5	4.5
Kazakhstan	2006	Liquid propane gas (LPG)	36.5	31.2	45.8	45.8	45.9
Kazakhstan	2006	Natural gas	36.1	41.4	17.8	18.5	13.9
Kazakhstan	2006	Kerosene			0.1	0.1	0.0
Kazakhstan	2006	Coal/lignite	6.2	5.6	20.0	19.4	23.9
Kazakhstan	2006	Charcoal	0.1	0.0	0.3	0.3	0.7
Kazakhstan	2006	Wood	0.6	0.4	4.3	4.0	6.5
Kazakhstan	2006	Animal dung	0.0	0.2	1.9	1.5	4.6
Kazakhstan	2006	Other					0.1
Kazakhstan	2006	**Solid fuel**	**6.8**	**6.3**	**26.6**	**25.2**	**35.6**
Kyrgyzstan	2006	Electricity	28.7	29.5	32.1	33.3	27.4
Kyrgyzstan	2006	Liquid Propane Gas (LPG)	9.3	12.1	4.2	4.6	2.8
Kyrgyzstan	2006	Natural gas	49.2	28.4	14.4	17.6	2.1
Kyrgyzstan	2006	Coal/Lignite	6.2	12.7	16.3	17.1	12.8

COUNTRY	YEAR	TYPE OF COOKING OIL	URBAN	NON SLUM HOUSEHOLD	SLUM HOUSEHOLD	ONE SHELTER DEPRIVATION	TWO SHELTER DEPRIVATIONS
Kyrgyzstan	2006	Charcoal	2.4	3.2	4.9	3.0	12.2
Kyrgyzstan	2006	Wood	2.7	10.7	17.9	16.3	24.3
Kyrgyzstan	2006	Straw/shrubs/grass			0.1	0.1	
Kyrgyzstan	2006	Animal dung/pressed dung	0.4	2.4	6.7	6.2	8.8
Kyrgyzstan	2006	Agricultural crop residue	0.6	0.6	3.1	1.7	8.6
Kyrgyzstan	2006	Other (specify)	0.2	0.1	0.3	0.1	1.0
Kyrgyzstan	2006	Missing	0.3	0.2	0.1	0.1	0.0
Kyrgyzstan	2006	**Solid fuel**	**6.2**	**16.9**	**32.6**	**27.2**	**53.9**
Mongolia	2006	Electricity	38.5	80.0	18.3	28.2	11.5
Mongolia	2006	Liquid propane gas (LPG)	0.6	0.9	0.3	0.4	0.2
Mongolia	2006	Coal/lignite	31.0	5.3	20.5	27.8	15.5
Mongolia	2006	Briquette	0.2		0.2	0.1	0.3
Mongolia	2006	Wood	24.8	8.4	34.0	27.0	38.7
Mongolia	2006	Straw/shrubs/grass	0.2	0.2	1.1	0.5	1.5
Mongolia	2006	Animal dung	3.9	5.0	24.8	15.0	31.4
Mongolia	2006	Agricultural crop residue		0.2			
Mongolia	2006	Sawdust	0.7		0.5	0.8	0.3
Mongolia	2006	Other	0.1		0.3	0.1	0.4
Mongolia	2006	**Solid fuel**	**60.9**	**19.1**	**81.1**	**71.3**	**87.9**
Nepal	2006	Electricity	0.4	0.8			
Nepal	2006	LPG	40.2	59.9	20.9	35.2	6.2
Nepal	2006	Natural gas	0.2		0.3	0.6	
Nepal	2006	Biogas	3.3	3.2	3.4	4.6	2.1
Nepal	2006	Kerosene	15.8	16.0	15.6	20.2	10.7
Nepal	2006	Charcoal	0.1	0.2	0.1	0.2	
Nepal	2006	Wood	35.6	18.2	52.4	35.5	69.9
Nepal	2006	Straw/shrubs/grass	0.6		1.2	0.2	2.2
Nepal	2006	Agricultural crop	0.2		0.4	0.8	
Nepal	2006	Animal dung	2.5	0.3	4.7	1.4	8.1
Nepal	2006	No food cooked in HH	0.5	1.0	0.1		0.1
Nepal	2006	Other	0.6	0.3	0.9	1.3	0.5
Nepal	2006	**Solid fuel**	**39.1**	**18.7**	**58.9**	**38.1**	**80.3**
Tajikistan	2006	Electricity	52.0	47.8	46.4	46.1	46.7
Tajikistan	2006	Liquid propane gas (LPG)	10.5	13.4	3.6	5.0	2.3
Tajikistan	2006	Natural gas	29.8	34.2	11.5	15.7	7.7
Tajikistan	2006	Kerosene	0.0			0.1	
Tajikistan	2006	Coal/lignite	0.4	0.5	0.8	0.6	1.0
Tajikistan	2006	Wood	6.5	2.6	29.1	28.4	29.8
Tajikistan	2006	Straw/shrubs/grass	0.1	0.2	2.3	0.8	3.8
Tajikistan	2006	Animal dung	0.5	0.8	3.4	2.2	4.5
Tajikistan	2006	Agricultural crop residue		0.2	2.8	1.2	4.3
Tajikistan	2006	Other	0.1	0.3			
Tajikistan	2006	**Solid fuel**	**7.5**	**4.3**	**38.4**	**33.1**	**43.2**
Thailand	2006	Electricity	6.0	3.8	2.3	2.4	2.0
Thailand	2006	Liquid propane gas (LPG)	69.3	62.5	45.9	46.8	42.0
Thailand	2006	Biogas	0.2	0.3	0.3	0.3	0.3
Thailand	2006	Kerosene					0.1
Thailand	2006	Coal/lignite		0.1			
Thailand	2006	Charcoal	5.3	12.2	24.5	24.0	26.7
Thailand	2006	Wood	4.3	11.4	23.8	22.9	27.8
Thailand	2006	Straw/shrubs/grass					
Thailand	2006	Animal dung					
Thailand	2006	Agricultural crop residue			0.2	0.2	0.1
Thailand	2006	Other					
Thailand	2006	No Cooking	14.8	9.7	3.0	3.5	1.1
Thailand	2006	**Solid fuel**	**9.6**	**23.6**	**48.5**	**47.0**	**54.6**
Uzbekistan	2006	Electricity	2.0	1.2	1.1	1.0	1.4
Uzbekistan	2006	Liquid propane gas (LPG)	3.0	2.5	2.8	2.6	3.8
Uzbekistan	2006	Natural gas	94.4	81.7	79.8	82.5	67.5

COUNTRY	YEAR	TYPE OF COOKING OIL	URBAN	NON SLUM HOUSEHOLD	SLUM HOUSEHOLD	ONE SHELTER DEPRIVATION	TWO SHELTER DEPRIVATIONS
Uzbekistan	2006	Kerosene					0.1
Uzbekistan	2006	Coal/lignite					0.1
Uzbekistan	2006	Charcoal		0.1	0.1	0.1	0.2
Uzbekistan	2006	Wood	0.6	14.4	15.1	13.2	23.9
Uzbekistan	2006	Agricultural crop residue			0.9	0.5	2.9
Uzbekistan	2006	Other			0.1		0.2
Uzbekistan	2006	**Solid fuel**	**0.7**	**14.5**	**16.1**	**13.8**	**27.0**

COUNTRY	YEAR	TYPE OF COOKING OIL	URBAN	NON SLUM HOUSEHOLD	SLUM HOUSEHOLD	ONE SHELTER DEPRIVATION	TWO SHELTER DEPRIVATIONS
Belarus	2006	Electricity	13.7	16.9	4.7	4.2	17.0
Belarus	2006	Liquid propane gas (LPG)	9.2	8.5	38.3	37.7	52.4
Belarus	2006	Natural gas	76.7	74.1	51.4	52.5	26.0
Belarus	2006	Wood	0.4	0.5	5.5	5.6	4.6
Belarus	2006	**Solid fuel**	**0.4**	**0.5**	**5.5**	**5.6**	**4.6**
Belarus	2006	Electricity	66.9	47.4	21.5	22.9	8.7
Belarus	2006	Liquid propane gas (LPG)	9.4	6.2	1.5	1.6	0.6
Belarus	2006	Natural gas	5.2	2.7	0.3	0.3	
Belarus	2006	Coal/lignite	1.3	0.8			0.3
Belarus	2006	Charcoal	0.2	0.4	0.1	0.1	0.0
Belarus	2006	Wood	17.0	42.5	76.5	75.0	90.1
Belarus	2006	Straw/shrubs/grass		0.1	0.1		0.3
Belarus	2006	**Solid fuel**	**18.5**	**43.7**	**76.6**	**75.1**	**90.7**
Macedonia	2006	Electricity	71.5	64.9	51.4	54.3	37.6
Macedonia	2006	Liquid propane gas (LPG)	3.8	3.0	1.4	1.7	0.1
Macedonia	2006	Coal/lignite	0.3	0.3			
Macedonia	2006	Charcoal	0.3	0.3	0.1	0.1	0.2
Macedonia	2006	Wood	23.8	31.4	47.0	43.9	62.0
Macedonia	2006	Straw/shrubs/grass					
Macedonia	2006	Other	0.2	0.2			
Macedonia	2006	Missing					0.1
Macedonia	2006	**Solid fuel**	**24.5**	**32.0**	**47.1**	**44.0**	**62.2**
Moldova	2005	Electricity	5.4	6.0	2.8	2.9	2.3
Moldova	2005	LPG	18.3	13.7	35.5	34.1	41.3
Moldova	2005	Natural gas	74.8	79.5	57.6	60.0	47.2
Moldova	2005	Biogas	0.2	0.2	0.1	0.1	
Moldova	2005	Wood	0.8	0.3	2.8	1.8	6.8
Moldova	2005	Straw / shrubs / grass	0.2	0.1	0.6	0.6	0.6
Moldova	2005	Agricultural crop	0.1	0.1	0.3	0.2	0.6
Moldova	2005	Animal dung					
Moldova	2005	Other	0.1	0.1	0.3	0.2	1.1
Moldova	2005	**Solid fuel**	**1.2**	**0.5**	**3.7**	**2.7**	**8.0**
Montenegro	2006	Electricity	80.1	78.4	36.7	42.7	16.5
Montenegro	2006	Gas from bottle	2.1	2.2	1.4	1.5	0.8
Montenegro	2006	Coal/lignite	2.9	1.3	9.0	9.8	6.4
Montenegro	2006	Charcoal	0.7	0.2	1.2	0.8	2.7
Montenegro	2006	Wood	14.2	17.9	51.7	45.3	73.6
Montenegro	2006	**Solid fuel**	**17.9**	**19.4**	**61.9**	**55.8**	**82.7**
Serbia	2006	Electricity	70.4	57.2	29.7	32.2	13.2
Serbia	2006	Gas from bottle	9.2	9.1	6.1	7.0	0.5
Serbia	2006	Gas from gas pipeline	6.2	6.0	2.7	3.1	0.3
Serbia	2006	Coal/lignite	0.9	1.3	1.3	1.5	0.1
Serbia	2006	Charcoal		0.1			
Serbia	2006	Wood	12.9	25.8	59.6	55.8	84.1
Serbia	2006	Straw/shrubs/grass					0.1
Serbia	2006	Agricultural crop residue		0.1	0.4	0.3	1.0
Serbia	2006	Other	0.2	0.2	0.2	0.1	0.7
Serbia	2006	Missing	0.3	0.2	0.0		
Serbia	2006	**Solid fuel**	**13.7**	**27.3**	**61.3**	**57.5**	**85.3**

Gini coefficients for urban at national level, selected countries

AFRICA	URBAN Year	URBAN Gini Coefficient
Algeria1	1995ᵢ	0.35
Benin	2007ᶜ	0.47
Botswana	2001-02ᵢ	0.50
Burkina Faso	2003ᶜ	0.48
Burundi	2006ᶜ	0.49
Cameroon	2001ᵢ	0.41
Central African Republic	2003ᶜ	0.42
Côte d'Ivoire	2008ᵢ	0.44
Democratic Republic of Congo	2004-05ᶜ	0.40
Egypt	1997ᶜ	0.39
Ethiopia	2004-05ᶜ	0.44
Ethiopia	1999-00ᵢ	0.57
Kenya	1999ᵢ	0.55
Kenya	2006ᶜ	0.45
Malawi	1998ᶜ	0.52
Mauritania	2004ᶜ	0.39
Morocco	1998ᶜ	0.38
Mozambique	2002-03ᶜ	0.48
Namibia	1993ᵢ	0.63
Namibia	2003ᶜ	0.58
Nigeria	2006ᵢ	0.54
South Africa	2005ᵢ	0.76
Togo	2006ᶜ	0.31
Uganda	2005-06ᵢ	0.43
Zambia	2006ᵢ	0.66
Zimbabwe	1998ᵢ	0.60

ASIA		
Bangladesh	2000ᶜ	0.37
Cambodia	2004ᶜ	0.43
China	2002ᵢ	0.32
India	2004ᶜ	0.37
Indonesia	1999ᶜ	0.33
Malaysia	1999ᵢ	0.42
Mongolia	2006ᶜ	0.39
Nepal	1996ᵢ	0.43
Pakistan	2004ᶜ	0.34
Philippines	2003ᵢ	0.45
Sri Lanka	2006-07ᶜ	0.43
Sri Lanka	2006-07ᵢ	0.55
Viet Nam	2002ᵢ	0.41

LATIN AMERICA AND THE CARIBBEAN	URBAN Year	URBAN Gini Coefficient
Argentina	2006ᵢ	0.52
Bolivia	2007ᵢ	0.50
Brazil	2007ᵢ	0.58
Chile	2006ᵢ	0.52
Colombia	2005ᵢ	0.59
Costa Rica	2007ᵢ	0.48
Dominican Republic	2007ᵢ	0.56
Ecuador	2007ᵢ	0.52
El Salvador	2004ᵢ	0.46
Guatemala	2006ᵢ	0.55
Honduras	2007ᵢ	0.49
Mexico	2006ᵢ	0.48
Nicaragua	2005ᵢ	0.50
Panama	2007ᵢ	0.47
Paraguay	2007ᵢ	0.48
Peru	2004ᵢ	0.47
Uruguay	2007ᵢ	0.46
Venezuela	1990ᵢ	0.46

EASTERN EUROPE AND COMMONWEALTH INDEPENDENT STATES (CIS)		
Albania	2002ᵢ	0.29
Armenia	2001ᵢ	0.28
Azerbaijan	2001ᵢ	0.40
Belarus	2001ᵢ	0.24
Bulgaria	2001ᵢ	0.28
Georgia	2001ᵢ	0.36
Hungary	2000ᵢ	0.29
Kazakhstan	2001ᵢ	0.29
Kosovo	2002ᵢ	0.29
Kyrgyz Republic	2001ᵢ	0.28
Lithuania	2000ᵢ	0.31
Moldova	2001ᵢ	0.40
Poland	2001ᵢ	0.33
Romania	2002ᵢ	0.27
Russia	2001ᵢ	0.44
Serbia	2002ᵢ	0.29
Tajikistan	1999ᵢ	0.36
Turkmenistan	1998ᵢ	0.40
Uzbekistan	2000ᵢ	0.29

Gini coefficients for selected cities and provinces

Country	City	Year	Gini
AFRICA			
Burundi	Bujumbura	2006ᶜ	0.47
Cameroon	Yaounde	1996ⁱ	0.44
Cameroon	Douala	1996ⁱ	0.46
Central African Republic	Bangui	2003ᶜ	0.42
Congo	Brazzaville	2005ⁱ	0.45
Congo	Pointe-Noire	2005ⁱ	0.39
Côte d'Ivoire	Abidjan	2008ⁱ	0.50
D R Congo	Kinshasa	2004-05ᶜ	0.39
Ethiopia	Addis Ababa	2003ⁱ	0.61
Ethiopia	Addis Ababa	2003ᶜ	0.56
Ethiopia	Bahir Dar	2000ᶜ	0.36
Ethiopia	Jimma	2000ᶜ	0.36
Ethiopia	Dire Dawa	2000ᶜ	0.39
Ethiopia	Mekelle	2000ᶜ	0.39
Ethiopia	Awassa	2000ᶜ	0.41
Ethiopia	Dessie	2000ᶜ	0.49
Gabon	Libreville and Port Gentil	1996ⁱ	0.45
Ghana	Accra	1992ⁱ	0.50
Guinea- Bissau	Bissau	2006ᶜ	0.37
Kenya	Nairobi	2006ⁱ	0.59
Lesotho	Maseru	1993ⁱ	0.58
Morocco	Casablanca	2006ⁱ	0.52
Mozambique	Maputo	2002-03ᶜ	0.52
Nigeria	Lagos	2006	0.64
Rwanda	Kigali	2005ⁱ	0.47
Senegal	Dakar	2001-02ᶜ	0.37
Sierra Leone	Freetown	2002ᶜ	0.32
South Africa	Buffalo City (East London)	2005ⁱ	0.75
South Africa	Cape Town	2005ⁱ	0.67
South Africa	Ekurhuleni (East Rand)	2005ⁱ	0.74
South Africa	eThekwini (Durban)	2005ⁱ	0.72
South Africa	Johannesburg	2005ⁱ	0.75
South Africa	Mangaug (Bloemfontein)	2005ⁱ	0.74
South Africa	Msunduzi (Pietermaritzburg)	2005ⁱ	0.73
South Africa	Nelson Mandela Bay (Port Elizabeth)	2005ⁱ	0.72
South Africa	Tshwane (Pretoria)	2005ⁱ	0.72
Tanzania	Dar es Salaam	2007ᶜ	0.34

Country	City	Year	Gini
Togo	Lome	2006ᶜ	0.30
Uganda	Kampala	2002ᶜ	0.47
LATIN AMERICA AND THE CARIBBEAN			
Argentina	Buenos Aires	2005ⁱ	0.52
Argentina	Formosa	2005ⁱ	0.44
Argentina	Catamarca	2005ⁱ	0.55
Brazil	Belo Horizonte	2005ⁱ	0.61
Brazil	Brasilia	2007ⁱ	0.60
Brazil	Curitiba	2005ⁱ	0.59
Brazil	Fortaleza	2005ⁱ	0.61
Brazil	Goiania	2005ⁱ	0.65
Brazil	Rio de Janeiro	2007ⁱ	0.53
Brazil	São Paulo	2007ⁱ	0.50
Chile	Santiago	2006ⁱ	0.55
Chile	Chillan	2006ⁱ	0.51
Colombia	Bogotá	2005ⁱ	0.61
Colombia	Cali	1998ⁱ	0.54
Colombia	Medellín	1998ⁱ	0.51
Colombia	Barranquilla	1998ⁱ	0.57
Ecuador	Quito	1999ⁱ	0.54
Guatemala	Guatemala city	2004ⁱ	0.50
Mexico	Mexico city	2005ⁱ	0.56
Mexico	Guadalajara	2005ⁱ	0.40
Nicaragua	Managua	2001ⁱ	0.42
Haiti	Port-Au-Prince	2005ⁱ	0.52
Uruguay	Montevideo	2006ⁱ	0.45
Venezuela	Caracas	2007ⁱ	0.39
ASIA			
Bangladesh	Chittagong	2000ᶜ	0.29
Bangladesh	Dhaka	2000ᶜ	0.31
Bangladesh	Khulna	2000ᶜ	0.35
Cambodia	Phnom Penh	2004ᶜ	0.37
China	Beijing	2003ⁱ	0.22
China	Hong Kong	2001ⁱ	0.53
China	Shanghai	2004-05ⁱ	0.32
China	Wuhan	2004-05ⁱ	0.37
China	Shengyan	2004-05ⁱ	0.37
China	Fuzhou	2004-05ⁱ	0.34
China	Xian	2004-05ⁱ	0.35
China	Wuxi	2004-05ⁱ	0.39
China	Yichan	2004-05ⁱ	0.42
China	Benxi	2004-05ⁱ	0.29

Country	City	Year	Gini
China	Zhuhai	2004-05ⁱ	0.45
China	Baoji	2004-05ⁱ	0.34
China	Daqing	2004-05ⁱ	0.41
China	Shenzhen	2004-05ⁱ	0.49
India	Andhra Pradeshᵖ	2004ᶜ	0.37
India	Assamᵖ	2004ᶜ	0.31
India	Biharᵖ	2004ᶜ	0.33
India	Gujaratᵖ	2004ᶜ	0.30
India	Haryanaᵖ	2004ᶜ	0.36
India	Karnatakaᵖ	2004ᶜ	0.37
India	Keralaᵖ	2004ᶜ	0.40
India	Madhya Pradeshᵖ	2004ᶜ	0.39
India	Maharashtraᵖ	2004ᶜ	0.37
India	Orissaᵖ	2004ᶜ	0.35
India	Punjabᵖ	2004ᶜ	0.39
India	Rajasthanᵖ	2004ᶜ	0.37
India	Tamil Nadup	2004ᶜ	0.36
India	Uttar Pradeshᵖ	2004ᶜ	0.37
India	West Bengalᵖ	2004ᶜ	0.38
Indonesia	Jakarta	2005ᶜ	0.27
Jordan	Amman	1997ⁱ	0.39
Jordan	Irbid	1997ⁱ	0.31
Jordan	Zarqa & Mafrq	1997ⁱ	0.33
Jordan	Balqa & Madaba	1997ⁱ	0.35
Jordan	Jerash & Ajloun	1997ⁱ	0.31
Malaysia	Kuala Lumpur	1999ⁱ	0.41
Malaysia	Johor Bahru	1999ⁱ	0.37
Malaysia	Kuching	1999ⁱ	0.38
Malaysia	Ipoh	1999ⁱ	0.37
Mongolia	Ulaanbaatar	2006ᶜ	0.37
Philippines	Manila	2006ⁱ	0.40
Philippines	Cebu City	2003ⁱ	0.38
Philippines	Davao City	2003ⁱ	0.44
Philippines	Zamboanga	2003ⁱ	0.42

Country	City	Year	Gini
Sri Lanka	Colombo City	2002ⁱ	0.46
Viet Nam	Ha Noi (Red Delta region)	2002ⁱ	0.39
Thailand	Bangkok	2006	0.48
Thailand	Nonthaburiᵖ	2006	0.43
Thailand	Samutprakanᵖ	2006	0.34
Thailand	Nakhon Ratchasimaᵖ	2006	0.49
Thailand	Songkhlaᵖ	2006	0.49
Thailand	Chonburiᵖ	2006	0.36
Thailand	Udonthaniᵖ	2006	0.56
Thailand	Chiangmaiᵖ	2006	0.58
Viet Nam	Ho Chi Minh City	2002ⁱ	0.53

EASTERN EUROPE AND THE COMMONWEALTH INDEPENDENT STATES (CIS)			
Albania	Tirana	2002ⁱ	0.30
Bulgaria	Sofia	2001ⁱ	0.25
Hungary	Budapest	2000ⁱ	0.30
Lithuania	Vilnius	2000ⁱ	0.31
Moldova	Kishinev	2001ⁱ	0.37
Poland	Warsaw	2001ⁱ	0.31
Romania	Bucharest	2002ⁱ	0.26
Serbia	Belgrade	2002ⁱ	0.28
Armenia	Yerevan	2001ⁱ	0.31
Azerbaijan	Baku	2001ⁱ	0.38
Belarus	Minsk	2001ⁱ	0.23
Georgia	Tbilisi	2001ⁱ	0.37
Kazakhstan	Astana	2001ⁱ	0.26
Kyrgyz Republic	Bishkek	2001ⁱ	0.27
Russia	Moscow	2001ⁱ	0.47
Tajikistan	Dushanbe	1999ⁱ	0.36
Turkmenistan	Ashgabat	1998ⁱ	0.29
Uzbekistan	Tashkent	2000ⁱ	0.28

i. Refers to Gini coefficients based on Income
c. Refers to Gini Coefficients based on consumption
p. Province (urban)

Percentage of female and male aged 15-24 years non-employed by shelter deprivation

Country	Year	FEMALE							MALE						
		Urban	Rural	Non Slum	One Shelter Deprivation	Two Shelter Deprivations	Three Shelter Deprivations	All Slum	Urban	Rural	Non Slum	One Shelter Deprivation	Two Shelter Deprivations	Three Shelter Deprivations	All Slum
AFRICA															
Benin	1996	22.4	9.2	27.5	23.3	14.9	14.6	19.1	19.0	6.0	19.8	30.3	10.5		18.6
Benin	2001	14.4	5.5	20.1	13.4	7.9	9.5	11.3	47.5	28.7	59.3	45.0	28.9	21.8	38.7
Burkina Faso	1999	29.0	21.3	32.0	28.8	30.8		28.7	9.6	5.2	4.8	9.6	9.1	20.4	9.9
Burkina Faso	2003	13.8	1.4	14.2	13.0	12.6	8.3	12.7	2.7	4.7	2.8		24.5		2.7
Cameroon	1991	38.3	28.9	21.2	41.4	45.9	41.5	42.5	1.9						
Cameroon	1998	27.9	20.1	23.0	31.4	37.1	24.4	33.0	8.8	6.9					
Cameroon	2004	31.0	18.5	28.3	33.6	37.2	14.1	33.1	8.3	10.4					
Central African Republic	1994	31.8	17.6	26.9	32.5	37.5	29.3	30.9	9.3	8.1	7.4	9.4	8.8	5.7	13.0
Chad	1996	39.9	35.9	50.6	52.9	41.2	33.9	39.0	11.1	2.9	32.9	0.0	13.9	7.8	9.6
Chad	2004	11.3	1.4	13.7	10.9	12.5	12.3	7.9	8.4	8.2	6.8	8.6	7.6	10.0	9.6
Comoros	1996	42.4	43.5	38.2	41.2	50.3	64.3	45.0	21.8	29.1	19.0	20.7	18.8	60.0	23.5
Congo	2005	28.9	15.5	25.8	30.8	32.6	28.3	26.0							
Côte d'Ivoire	1994	36.1	26.2	33.2	41.4	40.8		40.8	15.4	3.3	16.7	15.0	7.5	31.7	14.3
Côte d'Ivoire	1999	29.3	11.5	25.8	35.7	27.1		33.6	13.3	7.2	10.4	15.7	17.6	12.7	15.6
Egypt	1992	77.3	77.3	74.7	78.6	88.2	100.0	80.91							
Egypt	1995	88.7	89.7	88.3	87.5	97.4	100.0	90.73							
Egypt	2000	90.6	93.0	90.6	85.6	96.0	100.0	90.80							
Egypt	2003	87.4	87.6	87.4	86.6	88.9		87.18							
Egypt	2005	91.2	90.0	91.9	90.0	90.4	90.5	50.0							
Ethiopia	2005	26.3	57.6	27.0	25.8	24.8	23.7	28.7							
Gabon	2000	32.2	37.2	28.1	37.2	37.5	38.0	37.3	8.2	9.9	5.0	11.3	12.0	15.8	11.8
Ghana	1993	38.6	28.7	39.7	38.5	37.0	20	38.0	32.4	19.1	25.5	30.2	46.7	37.5	35.9
Ghana	1999	29.5	25.2	29.0	29.0	33.3	75.0	30.3	21.8	14.1	26.8	21.7	14.9		19.5
Ghana	2003	29.6	18.7	31.0	25.5	33.2	58.3	27.5	22.5	14.6	28.2	21.6	14.3		19.5
Guinea	1999	26.1	17.6	26.0	28.1	22.3	30.8	26.1	12.3	5.1	15.7	8.9	13.1	14.2	12.1
Guinea	2005	17.4	16.9	18.8	14.4	10.2	23.2	18.8							
Kenya	1998	39.1	32.6	33.9	44.8	44.5	41.8	44.2	29.6	22.2	32.4	32.3	22.4	24.7	28.5
Kenya	2003	25.6	19.4	22.6	27.8	28.9	28.9	28.3	21.9	17.6	25.2	20.8	15.4	32.4	20.3
Madagascar	1997	25.4	17.3	22.3	27.3	27.7	21.5	25.6							
Mali	1996	40.5	43.7	32.8	38.6	38.5	49.1	40.9	18.0	13.4		12.7	23.0	23.7	18.7
Mali	2001	34.8	38.9	21.6	31.1	32.4		34.3	2.4	0.8	4.9	2.5			1.3
Morocco	1992	45.8	73.6	43.6	59.6	67.9	87.5	61.61							
Morocco	2004	49.6	78.3	47.7	61.5	73.1	87.5	62.5							
Mozambique	1997	55.6	29.4	22.3	55.5	55.8	78.0	59.8	19.5	28.7	13.7	19.1	16.8	30.7	20.2
Mozambique	2003	46.1	19.1	20.4	49.2	49.7	40.9	49.0	22.0	24.5	13.3	21.1	22.7	27.4	23.3
Niger	1998	66.1	45.3	54.9	65.1	64.7	78.3	66.4	17.2	3.8					
Nigeria	1990	36.8	43.5	34.6	37.6	37.8	37.0	37.5							
Nigeria	1999	32.8	44.2	27.6	31.6	35.6	64.4	35.2	18.8	14.5	25.8	15.9	18.1	17.8	16.9
Nigeria	2003	29.2	38.0	23.7	27.9	35.2	40.3	31.8	15.7	14.6	23.1	12.3	14.9	19.3	13.8
Rwanda	2000	35.6	8.7	15.1	50.4	32.4	26.6	39.3							

Country	Year	FEMALE							MALE						
		Urban	Rural	Non Slum	One Shelter Deprivation	Two Shelter Deprivations	Three Shelter Deprivations	All Slum	Urban	Rural	Non Slum	One Shelter Deprivation	Two Shelter Deprivations	Three Shelter Deprivations	All Slum
Rwanda	2005	26.7	20.1	29.1	25.2	29.6	22.8	16.7	17.5	30.9	14.6	19.9	14.6	18.9	36.6
Senegal	1997	49.4	48.1	37.9	49.4	51.7	62.9	50.7							
Senegal	2005	36.8	53.5	35.5	40.1	39.5	42.7	34.1	10.2	15.2	11.6	8.5	19.3	4.3	11.6
South Africa	1998	26.9	31.0	25.0	33.3	31.6	33.3	33.0							
Togo	1998	14.3	16.1	13.5	15.5	11.7	14.5	14.8	11.0	9.8					
Uganda	1995	41.7	32.7	28.9	39.8	46.8	46.6	43.7	8.7	5.9	7.0	12.2	9.0	4.2	8.9
Uganda	2001	39.3	21.4	25.2	41.0	39.9	41.3	41.8	11.6	7.6	7.9	20.3	9.6	5.3	11.7
Tanzania	1992	36.2	26.1	39.0	38.3	38.0	20.2	35.9							
Tanzania	1996	48.1	38.9	40.2	50.1	47.7	47.1	49.0							
Tanzania	1999	32.9	14.9	17.0	31.5	40.6	25.0	34.7							
Tanzania	2004	32.1	8.8	31.8	32.2	37.6	26.0	32.5	17.7	7.1	25.7	13.7	13.9	13.2	25.7
Zambia	1996	47.2	48.9	46.7	48.5	44.4	51.0	47.7							
Zambia	2002	46.1	38.2	46.0	49.5	41.6	48.1	47.3	19.3	17.5	19.9	14.3	24.0		16.3
Zimbabwe	1994	40.1	36.4	37.2	55.4	61.8	66.7	57.4							
Zimbabwe	1999	40.1	36.5	38.8	36.0	52.8		43.4	30.7	21.4	34.1	4.0			6.1

LATIN AMERICA AND THE CARRIBEAN

Country	Year	Urban	Rural	Non Slum	One Shelter Deprivation	Two Shelter Deprivations	Three Shelter Deprivations	All Slum	Urban	Rural	Non Slum	One Shelter Deprivation	Two Shelter Deprivations	Three Shelter Deprivations	All Slum
Bolivia	1994	19.0	26.7	12.7	22.3	25.4	44.9	25.0							
Bolivia	1998	13.3	37.6	7.3	13.0	23.9	31.4	16.5							
Bolivia	2004	11.2	30.2	6.4	10.6	18.9	29.4	13.5	3.5	4.6	3.7	3.7	3.2		3.1
Brazil	1996	18.7	35.6	17.5	18.8	22.3	41.2	20.1	2.8	1.0	3.5	2.9	0.5		2.1
Colombia	1995	20.2	41.7	18.9	34.3	36.9	50.0	35.4							
Colombia	2000	21.9	42.6	21.0	30.8	37.7	25.0	32.0							
Guatemala	1998	40.3	57.8	30.5	49.6	69.5	71.4	57.3							
Haiti	1994	31.0	39.8	24.9	34.0	42.0	53.5	36.2							
Haiti	2000	29.1	33.4	23.3	32.8	40.6	39.2	34.7	14.9	12.5					
Nicaragua	1998	27.8	61.7	16.8	29.6	39.1	40.7	34.4	4.4	6.9	2.2	4.9	5.5	5.2	5.3
Nicaragua	2001	26.6	60.5	17.2	26.2	35.5	57.2	31.3							
Paraguay	1990	13.1	43.4	8.5	18.0	15.6	24.7	17.7							
Peru	1991	13.1	43.4	8.5	18.0	15.6	24.7	17.7							
Peru	1996	17.3	34.6	13.9	18.5	23.4	30.1	22.0	5.6	1.4	7.7	2.6	3.7	8.5	3.9
Peru	2000	17.6	30.6	14.2	19.4	22.5	31.2	22.4							

ASIA

Country	Year	Urban	Rural	Non Slum	One Shelter Deprivation	Two Shelter Deprivations	Three Shelter Deprivations	All Slum	Urban	Rural	Non Slum	One Shelter Deprivation	Two Shelter Deprivations	Three Shelter Deprivations	All Slum
Armenia	2005	13.9	7.9	14.5	9.9	9.1	22.1								
Bangladesh	1996	69.4	66.4	67.8	81.6	57.3	100.0	70.7	7.2	2.6		20.9			13.9
Bangladesh	1999	72.8	80.0	66.8	79.2	78.1	75.0	78.3							
Bangladesh	2004	68.7	76.1	64.6	70.4	70.2	69.7	73.5							
India	1999	84.5	64.4	88.0	80.4	79.0		80.3							
Kazakhstan	1999	27.7	38.9	19.6	31.6	30.3	39.2	32.5	19.7	37.4	15.5	12.1	31.0	43.7	22.7
Kyrgyzstan	1997	26.1	47.2	16.2	14.0	32.8	54.8	29.4							
Moldova	2005	66.2	78.0	65.0	69.5	66.1	75.6	100.0							
Nepal	1996	52.7	19.4	84.8	71.3	38.0	6.1	47.8							
Nepal	2002	45.2	22.7	61.0	45.3	34.7	0.0	35.1							
Pakistan	1990	84.2	82.6	82.7	88.9	85.7	84.2	88.5							
Philippines	1998	15.3	30.6	12.6	19.8	28.6	33.3	22.2							
Philippines	2003	17.6	31.5	23.5	14.3	23.3	34.0	25.9							
Turkey	1993	84.5	53.3	85.6	82.5	89.7	33.3	81.4							
Turkey	1998	49.5	41.8	51.3	47.3	32.4	33.3	45.5	1.2	15.5	2.2				
Uzbekistan	1996	42.7	46.8	29.5	40.4	47.2	45.7	45.2							
Viet Nam	2002	16.7	10.4	18.8	12.5	16.7		12.5							
Yemen	1991	88.2	86.1	92.9	75.4	89.7	100.0	81.3							

Percentage of female and male aged 15-24 years in the informal employment by shelter deprivation

Country	Year	FEMALE							MALE						
		Urban	Rural	Non Slum	All Slum	One Shelter Deprivation	Two Shelter Deprivations	Three Shelter Deprivations	Urban	Rural	Non Slum	All Slum	One Shelter Deprivation	Two Shelter Deprivations	Three Shelter Deprivations
NORTHERN AFRICA															
Egypt	1992	4.7	18.1	0.0	12.8	14.3									
Egypt	1995	15.5	40.4	14.3	12.5	16.7									
Egypt	2000	13.7	17.5	12.5	20.0	28.6									
Egypt	2003	19.6	17.1	23.7											
Egypt	2005	22.4	27.1	17.6	29.3	40.6	19.9								
SUB-SAHARAN AFRICA															
Benin	1996	92.9	97.0	89.4	94.9	91.2	98.2		71.4	66.7					
Benin	2001	91.0	97.6	84.2	94.3	93.3	94.8		68.2	84.3	58.1	81.1	77.0	85.2	100.0
Benin	2006	79.8	91.7	87.6	79.3	87.2	78.3	88.8	69.8	82.3	28.3	76.5	64.5	79.8	
Burkina Faso	1992	87.5	97.6	76.9	88.1	88.5	87.7	88.2							
Burkina Faso	1999	84.0	99.1	42.9	85.2	85.7	81.8		55.7	85.7	40.0	68.4	58.3	71.7	81.1
Burkina Faso	2003	82.8	95.6	83.0	82.3	77.8	91.3		20.7	31.0					
Cameroon	1991	78.8	93.8	69.6	82.0	80.0	80.6	90.0							
Cameroon	1998	69.9	84.4	65.4	75.0	74.4	74.5	85.7	62.0	60.2					
Central African Republic	1994	96.8	98.0	88.9	97.2	96.8	97.0	98.0	75.2	81.1	100.0	77.0	86.2	82.9	70.0
Chad	1996	99.3	99.2	90.9	99.2	96.2	100.0	99.3	71.3	74.2					
Chad	2004	83.6	84.1	83.2	83.7	85.5	85.3	80.9	60.2	68.9	73.4	58.6	50.4	63.6	73.6
Comoros	1996	93.4	95.6	88.2	90.4	94.1	100.0	93.4	54.5	78.8	81.8	65.9	62.5	61.9	80.0
Congo	2005	92.5	97.5	90.3	93.7	94.8	90.9	97.7	52.0	66.3	50.6	52.7	52.3	51.3	67.0
Côte d'Ivoire	1994	88.0	95.0	84.8	93.6	94.1	92.0								
Côte d'Ivoire	1998	77.6	81.7	68.4	88.9	88.8	92.6		35.3	42.4	37.9	36.6	26.8	52.0	40.0
Ethiopia	2000	86.2	98.5	90.9	86.1	80.8	87.6	93.8							
Ethiopia	2005	69.9	93.4	55.7	73.0	65.2	73.3	90.4	16.8	30.6	11.5	17.7	21.7	18.5	9.7
Gabon	2000	75.6	83.0	74.1	77.2	79.3	73.1	70.0	71.0	62.1	68.8	70.9	73.8	66.7	62.5
Ghana	1993	80.8	94.0	82.1	79.9	80.0	81.5	50.0							
Ghana	1999	79.7	92.4	77.6	82.4	82.8	83.3	100.0	43.1	44.6	46.9	42.3	40.7	41.7	55.6
Ghana	2003	85.2	95.2	81.3	89.5	88.9	94.1		30.1	29.4	28.6	30.8	31.9	25.4	71.4
Guinea	1998	82.1	89.2	69.0	83.0	81.6	85.1	84.2	64.7	83.1	33.3	72.6	68.3	69.6	79.2
Guinea	2005	98.6	96.9	99.0	97.8	96.9	100.0	100.0							
Kenya	1993	45.4	64.2	35.3	58.2	53.7	60.0								
Kenya	1998	54.4	74.5	52.9	56.7	58.4	56.5	46.7	50.0	55.6	41.4	55.8	50.0	42.2	64.0
Kenya	2003	63.8	73.1	57.6	70.4	67.5	72.5	86.7	5.3	11.7	8.3	9.0	5.9	11.3	10.8
Madagascar	1997	77.7	90.5	78.3	77.3	78.1	69.7	94.7							
Malawi	2000	72.6	92.7	52.8	80.2	78.2	85.7	66.7							
Mali	1996	93.7	98.2	72.7	94.2	92.5	94.1	97.3	62.6	89.8					
Mali	2001	91.2	96.1	89.6	92.1	92.1	91.4		53.3	56.0					
Morocco	1992	23.4	62.5	22.1	25.1	21.8	50.0	66.7							
Morocco	2004	50.2	71.5	49.8	52.9	35.0	66.7								
Mozambique	1997	63.9	83.3	24.0	71.8	68.7	72.7	86.7	46.8	63.9	0.0	56.7	46.7	48.1	62.5
Mozambique	2003	70.9	88.6	65.6	71.7	68.9	72.8	88.2	8.5	12.9	7.1	9.8	7.9	5.0	18.5
Namibia	2000	38.0	46.5	33.6	53.1	65.4	43.2	100.0							
Niger	1998	92.1	98.7	87.5	92.7	92.2	93.5	86.4	57.2	84.0					
Nigeria	1990	68.6	87.7	58.0	71.6	69.4	75.5	66.7							
Nigeria	1999	77.2	89.7	67.6	81.1	71.4	90.9	100.0	59.2	67.3	58.3	65.2	60.5	67.9	68.6
Nigeria	2003	59.0	78.6	59.0	78.6	73.5	82.6	95.0	16.8	26.0	5.9	23.8	9.0	31.0	33.3
Rwanda	1992	22.2	51.9		29.3	19.0	42.9	40.0							
Rwanda	2000	65.2	61.3	60.9	67.9	62.5	71.4	87.5	47.5	60.5	10.0	55.2	50.8	55.3	60.0
Rwanda	2005	60.0	80.8	50.9	69.8	67.7	68.7	92.0	23.2	39.8	17.1	29.9	23.9	32.5	52.1
Senegal	2005	84.0	85.0	81.2	91.0	91.4	90.2	92.8	23.9	24.8	23.8	24.0	29.6	22.1	23.8
South Africa	1998	39.3	50.7	38.1	46.9	46.2	45.5								

Country	Year	FEMALE							MALE						
		Urban	Rural	Non Slum	All Slum	One Shelter Deprivation	Two Shelter Deprivations	Three Shelter Deprivations	Urban	Rural	Non Slum	All Slum	One Shelter Deprivation	Two Shelter Deprivations	Three Shelter Deprivations
Togo	1998	94.3	96.6	95.8	93.3	93.1	93.3	100.0	60.1	52.6					
Uganda	1995	58.8	83.7	38.5	62.9	56.3	65.4	87.5							
Uganda	2001	74.4	81.7	76.9	74.1	68.9	83.1		14.9	22.2	25.0	19.6	14.9	24.1	19.3
United Republic of Tanzania	1992	65.7	86.9	58.1	66.8	64.7	69.0	77.8							
United Republic of Tanzania	1996	100.0	100.0	100.0	100.0	100.0	100.0	100.0							
United Republic of Tanzania	1999	69.3	94.8	66.7	69.7	70.3	62.8		59.3	80.3	50.0	68.5	61.1	68.4	87.5
United Republic of Tanzania	2004	70.6	91.0	69.2	71.4	70.4	70.7	78.6	4.7	24.8	8.3	2.4	3.3		8.3
Zambia	1996	72.3	94.2	57.7	82.4	81.9	77.9	96.8	51.1	74.5	46.7	60.4	47.5	61.9	82.8
Zambia	2002	68.7	92.6	59.6	73.9	74.5	72.8	66.7	11.4	47.1	17.7	23.1	9.8	21.4	48.1
Zimbabwe	1994	55.2	60.8	53.9	67.9	65.2	80.0		38.7	40.3	37.7	41.6	40.7	40.0	46.2
Zimbabwe	1999	53.6	62.8	52.0	67.4	69.6	65.0								
LATIN AMERICA AND THE CARIBBEAN															
Brazil	1996	23.5	33.1	20.6	27.4	25.5	33.5	33.3	13.4	9.3	12.0	14.0	12.5	16.7	15.8
Bolivia	2004	65.7	74.4	61.3	71.5	69.8	73.8	81.7	68.3	70.5	60.7	72.7	71.7	70.7	77.7
Bolivia	1998	60.8	78.3	55.0	64.1	64.6	61.6	73.3	51.9	61.4	47.1	54.8	48.4	55.6	68.9
Colombia	2000	24.5	40.6	24.3	26.0	25.3	29.2	33.3							
Colombia	1995	47.7	63.5	47.6	49.0	44.1	60.0	66.7							
Colombia	1990	23.7	32.1	24.6	20.0	18.2	25.8	37.5							
Dominican Rep	2002	33.6	47.3	70.2	43.1	56.5	58.3	50.0	42.9	38.9	37.6	45.4	43.9	46.3	70.0
Guatemala	1998	45.2	62.0	35.7	69.1	71.7	62.5								
Haiti	2000	82.9	96.0	66.7	84.3	82.3	90.7	73.7	44.7	58.9					
Nicaragua	2001	52.4	63.9	48.8	54.9	48.2	63.2	66.7	54.6	50.0	54.0	53.4	49.3	59.0	52.4
Paraguay	1990	13.4	23.0	11.6	14.9	18.6	13.0	11.6							
Peru	2000	61.6	82.0	53.9	75.6	74.2	76.3	78.3							
Peru	1996	64.0	85.8	59.5	70.6	68.3	71.7	75.3	60.9	79.2	56.5	65.5	62.9	69.4	61.4
ASIA															
Armenia	2000	10.8	18.9	14.0	1.9	2.4									
Armenia	2005	9.5	19.9	8.3	21.3	26.0	5.7		70.7	89.3	81.2	68.6		68.6	
Bangladesh	1996	61.7	82.6	57.7	62.9	60.0	64.0		31.3	28.0	12.5	30.1	29.2	30.2	33.3
Bangladesh	1999	19.0	33.6	17.9	21.3	25.7	15.4		21.7	29.9	18.2	29.5	12.5	35.4	
Bangladesh	2004	27.6	46.8	25.1	28.7	27.8	33.8	9.0	37.6	58.0	25.0	53.1	49.1	51.5	55.3
India	1998	56.9	57.5	57.8	56.1	54.2	68.3								
Indonesia	1994	88.1	92.0		88.1	86.3	95.3	100.0							
Indonesia	1997	88.6	96.7		88.6	88.4	86.5								
Indonesia	2002	41.1	59.9	39.3	45.1	44.6	41.0								
Kazakhstan	1999	11.1	19.1	12.3	10.4	10.0	12.9	13.3	4.2	14.3	11.1	5.9	2.6	7.7	12.5
Kyrgyzstan	1997	19.2	31.3	11.8	21.2	17.9	23.5	16.7							
Moldova	2005	24.9	30.4	25.1	24.2	22.2	30.6								
Nepal	1996	72.7	84.3	100.0	70.0	66.7	76.9	80.0							
Nepal	2001	65.4	69.7	69.0	65.2	85.7	63.6	40.0	26.7	38.9	7.1	40.9	11.1	40.8	55.0
Pakistan	1990	84.2	79.3	81.5	90.0	88.9	100.0								
Philippines	1998	74.7	73.6	74.0	77.0	76.0	80.8	83.3							
Philippines	2003	51.3	68.6	50.5	57.6	53.3	67.7	100.0	7.3	18.9	10.0	15.3	11.7	25.9	27.3
Turkey	1993	75.3	94.4	71.2	90.5	88.9	100.0	100.0							
Turkey	1998	17.5	54.7	17.0	18.7	20.1	5.6		15.3	38.1	21.4	21.1	24.1		66.7
Uzbekistan	1996	14.1	8.7	19.4	13.0	18.0	11.1	7.1							
Viet Nam	2002	64.9	62.5	64.9	63.2	69.2	40.0	100.0							
Yemen	1991	38.5	44.4		62.5	50.0	100.0								

Enrolment in primary education in urban and rural areas (female and male)

		ENROLLMENT MALE								ENROLLMENT FEMALE							
Country	Year	Urban	Rural	Total	Non Slum Household	Slum Household	One Shelter Deprivation	Two Shelter Deprivations	Three Shelter Deprivations	Urban	Rural	Total	Non Slum Household	Slum Household	One Shelter Deprivation	Two Shelter Deprivations	Three Shelter Deprivations
AFRICA																	
Angola	2000	63.2	54.8	60.7	65.1	62.6	61.4	63.5	78.9	63.3	51.2	59.8	64.9	62.9	63.6	61.9	58.7
Benin	1996	70.6	41.5	51.5	81.8	67.5	82.4	65.0	46.3	50.3	24.5	33.9	64.6	45.5	55.7	48.3	24.8
Benin	2001	74.0	54.4	60.5	88.4	65.0	72.7	64.1	48.3	59.3	40.7	47.1	68.1	53.2	61.9	50.6	27.7
Benin	2006	76.9	58.6	64.6	89.1	73.1	83.9	75.2	54.3	68.6	51.2	57.2	77.6	65.6	74.5	69.4	45.3
Burkina Faso	1992	72.8	28.7	35.9	77.7	71.6	75.6	70.5	63.3	68.5	17.4	25.8	76.9	65.7	68.4	66.4	57.8
Burkina Faso	1999	74.4	26.2	32.0	80.4	72.7	72.1	74.0	73.9	68.3	15.1	22.2	66.7	69.0	70.3	67.7	63.1
Burkina Faso	2003	79.7	28.4	35.1	84.0	75.5	79.5	61.6	52.7	72.7	21.0	28.6	73.1	72.3	76.0	58.0	50.9
Cameroon	1991	75.0	64.1	68.0	86.0	71.0	82.4	70.8	45.6	70.9	52.8	59.1	81.5	67.1	77.0	65.9	49.0
Cameroon	1998	86.9	63.3	70.4	93.8	81.8	87.2	82.4	67.8	81.9	63.7	69.2	88.7	76.9	82.4	76.0	64.3
Cameroon	2004	87.8	73.2	79.4	93.5	83.6	84.8	83.9	76.7	87.4	68.7	76.9	90.0	85.6	88.2	82.6	80.6
Central African Republic	1994	73.6	52.6	61.3	79.8	72.8	76.6	75.6	69.5	65.4	33.8	47.8	82.2	63.1	70.4	65.2	56.9
Chad	1996	52.8	28.8	34.0	84.1	51.0	65.0	59.6	47.5	43.4	17.1	22.7	69.2	42.1	55.8	51.5	36.2
Chad	2004	59.9	33.7	38.4	83.9	57.9	65.1	60.0	49.9	49.2	25.3	29.6	62.0	48.1	62.5	50.4	38.3
Comoros	1996	55.5	41.8	45.0	76.1	47.9	60.0	42.3	29.4	56.1	36.4	41.2	72.6	50.5	66.3	33.8	38.7
Congo	2005	87.8	81.6	84.5	90.1	86.4	88.1	83.0	83.9	89.6	82.0	85.8	90.9	88.7	91.1	85.0	82.7
Côte d'Ivoire	1994	67.2	46.0	52.9	74.6	64.3	71.5	52.2	55.3	55.4	35.7	42.6	62.0	52.5	57.1	44.8	38.9
Côte d'Ivoire	1999	67.1	50.7	55.3	77.2	62.7	73.5	44.6	35.1	55.9	37.7	44.1	60.1	54.0	66.6	37.9	21.8
Côte d'Ivoire	2005	66.4	49.3	55.4	77.8	53.8	58.0	41.2	65.3	56.6	44.6	49.1	61.7	50.3	52.4	43.4	23.6
Democratic Republic of Congo	2000	72.9	47.0	54.6	88.5	70.7	80.5	71.5	55.2	69.6	39.3	48.4	82.9	67.7	78.6	69.1	48.8
Egypt	1992	90.5	84.7	87.2	91.4	89.8	92.1	90.0	76.6	89.1	67.7	76.8	93.2	85.6	86.3	88.1	70.0
Egypt	1995	91.6	85.9	88.2	94.8	88.6	90.5	87.9	80.2	91.0	69.1	78.1	95.7	86.5	90.2	84.0	73.3
Egypt	2000	87.1	86.8	86.9	89.3	81.8	82.9	82.1	43.6	88.2	79.6	83.0	90.9	82.3	83.5	80.9	59.6
Egypt	2003	84.1	82.6	83.2	85.0	81.2	83.7	77.6	36.8	84.5	79.3	81.4	87.6	75.5	75.8	75.5	69.8
Egypt	2005	88.1	85.4	86.4	88.6	86.2	88.0	77.8	89.8	86.8	82.5	84.1	87.8	83.0	83.2	83.7	61.5
Ethiopia	2000	75.1	27.3	32.6	91.1	74.1	87.0	79.3	66.9	71.7	20.7	27.2	71.0	71.8	80.7	74.5	66.1
Ethiopia	2005	77.6	39.0	42.1	85.0	76.6	85.9	75.9	71.5	79.7	38.3	42.3	86.7	78.8	86.1	81.8	70.6
Gabon	2000	93.0	92.3	92.8	92.8	93.1	94.6	90.1	88.6	93.6	90.3	92.7	94.1	93.0	93.9	91.0	89.4
Gambia	2000	58.3	43.7	48.5	65.6	55.6	55.6	57.5	56.9	58.7	35.7	44.1	66.9	55.0	58.8	46.5	52.9
Ghana	1993	88.2	71.6	76.6	86.1	88.8	90.7	89.9	74.0	87.6	68.9	74.3	90.0	86.8	87.8	85.4	86.5
Ghana	1999	85.2	70.5	74.4	87.8	84.1	87.5	79.4	76.3	84.0	70.0	74.0	82.6	84.6	86.9	83.6	51.9
Ghana	2003	70.5	56.2	61.2	75.4	64.4	66.4	55.8	53.7	66.9	55.5	59.8	70.1	61.9	64.7	59.4	14.9
Guinea	1999	46.6	18.0	25.9	44.9	47.1	50.8	43.6	36.1	40.8	11.1	19.7	47.1	38.7	45.4	31.0	27.2
Guinea	2005	71.2	35.9	45.2	76.8	61.2	65.2	52.4	30.1	63.5	30.1	39.3	69.0	52.9	58.4	40.3	17.8
Kenya	1993	75.3	74.9	74.9	72.2	76.4	82.6	68.3	73.1	73.6	74.3	74.2	80.2	70.7	74.5	65.4	62.4
Kenya	1998	85.7	81.3	81.9	97.3	79.3	81.1	76.4	79.1	84.7	82.1	82.5	92.1	81.7	81.9	83.5	79.5
Kenya	2003	82.4	77.8	78.4	87.6	80.2	83.7	81.8	76.0	82.5	78.1	78.8	86.1	81.0	84.7	82.2	76.0
Lesotho	2000	68.7	60.4	62.0	78.0	65.6	69.1	66.4	53.4	72.3	66.9	67.9	74.1	71.6	76.0	71.1	58.6
Lesotho	2004	81.3	81.4	81.4	81.7	80.8	83.4	70.7	84.8	87.7	86.9	87.0	87.0	89.0	88.9	88.8	96.1
Liberia	2007	35.9	13.2	21.2	49.2	32.2	33.1	33.0	27.5	32.1	12.1	19.9	48.9	27.1	31.4	25.1	17.4
Madagascar	1997	75.0	51.8	57.2	93.4	73.4	93.6	84.2	65.5	77.1	54.4	59.3	90.2	75.7	93.7	86.5	73.1
Madagascar	2003	84.5	70.5	73.1	91.5	82.0	88.0	82.7	70.6	86.6	73.9	76.4	93.6	84.1	88.2	83.8	76.7
Malawi	1992	78.2	55.4	58.1	87.0	75.4	85.8	72.0	53.8	76.5	55.1	57.8	83.7	74.2	81.0	72.8	57.9
Malawi	2000	89.5	73.4	75.4	92.5	87.3	88.5	87.0	60.1	87.3	76.3	77.8	87.6	87.1	88.3	85.5	75.3
Malawi	2004	89.0	78.7	80.1	89.8	88.6	92.7	87.2	76.9	89.2	83.0	83.9	91.5	88.2	92.4	84.5	80.5
Mali	1996	61.5	22.5	33.2	80.5	58.0	72.7	57.8	40.5	52.5	14.3	24.9	63.9	50.1	62.7	51.5	32.8

Country	Year	ENROLLMENT MALE								ENROLLMENT FEMALE							
		Urban	Rural	Total	Non Slum Household	Slum Household	One Shelter Deprivation	Two Shelter Deprivations	Three Shelter Deprivations	Urban	Rural	Total	Non Slum Household	Slum Household	One Shelter Deprivation	Two Shelter Deprivations	Three Shelter Deprivations
Mali	2001	70.2	36.5	44.4	81.5	64.5	69.1	61.6	51.0	58.6	24.9	32.8	74.5	50.9	59.3	43.5	33.5
Morocco	1992	71.7	44.5	54.8	76.5	67.7	69.1	64.0	62.5	71.7	24.2	41.8	73.2	70.5	71.5	66.7	75.0
Morocco	2004	95.5	85.0	90.4	96.6	91.2	90.5	98.4	100.0	95.3	76.9	86.4	95.7	93.5	93.6	92.0	100.0
Mozambique	1997	78.5	51.4	57.2	84.4	77.3	86.4	76.4	66.6	73.8	44.3	50.9	83.6	71.9	78.3	73.6	62.4
Mozambique	2003	76.5	56.9	62.8	91.8	73.4	83.2	79.6	52.7	75.1	48.0	56.6	89.6	71.9	83.6	78.6	50.0
Namibia	1992	82.5	83.7	83.4	83.6	81.4	82.8	80.5	76.1	88.4	85.7	86.4	87.6	89.0	90.8	81.3	87.1
Namibia	2000	92.3	83.1	85.4	95.1	89.1	91.7	87.0	79.5	90.8	84.6	86.2	93.9	86.9	89.8	75.6	86.8
Namibia	2007	85.4	83.1	83.9	88.4	81.1	83.7	80.4	71.4	86.5	84.9	85.4	88.9	83.3	87.5	80.2	73.7
Niger	1992	53.6	16.7	22.7	66.9	50.5	56.9	55.0	34.3	44.2	6.9	13.3	60.3	40.4	45.8	43.1	27.1
Niger	1998	64.4	22.3	30.6	78.0	61.1	70.0	64.0	39.6	56.3	11.6	20.8	66.7	53.2	64.2	56.7	32.3
Niger	2006	70.5	37.1	42.3	83.5	67.2	76.1	66.7	53.0	66.0	23.4	29.9	77.3	62.9	75.1	62.4	42.6
Nigeria	1999	69.0	53.1	57.5	78.1	66.9	76.4	63.2	44.7	64.6	49.0	53.5	68.9	63.3	70.6	64.1	38.6
Nigeria	2003	67.5	57.9	61.0	72.9	66.2	67.8	64.9	69.7	65.6	49.9	55.0	75.2	62.8	67.5	62.5	53.4
Rwanda	1992	76.4	60.4	61.2	94.0	71.7	75.2	74.4	69.9	79.9	61.0	61.8	88.8	76.8	82.4	77.6	72.6
Rwanda	2000	83.0	69.5	71.1	88.8	78.2	79.9	79.6	61.7	83.4	70.9	72.4	85.6	81.6	81.7	84.4	72.7
Rwanda	2005	87.7	83.5	84.1	89.8	86.8	89.9	84.8	83.9	90.2	85.8	86.4	93.9	88.6	90.3	87.9	85.4
Senegal	1993	55.6	18.8	31.0	62.7	52.8	55.8	50.7	47.2	48.4	12.5	24.7	59.3	44.5	49.5	37.8	32.8
Senegal	2005	66.4	40.2	49.4	68.8	60.9	60.7	60.8	63.7	68.2	40.8	50.7	71.4	61.2	63.5	51.7	70.6
Sierra Leone	2000	56.0	33.4	39.6	73.7	73.7	61.2	59.8	46.6	50.9	27.8	34.5	76.2	76.2	54.7	50.6	51.8
South Africa	1998	78.9	70.0	74.0	80.2	77.1	75.9	78.4	91.3	81.0	74.8	77.6	82.7	78.9	79.6	77.8	74.6
United Republic of Tanzania	1992	54.5	47.9	49.3	76.0	51.1	56.6	53.2	37.9	58.3	49.8	51.4	68.5	56.2	59.7	60.6	40.6
United Republic of Tanzania	1996	58.6	45.7	47.8	72.6	55.0	62.8	52.1	42.4	65.8	47.3	50.6	76.3	62.9	64.1	64.5	56.8
United Republic of Tanzania	1999	70.4	47.0	51.3	82.6	65.0	73.1	52.9	11.0	70.8	51.2	55.1	82.5	64.9	73.6	49.4	39.1
United Republic of Tanzania	2004	85.0	67.4	71.0	89.7	83.2	87.5	81.1	75.4	85.4	72.2	75.2	91.1	82.8	85.5	80.9	79.7
Togo	1998	87.6	67.7	72.1	90.6	87.0	88.9	87.4	67.8	81.2	56.2	63.4	83.0	80.7	82.3	80.3	65.0
Uganda	1995	82.0	73.5	74.3	87.2	81.3	91.4	81.6	71.1	80.1	70.3	71.5	74.4	80.9	85.4	81.8	74.0
Uganda	2001	90.8	86.0	86.5	93.0	89.3	90.2	89.2	75.0	88.5	87.2	87.4	88.4	88.5	89.1	85.2	100.0
Uganda	2006	86.4	78.8	79.5	91.1	85.2	86.0	84.0	94.1	83.3	78.5	79.0	82.9	83.5	86.2	84.7	80.2
Zambia	1996	78.7	57.5	65.6	87.3	73.9	79.6	64.0	59.4	79.5	58.4	66.6	82.6	77.7	83.5	69.0	65.1
Zambia	2002	77.3	61.6	67.2	83.1	67.8	71.0	62.4	55.7	78.7	59.9	66.8	82.4	72.0	74.4	67.6	64.2
Zambia	2007	87.0	73.3	77.8	90.2	84.8	89.1	81.2	79.6	86.0	73.8	78.0	89.7	83.7	84.5	85.3	79.0
Zimbabwe	1994	92.9	88.8	89.6	94.5	90.1	91.2	77.7	100.0	91.0	87.8	88.4	91.8	89.8	89.7	90.7	100.0
Zimbabwe	1999	89.2	88.6	88.7	89.0	100.0	100.0	100.0		90.2	89.1	89.4	90.6	77.0	77.0	.	
Zimbabwe	2005	92.2	84.8	86.6	92.5	91.2	91.0	100.0		91.4	86.9	88.0	91.4	91.6	91.3	100.0	

LATIN AMERICA AND THE CARIBBEAN

Country	Year	Urban	Rural	Total	Non Slum Household	Slum Household	One Shelter Deprivation	Two Shelter Deprivations	Three Shelter Deprivations	Urban	Rural	Total	Non Slum Household	Slum Household	One Shelter Deprivation	Two Shelter Deprivations	Three Shelter Deprivations
Bolivia	1998	93.2	89.9	91.8	96.7	92.4	94.2	91.1	91.4	94.8	87.9	91.9	95.7	94.6	96.4	93.2	94.0
Bolivia	2004	85.3	71.9	79.6	93.0	82.2	86.6	81.2	69.9	85.8	71.2	79.2	92.2	82.7	87.1	80.9	74.9
Brazil	1996	59.7	40.5	54.8	66.5	51.5	55.6	43.6	32.4	61.6	40.7	56.5	66.8	55.8	59.5	49.4	31.6
Colombia	1990	81.8	63.5	75.5	84.9	77.4	77.4	79.3	81.4	82.2	67.6	77.1	87.0	75.8	77.7	72.2	67.1
Colombia	1995	92.1	79.1	87.1	95.7	85.3	88.0	83.2	70.6	93.8	84.5	90.4	95.8	89.8	92.0	86.8	77.7
Colombia	2000	90.8	88.4	90.0	91.4	89.2	90.1	83.6	68.2	90.6	89.7	90.3	91.0	89.7	90.7	86.4	75.8
Colombia	2005	76.5	71.9	75.0	77.5	73.9	75.0	69.7	70.8	79.6	73.2	77.6	80.6	76.9	76.6	78.2	77.7
Dominican Republic	1991	58.2	27.4	44.2	65.9	44.9	49.2	34.5	27.5	61.3	32.5	48.2	69.8	43.8	44.9	43.7	25.0
Dominican Republic	1996	57.3	42.0	50.5	64.0	44.1	45.7	40.2	11.3	64.7	47.7	57.8	72.0	51.6	56.4	33.2	16.1
Dominican Republic	2002	85.8	84.3	85.3	89.7	78.8	80.8	69.2	69.3	88.7	88.0	88.4	90.9	84.0	86.1	70.7	86.1
Dominican Republic	2007	85.6	86.6	85.9	87.1	82.7	84.3	77.1	69.7	87.6	88.0	87.7	89.1	84.5	86.8	74.9	76.8
Guatemala	1995	72.3	52.5	58.9	85.3	65.9	74.0	63.6	57.8	64.7	47.5	53.1	74.7	60.1	72.5	53.1	51.0
Guatemala	1998	67.4	66.7	66.9	75.3	62.6	67.3	61.2	56.9	60.2	61.1	60.8	71.4	55.0	70.2	44.0	39.2
Guyana	2005	91.1	88.3	89.0	89.6	92.2	94.3	86.3	100.0	92.5	89.6	90.5	90.1	94.5	93.8	97.5	80.6
Haiti	1994	87.3	61.7	69.2	96.3	85.1	89.7	87.4	73.2	83.0	62.9	69.8	88.0	81.9	87.0	81.9	81.2
Haiti	2001	70.9	45.4	52.5	73.6	65.4	70.3	54.6	52.5	71.2	48.8	56.4	76.3	62.9	61.0	68.1	74.9

Country	Year	ENROLLMENT MALE								ENROLLMENT FEMALE							
		Urban	Rural	Total	Non Slum Household	Slum Household	One Shelter Deprivation	Two Shelter Deprivations	Three Shelter Deprivations	Urban	Rural	Total	Non Slum Household	Slum Household	One Shelter Deprivation	Two Shelter Deprivations	Three Shelter Deprivations
Haiti	2006	69.0	44.9	52.6	79.9	66.2	73.1	65.1	50.8	69.3	49.2	56.3	75.3	67.6	71.2	70.4	50.2
Honduras	2005	79.8	75.4	77.2	83.2	76.3	77.2	73.3	80.1	83.4	77.8	80.1	85.7	81.2	83.1	79.7	72.7
Nicaragua	1998	77.1	57.0	67.8	84.2	74.9	80.1	76.2	67.0	80.7	60.4	71.8	86.4	79.1	83.6	79.9	70.6
Nicaragua	2001	82.5	66.0	74.5	84.1	81.9	86.3	79.4	75.5	86.1	72.8	79.7	85.4	86.3	87.9	86.8	82.6
Peru	1991	86.7	80.6	84.6	85.3	87.5	88.7	88.0	85.6	87.1	79.5	84.5	88.3	86.4	88.9	84.8	85.4
Peru	1996	87.3	84.3	86.1	89.7	86.2	87.7	86.5	81.6	88.5	83.3	86.4	90.5	87.6	89.5	88.0	82.3
Peru	2000	77.8	70.3	74.4	79.4	76.8	77.1	78.3	78.1	78.0	69.5	74.1	81.5	75.7	77.3	75.8	74.2
Peru	2004	92.1	88.5	90.4	94.7	89.7	90.6	92.8	82.4	90.8	92.3	91.5	92.6	89.0	89.2	93.7	79.3

ASIA

Country	Year	Urban	Rural	Total	Non Slum Household	Slum Household	One Shelter Deprivation	Two Shelter Deprivations	Three Shelter Deprivations	Urban	Rural	Total	Non Slum Household	Slum Household	One Shelter Deprivation	Two Shelter Deprivations	Three Shelter Deprivations
Armenia	2000	55.7	58.7	57.1	55.5	57.9	56.6	100.0		57.0	58.5	57.7	56.7	60.1	59.8	63.3	
Armenia	2005	65.2	69.9	67.4	65.8	64.1	64.3	58.9	100.0	64.7	67.3	65.8	68.1	59.3	58.1	71.5	.
Azerbaijan	2000	89.4	87.2	88.3	88.2	89.6	90.6	88.2	89.4	90.5	86.2	88.4	93.0	90.0	89.2	91.0	93.3
Azerbaijan	2006	72.8	71.4	72.1	80.4	71.7	73.2	73.7	61.4	69.9	69.6	69.8	51.6	72.1	74.8	67.1	74.3
Bangladesh	1996	77.7	77.7	74.4	87.0	66.2	69.3	59.0	.	74.9	74.9	78.6	75.8	73.7	70.4	81.0	100.0
Bangladesh	1999	78.2	76.1	76.4	84.8	74.3	73.9	75.2	57.1	75.8	78.4	78.0	77.3	74.6	76.2	72.5	69.8
Bangladesh	2004	79.0	81.5	81.0	92.5	77.7	88.1	81.4	74.4	80.9	85.3	84.4	78.4	81.1	83.9	86.7	78.8
Cambodia	2000	73.8	64.6	65.9	85.8	71.4	88.3	71.4	62.2	70.0	62.5	63.5	82.7	67.2	74.8	69.7	61.2
Cambodia	2005	76.1	75.2	75.3	79.8	75.7	82.9	79.9	69.4	79.0	76.7	77.0	81.3	78.7	87.2	84.8	72.9
India	1993	73.2	57.4	61.1						71.3	43.5	50.1					
India	1998	91.0	82.6	84.5	96.6	86.8	90.0	81.0	79.2	88.2	74.7	77.8	95.2	83.2	87.5	74.6	77.3
India	2005	80.1	75.3	76.5	86.5	77.7	81.8	74.0	61.2	80.5	71.5	73.8	86.5	78.4	83.8	72.1	62.5
Indonesia	1991	77.1	70.5	72.4	80.9	75.0	76.3	74.0	71.6	76.8	71.0	72.7	78.7	75.8	76.6	77.5	68.1
Indonesia	1994	78.2	75.5	76.2	77.1	78.8	78.0	82.5	70.0	76.8	74.7	75.3	73.1	79.1	81.1	77.2	73.5
Indonesia	1997	77.0	78.1	77.8	76.2	78.2	77.9	79.6	77.4	77.0	77.1	77.1	76.8	77.4	76.3	82.3	74.2
Indonesia	2002	76.6	76.1	76.3	76.3	77.2	78.2	72.5	82.0	73.5	76.2	75.0	73.7	73.1	73.0	74.9	68.0
Indonesia	2007	75.9	76.5	76.3	74.1	79.4	78.4	82.0	82.7	72.7	74.8	74.0	71.7	74.6	74.7	76.0	68.7
Iraq	2000	78.4	61.8	72.8	79.4	74.7	75.4	70.0	60.0	72.5	44.9	63.2	75.0	63.8	65.0	57.5	32.6
Jordan	1997	87.1	88.2	87.3	87.4	86.8	87.2	79.6	100.0	88.5	85.1	87.8	89.1	88.0	88.2	83.9	100.0
Jordan	2002	86.6	85.2	86.3	84.7	89.2	89.7	82.1	100.0	87.8	88.4	87.9	87.1	88.7	88.8	86.8	100.0
Jordan	2007	87.3	88.0	87.4	86.7	88.2	88.4	78.9		90.5	89.2	90.3	91.2	89.5	91.2	89.5	
Kazakhstan	1995	90.6	89.3	89.8	92.9	89.5	87.2	93.8	100.0	86.6	93.3	90.5	81.7	89.3	88.7	92.0	83.4
Kazakhstan	1999	86.5	87.3	86.9	89.6	84.7	84.2	85.4	87.8	85.4	90.1	88.3	88.9	82.7	83.3	86.5	68.2
Kazakhstan	1997	77.0	78.6	78.1	77.4	76.4	76.1	78.8		76.1	75.0	75.3	81.5	69.9	69.7	71.5	
Moldova	2005	86.3	86.6	86.5	86.7	85.1	89.1	64.2	100.0	85.4	88.0	87.2	84.7	87.1	87.3	83.9	100.0
Mongolia	2000	65.2	57.8	61.0	67.1	64.9	70.2	63.4	61.2	63.7	59.3	61.1	68.7	62.6	66.2	61.7	57.1
Myanmar	2000	84.8	75.9	77.9	87.5	84.3	85.3	83.2	73.7	84.7	75.7	77.5	84.0	84.9	86.5	83.0	72.6
Nepal	1996	83.8	72.6	73.5	93.5	80.7	93.9	83.0	69.8	85.5	54.2	56.3	97.4	81.5	92.9	79.9	69.2
Nepal	2001	92.3	78.8	80.0	97.6	87.4	88.5	88.8	71.2	87.5	64.7	66.6	94.6	81.0	90.6	71.8	83.1
Nepal	2006	93.5	89.1	89.7	98.5	91.6	94.3	92.8	84.8	89.4	83.3	84.0	97.7	85.8	94.4	81.3	72.6
Pakistan	1990	75.0	55.2	60.6	83.0	73.7	78.5	64.9	46.2	69.9	32.8	43.8	83.5	67.7	75.2	51.7	25.1
Pakistan	2006	78.1	66.4	69.7	83.4	76.9	82.6	73.1	54.8	76.4	56.2	62.2	87.1	73.7	81.5	65.9	51.0
Philippines	1993	66.2	62.1	64.0	74.5	64.6	71.0	63.9	60.6	67.9	65.5	66.6	72.1	67.1	72.8	68.2	59.3
Philippines	1998	86.5	76.3	80.8	91.9	82.9	86.2	80.0	72.5	89.9	80.3	84.5	95.6	86.3	90.3	83.6	77.6
Philippines	2003	88.7	84.0	86.2	89.9	86.4	87.9	83.6	68.1	89.3	85.6	87.3	90.6	86.7	89.1	82.9	49.2
Tajikistan	2000	71.1	74.7	73.9	88.5	69.9	70.7	71.0	65.0	73.9	76.8	76.2	75.0	73.8	81.1	73.5	59.0
Turkey	1993	75.1	71.3	73.5	80.9	65.5	67.4	64.8	53.0	72.2	67.7	70.2	75.8	65.5	67.6	66.1	41.3
Turkey	1998	77.0	67.5	73.4	81.3	68.0	70.4	54.9	70.4	73.3	64.3	69.9	83.1	57.6	57.0	59.4	64.2
Turkey	2004	69.2	65.9	68.1	72.7	61.4	60.6	69.0	70.7	69.3	63.3	67.3	73.3	60.4	61.1	51.2	71.6
Uzbekistan	1996	56.1	60.1	58.7	55.8	56.6	57.6	48.1	70.8	55.9	54.1	54.7	59.1	51.8	48.5	63.9	100.0
Uzbekistan	2000	78.9	75.0	76.1	78.8	79.0	81.7	76.2	78.9	73.8	75.1	74.7	74.7	73.7	75.9	72.2	68.3
Viet Nam	1997	86.6	83.1	83.5	91.8	84.5	89.8	86.2	62.0	90.0	85.0	85.6	93.0	88.4	90.9	96.0	76.1
Viet Nam	2002	96.8	96.4	96.4	98.2	95.4	98.1	90.6	96.4	96.7	95.4	95.5	98.1	95.5	98.0	88.3	100.0
Viet Nam	1991	61.3	51.8	53.3	70.1	59.5	62.7	62.5	45.3	58.5	20.4	26.8	65.8	56.6	59.6	57.7	46.9

Proportion of malnourished (underweight) children (under five)

Country	Year	Urban	Rural	Total	Non slum	Slum	One Shelter Depv	Two Shelter Depv	Three Shelter Depv	Four Shelter Depv
AFRICA										
Benin	1996	21.4	26.6	25.0	18.1	22.3	16.0	24.3	27.8	39.4
Benin	2001	24.2	33.4	30.4	19.1	27.4	23.4	28.2	38.8	
Benin	2006	32.3	41.3	38.1	24.4	34.8	30.7	37.1	38.1	44.5
Burkina Faso	1992	19.8	35.8	33.3	14.1	21.2	18.6	21.2	26.9	32.8
Burkina Faso	1999	22.7	38.8	36.8	23.1	22.6	18.6	27.2	29.1	
Burkina Faso	1999	19.8	41.4	38.6	21.2	18.8	17.9	21.4	45.5	
Cameroon	2004	23.1	38.2	31.7	15.9	27.2	24.4	30.1	35.0	
Central African Republic	1994	28.6	37.2	33.6	25.9	28.9	21.8	28.1	36.5	39.0
Chad	2004	32.3	43.0	40.9	19.5	33.2	28.3	31.7	35.4	39.8
Comoros	1996	29.9	35.0	33.8	25.8	31.5	26.7	34.5	47.1	
Congo	2005	21.7	28.1	25.2	19.4	22.7	22.9	22.2	23.1	22.3
Côte d'Ivoire	1994	15.3	29.2	24.4	13.0	16.0	14.2	16.9	21.0	22.9
Democratic Republic of Congo	2007	31.3	44.0	38.9	15.9	36.9	34.1	41.1	31.9	
Egypt	1992	20.0	29.6	26.0	14.8	24.3	22.5	26.8	26.6	40.6
Egypt	1995	22.8	34.4	29.8	19.3	26.2	23.7	28.8	31.2	58.0
Egypt	2000	13.8	21.8	18.7	13.0	15.6	15.3	15.7	23.1	
Egypt	2003	14.1	16.6	15.6	12.7	17.9	15.0	21.8	32.3	
Egypt	2005	16.2	18.5	17.6	14.7	20.2	22.4	17.8		
Ethiopia	2000	41.6	52.3	51.2	31.0	42.1	31.5	37.0	52.3	47.6
Ethiopia	2004	31.7	47.6	46.4	4.9	34.5	15.1	38.5	45.7	45.8
Ethiopia	2005	31.7	47.6	46.4	6.8	33.7	11.0	39.1	46.5	44.4
Gabon	2000	17.4	29.0	20.6	13.8	20.1	16.2	23.5	35.3	51.2
Ghana	1993	15.5	30.0	25.9	12.9	17.5	14.9	23.9	40.0	
Ghana	1999	14.3	29.7	25.9	13.6	15.2	14.7	17.4	25.7	
Ghana	2003	19.9	34.0	29.4	17.5	21.4	20.7	22.6	30.0	
Guinea	1999	18.2	29.4	26.1	14.0	19.7	17.1	20.8	31.9	
Guinea	2005	23.1	38.1	34.7	21.8	24.6	22.6	29.6	27.2	
Kenya	1993	21.3	34.8	33.3	19.2	34.1	33.5	25.1	75.0	
Kenya	1998	22.7	32.7	30.9	16.8	24.5	22.3	23.9	35.7	
Kenya	2003	23.8	32.0	30.6	9.2	29.0	25.8	27.4	32.9	57.2
Lesotho	2003	32.7	37.3	36.7	33.5	31.7	30.5	32.9	51.9	
Liberia	2007	24.9	37.1	33.5	16.8	26.3	20.5	26.5	38.8	38.4

STATE OF THE WORLD'S CITIES 2010/2011

Country	Year	Urban	Rural	Total	Non slum	Slum	One Shelter Depv	Two Shelter Depv	Three Shelter Depv	Four Shelter Depv
Madagascar	1997	44.6	49.2	48.3	25.5	44.8	35.3	49.6	46.2	50.0
Madagascar	2003	40.9	48.9	47.3	36.2	42.3	42.2	41.9	43.0	
Malawi	1992	35.2	50.9	49.2	16.3	36.9	30.8	35.8	45.1	
Malawi	2000	34.2	51.3	49.0	27.6	38.4	34.5	45.0	42.7	
Malawi	2004	37.3	49.0	47.5	27.0	41.0	32.3	44.5	54.2	57.1
Mali	1996	21.8	33.1	30.1	19.6	22.1	17.3	23.4	25.8	28.5
Mali	2001	23.2	42.1	37.6	18.3	24.3	21.9	26.0	29.8	
Mali	2006	23.9	37.8	33.9	18.8	26.1	25.3	24.0	31.0	45.4
Morocco	1992	13.2	30.0	24.2	9.5	16.8	15.3	25.8	7.1	18.2
Morocco	2004	13.0	23.6	18.2	11.2	15.9	15.9	15.4		
Mozambique	1997	27.3	38.9	35.9	29.3	14.2	27.4	46.3	62.6	
Namibia	1992	21.8	31.4	28.5	13.9	27.5	26.1	22.2	37.2	
Namibia	2000	21.7	23.0	22.6	18.8	27.7	31.1	21.8	33.3	
Namibia	2007	20.6	25.9	23.9	12.1	29.7	27.4	28.6	40.5	
Niger	1992	26.9	42.4	39.5	25.0	28.3	23.6	31.2	39.5	
Niger	1998	31.2	43.0	27.0	34.2	29.9	36.8	44.9		
Niger	2006	30.6	53.3	49.9	25.5	32.3	27.9	34.7	40.0	
Nigeria	1999	41.6	47.0	45.5	43.3	41.3	37.9	45.0	48.0	
Nigeria	2003	28.9	42.9	38.5	18.8	31.9	30.0	28.8	45.9	41.4
Rwanda	1992	34.2	49.4	48.7	16.0	39.4	32.2	39.7	42.1	61.8
Rwanda	2000	27.8	44.9	42.4	22.4	30.0	29.2	33.4		
Rwanda	2005	31.9	47.3	45.1	21.1	36.5	30.0	38.7	47.0	
Senegal	1993	14.8	30.6	24.7	13.1	15.3	11.8	17.9	26.8	
Senegal	2005	8.6	19.9	15.9	7.4	10.6	9.1	15.0		
Senegal	2005									
Swaziland	2006	17.6	23.3	22.3	17.0	18.0	15.1	27.7	30.5	
Tanzania	1992	37.9	44.6	43.2	20.0	41.0	33.2	47.7	41.2	
Tanzania	1996	32.4	45.8	43.4	25.4	34.1	30.8	34.8	40.7	
Tanzania	1999	24.5	46.5	42.6	21.2	26.1	21.6	32.6	30.4	
Tanzania	2004	25.7	39.7	37.1	18.2	27.8	23.2	28.0	41.2	
Togo	1998	14.8	23.9	21.7	12.7	16.6	16.0	15.5	53.5	
Uganda	1995	22.5	40.3	38.3	16.5	23.1	17.3	22.8	28.7	36.2
Uganda	2001	26.5	39.9	38.6	21.9	29.1	24.3	38.3	35.0	
Uganda	2006	22.5	32.6	31.5	22.0	22.6	19.0	25.1	37.3	
Zambia	1992	32.6	46.3	39.8	27.9	34.8	34.0	34.5	41.7	
Zambia	1996	32.7	48.7	42.4	26.7	35.4	30.8	39.4	49.0	48.8
Zambia	2002	37.1	51.1	46.8	35.7	38.8	37.3	42.0	38.4	
Zambia	2007	33.2	41.5	39.1	29.4	35.1	35.4	33.2	35.2	40.5
Zimbabwe	1994	17.6	22.8	21.4	14.0	22.2	22.0	23.3	30.7	
Zimbabwe	1999	20.6	29.2	26.5	20.5	23.0	30.7	16.5		
Zimbabwe	2005	23.3	29.8	28.1	22.7	24.4	25.0	5.7		

Country	Year	Urban	Rural	Total	Non Slum	Slum	One Shelter Depv	Two Shelter Depv	Three Shelter Depv	Four Shelter Depv
LATIN AMERICA & THE CARIBBEAN										
Bolivia	1994	64.9	46.1	55.7	72.0	59.3	61.6	56.7	55.5	
Bolivia	1998	18.9	37.8	26.8	11.4	23.9	22.4	27.0	30.7	
Bolivia	2004	18.6	36.9	26.4	13.6	24.6	21.1	29.8	31.7	
Brazil	1991									
Brazil	1996	7.8	19.0	10.5	4.6	12.9	10.8	17.2	31.9	
Colombia	1990									
Colombia	1995	12.5	19.1	15.0	11.2	22.9	21.6	24.8	27.2	
Colombia	2000	10.8	19.4	13.5	10.1	16.7	15.3	20.3	32.7	
Colombia	2005	9.0	16.9	11.5	6.0	14.5	13.1	20.8	14.2	38.1
Dominican Republic	1991	12.0	22.8	16.5	7.5	16.1	12.8	21.8	30.3	47.8
Dominican Republic	1996	7.3	15.2	10.7	6.2	10.3	8.6	27.9	24.0	
Dominican Republic	2002	7.7	11.0	8.8	7.0	12.1	12.8	9.4	31.3	
Dominican Republic	2007	6.3	9.0	7.2	4.8	8.8	7.5	13.3	12.6	16.2
Guatemala	1995	35.3	56.6	49.7	22.8	49.1	42.0	61.3	48.6	
Guatemala	1998	32.4	54.4	46.4	20.4	55.1	58.6	48.7	15.7	
Haiti	1994	24.2	35.1	31.9	10.8	26.1	21.6	25.5	32.7	55.5
Haiti	2000	11.5	26.5	21.9	9.0	15.7	13.7	20.0	22.6	
Honduras	2005	13.6	31.6	24.2	6.9	17.3	16.4	19.4	24.8	
ASIA										
Armenia	2000	10.1	16.0	13.0	11.1	8.5	7.4	16.5		
Armenia	2005	14.0	11.5	13.0	15.2	12.3	13.4	7.7	20.9	
Bangladesh	1996	39.4	56.2	54.6	28.5	51.1	49.3	55.9		
Bangladesh	1999	35.0	46.6	44.6	22.7	44.0	41.8	49.8	38.6	
Bangladesh	2004	37.7	44.3	43.0	23.7	47.6	44.8	51.4	66.5	
Bangladesh	2007	30.6	37.4	36.0	11.2	37.2	29.0	40.6	45.8	
India	1992	44.5	54.0	51.8	39.0	52.6	51.1	58.6		
India	1998	35.2	47.9	44.9	29.5	46.0	46.1	44.7		
India	2005	34.3	45.2	42.5	21.0	39.5	33.9	42.3	53.7	48.8
Indonesia	1992									
Indonesia	1994									
Indonesia	1997									
Indonesia	2002									
Jordan	2007	11.8	13.5	12.1	10.6	13.5	12.8	32.8		
Kazakhstan	1995	7.5	21.8	15.8	1.7	9.9	6.0	19.1	24.3	
Kazakhstan	1999	5.8	12.3	9.7	5.3	6.1	6.4	7.4		
Kyrgyzstan	1997	14.8	27.7	24.8	10.1	16.5	13.3	19.2	47.1	
Moldova	2005	7.1	9.4	8.6	6.6	8.8	7.3	11.9		
Nepal	1996	35.4	49.3	48.4	15.7	38.1	29.0	42.0	54.6	
Nepal	2001	36.3	51.5	50.5	30.1	40.7	32.5	46.3	52.2	
Nepal	2006	29.0	44.6	42.7	15.6	34.8	30.7	30.5	46.5	55.5
Pakistan	1990	40.4	54.5	49.6	37.2	50.7	51.1	45.6		
Pakistan	2006									
Philippines	1993									
Philippines	1998									

Source: Global Urban Indicators Database, 2010

Bibliography

A

Abbott, D. (n.d.). *Pro-poor policies: What are they? How do they contribute to the achievement of the MDGs?* (Presentation notes). Sub-Regional Workshop for the North Pacific: Integrating MDGs into National Development Strategies and Budgets. UNDP Pacific Centre.

The African Child Policy Forum. (2008). Postscript: The global food crisis and its implications for child wellbeing in Africa. In The African report of child well-being 2008 (pp. 99-103). Addis Ababa: Author.

Agarwal, S., Srivastava, A., Srivastava, K., Sangar, K., & Agnihotri, A. (2002). *Nutrition and health services to the urban poor*. Retrieved from: http://www.uhrc.in/downloads/Articles/Nutrition_Health_Urban_Poor.pdf

Agbola, B. (2009a, August). *Background document City of Abuja, Nigeria*. Unpublished UN-HABITAT background study for the *State of the World's Cities Report 2009/10*.

Agbola, B. (2009b). *Africa regional summary report*. Unpublished UN-HABITAT background study for the *State of the World's Cities Report 2009/10*.

Agevi, E. (2009). *Cities for all: Bridging the urban divide – a case of Nairobi City*. Unpublished UN-HABITAT background study for the *State of the World's Cities Report 2009/10*.

Akpo, M. (2008). Combating gender-based violence in Benin. In M. Tembon & L. Fort (Eds.), *Girls' education in the 21st century: Gender equality, empowerment, and economic growth* (pp. 143-151). Washington, D.C.: The World Bank.

Albalak, R., Bruce, N., McCracken, J.P., Smith, K.R., & de Gallardo, T. (2001). Indoor respirable particulate matter concentrations from an open fire, improved cookstove, and LPG/open fire combination in a rural Guatemalan community. *Environmental Science and Technology*, 35(13), 2650-2655.

Alberdi, I. (2009, 13 July). The world economic and financial crisis: What will it mean for gender equality? Speech given at the Fifth Annual Meeting of Women Speakers of Parliament, Vienna, Austria. Retrieved from: http://www.unifem.org/news_events/story_detail.php?StoryID=901

Albritton, R. & Bureekul, T. (2002). *Civil society and the consolidation of democracy in Thailand*. (Working Paper Series No. 4). Taipei: Asian Barometer Project Office. Retrieved from: http://www.asianbarometer.org

Alemayehu Gebremedhin, T. (2006). *The analysis of urban poverty in Ethiopia*. Retrieved from https://editorialexpress.com/cgi-bin/conference/download.cgi?db_name=ACE2004&paper_id=168

Al-Mekhlafy, T.A. (2008). Strategies for gender equality in basic and secondary education: A comprehensive and integrated approach in the Republic of Yemen. In M. Tembon & L. Fort (Eds.), *Girls' education in the 21st century: Gender equality, empowerment, and economic growth* (pp. 269-277). Washington, D.C.: The World Bank.

Annez, P.C. & Buckley, R. (2008). Urbanization and growth: Setting the context. In *Urbanization and growth*, M. Spence, P.C. Annez, & R. Buckley (Eds.). Washington, D.C.: Commission on Growth and Development/The World Bank.

Asian Development Bank. (2004). *City development strategies to reduce poverty*. Manila: Author.

Asian Development Bank. (2007). *Inequality in Asia: Key indicators 2007 special chapter, highlights*. Manila: Author. Retrieved from: http://www.adb.org/Documents/Books/Key_Indicators/2007/pdf/Inequality-in-Asia-Highlights.pdf

Asian Development Bank. (2008, June). *Managing Asian cities*. Manila: Author.

Aslam, M., Kingdom, G., & Söderbom, M. (2008). Is female education a pathway to gender equality in the labor market? Some evidence from Pakistan. In M. Tembon & L. Fort (Eds.), *Girls' education in the 21st century: Gender equality, empowerment, and economic growth* (pp. 67-92). Washington, D.C.: The World Bank.

Australian Government. (2009). Social inclusion in the Australian Government. Retrieved from: http://www.socialinclusion.gov.au

Awuor-Hayangah, R. (2009a). *A case of city of Johannesburg, South Africa*. Unpublished paper prepared for the *State of the World's Cities Report 2009/10*.

Awuor-Hayangah, R. (2009b). *South Africa summary report*. Unpublished UN-HABITAT background study for the *State of the World's Cities Report 2009/10*.

B

Baldares, T.M. (2009, August). *City report on Cartago*. Unpublished UN-HABITAT background study for the *State of the World's Cities Report 2009/10*.

Bangladesh Dalit and Excluded Rights Movement, Nagorik Uddyog & the International Dalit Solidarity Network. (2009, February). *The human rights situation of Dalits in Bangladesh*. (Joint NGO submission to 4th UPR session). Retrieved from: http://www.dalits.nl/pdf/UPR-Bangladesh.pdf

Barber, S., Bertiozzio, S. & Gertler, P. (2005). *Variations in prenatal care quality in Mexico mirror health inequalities*. Washington, D.C.: World Bank.

Barrera-Osorio, F. (2008). The effects of a reduction in user fees on school enrollment: Evidence from Colombia. In M. Tembon & L. Fort (Eds.), *Girls' education in the 21st century: Gender equality, empowerment, and economic growth* (pp. 201-207). Washington, D.C.: The World Bank.

Barrios, S., Bertinelli, L., & Strobl, E. (2006). Climate change and rural-urban migration: The case of sub-Saharan Africa. *Journal of Urban Economics*, 60 (3): 357-71.

Bazoglu, N. (2007, July). *Cities in transition: Demographics and the development of cities*. Unpublished paper presented at Innovations for an Urban World: A Global Urban Summit, at the Bellagio Study and Conference Center, Rockefeller Foundation, Bellagio, Italy.

Becker, G.S. (1991). A treatise on the family. Cambridge, MA: Harvard University Press.

Birdsall, N. (2006). *The world is not flat: Inequality and injustice in our global economy*. (WIDER Annual Lecture 9). Helsinki: UNU-WIDER. Retrieved from:http://www.cgdev.org.doc/commentary/sppeches/Bidsall_WIDERpaper.pdf

Birdsall, N., & Londoño, J. (1997). Asset inequality matters: An assessment of the World Bank's approach to poverty reduction. *American Economic Review*, 87(2), 32-37.

Borja, J. & Drnda, M. (2003). *La ciudad conquistada*. Madrid: Alianza.

Brennan, M.A. (2005). *The importance of incorporating local culture into community development*. (University of Florida FCS9232). Retrieved from: http://edis.ifas.ufl.edu/pdffiles/FY/FY77300.pdf

Brown, A. & Kristiansen, A. (2009, March). *Urban policies and the right to the city: Rights, responsibilities and citizenship.* (MOST-2 Policy Papers Series). Retrieved from: http://unesdoc.unesco.org/images/0017/001780/178090e.pdf

Bruce, N., Perez-Padilla, R., & Albalak, R. (2000). Indoor air pollution in developing countries: A major environmental and public health challenge. *Bulletin of the World Health Organization,* 78(9), 1078-1092.

Brunn, S.D., Williams, J.F., & Zeigler, D.J. (2003). *Cities of the world*. Lanham, MD: Rowman & Littlefield.

C

Caldeira, T. (2001). *City of walls: Crime, segregation, and citizenship in São Paulo*. Berkeley, CA: University of California Press.

Campos, J.E. & Pradhan, S. (2007). *The many faces of corruption*. Washington, D.C.: The World Bank.

Cárdenas, M. & Bernal, R. (1999, November). *Changes in the distribution of income and the new economic model in Colombia*. (Study for the Ford Foundation for the project, "Growth, employment and equity: Latin America in the 1990s"). Washington, D.C.: ECLAC.

Catholic Relief Services. (2008). *Using market forces to improve urban food security*. Retrieved from: http://crs.org/zimbabwe/market-assistance/

Central Intelligence Agency. (n.d.). Rwanda. In *The CIA world fact book*. Retrieved from https://www.cia.gov/library/publications/the-world-factbook

Centre for Development and Enterprise (CDE). (2002, October). *Johannesburg, Africa's world city: A challenge to action*. (CDE Research 11.) Johannesburg: Author.

Chakrabarti, R. & Subramanian, A. (2003). *Compensation, inequality and corruption*. Retrieved from: http://www.idfresearch.org/pdf/wp0302.pdf

Chowdhury, T. (2006). *Taking slums seriously*. Unpublished document prepared for the *State of the World's Cities Report 2006/7*. Nairobi: UN-HABITAT.

City Mayors. (n.d.). The 150 richest cities in the world by GDP in 2005. In *City Mayors Statistics*. Retrieved from http://www.citymayors.com/statistics/richest-cities-2005.html

City of Johannesburg. (2009). *Growth and development strategy 2006*. Retrieved from: http://www.joburg.org.za/content/view/139/114/

City of Portland. (n.d.). Voices from the Community: The VisionPDX input report. *Vision Into Action*. Retrieved from http://www.visionpdx.com/reading/inputsummary/

City of Stonnington. (n.d.). *Charter of human rights*. Retrieved from: http://www.stonnington.vic.gov.au/www/html/2790-charter-of-humanrights.asp

Cohen, B. (2004). Urban growth in developing countries: A review of current trends and a caution regarding existing forecasts. *World Development*, 32:1, 23-51.

COHRE. (2007). *Fair play for housing rights*. Retrieved from: http://www.cohre.org/store/attachments/COHRE's%20Olympics%20Report.pdf

COHRE. (2008, 28 October). *Violations of women's housing rights in Kenya's slum communities*. Retrieved from http://www2.ohchr.org/english/bodies/cescr/docs/info-ngos/COHREKenya41.pdf

COHRE & Hakijami Trust. (2007, 5 November). *Submission to the United Nations Committee on Economic, Social and Cultural Rights on the occasion of pre-sessional working group discussion*, Kenya Right to Housing and Water (Article 11(1)). Retrieved from http://www2.ohchr.org/english/bodies/cescr/docs/info-ngos/cohrekenya39.pdf

Collier, P. (2007). *The bottom billion: Why the poorest countries are failing and what can be done about it*. Oxford: Oxford University Press.

Commission for Africa. (2005, March). *Our common interest: Report of the Commission for Africa*. Retrieved from: http://www.commissionforafrica.org/english/report/thereport/english/11-03-05_cr_report.pdf

Commission on Growth and Development. (2009). *Urbanization and growth*. M. Spence, A.P. Clarke, & R. Buckley (Eds.). Washington, D.C.: Author/The World Bank.

Corvalán, C.F., Kjellstrom, T., & Smith, K.R. (1999). Health, environment and sustainable development: Identifying links and indicators to promote action. *Epidemiology*, 10(5), 656–660.

Coward, S. (2006, 5 December). Poverty in Latin America continues to decrease for the third consecutive year – ECLAC. *Caribbean PressReleases.com*. Retrieved from: http://www.caribbeanpressreleases.com/articles/940/1/Poverty-in-Latin-America-Continues-to-Decrease-for-the-Third-Consecutive-Year---ECLAC/Page1.html

Crowe, S. (2009). 'A silent emergency' as Bangladesh's poor suffer from economic downturn. *UNICEF*. Retrieved from: http://www.unicef.org/infobycountry/bangladesh_49247.html

D

Delavallade, C. (2006). Corruption and distribution of public spending in developing countries. *Journal of Economics and Finance*, 30 (2), 222-239.

Departamento Administrativo Nacional de Estadística. (n.d.). *Encuesta de cultura política 2008*. Retrieved from: www.dane.gov.co

Department for International Development (UK). (n.d.). Inequality in middle income countries: South Africa case. (Section 2. An overview of inequality, poverty and growth in SA.) Retrieved from: *http://www.sarpn.org.za/documents/d0000671/P686-Gelb_Inequality_in_SA_section2.pdf*

Diop, B.A. (2009). *Plan directeur D'urbanisme de Dakar horizon «2025»*. Retrieved from: http://www.cifal-ouaga.org/niamey/exposes/Module3/Pr%C3%A9sentation%20PDU%20DAKAR%20HORIZON%202025.pdf

Diop, M. (2008). *Le Sénégal des migrations: Mobilités, identités et sociétés*. Dakar: Crepos, Karthala, ONU Habitat.

Djagba, B.K., Mboup, G., Guedeme, A., & Nouatin, B.M. (1999). Facteurs de surmortalité post-néonatale au Bénin. In G. Mboup & N. Kodjobé (Eds.), *Perspectives sur la planification et la santé de la reproduction au Bénin* (pp. 73-102). Calverton, MD: Macro International Inc. Retrieved from: http://www.measuredhs.com/pubs/pdf/FA27/FA27.pdf

Douglass, M. & Liling, H. (2007). Globalizing the city in Southeast Asia: Utopia on the urban edge. The case of Phu My Hung, Saigon. *IJAPS*, 3(2), 1-42.

Dreier, P. (2009, 22 July). RE: Richard Florida gets the boot – not. Message posted to ComUrb listserve: comurb_r21@email.rutgers.edu

Duru-Bellat, M., Kieffer, A., & Reimer, D. (2008). Patterns of social inequalities in access to higher education in France and Germany. *International Journal of Comparative Sociology*, 49(4-5), 347-368.

E

ECLAC/ILO. (2009, June). The employment situation in Latin America and the Caribbean. (Bulletin No. 1). *The Inter-American Centre for Knowledge Development in Vocational Training*. Retrieved from: http://www.oitcinterfor.org/public/english/region/ampro/cinterfor/news/biblio/ec_ilo.htm

Embassy of the Socialist Republic of Viet Nam in the United States. (2002, 25 October). Viet Nam leading developing world in poverty reduction. *News*. Retrieved from: http://www.vietnamembassy-usa.org/news/story.php?d=20021025181158

Engle, P., Hurtado, E., & Ruel, M. (1997). Smoke exposure of women and young children in highland Guatemala: Prediction and recall accuracy. *Human Organization*, 54(4), 408-417.

ESCAP. (2009, April). *Statistical yearbook for Asia and the Pacific*. Retrieved from http://www.unescap.org/stat/data/syb2008

Ethiopian Ministry of Finance and Economic Development. (2006, September). *Ethiopia: Building on progress; a plan for accelerated and sustained development to end poverty*. Retrieved from: http://planipolis.iiep.unesco.org/upload/Ethiopia/Ethiopia_PASDEP_2005_2010.pdf

Ethkwini Municipality. (2006). *Integrated development plan 2010 and beyond*. Retrieved from: http://www.durban.gov.za/durban/government/policy/idp/idp/idp2011/idp1

European Centre for Development Policy Management (ECDPM 2004) & Netherlands Ministry for Foreign Affairs. (n.d.). *Institutional development: Learning by doing and sharing; approaches and tools for supporting institutional development*. Retrieved from: http://www.capacity.org

European Commission. (n.d.). Eurostat statistics database. Accessed through: http://epp.eurostat.ec.europa.eu/portal/page/portal/eurostat/home/

European Environmental Agency. (2006). *Urban sprawl in Europe: The ignored challenge*. Copenhagen: Author. Retrieved from: http://www.eea.europa.eu/publications/eea_report_2006_10/eea_report_10_2006.pdf

Evans, B. & Haller, L. (2005*). Securing sanitation: The compelling case to address the crisis*. (Report commissioned by the Government of Norway as input to the Commission on Sustainable Development and its 2004-2005 focus on water, sanitation and related issues). Stockholm: Stockholm International Water Institute. Retrieved from: http://www.siwi.org/documents/Resources/Reports/CSD_Securing_Sanitation_2005.pdf

Ezzati, M. & Kammen, D.M. (2002). The health impacts of exposure to indoor air pollution from solid fuels in developing countries: Knowledge, gaps, and data needs. *Environmental Health Perspectives*, 110(11), 1057-1068.

F

ECLAC/ILO. (2009, June). The employment FAFO. (2009). *Cities and citizens report*. Unpublished document created for the UN-HABITAT Monitoring Urban Inequities Programme, Nairobi.

Fausto Brito, A. (2008). *Les marchés des vides urbains. Enjeux et stratégies d'acteurs à Guadalajara, Mexique*. Paris: Adef.

Fay, M. & Opal, C. (2000). *Urbanization without growth: A not-so-uncommon phenomenon*. (World Bank Policy Research Working Paper 2412.) Washington, D.C.: World Bank Urban Development and Transportation Division.

Fernández Güell, J.M. (2006). *Planificación estratégica de ciudades*. Barcelona: Estudios Universitarios de Arquitectura, Editorial Reverté.

Ferreira, F. & Walton, M. (2006, January). Inequality of opportunity and economic development. (World Bank Policy Research Working Paper 3816). Washington, D.C.: The World Bank.

Filmer, D. (2000). *The structure of social disparities in education*. (Policy Research Working Paper 2268). Washington, D.C.: The World Bank Development Research Group.

Florida, R. (2008). *Who's your city?* New York: Basic Books.

Florida, R., Gulden, T., & Mellander, C. (2007, October). *The rise of the mega-region*. Retrieved from http://creativeclass.typepad.com/thecreativityexchange/files/florida_gulden_mellander_megaregions.pdf

Friedman, S. (n.d.). *Comments on the inclusive cities project concept paper and proposals for a revised research topic*. Retrieved from: http://www.wilsoncenter.org/news/docs/1.4%20Steven%20Friedman.doc

G

Garelli, S. (2002). *Competitiveness of nations: The fundamentals*. Retrieved from: http://members.shaw.ca/compilerpress1/Anno%20Garelli%20CN%20Fundamentals.htm

Gervais-Lambony, P. (2008). *Space matters: Identity, justice and democracy at the ward level in South African cities. Transformation: Critical Perspectives on Southern Africa*, 66/67, 83-97. Retrieved from: http://muse.jhu.edu/journals/transformation/summary/v066/66.gervais-lambony.html

Government of Brazil, Institute for Applied Economic Research (2007). *Millennium Development Goals: National monitoring report*. Brasilia: IPEA.

Grobler-Tanner, C. (2006). *Understanding nutrition data and the causes of malnutrition in Niger: A special report by the Famine Early Warning Systems Network (FEWS NET)*. Washington, D.C.: United States Agency for International Development.

Grusky, D. B. & Kanbur, R. (Eds.) (2006). *Poverty and inequality: Studies in social inequality*. Stanford, CA: Stanford University Press.

Gustafsson, B. & Nivorzhkina, L. (2005). How and why transition made income inequality increase in urban Russia: A local study. *Journal of Comparative Economics*, 33, 772-787.

Gyimah-Brempong, K. (2002). Corruption, economic growth and income inequality in Africa. *Economics of Governance*, 3, 183-209.

H

Habitat International Coalition. (2008, 3 October). *Ecuador's new constitution includes several housing-related rights*. Retrieved from: http://www.hicnet.org/news.php?pid=59

Hanushek, E. (2008). Schooling, gender equity, and economic outcomes. In M. Tembon & L. Fort (Eds.), *Girls' education in the 21st century: Gender equality, empowerment, and economic growth* (pp. 23-40). Washington, D.C.: The World Bank.

Haworth, C., Long, J., & Rasmussen, D. (1978). Income distribution, city size, and urban growth. *Urban Studies*, 15, 1-7.

HCM City People's Committee. (n.d.). *Prosperity leads city to lift poverty line*. Retrieved from: http://english.vietnamnet.vn/social/2009/01/822264/

Helen Keller International. (2006, August). *Trends in child malnutrition, 1990-2005*. (Nutritional Surveillance Project Bulletin No. 19). Retrieved from: http://www.hki.org/research/nsp_storage/NSP%20Bulletin%2019.pdf

Huchzermeyer, M. (2009). *Interpreting the right to the city: Mediation, meaningful engagement and access to services in recent Constitutional Court litigation in South Africa*. Unpublished paper prepared for the *State of the World's Cities Report 2009/10*.

Hyun, H.S. (2008, July). *Conditional cash transfer programmes: An effective tool for poverty alleviation*. (ERD Policy Brief Series No. 51). Manila: Asian Development Bank.

I

Ilako, F. & Kimura, M. (2004, July). Provision of ARVs in a resource-poor setting: Kibera slum, Kenya. Paper submitted to the International Conference on AIDS, African Medical and Research Foundation (AMREF), Nairobi, Kenya. Abstract retrieved from: http://gateway.nlm.nih.gov/MeetingAbstracts/ma?f=102281024.html

Indermit, G. & Homi, K. (2007). *An East Asian renaissance: Ideas for economic growth.* Washington, D.C.: World Bank.

Inglehart, R. (1997). *Modernization and postmodernization: Cultural, economic, and political change in 43 societies.* Princeton, N.J.: Princeton University Press.

Instituto Pólis. (n.d.). *The statute of the city: New tools for assuring the right to the city in Brasil.* Retrieved from: http://www.polis.org.br/obras/arquivo_163.pdf

Inter-American Development Bank (2007). *OUTSIDERS? The changing patterns of exclusion in Latin America and the Caribbean, 2008 Report.* Washington, D.C.: Author.

International Labour Organization. (2001). *Decent work: A common goal of youth and trade unions.* Geneva: Author.

International Labour Organization. (2004, August). *Global employment trends for youth.* Geneva: Author.

International Labour Organization. (2009, January). *Global employment trends.* Geneva: Author.

International Monetary Fund. (2004, February). *The Federal Democratic Republic of Ethiopia: Poverty reduction strategy paper, annual progress report.* Retrieved from: http://www.imf.org/external/pubs/ft/scr/2004/cr0437.pdf

International Monetary Fund. (2008). *Food and fuel prices: Recent developments, macroeconomic impact, and policy responses.* Retrieved from: https://www.imf.org/external/np/pp/eng/2008/063008.pdf

International Monetary Fund, (2009, April). *World economic outlook: Crisis and recovery.* Washington, D.C.: Author.

International Policy Center for Inclusive Growth, UNDP. (2009, July). *What explains the decline in Brazil's inequality?* (One Pager No. 89). Brasilia: Author.

Investopiedia. (n.d.) *Rent-seeking.* Retrieved from: http://www.investopedia.com/terms/r/rentseeking.asp

IPEA. (2009, Junio). Revista desafíos *Desenvolvimento.* Retrieved from: http://desafios2.ipea.gov.br/sites/ooo/17/edicoes/51/pdfs/rd51not03.pdf

J

Jacobs, J. (1961). *The death and life of great American cities.* New York: Random House.

James, R., Arndt, C., & Simler, K. (2005, January). *Has economic growth in Mozambique been pro-poor?* Washington, D.C.: International Food Policy Research Institute.

K

Kasarda, J.D. & Krenshaw, E.M. (1991). Third world urbanization: Dimensions, theories, and determinants. *Annual Review of Sociology,* 17: 467-501.

Kessides, C. (2006). *The urban transition in sub-Saharan Africa: Implications for economic growth and poverty reduction.* Washington, D.C.: World Bank.

Kirk, J. (2008). Addressing gender disparities in education in contexts of crisis, postcrisis, and state fragility. In M. Tembon & L. Fort (Eds.), *Girls' education in the 21st century: Gender equality, empowerment, and economic growth* (pp. 153-178). Washington, D.C.: The World Bank.

Knight D. (2008, October). *What is a city region?* City Region Studies Centre, University of Alberta, Canada. Retrieved from: http://www.crsc.ualberta.ca/pdf/whatiscityregion.pdf

Kothari, M. (2003). *Privatising human rights: The impact of globalization on adequate housing, water and sanitation.* Retrieved from: http://unpan1.un.org/intradoc/groups/public/documents/apcity/unpan010131.pdf

Kothari, M. & Chaudhry, S. (2009, October). *Taking the right to the city forward: Obstacles and promises.* Unpublished background paper prepared for UN-HABITAT.

Kruger, J.S. & Chawla, L. (2002). "We know something someone doesn't know": Children speak out on local conditions in Johannesburg. *Environment and Urbanization* 14(2): 85-96.

Kuala Lumpur City Hall. (2008). *KL city plan 2020.* Retrieved from: http://klcityplan2020.dbkl.gov.my/eis/

L

Lambsdorff, J. G. (2006). What is bad about corruption? The contribution of the new institutional economics. In H. Hemmer (Ed.), *Seminar on good governance* (pp. 11-55) [Meeting notes]. Kaiserin Augusta Hotel, Weimar, Germany, 18-21 January.

Landman, K. & Schönteich, M. (2002). Urban fortresses. *African Security Review,* 11(4). Retrieved from: http://www.iss.co.za/Pubs/ASR/11No4/Landman.html

Lavalle, G. A, Houtzager P.P, & Castello, G. (2005). *In whose name? Political representation and civil organisations in Brazil.* (IDS Working Paper 249.) Retrieved from: http://www.cebrap.org.br/imagens/Arquivos/IDSWp249InWhoseName.pdf

Lemanski, C. (2004). A new apartheid ? The spatial implications of fear of crime in Cape Town South Africa. *Environment and Urbanization,* 16(2), 101-112.

Liu, Z., Li, J., Lu, Q., & Liu, Y. (2009). Evolution rules of urban-rural development and inspiration for China's agriculture. *Chinese Journal of Population, Resources and Environment,* 7(3), 48-54.

Lockheed, M. (2008). The double disadvantage of gender and social exclusion in education. In M. Tembon & L. Fort (Eds.), *Girls' education in the 21st century: Gender equality, empowerment, and economic growth* (pp. 115-126). Washington, D.C.: The World Bank.

López Moreno Eduardo (1997), *"Regular o No Regular: El Dilema de las Reservas Territoriales",* Cuaderno Metodológico 1, CONACYT, Universidad de Guadalajara, México.

López Moreno, E. (2003). *Slums of the world: The face of urban Poverty in the new millennium.* Nairobi: UN-HABITAT.

López Moreno, E., (2007). How far is the world from the slum target? *International Aid + Trade 2006/2007 Review: Driving aid, relief and development.* London: Sustainable Development International. pp. 117-119.

López Moreno, E. (2009, Marzo). *Desanimo o esperanza en un mundo de realidades contrastadas.* II Congreso Internacional de Desarrollo Humano – Ciudad Sostenible: Los Retos De La Pobreza Urbana, Madrid, España, Red Universitaria, en prensa.

M

Malloy, T., Gazzola, M. (2006). *The aspect of culture in the social inclusion of ethnic minorities.* Retrieved from http://www.ecmi-eu.org

Mannathoko, C. (2008). Promoting education quality through gender-friendly schools. In M. Tembon & L. Fort (Eds.), *Girls' education in the 21st century: Gender equality, empowerment, and economic growth* (pp. 127-142). Washington, D.C.: The World Bank.

Marras, S. (n.d.). Mapping the unmapped. *Afronline*. Retrieved from http://www.afronline. org/wp-content/uploads/2009/06/kibera_ mapping_the_unmapped.pdf

Martinez, R. & Fernandez, A. (2006, April). Child malnutrition in Latin America and the Caribbean. *Challenges: Newsletter on progress towards the Millennium Development Goals from a child rights perspective*, 2, 4-9. Retrieved from: http:// www.unicef.org/lac/Desafios_2_ing(9).pdf

Marx, V. & Nobile, R. (2009, August). *City report on São Paulo*. Unpublished UN-HABITAT background study for the *State of the World's Cities Report 2009/10*.

Mathon, D. (2009, August). *City report on Port-au-Prince*. Unpublished UN-HABITAT background study for the *State of the World's Cities Report 2009/10*.

Mboup, G. (1997). Evaluation de la Cohérence des Objectifs du Programme de Coopération 199-2003. Programme, Planification, Suivi et Evaluation. Cotonou, Benin: UNICEF.

McElfish, J. (2007). An additional 100 million Americans must not be housed in urban sprawls. *City Mayors*. Retrieved from: http://www. citymayors.com/development/sprawl-usa.html

Mingione, E. & Vicari Haddock, S. (2008). *European urban inequality*. Unpublished background paper commissioned by UN-HABITAT.

Ministry of Nairobi Metropolitan Development. (2009). *A world class African metropolis*. Retrieved from: http://www.nairobimetro.go.ke/ index.php.

Mitra, A. (1990). Duality, employment structure and poverty incidence: The slum perspective. *Indian Economic Review*, 25(1), 57-73.

Montezuma, R. (2009, August). *City report on Bogotá*. Unpublished UN-HABITAT background study for the *State of the World's Cities Report 2009/10*.

Municipal Corporation of Visakhapatnam. (n.d.) *Citizens charter*. Retrieved from: http://www. gvmc.gov.in/CitizensCharter/CitizensCharter1.html

Murillo, M. (2008). Social inequality and child malnutrition are the main threats of the food crisis in Latin America and the Caribbean. *Food crisis*. Retrieved from: http://www.visionmundial.org/ archivos-de-usuario/File/2008/crisisalimentaria/ crisisalimentaria_ing.pdf

N

Naudé, W.A. & Krugell, W. (2004). *An inquiry into cities and their role in subnational economic growth in South Africa*. WIDER Research Paper. Helsinki: UNU-WIDER.

Njoh, A. J. (2003). Urbanization and development in sub-Saharan Africa. *Cities*, 20(3), 167-174.

Nord, S. (1980, January). An empirical analysis of income inequality and city size. *Southern Economic Journal*, 46(3), 863-872.

Noronha, P. (2007, 3 July). Delhi-Mumbai industrial corridor: India, Japan sign MoU. *The Hindu Business Line*. Retrieved from http:// www.thehindubusinessline.com/2007/07/04/ stories/2007070452120200.htm

Notti, F. & Meyer, N. (2009, 15 April). *OHCHR contribution to VEGM: Mission report on excluded groups in Nepal*. Retrieved from: http:// www.unescap.org/ESID/hds/development_ac-count/mtg/Virtual%20EGM/V-EGM%2015%20 April%202009%20OHCHR%20Mission%20 Report%20on%20Excluded%20Groups%20in%20 Nepal.pdf

Nunoo, F.K.E. (2009, August). *Background document City of Accra, Ghana*. Unpublished UN-HABITAT background study for the *State of the World's Cities Report 2009/10*.

O

Ocampo, J.A. (2008, March). *Income distribution, poverty and social expenditure in Latin America*. Paper presented at the Conference of the Americas, Organization of American States, Washington, D.C.

Ojima, R. & Hogan, D.J. (2009). *Mobility, urban sprawl and environmental risks in Brazilian urban agglomerations: challenges for urban sustainability*. Retrieved from: http://iussp2009.princeton.edu/download. aspx?submissionId=90294

Okojie, C. & Shimeles, A. (2006, February). *Inequality in sub-Saharan Africa: A synthesis of recent research on the levels, trends, effects and determinants of inequality in its different dimensions*. London: Overseas Development Institute.

Olatubara, C.O., Omirin O.J. & Kasim, F. F. (2009, August). *State of the world's cities report 2010/11: Ibadan*. Unpublished UN-HABITAT background study for the *State of the World's Cities Report 2009/10*.

Ooi, G.L. & Yuen, B. (Eds.) (2009). *World cities: Achieving liveability and vibrancy*. Singapore: Civil Service College, Institute of Policy Studies and World Scientific Publishing.

Organization for Economic Cooperation and Development (OECD). (2008). *OECD environmental outlook to 2030*. Paris: OECD Publishing.

Organization for Economic Cooperation and Development (OECD). (n.d.). Regional statistics database. Accessed through: http://stats.oecd. org/OECDregionalstatistics

Oyelaran-Oyeyinka, B. & McCormick, D. (2007). *Industrial clusters and innovation systems in Africa: Institutions, markets and policy*. New York: United Nations University Press.

P

Paes de Barros, R.P., Ferreira, F.H.G., Vega, J.R.M., & Chanduvi, J.S. (2009). *Measuring inequality of opportunities in Latin America and the Caribbean*. (report No. 46827, The World Bank). New York: Palgrave MacMillan.

The People's Movement for Human Rights Education. (2007, March). *Human rights learning and human rights cities: Achievements report*. Retrieved from: http://www.pdhre.org/achieve-ments-HR-cities-mar-07.pdf

Postiglione, G.A. (Ed.) (2006). *Education and social change in China: Inequality in a market economy*. New York: East Gate.

Pow, C. (2007). Securing the 'civilised' enclaves: Gated communities and the moral geographies of exclusion in (post-)socialist Shanghai. *Urban Studies*, 44(8), 1539–1558.

PricewaterhouseCoopers. (2008). *Cities of opportunity*. Retrieved from: http://www.pwc. com/us/en/cities-of-opportunity/summary-download.jhtml.

Proceedings from the 2nd South Asian Confer-ence on Sanitation. (SACOSAN-2, 2006, 20-22 September). Islamabad, Pakistan.

R

Raffensperger, L. (2007, 9 November). October 2007 monthly update: Solid fuel use and indoor air pollution. Message posted to: http://earthtrends. wri.org/updates/node/257

Rakodi, C. (2001, November). City politics: A voice for the poor? *ID21 Insights*, 38. Retrieved from: http://www.id21.org/insights/insights38/insights-iss38-art00.html

Rambla, X., Ferrer, F., Tarabini, A., & Verger, A. (2008). Inclusive education and social inequality: an update of the question and some geographical considerations. *Prospects*, 38(1), 65-76.

Rashid, S. F. & Hossain, Y. (2005). Constraints in delivering services to the urban poor living in slums in Dhaka, Bangladesh. Washington, D.C.: The World Bank.

Ravallion, M. (1997). Can high-inequality developing countries escape absolute poverty? *Economic Letters*, 56(1), 51-57.

Ravallion, M., Chen, S., & Sangraula, P. (2006). *New evidence on the urbanization of global poverty*. (Background Paper for the *World Development Report 2008*.) Washington, D.C.: The World Bank.

Rehfuess, E., Mehta, S., & Prüss-Üstün, A. (2006). Assessing household solid fuel use: Multiple implications for the Millennium Development Goals. *Environmental Health Perspectives*, 114(3). Retrieved from: http://www.ehponline.org/members/2006/8603/8603.pdf

Reynals, C. (2009, August). *City report on inclusiveness on Buenos Aires*. Unpublished UN-HABITAT background study for the *State of the World's Cities Report 2009/10*.

S

Salazar-Xirinachs, J.M. (2009, 20 March). *The impact of the global financial and economic crisis on developing countries, in particular Africa, and the prospects for attaining the MDGs*. [Speech transcript]. Africa Group Meeting, International Labour Organization, Geneva, Switzerland.

Santandreu, A. & Price, J. (2009, August). *Background document City of Callao, Peru*. Unpublished UN-HABITAT background study for the *State of the World's Cities Report 2009/10*.

Satterthwaite, D. (2000, 4 November). *Will most people live in cities?* Retrieved from: http://www.bmj.com/cgi/content/full/321/7269/1143.

Satterthwaite, D. (2007). *The transition to a predominantly urban world and its underpinnings* (Human Settlements Discussion Paper Series, Urban Change-4). London: International Institute for Environment and Development.

Science Daily. (2007, 25 May). Mayday 23: World population becomes more urban than rural. In *Science Daily*. Retrieved from: http://www.sciencedaily.com/releases/2007/05/070525000642.htm

Sen, A. (1999). *Development as freedom*. Oxford: Oxford University Press.

Sharma, P. (2003). Urbanization and development. In *Population monograph of Nepal 2003*, Government of Nepal Central Bureau of Statistics (Ed.), pp. 375-412. Retrieved from: http://www.cbs.gov.np/population_1_contents.php

Smith, K.R., Samet, J.M., Romieu, I., & Bruce, N. (2000). Indoor air pollution in developing countries and acute lower respiratory infections in children. *Thorax*, 55(6), 518-532.

Soares, S., Perez Ribas, R., & Veras Soares, F. (2009, March). Focalização e cobertura do programa Bolsa-Família: Qual o significado dos 11 milhões de famílias? Texto Para Discussão No. 1396. Rio de Janiero: IPEA. Retrieved from: http://www.ipea.gov.br/sites/000/2/publicacoes/tds/td_1396.pdf

Social Planning Council of Ottawa. (2003, 20 September). *Our homes, our neighbourhoods: Building an inclusive city*. Retrieved from: http://www.spcottawa.on.ca/PDFs/Publications/InclusiveHousing_Forum_Eng.pdf

Society for Development Studies. (2009a, August). *City report on Jaipur*. Unpublished UN-HABITAT background study for the *State of the World's Cities Report 2009/10*.

Society for Development Studies. (2009b, August). *City report on Mumbai*. Unpublished UN-HABITAT background study for the *State of the World's Cities Report 2009/10*.

Society for Development Studies. (2009c, August). *City report on New Delhi*. Unpublished UN-HABITAT background study for the *State of the World's Cities Report 2009/10*.

Spence, M., Annez, P.C., & Buckley, R.M. (Eds.) (2009). *Urbanization and growth*. Washington, D.C.: Commission on Growth and Development/ The World Bank.

Stiglitz, J. (2003). Towards a new paradigm of development. In J.H. Dunning (Ed.), *Making globalization good: The moral challenges of global capitalism* (pp. 76-107). Oxford: Oxford University Press.

Sumarto, S. & Suryahadi, A. (2001, 22-23 May). *Principles and approaches to targeting with reference to the Indonesian safety net*. Paper presented at Workshop on Targeting and Rapid Assessment Methodologies, the Australian National Univesity and Insan Hitawasana Sejahtera, Jakarta. Retrieved from: http://www.aseansec.org/paper01.doc

Svensson, J. (2005). Eight questions about corruption. *Journal of Economic Perspectives*, 19 (3), 19-42.

T

Taher, M. & Chowdhury, I.U. (2009, August). *City report on Chittagong*. Unpublished UN-HABITAT background study for the *State of the World's Cities Report 2009/10*.

Taher, M. & Islam, K.M. (2009). *City report on Rajshahi*. Unpublished UN-HABITAT background study for the *State of the World's Cities Report 2009/10*.

Taher, M. & Islam Nazem, N. (2009). *Dhaka City*. Unpublished UN-HABITAT background study for the *State of the World's Cities Report 2009/10*.

Tan, J.L.H. (Ed.). (1999). *Human capital formation as an engine of growth*. Singapore: Institute of Southeast Asian Studies.

Tembon, M. & Fort, L. (Eds.) (2008). *Girls' education in the 21st century: Gender equality, empowerment, and economic growth*. Washington, D.C.: The World Bank.

U

UCLG. (2008). *Let's build the inclusive cities of the 21st century*. Istanbul: Author. Retrieved from: http://www.cities-localgovernments.org/uclg/upload/template/templatedocs/informe_debate_inclusion_en.pdf

UNDP (1990). *Human development report*. New York: Oxford University Press.

UNDP. (2004). *Human development report 2004: Cultural liberty in today's diverse world*. New York: Author.

UNDP. (2009). *Latin American and the Caribbean: Democratic governance*. Retrieved from: http://www.undp.org/latinamerica/governance.shtml

UNESCO. (2000). *Cultural diversity, conflict and pluralism: World culture report 2000*. Paris: Author.

UNESCO. (2008). *UNESCO country programming document for the Eastern Republic of Uruguay 2008-2009*. Retrieved from: http://unesdoc.unesco.org/images/0018/001835/183588e.pdf

UNICEF. (2008). *State of the world's children 2008*. New York: Author.

UN-HABITAT. (1996). *The Habitat Agenda: Chapter I – Preamble*. Retrieved from http://www.unhabitat.org

UN-HABITAT. (2002). *Rights and reality*. Retrieved from http://ww2.unhabitat.org/publication/hs66702e/default.asp

UN-HABITAT. (2003). *Global Report on Human Settlements 2003: The challenge of slums*. London: Earthscan.

UN-HABITAT. (2004, 15 November). *How Medellín became a city of opportunities*. Retrieved from: http://www.unhabitat.org/content.asp?cid=2450&catid=5&typeid=6&subMenuId

UN-HABITAT. (2005). *Good policies and enabling legislation for attaining the Millennium Development Goals: A methodology for participatory review and assessment*. Nairobi: Author.

UN-HABITAT. (2006). *The state of the world's cities report 2006/7: The Millennium Development Goals and urban sustainability*. London: Earthscan.

UN-HABITAT. (2008). *The state of the world's cities report 2008/9: Harmonious cities*. London: Earthscan.

UN-HABITAT & United Nations Economic Commission for Africa. (2008). *The state of African cities 2008: A framework for addressing urban challenges in Africa*. Nairobi: Author.

UN-HABITAT. (2009a). *The 2009 Scroll of Honour Award winners: Alexandra renewal project (South Africa)*. Retrieved from: http://www.unhabitat.org/content.asp?typeid=19&catid=588&cid=7291#SouthAfrica

UN-HABITAT. (2009b). *Global report on human settlements 2009: Planning sustainable cities*. London: Earthscan.

UN-HABITAT Best Practice Database. (2008a). *Change management unit (CMU) under Municipal Affairs Department, Government of West Bengal, India*. Retrieved from: http://www.unhabitat.org/bestpractices/2008/mainview04.asp?BPID=2155

UN-HABITAT Best Practice Database. (2008b). *Imihigo, Ministry of Local Governments, Community Development and Social Affairs, Rwanda*. Retrieved from: http://unpan3.un.org/unps/Public_NominationProfile.aspx?id=291

UN-HABITAT Best Practice Database. (2008c). *Upgrading slum system, Brazil*. Retrieved from: http://www.unhabitat.org/bestpractices/2008/mainview04.asp?BPID=1918

UNIFEM. (2008). *Who answers to women? Progress of the world's women 2008/9*. New York: Author.

United Nations Administrative Committee on Coordination, Subcommittee on Nutrition. (1988, March). Rapid urbanization poses challenge to health, nutrition. *SCN News*, 2, 5-7.

United Nations DESA. (2008a). *The Millennium Development Goals report 2008*. New York: Author.

United Nations Department of Economic and Social Affairs (DESA). (2008b). *World urbanization prospects: The 2007 revision.* New York: Author.

United Nations DESA. (2008c). *People matter: Civic engagement in public governance*. Retrieved from: http://unpan1.un.org/intradoc/groups/public/documents/UN/UNPAN028608.pdf

United Nations Economic and Social Council. (2009, 4-22 May). *Implementation of the international covenant on economic, social and cultural rights*. (Reply by the Government of Brazil). Retrieved from: http://www2.ohchr.org/english/bodies/cescr/docs/E.C.12.BRA.Q.2.Add.1.pdf

United Nations Industrial Development Organization. (2004). Industrialization, environment and the Millennium Development Goals in sub-Saharan Africa: The new frontier in the fight against poverty. Vienna: Author. Retrieved from: http://www.unido.org/index.php?id=7676

Uslaner, E.M. (2005). *Economic inequality and the quality of government*. Paper presented at the Annual Meeting of the Society for the Advancement of Socio-Economics, Budapest, Hungary, 30 June-2 July.

V

Van Damme, D. (2009, 10 September). *Human capital development in cities and regions*. (Presentation notes). Retrieved from: http://www.oecd.org/dataoecd/14/33/43684473.pdf

Van Dijk, M.P. (2007, 1 March). *The contribution of cities to economic development: An explanation based on Chinese and Indian cities*. Inaugural Address as Affiliate Professor of Urban Management, Institute of Social Studies, The Hague.

Vásconez, J. (2009, August). *City report on inclusiveness in Quito*. Unpublished UN-HABITAT background study for the *State of the World's Cities Report 2009/10,* prepared by the Centro Internacional de Gestión Urbana (CIGU).

W

Wafula, E.M., Kinyanjui, M.M., Nyabola, L., & Tenambergen, E.D. (2000). Effect of improved stoves on prevalence of acute respiration infection and conjunctivitis among children and women in a rural community in Kenya. *East African Medical Journal*, 77(1), 37-41.

Wahlberg, K. (2008). Are we approaching a global food crisis? Between soaring food prices and food aid shortage. *World Economy & Development in Brief*. Retrieved from: http://www.globalpolicy.org/component/content/article/217/46194.html

Warah, R. (1999). Divided loyalties: The African identity crisis. *Habitat Debate*, 5(1), 20-21.

Warnakula, J. (2009). *Colombo City, Sri Lanka*. Unpublished UN-HABITAT background study for the *State of the World's Cities Report 2009/10*.

Weisman, S. (2006, 14 September). Wolfowitz corruption drive rattles World Bank. *The New York Times*. Retrieved from: http://www.nytimes.com/2006/09/14/business/14wolf.html?_r=1&pagewanted=1

Whebell, C.F.G. (1969). Corridors: A theory of urban systems. *Annals of the Association of American Geographers*, 59(1), 1-26.

World Bank. (n.d.). CCT programs: Now on every continent. *Conditional cash transfers: Reducing present and future poverty*. Retrieved from: http://web.worldbank.org

World Bank. (2007). *World development indicators*. Washington, D.C.: Author.

World Bank. (2008a, 14 April). Food price crisis imperils 100 million in poor countries, Zoellick says. *News & Broadcast*. Retrieved from: http://web.worldbank.org

World Bank. (2008b). *World Bank researchers release worldwide governance indicators 1996-2007*. News Release accesed online on 24/09/09 from http://siteresources.worldbank.org/EXTWBIGOVANTCOR/Resources/Newsrelease.pdf

World Bank. (2009). *World development indicators 2009*. Washington, D.C.: Author.

X

Xueyong, Z. (n.d.) *The economic role of community-based NGOs in environmental governance*. Retrieved from: http://arnova.omnibooksonline.com/2006/data/papers/PA061373.pdf

Y

Yeung, Y. & Lo, F. (1996). Global restructuring and emerging urban corridors in Pacific Asia. In Y. Yeung & F. Lo (Eds.), *Emerging World Cities in Pacific Asia* (pp. 17-47). Tokyo: United Nations University Press.

You, J. & Khagram, S. (2005). A comparative study of inequality and corruption. *American Sociological Review*, 70, 136-157.

Z

Xueyong, Z. (n.d.) *The economic role of* Zetter, R. (2002). Market enablement or sustainable development: The conflicting paradigms of urbanization. In R. Zetter & R. White (Eds.), *Planning in cities: Sustainability and growth in the developing world*. London: ITDG Publishing.

Index

Note: Page numbers in *italics* refer to maps, figures, tables, boxes and illustrations. Those followed by 'n' refer to notes.